The Way We Lived

Volume I
1492–1877

The Way We Lived

Essays and Documents
in American Social History
Sixth Edition

Frederick M. Binder

City University of New York, College of Staten Island

David M. Reimers

New York University

Houghton Mifflin Company   Boston   New York

Publisher for History and Political Science: Suzanne Jeans
Senior Sponsoring Editor: Ann West
Senior Marketing Manager: Katherine Bates
Senior Development Editor: Jeff Green
Senior Project Editor: Carol Newman
Cover Design Director: Tony Saizon
New Title Project Manager: Susan Peltier
Marketing Assistant: Lauren Bussard
Editorial Assistant: Evangeline Bermas

Printed in the U.S.A.

Library of Congress Catalog Card Number: 2007924342

ISBN 13: 978-0-618-89466-6
ISBN: 10: 0-618-89466-7

1 2 3 4 5 6 7 8 9 10- CRS-11 10 09 08 07

Contents

Preface

History courses have traditionally emphasized the momentous events of our past. Wars and laws, technological advances and economic crises, ideas and ideologies, and the roles of famous heroes and infamous villains have been central to these studies. Yet what made events momentous is the impact they had on society at large, on people from all walks of life. Modern scholars' growing attention to social history is in part a recognition that knowledge of the experiences, values, and attitudes of these people is crucial to gaining an understanding of our past.

America's history as reflected in the everyday lives of its people provides the focus of these volumes. In preparing a work of selected readings, we have had to make choices about which episodes from our past to highlight. Each of those included, we believe, was significant in the shaping of our society. Every essay is followed by original documents that serve several purposes. They provide examples of the kinds of source materials used by social historians in their research; they help to illuminate and expand upon the subject dealt with in the essays; and they bring the reader into direct contact with the people of the past—people who helped shape, and people who were affected by, the "momentous events."

Our introduction to each essay and its accompanying documents is designed to set the historical scene and to call attention to particular points in the selections, raising questions for students to ponder as they read. A list of suggested readings follows after each of the major divisions of the text. We trust that these volumes will prove to be what written history at its best can be—interesting and enlightening.

We are pleased to note that favorable comments by faculty and students as well as the large number of course adoptions attest to the success of our first five editions. Quite naturally, we thus have no desire in our sixth edition to alter the basic focus, style, and organization of *The Way We Lived*. Many of those essays that our readers and we consider to have been the earlier editions' best remain intact. However, it is our belief that the new selections, reflecting recent scholarship, will identify and clarify significant issues in American social history even more effectively than those they replaced. In choosing new essays and documents for inclusion, we have sought to present a broader view of historical events and to illustrate the impact these events have had on the lives of people.

Thus, in Volume 1 we include an essay relating the story of an indentured servant from the time he left his home in England to his rise as a man of substance in colonial Maryland. Our new essay on the Revolution focuses on the foot soldiers of the army, identifying their backgrounds and describing their experiences. Another new essay enables the reader to follow a wagon train as it travels from Missouri to the Pacific coast on the Oregon

Trail. We have replaced our essay on the Second Great Awakening, which dealt with the revival in the urban Northeast, with one describing and comparing the movement in both the North and the South.

In Volume 2 we have shifted our emphasis somewhat from the experiences of eastern and southern European immigrants in urban settings to present a new essay examining the lives of Polish immigrants in rural Minnesota. The new essay describing society in post–World War I America paints a picture of an economic boom coupled with a nativist and racist prejudice. We believe that readers will find the new essay on the Great Depression most interesting. It relates the impact of both economic disaster and the destructive force of nature on a small Texas town. Also new to the sixth edition is an essay focusing on the impact of recent immigration both on the residents of suburban Long Island, New York, as well as the Hispanic immigrants who labor in what the author terms the "new sweatshops." Readers will also discover several new documents in both volumes of *The Way We Lived*.

We would like to thank the following reviewers for their excellent and helpful comments:

Ginette Aley, University of Southern Indiana;
John S. Baick, Western New England College;
Garna L. Christian, University of Houston—Downtown;
Michael B. Dougan, Arkansas State University;
Darryl C. Mace, Cabrini College;
Martin R. Menke, Rivier College;
Patrick D. Reagan, Tennessee Tech University;
Stephen Rockenbach, Northern Kentucky University; and
Michael Schaller, University of Arizona.

It is our hope that students will find as much pleasure in reading this new edition as we have had in creating it.

F. M. B.

D. M. R.

PART I

Colonial Society
1492–1783

Chapter 1

The First Americans

A Native American couple share a meal, as drawn by John White, member of the ill-fated Roanoke Colony, circa 1856.

Up until a few short decades ago, students of history were taught that the story of America began with Columbus's voyage of discovery, followed by settlement of the land by Europeans. Native Americans were depicted primarily as part of the unfamiliar, exotic, and somewhat threatening natural landscape that had to be tamed. Fortunately, scholars in recent years have come to appreciate and to illustrate that American history predated European colonization by thousands of years. America's first settlers had begun their migration—that would continue for centuries—across the land bridge that emerged periodically in the Bering Sea. Drawing from a variety of Asiatic peoples, the hundreds of native tribes that settled across America prior to the arrival of Europeans differed profoundly in language, religion, economy, and social and political organization. Before the first white men set foot on American soil, Indian nations used the land effectively and flourished.

The essay that follows, from Peter Nabokov and Dean Snow's "Farmers of the Woodlands," illustrates the complexity and vitality of the societies and cultures of

3

two groups of Indians, the Algonquians and Iroquoians, as they existed in 1492. Situated between the Atlantic coastline and the foothills of the Appalachians, both groups figured prominently in the drama of initial contact between Europeans and Native Americans. As you read, make note of the ways in which the Indians, in the authors' words, "made extremely efficient use of the natural resources in their river and forest world." What factors appeared to be most significant in leading some Eastern Indians toward a primarily seminomadic hunting-and-gathering pattern of existence and others toward an agrarian, semi-sedentary, village-based way of life? In what ways do the descriptions of Indian culture found in the essay complement or contrast with popular film depictions of Native Americans?

The image of the Indian portrayed by the early English colonists differs in many respects from that of modern scholars. Using their own culture as the guideline by which to evaluate others, colonists found some aspects of Indian life exotic, some even admirable, but on the whole they deemed Indians inferior savages. Thus, the prevailing attitude of the Europeans was that the Indians had to adopt white man's civilization or be vanquished. One of the earliest and most influential proponents of this view was Captain John Smith, swashbuckling adventurer and a leader of the Jamestown, Virginia, settlement of 1607. In his *A Generall Historie of Virginia,* published in 1624, Smith describes the land and native people of England's first North American colony. The first document includes some of Smith's descriptions of Virginia's "Naturall Inhabitants." What evidence is there that Smith evaluated these people's culture by European standards?

The Indians' resistance to attempts to subjugate them both culturally and physically during the colonial period contributed to the general consensus among the European settlers that they faced a truly barbarous and savage people. However, while few Indians embraced white society, evidence exists of a considerable number of English colonists who ran off to join the Indians and of white captives who, when given the opportunity to return home, chose to remain among the Indians. Look for clues to explain these phenomena in the experiences of Mary Jemison, related in the second document. The daughter of colonists, Jemison was captured and adopted by Seneca Indians in 1755, when she was twelve years old. Mary, in turn, assimilated the Seneca's way of life. When she related the story of her adventure to Dr. James Seaver in 1823, she still lived among the Seneca. In the excerpt that follows, she recalls her thoughts and experiences after four years in captivity.

The Seneca Indians were members of the New York–based League of the Iroquois, a confederation that was able—through their unity, courage, and military and diplomatic skills—to withstand European incursions for more than a hundred years. Their ill-fated alliance with the British during the Revolutionary War led to their downfall. By 1805, the time of the final document, the once mighty Iroquois shared the fate of other Indians before them: encroachment on their lands and pressure to abandon their religion and way of life. The third document presents a speech by Red Jacket, a Seneca warrior and subchief. Born in 1751,

Red Jacket was old enough to have served during the years when Iroquois power and prestige were at their height. Now he headed what detractors called the "pagan faction"—Iroquois who sought to maintain their traditional culture and to keep European influences outside the borders of their reservation. In his speech, Red Jacket responds to Missionary Cram's suggestion that Native Americans convert to Christianity and accept European ways. What is Red Jacket's view of the European assault on Indian life?

Although the readings in this chapter have focused on the Native Americans of the eastern coast of British North America, it is important to remember that Spanish colonizers of territory that would later be part of the United States also encountered and interacted with Indians. In 1598, Juan de Oñate established the colony of New Mexico. The final document is from a letter he wrote to the Spanish viceroy in Mexico in which he described the nature and society of the native inhabitants. In what ways does the document serve to illustrate the wide variety of Native American cultures existing in North America during the colonial period?

ESSAY

Algonquians and Iroquoians: Farmers of the Woodlands

Peter Nabokov with Dean Snow

When the hunting party of three Penobscot River Indian families arrived at the frozen creek in the spring of 1492, the men tested the ice with their five-foot staves. It would support them today, but not much longer. The wintry season which they called "still-hunting and stalking" was ending quickly. A warm spell a few days earlier caused sticky snow to cling to their moose-hide snowshoes, slowing them down.

It was time to head downstream, following creeks to the broad river and continuing to where it widened to the sea. Other hunters and their families, whom they had not seen since autumn, would also be returning to the summer villages. The warmer evenings would offer time for recounting the past winter—all the deaths, births, hunts, and tragic, funny, and supernatural happenings of which human memory and history are made.

The hunting parties were traversing a well-watered and heavily forested landscape which white men would one day call Maine. In their own language they knew themselves as "people of the white rocks country," a phrase which Europeans would later shorten to Penobscot. They

SOURCE: Peter Nabokov with Dean Snow, "Farmers of the Woodlands," *America in 1492: The World of the Indian People Before the Arrival of Columbus,* Alvin M. Josephy, Jr., ed. Copyright © 1992 by Alvin M. Josephy, Jr. Used by permission of Alfred A. Knopf, a division of Random House, Inc.

were one of six loosely organized eastern Algonquian-speaking tribes who would become known colloquially as Wabanakis, or "daybreak land people." Their territory marked the northern limits of Indian farming, for late thaws and early frosts permitted them to produce only a little corn, squash, and beans.

The annual shifts between seasonal camps up and down the Penobscot River valley were determined by the time-honored habits of fishing and hunting on which their survival depended. Branching out from this great stream were innumerable tributaries that were familiar to the hunters who revisited them, usually more than once, throughout the year. Each of these natural domains was dubbed a "river," which, to the Penobscot hunting families, evoked a stretch of stream and adjoining lands on which they held relatively exclusive hunting and fishing privileges. Deep in the heart of their homeland loomed their sacred Mount Katahdin, home to the fearsome spirit known as Pamola. Few hunters ventured above the tree line to trespass on his territory.

Waterways, and the well-trodden trails that connected them, served as the hunters' routes into the dense interior forests, where their arrows, snares, and deadfalls yielded moose, deer, beavers, muskrats, and otters in their "rivers." The central river was their highway down to the coast, where they collected clams and lobsters, speared seals, and caught porpoises.

Mobility was a necessity for the hunting life of the Penobscot. Hence, their social groups were small, and rules of residence were rather loose. Generally, it was up to the husband whether his family lived with his own or with his wife's parents. The opportunities and dictates of the hunt dominated all other concerns; social organization had to be flexible enough to let men make the most of the availability of game or shifts in the weather.

The hunters were not unhappy to leave winter behind. The "master of the animals" had blessed this group with a late-season moose cow, her unborn still in its slick, wet pouch. Their hunting had yielded enough beaver and other pelts, thick with luxuriant winter hair, to weigh down the toboggans the men dragged behind them. Their dogs also sniffed spring, and seemed happier. Ahead, everyone anticipated spearing and netting the shad, salmon, alewives, and sturgeon during their spring spawning runs.

This was also a time to harvest bark. It is hard to imagine northeastern Algonquian culture without the paper birch tree. Thin, speckled flats were peeled from the trunks at different times of year. Spring bark was thickest and was preferred for canoes, so the entire trunk would be cut down and the bark separated in the largest pieces possible. Then it would be sewn onto a canoe frame of steam-bent cedar wood and waterproofed at the seams with white-pine pitch colored with charcoal.

Summer bark was thinner, and was earmarked for roofing mats and receptacles. It could be stripped from the trunk in smaller flats without killing the tree. Then it could be folded and sewn into maple-sap buckets, baby cradleboards, and pitch-caulked cooking vessels in which heated stones were dropped to bring water to a boil. For more decorative items, floral designs were produced by careful scraping away to the darker, inner layer of the bark. Porcupine-quill or moose-hair embroidery might also ornament the bark surfaces.

In late spring, families planted gardens before heading for the coast and the pleasures of seabird eggs, escape from blackflies, summer berry picking, flirting among the young, easier fishing along the saltwater bays, and extended twilights. At summer's end, the "going about to find something" time, the forest lured them once more.

Hunting opened in earnest with moose mating season. To entice the fat summer bulls within arrow range, hunters trumpeted through birch-bark megaphones, imitating the sounds of cow moose. Then came winter, storytelling season, when a few families collected within wigwams and lulled children to sleep with the exploits of Glooskap, the trickster figure of Wabanaki folklore.

For Penobscot Indians in 1492, this cycle of tasks and pleasures seemed as predictable and everlasting as the seasons themselves. Their way of life also made extremely efficient use of the natural resources in their river and forest world. Woodlands, waterways, and—south of Penobscot country—open fields remain the ecological hallmarks of all of the North American East. However, in 1492, there was probably far more local variation in plant and animal life than we have today.

Indeed, if we are to believe the earliest European eyewitnesses, New England, for instance, resembled a checkerboard of natural preserves with dramatically contrasting ecological features. "It did all resemble a stately Parke, wherein appeare some old trees with high withered tops, and other flourishing with living green boughs," wrote James Rosier in 1605, after walking through the forests and fields not far from Indian Island in Maine. Yet in this stroll of less than four miles, the modern-day environmental historian William Cronon pointed out, Rosier's party actually passed beneath the leafy canopies of a number of quite different micro-environments.

The sylvan paradise of northern New England, lying at the northernmost extreme of the corn-growing region, was but one section of nearly one million square miles of the eastern half of North America that is commonly called the Woodland culture area. Farther west might be added 400,000 square miles of intermixed river foliage and tallgrass prairie, where—except on strips of narrow floodplain—Indians usually were not able to sustain substantial gardening.

By 1492, the native people of this huge eastern mass of the continent occupied a world already rich and complex in human history—many different histories, in fact. At least sixty-eight mutually unintelligible tongues, representing five of the twenty known language families of North America, were spoken in the region. The net effect of over 10,000 years of adaptation by contrasting native peoples who had grown deeply tied to a great diversity of environmental regions of the eastern woodlands had produced a complex cultural mosaic. . . .

It had taken time, new ideas, and experimentation for the woodland Indian peoples of 1492 to develop this annual round of land-use customs and mixed strategies of subsistence. Indian occupancy of the East is now believed to go back as far as 16,000 B.C., when Paleo-Indian foragers and hunters began settling the region in highly mobile bands. As these groups established local residency, they developed almost imperceptibly into the Indian world that archaeologists label the Archaic period, which lasted until about 700 B.C.

The domesticated dogs that accompanied the Penobscot hunters were introduced during Archaic times and were found throughout the East by 1492. Inherited from their Paleo-Indian forerunners, a principal Archaic weapon was the spear thrower. Archaic hunters improved this device to gain increased velocity during a throw by adding flexible shafts and by weighting the throwing stick with a ground stone to add leverage. . . .

By 1492, Indians in the East had been growing vegetables in two different ways for a long time. Both the Iroquoians and Algonquians practiced what is known as swidden, or slash-and-burn, horticulture. A plot of preferably well-drained land was cleared of its canopy of leaves and branches. The area was then burned and nutrient-rich ashes and organic materials were hoed into the forest floor. Seeds were dispersed within hand-formed mounds. The resulting fields did not have a very kempt appearance; generally, the corn stalks and squash vines flourished greenly amid a scatter of scorched or dead brush.

Among the semi-nomadic hunting-and-gathering Algonquian bands, who traveled relatively light and who fished, foraged, hunted, and gathered maple syrup, growing vegetables was but one subsistence activity. If a season's garden was beset by insects, or a hunt came up empty, the people generally could rely on stored foods or other options. The Iroquoians, however, who elevated swidden agriculture to their dominant means of support, might be considered true "farmers," rather than part-time "gardeners." Their sizable hillside lots were the mainstay for their matrilineal social system and for a semi-sedentary, village-based way of life. . . .

Prior to the advent of gardening, food foraging among woodland Indians had probably been the responsibility of women. The heightened importance of plant cultivation, processing, and storage steadily enhanced their role. By the time of Columbus, women were clearly the primary food producers in a number of woodland cultures whose political and religious systems reflected their status.

South of the northeastern territories of the Wabanaki peoples, the weather softened. Among the Indian groups of central and southern New England, the length of the summer allowed greater attention to gardening and so promoted a more settled village way of life. While for Penobscot hunters corn was a sometime delicacy, for the south it became a basic food staple. In present-day New Hampshire and Vermont, the western Abenakis were marginal farmers and fishermen. Among the Mahicans of eastern New York, like the Pocumtucks of the interior Connecticut River valley, work in the fields was still augmented by hunting in the woods and trapping migratory fish in local rivers.

Not surprisingly, this more temperate world had a larger native population than did the northern forests. It is estimated that the Massachusett, Wampanoag, and other Indian nations of southern New England possessed a population density of five people per square mile—ten times that of the hunters of Maine. Population densities at this high level also obtained for other eastern Algonquian-speakers farther south, the Lenapes (Delawares) and Nanticokes, and their linguistic kinfolk in coastal Delaware, Maryland, Virginia, and North Carolina. There, also, among the Powhatans and others, were permanent villages and more stable intertribal alliances.

All central and southern New England Indians spoke languages belonging to the same language family—Algonquian. Commonly, a tribesman was conversant with the words and pronunciation of his immediate neighbors, but communicated with decreasing fluency as trade, hunting, or warfare drew him farther from his home territory.

By 1492, techniques for growing and storing vegetables had been developing in the Northeast for four or five centuries. Wampanoag men cleared fields from the forests of oak, elm, ash, and chestnut. They felled the smaller trees and burned the thicker trunks at the base together with their branches, which left a coating of ash to enrich the soil. In Wampanoag society, rights to these cleared plots were inherited through the female line of descent.

Women broke up the ground with hoes edged with deer scapulae or clamshells. Around April, they began planting the seed corn in little mounds, often counting four kernels per hillock and perhaps adding heads of alewife fish for fertilizer. The corn came in many colors and kinds—flint, flour, dent, and pop.

By midsummer, an early crop yielded squash and beans and green corn, but the major harvest occurred in September. Apparently these crops helped each other out. The beans growing amid the corn added nitrogen, which corn consumes, while the heavy stalks offered support for the climbing bean vines. Finally, the corn provided the shade that the low-lying squash needed to reach maximum maturity.

When eaten together, beans, corn, and squash produced a greater protein intake, and Indians developed the mixed-vegetable dish which is still known by its Algonquian name, "succotash."

While garden caretakers weeded roots and protected the emerging crops from birds and pests, the majority of villagers headed for the coast to gather clams and oysters and to catch lobsters and fish. Wild greens, nuts, and fruits, which were also important to their diet, varied with season and habitat. They included blackberries, blueberries, raspberries, strawberries, and wild grapes, and walnuts, chestnuts, and acorns, which could also be dried and stored for leaner times.

In autumn, the Indians divided their time between preparing their agricultural surplus for winter storage and dispersing in hunting parties before winter set in. Deer were stalked by individuals, or were flushed into special game pens by communal drivers. For warm skins as well as meat, Indians stalked moose, elk, bears, bobcats, and mountain lions in late fall, winter, and early spring. In midwinter, they dangled lines into local ponds through the ice, but dipped nets or repaired fish weirs in milder seasons.

Villages came alive in summertime, their long, mat-covered multifamily structures busy with social activity. Those villages near cultural frontiers were surrounded by a protective stockade of fire-hardened, sharpened posts. A typical settlement included storage pits, menstrual huts, and sometimes special religious structures. Plaza-like areas were used for public feasts, and for dancing performed to the accompaniment of song, drum, and rattle.

Religious specialists among the Wampanoag of present-day Massachusetts were known as "powwows." Admired and feared for their association with extraordinarily strong "manitou," or spirits, they exhibited their spirit-bestowed powers at special events to benefit hunters, control weather, prophesy the future, cure the sick, or bewitch their enemies. They also mediated between the community and the spirit world at green-corn harvest feasts and at special midwinter rituals and memorials for the dead, and they concocted war magic against tribal enemies. Among some southern New England tribes, religious specialists who behaved more like formal priests maintained temples in which bones of the chiefly class were treasured.

Exchange was lively among these different peoples and probably bound them together in personal and group alliances. The eastern woods and riversides were laced with well-used trail systems along which goods and messages were conveyed. Individuals fortunate enough to be related to the resident "sachem," or chief, as well as powwows who were on intimate terms with them, benefited from the exchange of values and goods that moved back and forth.

In 1492, these Algonquian-speaking hunter-farmers were neighbors to more militarily powerful tribes who were representatives of another major eastern Indian language family, Iroquoian. Dwelling along the Carolina and Virginia portions of the Appalachian foothills were such Iroquoian-speaking peoples as the Nottoways, Meherrins, and Tuscaroras. The last of these would later migrate north to become the sixth member of the famous Iroquois confederacy in the eighteenth century.

Among the mountains, valleys, and flatlands that lay across what is now central New York State, the principal beacon of Iroquoian-speaking culture was positioned in the midst of a more extensive territory of

Algonquian-speaking groups. What these upper Iroquoian peoples may have lost in terms of sheer acreage, however, they more than made up for in the fertility of their agricultural lands, which they utilized most efficiently.

Inhabiting the mountains of eastern Tennessee and western North Carolina were southern Iroquoians, the ancestors of the populous Cherokees. Tutelos, who lived in Virginia, were speakers of the Siouan language, while the Catawbas, farther south, possessed a language with a more distant relationship to mainstream Siouan. West of Cherokee country were the Yuchis, whose language was vaguely related to Siouan.

If the birch was the emblematic tree of Algonquian culture, it was the white pine for the Iroquoians. In their cosmology, a cosmic evergreen was believed to stand at the center of the earth. Elm served more pragmatic purposes. Slabs of its heavy bark, sewn onto stout sapling frames, shrouded their barrel-roofed longhouses, which extended up to 300 feet or more in length.

These dormitorylike buildings were also an embodiment of the Iroquois social order, for women and children under one roof were linked by membership in the same clan, which was traced through the female line. Each of the ten or so Iroquois clans took its name from a particular animal or bird that was considered to be the original ancestor of the clan's members—thus there were, for example, the Eagle, Snipe, and Heron clans. Over the door at one end of a longhouse would be a depiction of the reigning clan animal of the house's inhabitants.

The year 1492 probably found this group of woodland Indians undergoing a profound social and political transformation. Sometime between 1450 and 1550, it is believed, the five major Iroquoian-speaking tribes south of the St. Lawrence River were developing an altogether innovative form of political union—a multitribal federation with members allied for mutual defense—and were deliberating with elaborately democratic rules of order. The story of the formation of the Iroquois League provides a strong argument against the notion that pre-contact Indian societies existed in a timeless vacuum and did not experience "history" until Columbus imported it.

At the dawn of this transformation, around A.D. 1450, northern Iroquoian groups were found across southern Ontario, New York, and central Pennsylvania in villages of slightly over 200 people each. As with the New England horticulturists, they practiced swidden agriculture, only to a far more intensive degree. Lacking direct access to coastal resources, they were more dependent upon gardening for survival. These tribes also appear to have been highly competitive and politically assertive.

Early Iroquoian life was divided into two domains, the clearings with their longhouses and gardens and the wider wilderness with its game and dangers. The clearings were the responsibility of women, and over each longhouse presided the oldest "clan mother." By contrast, the forests were a male domain, where the men gave offerings to the masked spirits, who responded by "giving" wild animals to respectful hunters.

Iroquois fields were cleared by hacking and burning around the base of tree trunks so that the heavier foliage died and, if necessary, the entire tree could be felled easily the following year. This also allowed sunlight to shine on the forest floor and provided ashes to energize the soil. Maize, beans, and squash were planted in hills among the fallen trees. Firewood was gathered as dead limbs dropped during the course of the year. Within a few years, however, the garden soil began to decline in productivity, and new acreage had to be opened up. Every twenty years or so, infestation from worms and other pests, plus depletion of easily available wood for fires and stockade or longhouse construction, forced relocation of the village. The entire community would rebuild not far away, often an easy walk from the old site.

For the Iroquoians, growing crops was not simply one of a number of food-gathering options; their fields were their lifeline. They were considerably more sedentary than their Algonquian neighbors. This heightened reliance upon cultigens and reliable food storage decisively elevated the prominence of women in political life. By 1492, not only was each longhouse under the authority of the eldest clan mother resident, but it was Iroquois women who handpicked candidates for the office of sachem.

However, the pattern of communities containing only a dozen or so longhouses changed by 1492, when Iroquois towns each began sheltering from 500 to 2,000 inhabitants. Perhaps a rise in intertribal warfare inspired consolidation for mutual defense, or improved farming strategies allowed for a dramatic aggregation of population. But the new social and political institutions that arose to cope with these mega-villages grew directly out of the old social fabric and residence patterns.

Traditionally, the center aisles of the Iroquoian longhouse split the buildings lengthwise. Paired family quarters faced each other like compartments in a sleeping car, with a shared cooking hearth in the central aisle. Men married "into" these longhouses—which were expanded if all existing quarters were spoken for. Although men appointed from senior households ran the affairs of the village as a council of equals, sometime around 1492 this changed. The matrilineal clans, which seem to have served originally as units that facilitated trade and exchange within the tribe, became the building blocks of a brand-new political institution. Within the century between 1450 and 1550, the Iroquois proper became known as the Five Nations, which held sway across present-day New York State. They consisted of the Seneca, Cayuga, Onondaga, Oneida, and Mohawk peoples.

According to Iroquois tradition, two legendary figures, Deganawidah and Hiawatha, conceived of a "great peace" among the incessantly feuding Iroquois peoples. They persuaded the Iroquois tribes, one by one, to accept their "good news of peace and power." Among the reforms they instituted was the abolition of cannibalism. The old social importance of the communal longhouse made it a perfect symbol for their political creation. All the member tribes talked of themselves as "fires" of an imagined "longhouse" that spanned the extent of Iroquois territory.

To its participants, this Iroquoian fraternity meant strength in numbers and security through allies. To outsiders such as the Hurons, neighboring Algonquians, and eventually the European powers, it meant a formidable foe. The full drama of Iroquois political destiny would actually unfold in the three centuries after 1492, but if Columbus had ventured northward, he would have witnessed a truly Native American representative government in the making. . . .

DOCUMENTS

"Of the Naturall Inhabitants of Virginia," 1624

The land is not populous, for the men be fewe; their far greater number is of women and children. Within 60 miles of *James* Towne there are about some 5000 people, but of able men fit for their warres scarse 1500. To nourish so many together they have yet no means, because they make so small a benefit of their land, be it never so fertill.

6 or 700 have beene the most [that] hath beene seene together, when they gathered themselves to have surprised *Captaine Smyth at Pamaunke,* having but 15 to withstand the worst of their furie. As small as the proportion of ground that hath yet beene discovered, is in comparison of that yet unknowne. The people differ very much in stature, especially in language, as before is expressed.

Since being very great as the *Sesquesahamocks,* others very little as the *Wighcocomocoes:* but generally tall and straight, of a comely proportion, and of a colour browne, when they are of any age, but they are borne white. Their haire is generally black; but few have any beards. The men weare halfe their heads shaven, the other halfe long. For Barbers they use their women, who with 2 shels will grate away the haire, of any fashion they please. The women are cut in many fashions agreeable to their yeares, but ever some part remaineth long.

They are very strong, of an able body and full of agilitie, able to endure to lie in the woods under a tree by the fire, in the worst of winter, or in the weedes and grasse, in *Ambuscado* in the Sommer.

They are inconstant in everie thing, but what feare constraineth them to keepe. Craftie, timerous, quicke of apprehension and very ingenious. Some

SOURCE: Edward Arber, ed., *Captain John Smith Works* (Birmingham, Eng.: The English Scholars Library, No. 16, 1884), 65–67.

are of disposition feareful, some bold, most cautelous, all *Savage*. Generally covetous of copper, beads, and such like trash. They are soone moved to anger, and so malitious, that they seldome forget an injury: they seldome steale one from another, least their conjurors should reveale it, and so they be pursued and punished. That they are thus feared is certaine, but that any can reveale their offences by conjuration I am doubtful. Their women are carefull not to bee suspected of dishonesty without the leave of their husbands.

Each household knoweth their owne lands and gardens, and most live of their owne labours.

For their apparell, they are some time covered with the skinnes of wilde beasts, which in winter are dressed with the haire, but in sommer without. The better sort use large mantels of deare skins not much differing in fashion from the Irish mantels. Some imbrodered with white beads, some with copper, other painted after their manner. But the common sort have scarce to cover their nakedness but with grasse, the leaves of trees, or such like. We have seen some use mantels made of Turkey feathers, so prettily wrought and woven with threeds that nothing could bee discerned but the feathers, that was exceeding warme and very handsome. But the women are alwaies covered about their midles with a skin and very shamefast to be seene bare.

They adorne themselves most with copper beads and paintings. Their women some have their legs, hands, breasts and face cunningly imbrodered with diverse workes, as beasts, serpentes, artificially wrought into their flesh with blacke spots. In each eare commonly they have 3 great holes, whereat they hange chaines, bracelets, or copper. Some of their men weare in those holes, a smal greene and yellow coloured snake, neare halfe a yard in length, which crawling and lapping her selfe about his necke often times familiarly would kiss his lips. Others wear a dead Rat tied by the tail. Some on their heads weare the wing of a bird or some large feather, with a Rattell. Those Rattels are somewhat like the chape of a Rapier but lesse, which they take from the taile of a snake. Many have the whole skinne of a hawke or some strange fowle, stuffed with the wings abroad. Others a broad peece of copper, and some the hand of their enemy dryed. Their heads and shoulders are painted red with the roote *Pocone* braied to powder mixed with oyle; this they hold in somer to preserve them from the heate, and in winter from the cold. Many other formes of paintings they use, but he is the most gallant that is the most monstrous to behould.

Their buildings and habitations are for the most part by the rivers or not farre distant from some fresh spring. Their houses are built like our Arbors of small young springs bowed and tyed, and so close covered with mats or the barkes of trees very handsomely, that notwithstanding either winde raine or weather, they are as warme as stooves, but very smoaky, yet at the toppe of the house there is a hole made for the smoake to goe into right over the fire.

Against the fire they lie on little hurdles of Reedes covered with a mat, borne from the ground a foote and more by a hurdle of wood. On these round about the house, they lie heads and points one by thother against the fire: some covered with mats, some with skins, and some starke naked lie on the ground, from 6 to 20 in a house.

Their houses are in the midst of their fields or gardens; which are smal plots of ground, some 20, some 40, some 100, some 200, some more, some lesse. Some times from 2 to 100 of these houses [are] togither, or but a little separated by groves of trees. Neare their habitations is little small wood, or old trees on the ground, by reason of their burning of them for fire. So that a man may gallop a horse amongst these woods any waie, but where the creekes or Rivers shall hinder.

Men women and children have their severall names according to the severall humor of their Parents. Their women (they say) are easilie delivered of childe, yet doe they love children verie dearly. To make them hardy, in the coldest mornings they wash them in the rivers, and by painting and oint-ments so tanne their skins, that after year or two, no weather will hurt them.

The men bestowe their times in fishing, hunting, wars, and such man-like exercises, scorning to be seene in any woman like exercise, which is the cause that the women be verie painefull and the men often idle. The women and children do the rest of the worke. They make mats, baskets, pots, morters, pound their corne, make their bread, prepare their victuals, plant their corne, gather their corne, beare all kind of burdens, and such like. . . .

Recollections of a "White Indian" (1759), 1823

I had then been with the Indians four summers and four winters, and had become so far accustomed to their mode of living, habits and dispositions, that my anxiety to get away, to be set at liberty, and leave them, had almost subsided. With them was my home; my family was there, and there I had many friends to whom I was warmly attached in consideration of the fa-vors, affection and friendship with which they had uniformly treated me, from the time of my adoption. Our labor was not severe; and that of one year was exactly similar, in almost every respect, to that of the others, with-out that endless variety that is to be observed in the common labor of the white people. Notwithstanding the Indian women have all the fuel and bread to procure, and the cooking to perform, their task is probably not harder than that of white women, who have those articles provided for them; and their cares certainly are not half as numerous, nor as great. In the summer season, we planted, tended and harvested our corn, and generally had all our children with us; but had no master to oversee or drive us, so

SOURCE: James E. Seaver, *A Narrative of the Life of Mrs. Mary Jemison* (Canandaigua, N.Y.: J. D. Bemis and Co., 1824), 46–49.

that we could work as leisurely as we pleased. We had no ploughs on the Ohio; but performed the whole process of planting and hoeing with a small tool that resembled, in some respects, a hoe with a very short handle.

Our cooking consisted in pounding our corn into samp or hommany,* boiling the hommany, making now and then a cake and baking it in the ashes, and in boiling or roasting our venison. As our cooking and eating utensils consisted of a hommany block and pestle, a small kettle, a knife or two, and a few vessels of bark or wood, it required but little time to keep them in order for use.

Spinning, weaving, sewing, stocking knitting, and the like, are arts which have never been practised in the Indian tribes generally. After the revolutionary war, I learned to sew, so that I could make my own clothing after a poor fashion; but the other domestic arts I have been wholly ignorant of the application of, since my captivity. In the season of hunting, it was our business, in addition to our cooking, to bring home the game that was taken by the Indians, dress it, and carefully preserve the eatable meat, and prepare or dress the skins. Our clothing was fastened together with strings of deer skin, and tied on with the same.

In that manner we lived, without any of those jealousies, quarrels, and revengeful battles between families and individuals, which have been common in the Indian tribes since the introduction of ardent spirits amongst them.

The use of ardent spirits amongst the Indians, and the attempts which have been made to civilize and christianize them by the white people, has constantly made them worse and worse; increased their vices, and robbed them of many of their virtues; and will ultimately produce their extermination. I have seen, in a number of instances, the effects of education upon some of our Indians, who were taken when young, from their families, and placed at school before they had had an opportunity to contract many Indian habits, and there kept till they arrived to manhood; but I have never seen one of those but what was an Indian in every respect after he returned. Indians must and will be Indians, in spite of all the means that can be used for their cultivation in the sciences and arts.

One thing only marred my happiness, while I lived with them on the Ohio; and that was the recollection that I had once had tender parents, and a home that I loved. Aside from that consideration, or, if I had been taken in infancy, I should have been contented in my situation. Notwithstanding all that has been said against the Indians, in consequence of their cruelties to their enemies—cruelties that I have witnessed, and had abundant proof of—it is a fact that they are naturally kind, tender and peaceable towards their friends, and strictly honest; and that those cruelties have been practised, only upon their enemies, according to their idea of justice.

Hominy (hommany) is shucked corn with the germ removed; *samp* is a boiled cereal made from hominy. (Eds.)

An Indian's View, 1805

Friend and brother, it was the will of the Great Spirit that we should meet together this day. He orders all things, and He has given us a fine day for our council. He has taken His garment from before the sun, and caused it to shine with brightness upon us; our eyes are opened, that we see clearly; our ears are unstopped, that we have been able to hear distinctly the words that you have spoken; for all these favours we thank the Great Spirit, and Him only. . . .

Brother, you say you want an answer to *your talk,* before you leave this place. It is right you should have one, as you are a great distance from home, and we do not wish to detain you; but we will first look back a little, and tell you what our fathers have told us, and what we have heard from the White people.

Brother, listen to what we say. There was a time when our forefathers owned this great land. Their seats extended from the rising to the setting sun. The Great Spirit had made it for the use of Indians. He had created the buffalo, the deer, and other animals for food. He made the bear and the beaver, and their skins served us for clothing. He had scattered them over the country, and taught us how to take them. He had caused the earth to produce corn for bread.

All this He had done for His Red children because he loved them. If we had any disputes about hunting grounds, they were generally settled without the shedding of much blood.

But an evil day came upon us; your forefathers [the Europeans] crossed the great waters, and landed on this island. Their numbers were small; they found friends, and not enemies; they told us they had fled from their own country for fear of wicked men, and come here to enjoy their religion. They asked for a small seat; we took pity on them, granted their request, and they sat down amongst us; we gave them corn and meat; they gave us poison in return. The White people had now found our country, tidings were carried back, and more came amongst us; yet we did not fear them, we took them to be friends; they called us brothers; we believed them, and gave them a larger seat. At length their numbers had greatly increased; they wanted more land; they wanted our country. Our eyes were opened; and our minds became uneasy. Wars took place; Indians were hired to fight against Indians, and many of our people were destroyed. They also brought strong liquors among us; it was strong and powerful, and has slain thousands.

Brother, our seats were once large, and yours were very small; you have now become a great people, and we have scarcely a place left to spread our blankets; you have got our country, but are not satisfied; you want to force your religion upon us.

SOURCE: Red Jacket's reply to Missionary Cram at Buffalo, New York, in Samuel G. Goodrich, *Lives of Celebrated American Indians* (Boston: Bradbury, Soden and Co., 1843), 283–287.

Brother, continue to listen. You say that you are sent to instruct us how to worship the Great Spirit agreeably to His mind, and if we do not take hold of the religion which you White people teach, we shall be unhappy hereafter; you say that you are right, and we are lost; how do we know this to be true? We understand that your religion is written in a book; if it was intended for us as well as you, why has not the Great Spirit given it to us, and not only to us, but why did He not give to our forefathers the knowledge of that book, with the means of understanding it rightly? We only know what you tell us about it; how shall we know when to believe, being so often deceived by the White people?

Brother, you say there is but one way to worship and serve the Great Spirit; if there is but one religion, why do you White people differ so much about it? Why not all agree, as you can all read the book?

Brother, we do not understand these things; we are told that your religion was given to your forefathers, and has been handed down from father to son. We also have a religion which was given to our forefathers, and has been handed down to us, their children. We worship that way. It teaches us to be thankful for all the favours we receive; to love each other, and to be united; we never quarrel about religion.

Brother, the Great Spirit has made us all; but He has made a great difference between His White and Red children; He has given us a different complexion and different customs; to you He has given the arts; to these He has not opened our eyes; we know these things to be true. Since He has made so great a difference between us in other things, why may we not conclude that He has given us a different religion according to our understanding? The Great spirit does right; He knows what is best for his children; we are satisfied.

Brother, we do not wish to destroy your religion, or take it from you. We want only to enjoy our own.

Brother, you say you have not come to get our land or our money, but to enlighten our minds. I will now tell you that I have been at your meetings, and saw you collecting money from the meeting. I cannot tell what this money was intended for, but suppose it was for your minister, and if we should conform to your way of thinking, perhaps you may want some from us.

Brother, we are told that you have been preaching to White people in this place; these people are our neighbors, we are acquainted with them; we will wait a little while and see what effect your preaching has upon them. If we find it does them good, makes them honest, and less disposed to cheat Indians, we will then consider again what you have said.

Brother, you have now heard our answer to your talk, and this is all we have to say at present. As we are going to part, we will come and take you by the hand, and hope the Great Spirit will protect you on your journey, and return you safe to your friends.

The Indians of New Mexico, 1599

Here . . . there must be, being conservative in my reckoning, sixty thousand Indians, with towns like ours and with houses built around rectangular plazas. They have no streets. At the pueblos where there are many plazas or large houses, they are joined by narrow passageways between the buildings. Where there are fewer people, the houses are two and three stories high . . . but there are some houses and even entire pueblos with four, five, six, and seven stories.

The dress of the Indians consists of cotton or agave blankets, well decorated, white or black; it is very good clothing. Others dress in buffalo skins, of which there is a great abundance. These furs have a beautiful wool; I am sending you some samples of what they make of it. This land is plentiful in meat of the buffalo, sheep with huge antlers, and native turkeys. At Mohoce and Zuñi there is game of all kinds. There are many wild animals and beasts; lions, bears, tigers, wolves, penicas, ferrets, porcupines, and others. The natives tan and use their skins. To the west there are bees and very white honey, of which I am sending a sample. Their corn and vegetables, and their salines, are the best and largest to be found anywhere in the world.

There is great abundance and variety of ores; those I mentioned above are very rich. Some discovered around here do not seem so, although we hardly started to examine the many things that there are. There are fine grape vines, rivers, and woods with many oak and some cork trees; there are also fruits, melons, grapes, watermelons, Castilian plums, capulins, piñon, acorns, native nuts, *coralejo,* which is a delicate fruit, and other wild plants. There are also many fine fish in this Río del Norte* and other streams. From the metals that we find here, we can obtain all colors and the finest.

The people are as a rule of good disposition, generally of the color of those of New Spain,** and almost the same in customs, dress, grinding of meal, food, dances, songs, and in many other respects. This is not true of their languages, which here are numerous and different from those in Mexico. Their religion consists in worshiping of idols, of which they have many; in their temples they worship them in their own way with fire, painted reeds, feathers, and general offerings of almost everything: little animals, birds, vegetables, etc. Their government is one of complete freedom, for although they have some chieftains they obey them badly and in very few matters.

SOURCE: From *Don Juan de Oñate: Colonizer of New Mexico, 1595–1628,* by George P. Hammond and Agapito Rey. Copyright © 1953 University of New Mexico Press.
   *The Rio Grande. (Eds.)
   **Refers to Spain's colonies south of the Rio Grande. (Eds.)

We have seen other nations, such as the Querechos or Vaqueros, who live among the Cíbola cattle in tents of tanned hides. The Apaches, some of whom we also saw, are extremely numerous. Although I was told that they lived in rancherías, in recent days I have learned that they live in pueblos the same as the people here. They have a pueblo eighteen leagues from here with fifteen plazas.

Chapter 2

Colonial Beginnings: Aspirations, Obstacles, and Opportunities

A trading post at St. Mary's, Maryland, c. 1640.

The colonial history of what today is the United States began in the early seventeenth century with the planting of settlements along the eastern seaboard. Almost all the early colonists were English; together, they suffered the hardships of the ocean voyage and the dangers and vicissitudes of frontier life. While their motives for leaving home varied, as did the kinds of colonial society they established, most viewed America as a land of opportunity. In the essay "The Rise of Daniel Clocker," Lois Green Carr presents an example of one who truly "made it." From the most humble beginnings in England, Clocker arrived in Maryland in 1636 as an indentured servant who ultimately attained personal freedom, economic well-being, and social respectability. What were the most difficult challenges facing Clocker as a new arrival seeking to adjust to life in Maryland? What do you identify as the key factors leading to his ultimate success?

The decade immediately following the arrival of Maryland's first colonists in 1634 witnessed steady growth and internal stability. Peace was established with the Indians; Catholic coreligionists of the colony's proprietor found a haven of toleration. The history of Virginia's early years, beginning at Jamestown in 1607, stands in marked contrast. Disease, mismanagement, greed, and the exploitation of people and natural resources threatened the very survival of the colony. The first document provides a vivid account of this period. Nathaniel Butler, governor of Bermuda, visited Virginia in 1622 and wrote a report of the conditions he saw there. What evidence did he provide that human failings were as much or perhaps even more to blame than natural causes for the sufferings of the colonists?

Those who invested in the Virginia venture as well those who led the settlement were motivated by what they believed was the opportunity for quick and easy profit attained by exploiting the colony's natural resources. As you read the second document, written by Governor John Winthrop of the Massachusetts Bay Colony, note the differences between the stated goals for that colony and conditions in Virginia. Composed during his journey to America in 1630, Winthrop's statement clearly expressed the religious motives of the Puritan adventurers and set forth the ideological objective that communal effort take precedence over individual ambition. What did Winthrop mean by his declaration that "we shall be as a City upon a Hill"?

Within little more than a generation after the founding of the three colonies discussed in this chapter, time and circumstances would do much to modify their original character. The Virginia colonists ultimately realized that their dreams of getting rich quickly would not find fulfillment; eventually, the expansion of agriculture furthered the development of a more stable—but nonetheless prosperous—society. Massachusetts also represented a success story, though not the kind John Winthrop envisioned. By the end of the seventeenth century, profits from agriculture, fishing, and commerce had moved the eastern half of the colony beyond wilderness status and diverted its citizens' attention from the mission of creating a new Zion. Although the Puritan spirit would long continue to influence the Massachusetts population, its dominance was broken. Unhappily, Maryland at the end of the eighteenth century presents a less positive example of change. Its minority Catholic population, which had initially found safe haven in the colony, suffered considerable social and political discrimination as a result of the anti-Catholic climate during the reign of James II and the subsequent Glorious Revolution in Britain.

ESSAY

The Rise of Daniel Clocker

Lois Green Carr

The Cumberland and Westmoreland area (now labeled Cumbria) is a rugged country of mountains, lakes, and fells. In the seventeenth century it was part of a border region considered savage by outsiders. Englishmen from further south found the inhabitants to be "primitive in their passions and morals, and entirely without understanding of the rules of a law-abiding society." Clans and powerful lords offered the more law-abiding inhabitants better protection from marauding Scots and outlaws than could officers of the crown or remote forces of law at Westminster. To make a living, people mined and quarried, grazed sheep and cattle on the mountain pastures, and raised grains in the valleys, although on soils poor in comparison to those of southern England.

Daniel Clocker probably grew up [in the north of England] in a family that combined mining with some self-sufficient husbandry, a common combination in the north, but he evidently left home to seek his fortune. In early seventeenth-century England, many Englishmen were on the move, often from countryside to towns and ultimately to major urban centers. For a century, population had been growing, and opportunities to work were becoming scarce with increasing unemployment and underemployment. In the north, furthermore, grain harvests could be meager, and in the more inaccessible mountain parts, the 1620s saw several years of famine. The particulars of why and when Daniel Clocker made up his mind to try his luck elsewhere are not yet known, but by 1636, he had reached a port—probably London—from which emigrants were sailing to the New World. In London, he had a likely kinsman, Jasper Clocker—possibly the youngest child of Gosper and Mabell—who lived in St. Botolph-without-Aldgate parish.

Little is known about the ways in which emigrants learned of opportunities to sail for America, especially at this early time. Daniel Clocker probably did not have America, much less Maryland, in mind when he left home, but he may well have been seeking adventure. Lord Baltimore, the Proprietor of Maryland, published a series of pamphlets advertising his colony and its opportunities, but Clocker, who could not write his name, may not have been able to read, and in any case, such literature was aimed at investors, not servants. Most news came to people by word of mouth. Perhaps Daniel looked for work as a laborer at the waterfront and heard talk of a

SOURCE: Lois Green Carr, "From Servant to Freeholder: Daniel Clocker's Adventure," *Maryland Historical Magazine* 99, no. 3, 288–302.

ship traveling to "Virginia," as the whole Chesapeake region was then known. Or he may have worked at an inn where he could overhear the conversation of a merchant looking for servants for colonists in need of labor. It is even possible that Captain Thomas Cornwaleys had commissioned such a merchant to find him the five young servants he imported in 1636. The only fact we know for certain is that in 1636, Clocker arrived in Maryland; he had come to a New World settlement barely established, but where tobacco was quickly becoming a profitable product for export; and he became an indentured servant to Captain Thomas Cornwaleys, one of the major investors and first leaders of the new province.

Indentured servitude was the chief mechanism for transporting poor people in need of work across the ocean to the English North American colonies. In seventeenth-century Maryland, 70 to 80 percent of immigrants came this way. Most were young men; the sex ratio was six men to a woman in the 1630s and three men to a woman by mid-century and after. Passage cost about £6 sterling, which the servant repaid to his master by four or more years of labor. During this time the master provided shelter, food, clothing, and medical care, and when the servant's time was up, gave him or her freedom dues. These were a new set of clothes, three barrels of Indian corn, and (for men) an axe and a hoe. The corn was enough to feed the ex-servant for a year, with seed for the next year's crop. The axe and hoe were the basic tools needed for raising corn to eat and tobacco to sell. In all, here was food and equipment to make a start. The master, in turn, received several years of labor he needed to make profits from the export of tobacco to a European market. In theory, at least, the indenture system benefited both the master and his laborer.

The form of indenture that Lord Baltimore published in a recruiting pamphlet also specified fifty acres of land as a part of freedom dues, but the Maryland records make clear that what was intended was a warrant for fifty acres. A warrant enabled its owner to locate a piece of land and pay for a survey and patent. The land was not free to the holder of a warrant, but it was worth close to nothing compared to the price of freehold land in England. There the great majority of people owned none. Since the master was due a warrant for one hundred acres for paying the transportation costs of the servant, he was in effect giving his former servant half. However, it appears that either many indentures did not have such a clause or that many masters simply ignored it. Lord Baltimore soon found it expedient to reduce the warrant for transportation of a settler to fifty acres and himself grant a fifty-acre warrant to any ex-servant who applied for it.

Lord Baltimore offered two lures to his settlers. First was the land [50 acres], which he granted to anyone who paid his own way or that of another and to servants who completed their terms. To attract leaders like Cornwaleys, he made extra-large land grants—for the earliest adventurers as much as two thousand acres for each five men imported, or four hundred acres per man. With these grants went the right to hold the title lord of the manor and the powers of English manor lords to hold manorial courts. The proprietor intended that these lords would hold the major offices in his colony.*

Second was freedom of conscience in religion. Maryland was to be a land where Catholics would be free of the English penal laws. In England, these laws forbade Catholics to worship in secret, heavily fined or imprisoned them for not taking communion in the Church of England, and prevented them from holding public office. Catholics could not provide their Catholic children a Catholic education nor give or bequeath them land. These and other severe restrictions were not always strictly enforced, but the danger was always present. In Maryland, Catholics were to be free of these laws. Evidently both George and Cecil Calvert assumed that they would not automatically extend to the colony.

In protecting Maryland Catholics, the proprietor was not trying to create a Catholic colony. He envisioned a country where all Christians could worship as they pleased; no one could be excluded from public office for his religion; and no public taxes could be demanded for the support of any church. With these policies, he believed, religious peace would be kept and prosperity for all would follow.

What were the lures for Daniel Clocker? Would that we knew! Was he simply hungry and basically in search of survival? Or did he hope that with hard work a better life awaited him? His later career tells us that he was not a Catholic. Probably religion did not enter into his decision, but the possibility of acquiring land may have had a heady impact.

Did he consider the risks: of shipwreck, of the likelihood that he would never again see family and friends? Did he fear a destination of which he knew little or nothing, except, perhaps, that "savages" inhabited it? Perhaps not. He was young, as were most seventeenth-century Chesapeake immigrants. If Daniel was the son of Hans and Bridgid Clocker, he was about seventeen. Probably then, as now, a young man was unlikely to believe that *he* was going to die, no matter what dangers he faced. Lord Baltimore offered servants a chance to acquire land, and in England there was no such promise. Doubtless Daniel Clocker did not expect to attain great wealth, but he surely hoped for a better future than he could see in England.

Nevertheless, the risk of early death for Clocker was large. All newcomers to the Chesapeake fell ill during the first year. They had moved to a new disease environment. Although many of the illnesses were familiar, the strains were different, and Englishmen had no immunities built up in childhood to such infections. In the very early years, 20 to 30 percent of new emigrants may have died in their "seasoning," the term settlers used to describe the experience. Furthermore, those who survived had life expectancies shorter than they would have had if they had stayed in England. Mean age

---

*Warrants of land came to be called headrights, but not all warrants were for taking up land.

at death for a seasoned man who arrived at age twenty was only forty-three, and 70 percent would die before age fifty. Luckily for Clocker, he won this gamble. He died at some point in his late fifties or early sixties.

Clocker arrived at Maryland's first settlement late in its second or early in its third year. In March 1634, Governor Leonard Calvert, with the help of Virginia fur trader Captain Henry Fleet, had selected a beautiful spot on the St. Mary's River, a small tributary of the Potomac River just above where it joins the Chesapeake Bay. Here had been a village of the Yaocomico Indians, who were ready to abandon it. They lived in fear of the fierce Susquehannock Indians, who lived along the Susquehanna River north of the bay. The spot was ideal. Soils were excellent, fields were already cleared, and timber and fresh water were ample. The Yaocomico sold their village to Governor Leonard Calvert for trade goods, and by the time Clocker arrived, all of them had moved away.

When Clocker disembarked, the fort built in 1634 was still in use. Leonard Calvert described it as "a palizado of one hundred and twentie yarde square, with flower flankes, we have mounted one peece of ordnance, and placed about six murderers in parts most convenient." About 140 people had occupied the fort in 1634 and about sixty had arrived the next year. Supposing 20 percent had died by 1636, Clocker joined a settlement of about 160 people, mostly young servant men. Doubtless many still lived in the fort, but others had probably built cabins nearby. The settlers were growing tobacco, Indian corn, beans and peas in nearby fields, and cabbages and other garden crops as well.

Lord Baltimore, who remained in England to defend his charter, had ordered that his first settlers lay out a town, and he expected them to build their houses there. To Europeans, towns were necessary to civilization, yet the cluster of settlement around the fort soon disappeared. The major investors were eager to start developing the large land tracts they were entitled to claim, and most other colonists were still indentured servants, who would follow their masters. Lord Baltimore recognized that more incentive would be needed to develop town properties. In 1636 he ordered that for the next two years the first adventurers, in addition to the land grants he had already offered, could have ten acres of Town Land on the fields of St. Mary's for each person they transported. Later adventurers could have five acres per person. The investors responded, but the result was not a village. By 1641 there were perhaps eleven houses spread out over about 1,500 acres, not all of it yet surveyed. It was to be another twenty-five years before even a hamlet such as Daniel had known at home came into being on the Town Lands.

Daniel must have blessed his good luck for his safe arrival, but he undoubtedly was soon sick in his seasoning. Probably he caught malaria early on, an intermittent disease that stayed with him the rest of his life. He may also have suffered dysentery, another common ailment, or typhoid or typhus. Once he was well, he was put to hard work. Cornwaleys had been

26

using his servants to build the fort, erect temporary housing for settlers, and raise tobacco. Daniel doubtless helped in the fields and on the various construction projects, where he may have gained experience in planting and carpentry that was to prove useful in later life.

Clocker's status as a servant was different from what he likely had experienced in England. There, boys and girls customarily left home after age fourteen to work in the households of others until they could marry and establish their own. Some were apprenticed for several years in return for education in a skill, but most worked as servants in husbandry on yearly contracts, giving them chances to escape harsh or incompatible masters. By contrast, Clocker's service to Cornwaleys was payment for ocean passage. He began with a debt to his master. Consequently his contracted term was much longer, and even more important, his master could sell him without his consent. He could not choose a master. Furthermore, penalties for running away could be severe. Servants—most were caught or returned on their own, if they did not perish—had to pay extra days of service for each day they were absent. Some unhappy Chesapeake indentured servants called their circumstances slavery.

Nevertheless, Maryland custom, later established in law, gave Clocker and his fellow servants important protections. They could complain to the county court if food, clothing, shelter, or medical care were insufficient, or if beatings for correction had produced serious injury. The court would order masters to remedy deficiencies and forbid punishment of servants for bringing complaints. Early court records are missing that might show whether Daniel Clocker had occasion for complaint against Cornwaleys, and if so, what the outcome was; but clearly on the whole, the system worked. From the standpoint of colony leaders, the shortage of labor was too severe to risk developing a reputation for Maryland as a place poor Englishmen should avoid. From the standpoint of the servant, he or she could seek redress for serious neglect or mistreatment and could look forward to being free in a society that, for several decades, at least, offered real opportunities, provided early death did not intervene.

Living conditions in the region were also new for Clocker. For one thing, he had to adjust to a new climate. Winters were colder and summers much hotter than in England. For another, he had to accept new foods. English settlers could not grow wheat, the staple of the English diet. Growing wheat required plowing the ground, and in the Chesapeake for many decades plowing was usually impractical. The root systems of trees in forests never before cleared took too long to dig out. Settlers adopted Indian agriculture, which produced maize or Indian corn. They learned how to kill the trees by girdling so that the sap could not rise. When the leaves fell off, the sun reached the ground, and one could then use a hoe to make hills of earth beneath the branches and plant kernels of corn. The yield was extraordinary to English eyes. The productivity per acre was twice that of wheat.

Furthermore, once the land was ready, the crop was simple to produce. In about four days, and armed only with a hoe, a man could make hills and plant enough seed to feed himself for a year. He had to spend a few days here and there weeding until his corn plants were high enough to shade out competing plants, but otherwise the crop required little attention until the planter was ready to harvest it. This was in many ways an ideal food crop.

Daniel may have missed English bread and at first disliked corn bread and corn mush or hominy. In addition, he probably found the preparation of the kernels for making them edible an onerous task. Like the Indians, the settlers had to soak the kernels for several hours to soften the shells a little and then pound them in a mortar with a pestle. After sifting, the cook used the fine grains to make bread and boiled the coarse grains to make hominy. It took ten minutes to pound a cup, and the ration per man was about four and a half cups per day, or nearly an hour of pounding. Some settlers complained that they could not digest the bread or the hominy. If the kernels they ate had not been sufficiently pounded, undoubtedly they could not. Most settlers did adjust quickly to maize, which continued as a staple of the Maryland diet long after wheat or rye or barley became a practical alternative.

Maize has one disadvantage. It is not as complete in nutrients as wheat or rye or barley. It is lacking in niacin, an essential element, and a diet confined to maize brings on a debilitating disease, pellagra, with its painful sores and severe gastritis. The Indians avoided this illness by supplementing their corn with beans and peas, which they grew among the corn stalks, and by hunting for meat and fish. The English did the same.

In consequence, Clocker ate some foods not so easily procured in England. In 1636, little domestic livestock was as yet on hand at St. Mary's, but deer, small mammals, and birds were abundant, oyster beds lined the shores of the St. Mary's River, and fish of many kinds were easily caught. He probably had the first deer meat, the first oysters, the first sturgeon, perhaps the first wild duck or goose he had ever eaten. Archaeologists working on seventeenth-century Chesapeake sites have found ample evidence of such consumption. Cornwaleys doubtless supplied all his servants with protein from such sources or they would have become too weak to work. Clocker may have eaten better than he ever had in England.

More than English bread, Clocker may have missed the beer and cider he was used to drinking. Barley for English beer could not easily be grown on unplowed land, and corn did not make good beer. While the settlers brought seeds for planting fruit trees, orchards were few in 1636 and were not yet producing. Peaches grew for three years and apple trees for seven before they bore fruit. Local cider would soon be generally available and an important source of nutrition, but for the moment colonists drank water. Luckily there was an abundance of good springs on the Town Lands and nearby.

Also different from England, and far less satisfactory than the food and drink, was the housing available, and not just to servants like Clocker.

Houses were made of wood and the framing posts were not set on foundations but put in the ground, where moisture and termites soon attacked them. Many houses were very small one-room structures with earthen floors, and at first probably few were more than one story high, with a loft above. In some, smoke from the fire escaped from a hole in the roof, although most householders probably built chimneys of wattle and daub as soon as possible. All were covered by rived clapboard siding and roofing, easily penetrated by wind and rain. Such buildings rotted quickly, requiring major repairs within about fifteen years. English houses, put on foundations of stone or brick, constructed of timber filled in with wattle and daub and covered with thatched roofs, were more permanent and in every way more comfortable: much warmer and drier and usually larger. However, travelers' descriptions, builder's contracts, and archaeological excavations tell that over the whole seventeenth century, most Chesapeake settlers continued to live in impermanent leaky structures, although, as time went on, more often than earlier improved with extra rooms and occasionally a brick chimney. Such houses were quickly built and hence inexpensive to construct in a labor-short society.

Furnishings for the early houses were minimal. Twenty-six estate inventories that survive from 1638 to 1642 show that people slept on the floor on tickings filled with flock and used wool blankets or rugs for a covering. The masters might have sheets, but most buildings were too small and crowded to permit bedsteads, which could not be rolled away during the day. Only two inventories indicated their presence. Nor were tables or seats usually listed; such items appeared in only five inventories. People sat on chests or brought in stumps or perhaps simply squatted; and large chests doubled as beds and tables. In turn, these quarters must have been dark unless the window shutters were open, in which case the rooms were undoubtedly very cold. If Daniel Clocker lived in Cornwaleys' house, he may have been more comfortable than most settlers, but his master likely crowded most of his many servants into separate housing and provided few furnishings.

Finally, Clocker had to learn a whole new system of husbandry organized around tobacco and corn. Tobacco had two characteristics that dominated all planter decisions. First, it required a great deal of land. It was a crop so demanding of nutrients that the planter had to move to new land after three years. He could grow corn on the old land for another three or four years, since the deeper root systems of corn tapped a new level of nutrients, but thereafter—in the absence of manuring, which gave tobacco an unpleasant aroma and taste—the land had to lie fallow for twenty years. In any one year, the planter did not use much of his land. One hand could handle only two to three acres in tobacco plants, plus two acres in corn that custom, and then law, required to ensure the colony's subsistence. However, over the long term, a planter needed twenty acres per hand growing

29

tobacco if he was not to deplete his land. Since he also needed land for wood and for livestock to range in, contemporaries considered fifty acres to be the minimum acreage for a farm.

Second, tobacco was a very labor intensive crop, and one that required careful tending and observation nearly all year round. Work began in February with clearing and planting a small tobacco seed bed. It ended in December with packing the leaf in casks for shipment to overseas markets. In between were months of hoeing unplowed ground into hills; planting corn and transplanting tobacco seedlings; weeding, deworming, and pruning the tobacco; and curing the crop and hanging it to dry in the tobacco barn. Clocker and his fellow servants learned from their overseers how to judge when the leaf was ripe for curing, how to hang it to ensure proper drying, and how to judge when it was ready to be stripped and packed. They hoped one day to be planters themselves, and mistakes would spoil the crop.

Taking care of animals was a daily routine for English farmers that was missing from Clocker's new life. Cattle and hogs ranged for their food in the forest, and planters did not stable or feed them in winter. To feed their cattle, planters would have had to raise corn beyond what they needed for their own subsistence, and the tight schedules for hilling and planting in the spring meant that hills for more corn would mean fewer for the cash crop. Since the animals had to fend for themselves, planters fenced in their crops, not their livestock, another difference from English practices, and one that discouraged the collection of manure.

Throughout the seventeenth century visiting Englishmen were dismayed at what seemed to them inefficiency and neglect in the Chesapeake: cattle running loose, unstabled and starving in winter; houses leaky and rotting; crops unmanured; old fields full of dead stumps, growing up in weeds, and looking forsaken, although as the land renewed itself, it produced good timber. The English farmer fertilized his land with animal manure, making long-term fallows unneeded. He found or made grass pasture for his cattle and, as necessary, stabled and fed them in winter. His wife or his dairy maid milked his cows and made butter and cheese, often to sell. What English critics did not understand were the constraints that faced colonists in the Chesapeake. Unlike England, land in the Chesapeake was plentiful and cheap, whereas labor was scarce and expensive. Virgin forest provided ample timber but made plowing and hence production of English grains impractical. At the same time these woodlands supplied sufficient forage for animals nearly all year round. A long fallow agriculture, range-fed cattle, and earthfast clapboarded houses that could be quickly constructed were efficient solutions to new circumstances.

By 1640, Clocker was free of his service. What were his choices then? He was a laborer in a labor-short economy, where wages were high. He could make a contract to serve Cornwaleys or another employer for wages. This arrangement would probably provide him with room, board, and washing but would deprive him of some autonomy. His master would dictate his activity and have power to discipline him as a member of the household. Or Clocker could persuade a planter to lease him land on which he could set up his own household and plant his own crops, perhaps paying part of his rent with labor. However, he then would have to supply his own house-keeping, grow his own food, and perhaps even build himself a house to live in and a tobacco house for his crop. If he had to build housing, he would pay no rent for his land for several years, but even so, the capital necessary to begin this arrangement was most often not at hand for a newly freed servant, unless he could get credit from his landlord. Finally, he could use the headright Cornwaleys owed him to take up a fifty-acre tract and become not just a householder but a landowner. This last option was the least available as a first step. To take up land, he had to pay a surveyor and a clerk for his survey and patent. These additional costs required capital and/or credit that a newly freed servant usually did not have.

What Clocker decided is unknown. Probably he found another ex-servant to be his "mate" in establishing a tenancy on Cornwaleys's land. Besides the rent the captain charged—perhaps a third of the tobacco crop—his return was in the improvements Clocker and his mate made in housing and fencing and in planting and caring for the orchard always required in a lease. Once Clocker moved on, Cornwaleys could rent or sell the property at a higher price than unimproved land would bring. Such development leases, usually made for seven years, benefited both landlord and tenant in a newly settled colony.

As a freeman, Clocker was entitled to vote for a representative in the Maryland Assembly, or, if all freeman were called to attend, to cast his vote for any legislation the Assembly considered. Lord Baltimore's charter for Maryland gave the proprietor vast powers to create his own government and raise armies to defend his province. But the charter also provided a basic protection for his settlers: he could not make laws without "the Advice, Assent, and Approbation of the Free-Men . . . Or of the great Part of them, or of their Delegates or Deputies." Before 1650 all freemen were called to the Assembly or were permitted to vote for delegates. There were as yet no property requirements in law or custom, a situation without precedent in England. Of course, the leadership was in the hands of the few, mostly the governor and council—appointed by Lord Baltimore—which also sat as the Provincial Court. Nevertheless, the participation of free male settlers of any status was important to establishing the authority of the leaders. In such a small community, so isolated from its home base, cooperation was essential. However, actually attending the Assembly could be time-consuming and expensive, especially for poor men. Rather than appear, many freemen gave their proxies to one of the colony's leaders. In March 1642, so did Daniel Clocker.

The next stage in Clocker's career was marriage to Mary Lawne Courtney. She had arrived in 1638, at age twenty-four, as a servant indentured to

Margaret Brent, a prominent Catholic. However, Mary Lawne had not remained a servant long in this small woman-short society. In 1639, James Courtney, a free immigrant, had purchased her time and married her. By early 1643 she was a widow with a son, Thomas, at most a year old. Sometime in 1645 or very early 1646, she married Daniel Clocker.

Marriage gave Daniel new status. He was now truly the head of a family, a position that sharing with a male partner did not give him. As head, he was held responsible for the welfare and behavior of his wife and children and any other household members. The community expected him to keep good order and the law allowed him to correct any of his charges with physical punishment, provided that any stick used in beating was no thicker than a man's finger at its thickest end. Beating even his wife was permissible. Under English common law, he owned whatever property Mary brought to the marriage and he was in a position to control the assets of her child. As a married woman, Mary could not make a contract; her husband had to act for her. On the other hand, he owed her a maintenance and a share of his estate if he died before she did. Mary had had independence as a widow, but in this land three thousand miles away from any kin she might have in England, she had needed, and probably wanted, a husband more.

Still, her position was not as subordinate in reality as this description would suggest. Running a household, especially once there were children and perhaps servants, was necessarily a team effort. Mary pounded the corn, a daily two-hour task just for Daniel, herself, and little Thomas and a task that grew much longer as the family grew in size and age, although eventually the children could help. As well as keeping house and preparing meals, she gathered wild greens and berries, grew and administered medicinal herbs, raised cabbages, onions, and sweet potatoes, picked and dried apples or peaches from the orchard (once Daniel had one), and milked the cows. She watched the children when they were small and trained her daughters to housewifery as they grew older. When necessary, she assisted in the fields, perhaps watering or weeding the tobacco seedlings, or transplanting them into the hills, or hoeing weeds. All these activities contributed vitally to the family economy. A man without a wife was handicapped, unless he had a daughter old enough to take her mother's place. In this largely male society, wives had an especially high value. If husband and wife disagreed, the husband was likely to prevail, but family peace and efficiency required many shared decisions.

The Clockers began life together in troubled times for the Maryland colony. In 1642 civil war broke out in England between King Charles I and Parliament, and early in 1645 the conflict reached Maryland. A ship captain, Richard Ingle, who had been trading to Maryland and Virginia for tobacco, used letters of marque from Parliament—authorization to seize enemy ships—to atttack the St. Mary's settlement. His excuse was that

Maryland Catholics supported the king, as most Catholics did in England. He took the colony completely by surprise. Immediately he secured two Catholic leaders and two Jesuits as prisoners, and, with the help of disaffected Protestant settlers, pillaged the estates of Catholic leaders and burned the Catholic chapel. Governor Leonard Calvert, meanwhile, gathered supporters in a hastily fortified compound called St. Theomas's Fort but had no success in restablishing his rule. In April 1645, Ingle returned to England, taking his prisoners and plunder with him and leaving the colony in the hands of the rebels. Sometime afterward, Leonard Calvert finally departed to Virginia. He did not reestablish proprietary authority—with the help of soldiers he recruited in Virginia—until late in 1646. Why he took so long remains a mystery.

In early 1645, Maryland had had five hundred or more inhabitants; at Calvert's return, there were perhaps a hundred, fewer than had come in the first expedition in 1634. Ingle's raid and its aftermath were later referred to as the "time of troubles." Mary Courtney lost a cow during, in her words, "the time of the Plunder." In search of stability, most of the Maryland settlers pulled up stakes and moved acrosss the Potomac river to the as yet unsettled Northern Neck of Virginia.

The Clockers did not go, and the decision was undoubtedly wise. The late 1640s were a time of major expansion in the tobacco economy, and once Lord Baltimore's government was reestablished, new settlers rapidly piled into Maryland. Once more it was a place where a planter could work toward success. Clocker must have continued to raise corn and tobacco, and his skills as a carpenter were in some demand. By 1650 he was ready to pay the costs of acquiring freehold land.

In 1650 and 1651, Clocker obtained 150 acres. One hundred acres he patented, using his and Mary's service rights. These were rights to fifty acres that Lord Baltimore had established in 1648 for all servants who finished their terms. This hundred acres, on the Chesapeake Bay about seven miles east of the Town Lands, he called "Daniel Clocker's Hould." About the same time, he also purchased a fifty-acre Town Land tract known as St. Andrews from Margaret and Mary Brent, Mary Clocker's former mistresses, who were moving to Virginia. St. Andrews, on St. Andrews Creek, was adjacent to the sisters' own plantation, and they had probably been leasing it to the Clockers. Daniel must have jumped at the opportunity to buy it. The years of work he and Mary had put into building a farm there spared them the labor of building anew.

The Clockers lived on the Town Land at St. Andrews for the rest of their lives. They kept "Daniel Clocker's Hould" but later renamed it "Clocker's Marsh," a fact that suggests that the tract was more valuable for feeding livestock than for growing tobacco. They may have put cattle there instead of trying to farm it. By 1659, Daniel had also acquired a fifty-acre tract just across St. Andrews Creek, called Clark's Freehold. In all by that time he owned two hundred acres, enough to provide an inheritance for several children.

By 1661, the Clockers had five surviving children. They are named in a gift of cattle that their father made to them that year. Elizabeth had been born in 1646, Daniel in 1648 and Mary in 1650. Like most mothers in pre-industrial times, Mary Clocker nursed her babies herself, and the contraceptive effect of nursing, it was thought, meant the likelihood that a new pregnancy would not start until the baby was weaned shortly after his or her first birthday. Hence children often arrived about two years apart, as Mary Clocker's did. However, during the 1650s, Mary bore only two children who were still alive in 1661, John and Catheryn. Perhaps she had become less fertile; in 1659 she was forty-five. Or, she may have had miscarriages or carried to term two or three other children who died in infancy. Child mortality was very high everywhere in the seventeenth century. In Maryland, 45 to 55 percent of children born did not survive to adulthood, and most of these died before age four. Daniel Jr. and Mary—and Rebecca, not yet born when the gift was made—were to live to marry and establish their own families, but Elizabeth, John, and Catheryn and perhaps several other Clocker children did not.

The Clockers surely raised and sold tobacco, but they also gained income from other sources. An unusually substantial portion of immigrants from the late 1640s through the mid-1660s came in family groups. Unlike newly arrived servants, who would move into already established households, families needed dwelling houses, tobacco barns, and livestock. Daniel began to appear in the records as "Daniel Clocker, carpenter," especially after his stepson and sons reached the age when they could be of real help in the fields. Mary had skills as a dairy maid, an occupation confined to women, and there was a market among her neighbors for butter and cheese when she had time to make such products. Once the Clockers had well-established herds of cattle and pigs, they could sell pregnant cows and sows to households just starting out. The sale of a cow with her calf was a major supplement to income from tobacco, adding the value of more than half a tobacco crop from the late 1640s until the mid-1670s. And Mary was the local midwife. A court record in 1659 shows that in one difficult case she was owed two hundred pounds of tobacco, at that time about one-fifth of a year's crop.

What the Clockers could not do was purchase necessary manufactures locally. All such goods they imported from England in return for tobacco, a situation that prevailed over most of the seventeenth century. There was work for carpenters to build houses, coopers to make casks for the tobacco crop, and "taylors" to make clothing, but other crafts did not flourish. In all, it was simply more cost-efficient for settlers to import cloth, metal and leather products, and other manufactures in return for tobacco. Over these years, Daniel Clocker appeared in the remaining records from time to time as a participant in community affairs and government, although the absence of the county court records limits the amount and variety of information. Appointed by the Provincial Court, which acted as a probate court, he appraised the estates of dead neighbors to establish the value of their assets. This practice was a protection for both creditors and heirs or legatees of the deceased. As early as 1648, probably before he owned land, he was summoned to sit on a petit jury at the Provincial Court, and in 1653 he temporarily attained the address of "Mister" when he sat on a Provincial Court grand jury to investigate a murder. Clearly he was establishing himself as a reliable neighbor and citizen, whose word and judgment counted.

DOCUMENTS

Virginia, A Troubled Colony, 1622

I found the plantations generally seated upon meer salt marshes, full of infectious boggy and muddy creeks and lakes, and hereby subjected to all those inconveniences and diseases which are so commonly found in the most unsound and most unhealthy parts of England, whereof every country and climate hath some.

I found the shores and sides of those parts of the main river, where our plantations are settled, every where so shallow that no boats can approach the shores; so that besides the difficulty, danger and spoil of goods in the landing of them, the poor people are forced to the continual wading and wetting themselves, and that in the prime of winter, when the ships commonly arrive, and thereby get such violent surfeits of cold upon cold as seldom leave them until they leave to live.

The new people that are yearly sent over, which arrives here for the most part very unseasonably in winter, find neither guest-house, inn, nor any the like place to shroud themselves in at their arrival; no, not so much as a stroke given towards any such charitable work, so that many of them, by want hereof, are not only seen dying under hedges, and in the woods, but being dead lye some of them for many days unregarded and unburied.

The colony was this winter in much distress of victual, so that English meal was sold at the rate of thirty shillings a bushel, their own native corn,

SOURCE: Report of Nathaniel Butler, Governor of Bermuda, 1622. Document from Bibliobase®, edited by Michael Bellesiles. Copyright © by Houghton Mifflin Company. Reprinted by permission.

called maize, at ten and fifteen shillings per bushel, the which, howsoever it lay heavy upon the shoulders of the generality, it may be suspected not to be unaffected by some of the chief, for they only having the means in those extremities to trade with the natives for corn, do hereby engross all into their own hands, and to sell it abroad at their own prices, and I myself have heard from the mouth of a prime one among them that he would never wish that their own corn should be cheaper amongst them than eight shillings the bushel.

Their houses are generally the worst that ever I saw, the meanest cottages in England being every way equal (if not superior) with the most of the best, and besides, so improvidently and scatteringly are they seated one from another, as partly by their distance, but especially by the interposition of creeks and swamps, as they call them, they offer all advantages to their savage enemies, and are utterly deprived of all sudden recollection of themselves upon any terms whatsoever.

I found not the least piece of fortification; three pieces of ordnance only mounted at James City, and one at Flowerde Hundreds, but never a one of them serviceable, so that it is most certain that a small bark of a hundred tun may take its time to pass up the river in spite of them, and coming to an anchor before the town may beat all their houses down about their ears, and so forcing them to retreat into the woods may land under the favour of their ordnance and rifle the town at pleasure.

Expecting, according to their printed books, a great forwardness of divers and sundry commodities at mine arrival, I found not any one of them so much as in any towardness of being, for the iron works were utterly wasted, and the men dead, the furnaces for glass and pots at a stay, and small hopes; as for the rest they were had in a general derision even amongst themselves, and the pamphlets that had published [there], being sent thither by hundreds, were laughed to scorn, and every base fellow boldly gave them the lye in divers particulars; so that tobacco only was the business, and for ought that I could hear every man madded upon that little thought or looked for anything else.

I found the ancient plantations of Henrico and Charles City wholly quitted and left to the spoil of the Indians, who not only burnt the houses, said to be once the best of all others, but fell upon the poultry, hogs, cows, goats and horses, whereof they killed great numbers, to the great grief as well as ruin of the old inhabitants, who stick not to affirm that these were not only the best and healthiest parts of all others, but might also, by their natural strength of situation, have been the most easily preserved of all others.

Whereas, according to his Majesty's most gracious letters-patents, his people are as near as possibly may be to be governed after the excellent laws and customs of England, I found in the Government here not only ignorant and enforced strayings in divers particulars, but wilful and intended ones; in so much as some who urged due conformity have in contempt been termed men of law, and were excluded from those rights which by orderly proceedings they were elected and sworn unto here.

There having been, as it is thought, not fewer than ten thousand souls transported thither, there are not, thro' the aforementioned abuses and neglects, above two thousand of them to be found alive at this present . . . many of them also in a sickly and desperate state. So that it may undoubtedly be expected that unless the confusions and private ends of some of the Company here, and the bad execution in seconding them by their agents there, be redressed with speed by some divine and supream hand, that instead of a plantation it will get the name of a slaughter-house, and so justly become both odious to ourselves and contemptible to all the world.

"We shall be as a City upon a Hill," 1630

1. For the persons, we are a Company professing ourselves fellow members of Christ, In which respect only though we were absent from each other many miles, and had our employments as far distant, yet we ought to account ourselves knit together by this bond of love, and live in the exercise of it, if we would have comfort of our being in Christ. . . .

2. for the work we have in hand, it is by a mutual consent through a special overruling providence, and a more than an ordinary approbation of the Churches of Christ to seek out a place of Cohabitation and Consortship under a due form of Government both civil and ecclesiastical. In such cases as this the care of the public must oversway all private respects, by which not only conscience, but mere Civil policy doth bind us; for it is a true rule that particular estates cannot subsist in the ruin of the public.

3. The end is to improve our lives to do more service to the Lord the comfort and increase of the body of christ whereof we are members that ourselves and posterity may be the better preserved from the Common corruptions of this evil world to serve the Lord and work out our Salvation under the power and purity of his holy Ordinances.

4. for the means whereby this must be effected, they are 2fold, a Conformity with the work and end we aim at, these we see are extraordinary, therefore we must not content ourselves with usual ordinary means

SOURCE: Karen Ordahl Kupperman, ed., *Major Problems in American Colonial History* (Lexington, Mass.: D. C. Heath and Co., 1993), 124–126. Reprinted with permission of Houghton Mifflin Company.

Some of the spelling in this document has been modernized.

whatsoever we did or ought to have done when we lived in England, the same must we do and more also where we go: That which the most in their Churches maintain as a truth in profession only, we must bring into familiar and constant practice, as in this duty of love we must love brotherly without dissimulation, we must love one another with a pure heart fervently we must bear one another's burdens, we must not look only on our own things, but also on the things of our brethren, neither must we think that the lord will bear with such failings at our hands as he doth from those among whom we have lived. . . .

. . . Thus stands the cause between God and us, we are entered into Covenant with him for this worke, we have taken out a Commission, the Lord have given us leave to draw our own Articles we have professed to enterprise these Actions upon these and these ends, we have hereupon besought him of favour and blessing: Now if the Lord shall please to hear us, and bring us in peace to the place we desire, then hath he ratified this Covenant and sealed our Commission, [and] will expect a strict performance of the Articles contained in it, but if we shall neglect the observation of these Articles which are the ends we have propounded, and dissembling with our God, shall fall to embrace this present world and prosecute our carnal intensions, seeking great things for ourselves and our posterity, the Lord will surely break out in wrath against us be revenged of such a perjured people and make us know the price of the breach of such a Covenant.

Now the only way to avoid this shipwreck and to provide for our posterity is to follow the Counsel of Micah, to do Justly, to love mercy, to walk humbly with our God, for this end, we must be knit together in this work as one man, we must entertain each other in brotherly Affection, we must be willing to abridge ourselves of our superfluities, for the supply of others' necessities, we must uphold a familiar Commerce together in all meekness, gentleness, patience and liberality, we must delight in each other, make others' Conditions our own, rejoice together, mourn together, labour, and suffer together, always having before our eyes our Commission and Community in the work, our Community as members of the same body, so shall we keep the unity of the spirit in the bond of peace, the Lord will be our God and delight to dwell among us, as his own people and will command a blessing upon us in all our ways, so that we shall see much more of his wisdom power goodness and truth than formerly we have been acquainted with, we shall find that the God of Israel is among us, when ten of us shall be able to resist a thousand of our enemies, when he shall make us a praise and glory, that men shall say of succeeding plantations: the lord make it like that of New England: for we must Consider that we shall be as a City upon a Hill, the eyes of all people are upon us; so that if we shall deal falsely with our god in this work we have undertaken and so cause him to withdraw his present help from us, we shall be made a story and a by-word through the world, we shall open the mouths of enemies to speak evil of the ways of god and all professors for Gods sake; we shall shame the faces of many of gods worthy servants, and cause their prayers to be turned in Curses upon us till we be consumed out of the good land whether we are going. . . .

Chapter 3

The Enslavement of Africans in Britain's American Colonies

A slave auction in 18th century New York, a major center of the slave trade in colonial America.

Africans contributed to the population of the developing American colonies. Although the first blacks brought to Virginia in 1619 were forcibly removed from West Africa, the English colonists probably did not view them as slaves; slavery did not exist in the laws of the colonies prior to the 1660s. Thus the fate of blacks brought to the colonies before that decade varied. Some, like white servants, eventually gained their freedom and obtained land and even servants of their own. Others spent their lives in servitude. But beginning in law during the decade of the 1660s and rapidly increasing in practice after 1680, slavery spread throughout the colonies and became the primary source of labor from the Chesapeake colonies south to Georgia.

In the essay that follows, historian Jon Butler traces the evolution of slavery, explains the reasons for its virtual displacement of white indentured servitude in the southern colonies, and describes in detail the experiences of the Africans from capture in their native lands, to the horrors of their sea voyage to America, and finally to their existence under what he terms the "increasingly authoritarian institution" of slavery. With whites and Native Americans far outnumbering blacks in the American colonies during most of the seventeenth century, how does the author account for the decision to turn to Africa for the supply of laborers and to slavery as the system of work-force control? The essay describes the gradual emergence of a sense of community among African Americans during the eighteenth century. What do you consider to be the most significant manifestations of their communal life?

As the essay makes clear, slavery was by no means restricted to the South. In New York City, a major center of the slave trade, nearly half of its citizens owned slaves. As you read the first document, a 1731 New York law regulating the movement of slaves at night, be aware of the fact that the city had experienced a major slave rebellion in 1712 that began with arson and ended with the execution of twenty-three slaves. Then consider the role played by fear in encouraging the passage of laws such as this as well as the brutality often associated with slave owning.

Probably slavery's most brutal aspect was the slave trade, which included capture and forced removal to ports in Africa, the sea journey across the Atlantic, and finally sale in the slave markets of America. Undoubtedly, the cruelest segment of that three-part horror story took place on the slave ships during the transatlantic voyage, termed the Middle Passage. The second document is from an account by Englishman Alexander Falconbridge of the conditions he witnessed as a ship's doctor aboard slave ships in the 1780s. In what ways did some of the Africans, under the most hopeless conditions, still manage to offer resistance to their captors?

ESSAY

The Evolution of Slavery in Colonial America

Jon Butler

The history of Africans in America differs dramatically from the history of Europeans in America. Where the African experience in America centered on themes of capture, enslavement, and coercion, the history of Europeans in America centered on themes of choice, profit, and considerable freedom.

SOURCE: Reprinted by permission of the publisher from "Peoples" in *Becoming America: The Revolution Before 1776* by Jon Butler, pp. 36–48, Cambridge, Mass.: Harvard University Press. Copyright © 2000 by the President and Fellows of Harvard College.

The African and European experiences never duplicated and seldom paralleled each other. Yet Africans and their experience in America powerfully intersected the decline of the Indian population and the outpouring of non-English immigrants to America to recast the seventeenth-century colonies and become the American future.

In 1680 slavery was uncommon, strange, and even exotic in the British mainland colonies. British colonists certainly knew what it was. They knew it meant ownership of other human beings. They knew it gave owners untrammeled power to buy, sell, and compel labor from the enslaved and to own their offspring. As the eighteenth century progressed, they tightened slaveholding and treated bonded men and women with ever greater severity. They consistently corralled Africans' behavior and wrung from them every conceivable advantage of labor and creativity, often through unimaginable mental and physical cruelty. The principal impetus for this action was simple: profit. Slaveholding attracted European colonists intent on realizing the dreams that brought them to America even when it subjected others to horrific suffering.

As late as 1680 the English mainland colonies knew few Africans and little slavery. In the Chesapeake colonies of Maryland and Virginia, Africans accounted for only 5 percent of the population in 1680, and English indentured servants comprised more than 90 percent of the hired labor force. Between 1650 and 1680 the minor slavery that existed in the Chesapeake remained loose and relatively informal. Its legal articulation was sparse, and its social leakage substantial. The Maryland and Virginia legislatures passed few laws enunciating a comprehensive slave "code" before 1690, and from the 1650s into the 1680s, surprising numbers of Africans lived as free residents, completing labor terms more akin to those of indentured servants, after which they were freed by their owners. Some free Africans farmed land they owned, and a few, like Anthony Johnson of Accomack County, Virginia, owned African slaves themselves. Yet by 1700 the free Africans had disappeared—fled or been reenslaved, no one knows—probably because the English settlers' sudden turn to extensive slaveholding after 1680 made them a threat, a preview of the ways that increased slaveholding would transform seventeenth-century colonial society almost beyond recognition.

Why the rush to slaveholding after 1680? Complex causes created the change. First, the supply of British and continental European indentured servants declined as the colonial demand for labor continued and accelerated, especially after 1680. English officials complained less about overcrowding at home, and rumors of mistreatment of indentured servants in America abounded. As a result, the immigration of servants from England to America declined in the last quarter of the seventeenth century and failed to satisfy the rising labor demands of colonial farmers, especially in the Chesapeake and the Carolinas. The immigration statistics for the first decade of the eighteenth century reflect the result: between 1700 and 1709, only 1,500 indentured English, Scottish, and continental European indentured servants arrived in America, while imported Africans numbered 9,000. By the first decade of the eighteenth century, then, captured Africans outstripped indentured servants by a ratio of at least 6–1 and established a pattern of colonial labor consumption not broken until the American Revolution.

Second, captive Africans consistently became easier to obtain. The Royal African Company, which had been granted a monopoly for the British slave trade in 1672, eagerly exploited the growing market in the still small British mainland colonies. By the 1690s the company's success produced demands to open the market to competitors, and when the Crown ended the monopoly in 1698 new entrepreneurs plunged into the trade. London, Liverpool, and especially Bristol slave traders soon accounted for the great bulk of eighteenth-century mainland colony slave imports, but colonists also entered the trade. Between 1680 and the 1740s colonial merchants and ship owners began to specialize in slave trading—John Guerard, Richard Hill, Benjamin Savage, and Joseph Wragg in Charleston and Godfrey Malbone, Abraham Redwood, the Wanton family, and Samuel Vernon in Newport, Rhode Island, among others. In addition, the increasing reach of international commerce into all the colonies meant that enslaved Africans were also more easily available from Spanish, French, and especially Dutch traders. By 1710, then, the increasing numbers of colonists who wanted Africans enjoyed considerable choice in both Africans and merchants.

But why slaves? Why not some form of indentured servitude, especially since the English treated at least some Africans as indentured servants before 1650 and since both the English Civil War (1645–1649) and the Glorious Revolution (1688–1689) raised the English commitment to personal freedom? The reasons lodged in slaveholding's attraction. Slavery furnished laborers that European immigration could not stock. Slavery ameliorated the uncertainties that indentured servitude engendered. Slavery imposed a formal legal silence upon laborers denied the rights that indentured servants claimed for shelter, clothing, and even education. And slavery offered lifetime service while indentured servants completed their labor in three or four years. Even if masters breached indenture contracts without fearing lawsuits and even if few servants actually pursued complaints, the comparative point was obvious: slaves offered more attractive, longer-term investments even as they also conveyed new kinds of status to their owners.

But why not Indians rather than Africans? Indian slavery existed in the American colonies from the mid-seventeenth century past the American Revolution. But Indian slavery never prospered. Too many Indians remained free, too many resisted slavery, and too many escaped too easily into a countryside they knew intimately, in striking contrast to captured Africans, who found the countryside even more unfamiliar than did the

Europeans in America. Indian slavery existed in colonial America, but it remained an oddity.

The focus on Africans had two causes. Again, one involved convenience. In the sixteenth and seventeenth centuries Europeans discovered in Africa a ready and rapidly expanding supply of slaves. Europeans could purchase captives in African wars that they could then sell as laborers in the New World colonies. A fateful Benin agreement with a Portuguese trade in 1472 to allow the trade of precious metals and "slaves" began a trade that devastated Old World Africa. A rapidly accelerating New World demand for slaves escalated wars among African nations. Previously incidental captives became prime booty to be sold to multiplying numbers of European traders hurrying back to Africa to acquire fresh captives for eager New World markets.

Second, Western perceptions of African culture induced Europeans to ask few, if any, questions about the legal and moral basis of their own behavior. Europeans had long labeled Africans as foreign, heathen, and differently colored, regardless of African national and cultural differences and without help from pseudo-specific nineteenth-century concepts of "race." African "government" seemed chaotic and incapable. Africans were "savage" and libidinous. And they were not white, or not what passed for "white" in a Europe actually overflowing with considerable varieties of skin color among its peoples. In short, Africans might be human, but Europeans also perceived them as different, disagreeable, and dispensable, ideal candidates for an enslavement that very quickly became indelibly American.

In turning to slavery so widely after 1680, English and other European colonists in America joined a slave trade that became the largest forced human migration in history. Anomalies typified this transformation. Even at its height slave imports to Britain's mainland colonies remained a minor part of the much larger New World slave trade. Ninety-five percent of the captured Africans brought to the New World between 1700 and 1760 went to places other than the British mainland colonies: 400,000 arrived in the Dutch Caribbean, 400,000 in Spanish America, 1,000,000 in the British Caribbean, 1,000,000 in the French Caribbean, and 1,300,000 in Portuguese Brazil. By contrast, only about 250,000 captured Africans came to the British mainland colonies.

The dramatic rise in slave imports after 1680 nonetheless held immense implications for the development of Britain's eighteenth-century mainland colonies. Before 1680 English immigrants constituted the single largest group arriving in the mainland colonies and made up nearly 90 percent of all foreign arrivals in the colonies. But after 1700 and down to the American Revolution, Africans constituted the largest group of arrivals in the colonies and outstripped all European immigrants combined. Africans failed to outnumber European immigrants only between 1750 and 1759 and between 1770 and 1775, although even in those years they still outnumbered any single group of European immigrants. The number of imported Africans climbed from 9,000 between 1700 and 1709 to 40,000 in the 1730s, then doubling to 80,000 in the 1760s, with a dip to 50,000 in the 1750s. Between 1770 and 1775, African imports dropped to less than 20,000, largely because prerevolutionary political tension reduced the demand for slaves among anxious farmers and planters.

Slaveholding became especially prominent in the southern colonies but also prospered in the north. Through the 1670s indentured servants outnumbered slaves in Maryland estate inventories almost four to one. But by the 1690s slaves outnumbered indentured servants four to one. Africans constituted 13 percent of the Maryland population by 1704 and 30 percent of it by 1764. Africans constituted 6 percent of Virginia's population in 1680, 20 percent by 1720, and almost 40 percent by 1760. In South Carolina, this rate grew both higher and faster. The West Indies planters who settled the colony in the 1680s overwhelmingly rejected indentured servitude and turned to slaveholding for imported agricultural labor, just as they had done in the West Indies. Enslaved Africans outnumbered Europeans there by 1710 and constituted two-thirds of the colony's population by 1720.

Population changes in the middle and northern colonies were impressive but not so dramatic. By 1770 Pennsylvania contained more than 4,000 slaves, although the proportion of slaves seldom exceeded 3 percent between 1690 and 1770. As early as 1698 New York contained about 2,000 slaves, or about 12 percent of the population, a legacy, in part, of long-standing Dutch slave trading. But Africans climbed to about 15 percent of the colony's population at mid-century, and in 1771 the colony still contained 20,000 Africans amid 150,000 Europeans.

Even New England knew slavery. Rhode Island always contained the largest percentage of slaves in the region, a by-product of the extensive slave trading pursued by its merchants and shippers. Perhaps reflecting this fact, Rhode Island's enslaved population also fluctuated considerably, 6 percent in 1708, almost 12 percent in 1755, then back to 6 percent in 1771. In Connecticut, enslaved Africans never topped 3.2 percent of the population (in 1762), although this low ratio still placed more than 4,500 slaves in the colony. In Massachusetts, the most "English" of all the colonies, enslaved Africans made up only 2.1 percent of the population in 1764. Yet by the Revolution, more than 5,000 Africans lived in this northern colony, where captured Africans had been present since the 1630s and where their antiquity in the land was scarcely younger than the settlement of their Puritan owners.

Death, agony, and bittersweet resilience characterized the African experience in the mainland colonies. Death not only came unusually early, at least by comparison to the experience of European colonists, but in circumstances Europeans never knew. The experience of slavery for Africans began with the deaths of compatriots and kin in local wars. Then more of it came in the infamous middle passage from Africa to America, where 10 percent of slaves packed aboard a vessel died regularly and where entrapment on a ship fraught with disease or commanded by an incompetent captain sometimes brought the death rate higher. Then death stalked Africans in America. Typically, they survived less than five years. Sometimes they did not make it through even one year in America: eight of the thirty-two slaves John Mercer bought in Virginia between 1733 and 1742 died in their first year of service, for example. The causes were not difficult to locate: lack of resistance to European and American diseases, unfamiliar foods, poor housing, and depression and anomie, which produced sufficient suicides to prompt owners to complain about the problem. Unlike inanimate property, Africans could and did destroy themselves, a prospect owners feared and resented.

The agony centered on slaveholding itself, and after 1680 European colonists in the mainland settlements constructed a slaveholding of intense control and manipulativeness, a distinctly modern institution that laid the foundation for the even more powerful slaveholding of the postrevolutionary antebellum era. Everywhere in the eighteenth-century mainland colonies, European slaveholders produced an increasingly authoritarian institution ever more concerned with owners' power, slave discipline, and what they regarded as African "misbehavior." Seventeenth-century legislation was often brief in the extreme. But after 1680 assemblies from the Carolinas to New England continuously expanded "slave law" to tighten owners' control and better control slave behavior. Sometimes this happened fitfully, as after "incidents" like the 1712 New York City slave revolt, the 1739 Stono Rebellion in South Carolina, and the rumor of a slave revolt in New York City in 1741. Legislators felt that the rapidly growing enslaved population needed taming, as did those who employed slaves. Thus when New York revised its slave code in 1731 it prohibited Africans from owning or possessing guns and also fined owners for letting slaves wander alone at night.

The eighteenth-century colonial slave laws were not uniform. South Carolina's slave laws were more brutal than those of Virginia and Maryland, though all were harsh enough. South Carolina more readily subjected Africans to death and specified cutting ankle cords, slitting noses, and "gelding," or castration, than did Virginia, although everyone sanctioned the whip for almost all offenses. Yet from South Carolina to New York and Rhode Island, legislation everywhere tightened slaveholding. In the process American colonists made modern American slavery primarily between 1680 and 1770. They did not inherit it. Seventeenth-century mainland colony slavery established crucial principles about the ability of one person to own another. Eighteenth-century mainland colony slavery created the modern system of human and legal interrelationships that left a devastating and indelible imprint on America, its society, and its conscience.

The increasingly restrictive law measured slavery's coercion only partially. For most captured Africans, the experience of slavery far outstripped any legal description of its parameters. To be captured in wars among African nations, shipped to America on boats where many passengers died from exposure and malnourishment, sold to quizzical Europeans who eagerly purchased a body, labor, and possible offspring—but who had no interest in the person—then to be carted, often in chains, to a farm to perform an unknown labor for a complete stranger who was now one's "owner" but with whom one could not share a single word, much less a sentiment, all led to grudging, difficult labor and sometimes to sickness and worse. Owners might farm with slaves, as did the Huguenot immigrant Elias Horry, whose grandson remembered that Horry "worked many days with a Negro man at the Whip saw" in the early 1700s. But they shared only work, which more often bred contempt than affection.

Slave resistance brought punishment, sometimes gruesome, even when the law prohibited capricious retribution by owners. Whipping occurred routinely and often was accomplished publicly in ritual-like settings as an example to others. But owners went far beyond whipping without fear of punishment, rationalizing their behavior with reference to "necessity" and even self-pity. When an African lost a bundle of rice in 1713, the local Anglican minister described how a South Carolina planter forced a slave "into a hellish Machine . . . [in] the shape of a Coffin where he could not Stirr," there to await death by starvation or heat stroke; the slave's child resolved the affair by slipping a knife inside the coffin so his father could commit suicide. Seventy years later, Crèvecoeur* described a depressingly similar episode, the well-known scene in *Letters from an American Farmer* in which an enslaved African awaited death from wild animals, having been locked in a cage hanging from a tree. Birds had "already picked out his eyes; . . . his arms had been attacked in several places; . . . the blood slowly dropped and tinged the ground beneath." The slave begged for a means for suicide: "Tanky you, white man; tanky you; puta some poison and give me." Unlike the slave's son seventy years earlier, Crèvecoeur walked on. A rationalization for the execution came quickly: "Soon [I] reached the house at which I intended to dine. There I heard that the reason for this slave's being thus punished was on account of his having killed the overseer of the plantation. They told me that the laws of self-preservation rendered such executions necessary." Little wonder that retribution for slave misdeeds soon produced its own gruesome material culture—whips, mouthpieces, "iron negro fetters," and "Negro spurs" that appeared in estate inventories catalogued alongside farm implements and household goods as tools of the day.

The enslavement fashioned by European colonists in Britain's mainland colonies devastated traditional culture among captured Africans. Slaves came from increasing numbers of African societies in the eighteenth century,

---

*J. Hector St. John Crèvecoeur, a native of France who settled for a time in Orange County, New York. His writings described agriculture and rural society in America. (Eds.)

including Ibo, Ashanti, and Yoruba societies on the African west coast, and later from Muslim societies deeper inside the African continent as the century progressed. This growing diversity, combined with European fears and opposition, impeded "ethnic" cultures among mainland colony slaves. African diversity meant that slaves shared relatively little traditional culture, and European fears of assertive individual and group consciousness led slaveholders to prohibit the expression of cultural cohesiveness among Africans they owned. Much of traditional Ibo, Ashanti, and Yoruba secular culture languished in the aftermath even when smaller specific features might survive. Ibo, Ashanti, and Yoruba religious systems likewise failed to reproduce themselves in America. The result was a spiritual and cultural holocaust that shattered the breadth of traditional African culture and religion throughout the mainland colonies. Certain discrete rites persevered, especially those that concerned magic, healing, and burial. But Ashanti, Ibo, or Yoruba religious and cultural systems, among others, never survived in any holistic fashion, and no New World Ashanti, Ibo, or Yoruba ethnicity blossomed in Britain's mainland colonies.

The contrast between the African and European experiences could not have been more startling. The Scots, Scots-Irish, and Germans, among others, replicated Old World cultures in New World society with considerable success. Religiously motivated European immigrants like the Moravians and Mennonites achieved Old World ideals they frequently could not realize at home. Other Europeans, particularly Huguenots but also Scots and Scots-Irish, chose to assimilate within a dominant English culture (and were welcomed in doing so), abandoning their own distinctive cultures and beliefs. But captured and enslaved Africans moved within extraordinarily constricted boundaries. Captivity and slavery prevented them from realizing the goals that Europeans eagerly pursued, especially the freedom and power that arose from improving one's material circumstances.

Yet, with bittersweet persistence, enslaved Africans nonetheless turned an African holocaust into New World culture. Despite incredible difficulties, they reshaped Old World traditions and New World experiences into a new culture and society in the British mainland colonies that proved to be among the most noteworthy of all the New World's creation. Family life underwrote this achievement. This foundation in the family was particularly surprising because the law did not protect slave marriages (nothing prohibited owners from separating couples), and drastically unbalanced sex ratios in the mainland colonies' African population made conjugal relationships difficult. Between 1680 and the 1740s African men outnumbered women by substantial margins, 180 to 250 men for every 100 women in the Chesapeake, and 400 to 100 in South Carolina. Yet a social life rooted in a renewed family structure emerged nonetheless. Most important, captured Africans slowly formed conjugal units and raised children. The law never recognized this reality, but owners embraced it, enjoying social benefits that carried no legal responsibilities or moral obligations. Slave "marriage" fit traditional European social and religious expectations, could be disregarded at will, decreased tensions among the slaves, organized and disciplined the work force, and, conveniently, provided offspring who, as the owners' property, immediately could be bought and sold.

Reconstructed African-American family life merged African past and colonial present. Kinship crisscrossed and reinforced a surrounding culture of visiting and friendship, all of which molded buoyant communities and family life among captured Africans from the Carolinas to New England. Captured Africans traveled to see friends and uncles, lodged with cousins, and fell in love with acquaintances. When owners broke the Africans' extralegal marriages by selling spouses and children, Africans traveled far to see detached spouses and children. They sustained kinship beyond the conjugal family and reconstructed family life when capricious circumstances suddenly brought relatives together years later.

Captured Africans slowly forged a public culture in the colonies. This culture first centered, perhaps not surprisingly, on emerging rituals of family and kinship. The rare contemporary watercolor, *The Old Plantation,* of a late-eighteenth-century African-American celebration in the Chesapeake . . . conveys community most obviously in the numerous social groupings—two couples, a cluster of women, and several groups of men—held together with a caring expressed in the joy of the observers, the liveliness of the dancer, and the pleasure in the music. New England, despite its small captive African population, demonstrated the resilience of this thrust; it too produced a public African-American culture after 1730. A developing folk life took public expression in games (paw paw, a cowrie shell gambling game, for example), music (especially fiddle playing, as in the Chesapeake), dancing, public story-telling, and, in New England, African-American election day celebrations, in which captive Africans elected "kings" and "governors" for one day, a satire that spoofed both European and captive African pretensions yet also symbolized a substantial African-American community.

The advancing realization of community among Africans deepened fear of rebellion among Europeans in America. The two principal rebellions of the colonial era, the 1712 New York City revolt and South Carolina's 1739 Stono Rebellion, never freed captured Africans as their planners hoped. The New York City rebellion lasted only one evening and the Stono Rebellion several days and both cost many African lives. But the two rebellions, plus rumors of revolts in Annapolis, Maryland, in 1740 and in New York City again in 1741, terrorized Europeans. They gave ominous meaning to signs of African-American community and resolve: sustained, persistent labor resistance that ranged from tool breakage, slack work, and running away to assault against Europeans and even homicide.

Running away and work resistance, not revolution, became the most common form of African resistance to slavery and also helped to create community and strengthen individual resolve. Few captured Africans were lucky enough to manage permanent escapes. The wilderness was as strange to them as to Europeans, and slave owners possessed overwhelming powers of chase, detection, and capture. Despite these difficulties, Africans continually resisted owners by running away, even if only for short periods of time, and by resisting work. Runaways produced a peculiar newspaper culture in which runaway advertisements in the *Virginia Gazette* and the *South Carolina Gazette* became a small literary genre. Owners tried to raise alarm among slaveholders almost inured to such departures while attempting to describe the uniqueness of the missing African in ways that would engineer his or her return.

Work resistance could be more subtle. In South Carolina, slaves resisted the arduous labor of pounding rice by hand. Owners recognized the hardship and the cost: one observer described rice pounding as "the severest work the negroes undergo and costs every planter the lives of several slaves annually." Africans sometimes complained about particular jobs, occasionally winning an owner's understanding but most often suffering punishment and a return to work. Some resistance verged on rebellion. Africans sabotaged tools, ruined processed crops, and burned barns. They murdered owners with a wide range of techniques from assault to poisoning. After the 1739 Stono Rebellion, planters in South Carolina and elsewhere feared that such episodes were bringing them closer to an even larger confrontation.

Resistance, flight, and murder reinforced community among Africans. Initiating resistance required cooperation from friends, who made identification of individual culprits difficult, and from relatives, who hid runaway Africans who bolted. Resistance took root in the growing reality of kinship among Africans originally from highly diverse cultures, in a growing sense of place, and in a knowledge that Africans were the backbone of a burgeoning economy and culture whose achievement they guaranteed but whose reward they were denied. Even in the face of retributive Europeans, captured Africans had created community under conditions experienced by no other immigrants to America.

Memories of Africa stood at the center of that community, even if the expression of community remained frustrated and often unfulfilled in America and even if . . . America helped reshape some African traditions. Although difficult to capture, one expression of those memories came from a most unlikely source. Sometime in 1752 or 1753, a white Virginia blacksmith, Charles Hansford, filled a small manuscript notebook with three poems, two on love and religion and a third, "My Country's Worth," on Virginia. Knowledgeable about the 1739 Stono Rebellion and the rumors of revolts in Annapolis and New York City, Hansford compared Virginia to Rome and ancient Egypt, who "bought and bred up slaves as we do not / and yet neglected (or they knew not how) / Those slaves to manage. Sometimes they rebell'd / Which cost much sweat and blood ere they were quell'd."

Yet Hansford's comments on rebellion paled beside his startling observations about the captured Africans' memories of home.

> That most men have a great respect and love
> To their own place of birth I need not prove—
> Experience shows 'tis true; and the black brood
> Of sunburnt Affrick makes the assertion good.
> I oft with pleasure have observ'd how they
> Their sultry country's worth strive to display
> In broken language, how they praise their case
> And happiness when in their native place.
> Such tales and descriptions, when I'd leisure,
> I often have attended to with pleasure,
> And many times with questions would assail
> The sable lad to lengthen out his tale.
> If, then, those wretched people so admire
> Their native place and have so great desire
> To reenjoy and visit it again—
> Which, if by any means they might attain,
> How would they dangers court and pains endure
> If to their country they could get secure!
> But, barr'd of that, some into madness fly,
> Destroy themselves, and wretchedly they die.

DOCUMENTS

Slavery in New York City, *1731*

A LAW

For Regulating Negroes and Slaves in the Night Time*

Be it ordained by the Mayor, Recorder, Alderman and Assistants of the City of New York, convened in Common-Council, and it is Herby Ordained by the Authority of the same, That from hence-forth no Negro, Mulatto or Indian Slave, above the Age of Fourteen Years, do presume to be or appear in any of the Streets of this City, on the South side of the Fresh-Water, in the

---

*Grammar, sentence structure, and the use of capitals are as they were in the original document. (Eds.)

SOURCE: City of New-York, ss. A law for Regulating Negroes and slaves in the night time (1731), *Archives of Americana Collection: Early American Imprints, Series 1*: Evans, 1639–1800.

Night-time, above one hour after Sun-set, without a Lanthorn** and lighted Candle in it, so as the light may be plainly seen (and not in company with his, her or their Master or Mistress, or some White Person or White Servant belonging to the Family whose Slave he or she is, or in whose Service he and she then are). That then and in such case it shall and may be lawful for any of his Majesty's Subjects within this said City to apprehend such Slave or Slaves, not having such Lanthorn and Candle, and forth-with carry him, her or them before the mayor or Recorder, or any one of the Aldermen of the said City (if at a seasonable hour) and if at an unseasonable hour, to the Watch House, there to be confined until the next morning) who are therefore authorized, upon Proof of the Offense, to commit such Slave or Slaves to the common Gaol, for such his, her or their Contempt, and there to remain until the Master, Mistress or Owner of such Slave or Slaves, shall pay to the Person or Persons who apprehended and committed every such Slave or Slaves, the Sum of Four Shillings current Money of New-York, for his, her or their pains and Trouble therein, with Reasonable Charges of Prosecution.

And be it further Ordained by the Authority aforesaid, That every Slave or Slaves that shall be convicted of the Offence aforesaid, before he, she or they be discharged out of Custody, shall be Whipped at the Public Whipping-Post (not exceeding Forty Lashes) if desired by the Master or Owner of Such Slave or Slaves.

Provided always, and it is the intent hereof, That if two or More Slaves (not exceeding the Number of Three) be together in any lawful Employ or Labour for the Service of their Master or Mistress (and not otherwise) and only one of them have and carry such Lanthorn with a lighted Candle, the other Slaves in such Company not carrying a Lanthorn and lighted Candle, shall not be construed and intended to be within the meaning and Penalty of this Law, any thing in this Law contained to the contrary hereof in any wise notwithstanding. Dated at the City-Hall this Two and Twentieth Day of April, in the fourth year of His Majesty's Reign, Annoq; Domini 1731.

By Order of the Common Council

Recollections of the Middle Passage, 1788

The men Negroes, on being brought aboard the ship, are immediately fastened together, two and two, by handcuffs on their wrists, and by irons riveted on their legs. They are then sent down between the decks, and placed in

---

**"Lantern" in today's usage. (Eds.)

SOURCE: Noel Rae, *Witnessing America: The Library of Congress Book of First Accounts of Life in America, 1600–1900* (New York: Penguin Books, 1996), 35–39. Originally published in London, 1788, by Alexander Falconbridge, late surgeon in the African slave trade.

an apartment partitioned off for that purpose. The women likewise are placed in a separate apartment between decks, but without being ironed. And an adjoining room, on the same deck, is besides appointed for the boys. Thus are they all placed in different apartments.

But at the same time, they are frequently stowed so close, as to admit of no other posture than lying on their sides. Neither will the height between decks, unless directly under the grating, permit them the indulgence of an erect posture; especially where there are platforms, which is generally the case. These platforms are a kind of shelf, about eight or nine feet in breadth, extending from the side of the ship towards the centre. They are placed nearly midway between the decks, at the distance of two or three feet from each deck. Upon these the Negroes are stowed in the same manner as they are on the deck underneath.

In each of the apartments are placed three or four large buckets, of a conical form, being near two feet in diameter at the bottom, and only one foot at the top, and in depth about twenty-eight inches; to which, when necessary, the Negroes have recourse. It often happens that those who are placed at a distance from the buckets, in endeavouring to get to them, tumble over their companions, in consequence of their being shackled. These accidents, although unavoidable, are productive of continual quarrels, in which some of them are always bruised. In this distressed situation, unable to proceed, and prevented from getting to the tubs, they desist from the attempt; and, as the necessities of nature are not to be repelled, ease themselves as they lie. This becomes a fresh source of broils and disturbances, and tends to render the condition of the poor captive wretches still more uncomfortable. The nuisance arising from these circumstances, is not unfrequently increased by the tubs being much too small for the purpose intended, and their being usually emptied but once every day. . . .

About eight o'clock in the morning the Negroes are generally brought upon deck. Their irons being examined, a long chain, which is locked to a ring-bolt, fixed in the deck, is run through the rings of the shackles of the men, and then locked to another ring-bolt, fixed also in the deck. By this means fifty or sixty, and sometimes more, are fastened to one chain, in order to prevent them from rising, or endeavouring to escape. If the weather proves favourable, they are permitted to remain in that situation till four or five in the afternoon, when they are disengaged from the chain, and sent down.

The diet of the Negroes, while on board, consists chiefly of horse beans, boiled to the consistence of a pulp; of boiled yams and rice, and sometimes a small quantity of beef or pork. The latter are frequently taken from the provisions laid in for the sailors. They sometimes make use of a sauce, composed of palm oil, mixed with flour, water, and pepper, which the sailors call *slabber sauce.* Yams are the favourite food of the Eboe, or Bight Negroes, and rice or corn, of those from the Gold and Windward Coasts.

Most of the slaves have such an aversion to the horse beans that unless they are narrowly watched, when fed upon deck, they will throw them overboard, or in each other's faces when they quarrel.

Their food is served up to them in tubs, about the size of a small water bucket. They are placed round these tubs in companies of ten to each tub, out of which they feed themselves with wooden spoons. These they soon lose, and when they are not allowed others, they feed themselves with their hands. In favourable weather they are fed upon deck, but in bad weather their food is given them below. Numberless quarrels take place among them during their meals; more especially when they are put upon short allowance.

Upon the Negroes refusing to take sustenance, I have seen coals of fire, glowing hot, put on a shovel, and placed so near their lips, as to scorch and burn them. And this has been accompanied with threats, of forcing them to swallow the coals, if they any longer persisted in refusing to eat. These means have generally had the desired effect. I have also been credibly informed that a certain captain in the slave trade poured melted lead on such of the Negroes as obstinately refused their food.

Exercise being deemed necessary for the preservation of their health, they are sometimes obliged to dance, when the weather will permit their coming on deck. If they go about it reluctantly, or do not move with agility, they are flogged; a person standing by them all the time with a cat-ó-nine-tails in his hand for that purpose. Their music, upon these occasions, consists of a drum, sometimes with only one head; and when that is worn out, they do not scruple to make use of the bottom of one of the tubs before described. The poor wretches are frequently compelled to sing also; but when they do so, their songs are generally, as may naturally be expected, melancholy lamentations of their exile from their native country.

The hardships and inconveniences suffered by the Negroes during the passage are scarcely to be enumerated or conceived. They are far more violently affected by the seasickness than the Europeans. It frequently terminates in death, especially among the women. But the exclusion of the fresh air is among the most intolerable. For the purpose of admitting this needful refreshment, most of the ships in the slave trade are provided, between the decks, with five or six air-ports on each side of the ship of about six inches in length, and four in breadth; in addition to which, some few ships, but not one in twenty, have what they denominate *wind-sails*. But whenever the sea is rough and the rain heavy, it becomes necessary to shut these, and every other conveyance by which the air is admitted. The fresh air being thus excluded, the Negroes' rooms very soon grow intolerably hot. The confined air, rendered noxious by the effluvia exhaled from their bodies, and by being repeatedly breathed, soon produces fever and fluxes, which generally carries off great numbers of them.

. . . One half, sometimes two-thirds, and even beyond that, have been known to perish.

As very few of the Negroes can so far brook the loss of their liberty, and the hardships they endure, as to bear them with any degree of patience, they are ever upon the watch to take advantage of the least negligence in their oppressors. Insurrections are frequently the consequence; which are seldom suppressed without much bloodshed. Sometimes these are successful, and the whole ship's company is cut off. They are likewise always ready to seize every opportunity for committing some act of desperation to free themselves from their miserable state; and notwithstanding the restraints under which they are laid, they often succeed.

While a ship, to which I belonged, lay in Bonny River,* one evening, a short time before our departure, a lot of Negroes, consisting of about ten, was brought on board; when one of them, in a favourable moment, forced his way through the network on the larboard side of the vessel, jumped overboard and was devoured by the sharks.

During the time we were there, fifteen Negroes belonging to a vessel from Liverpool, found means to throw themselves into the river; very few were saved; and the residue fell a sacrifice to the sharks. A similar instance took place in a French ship while we lay there.

*The river flows into the Atlantic by the town of Bonny in Nigeria, western Africa. (Eds.)

Chapter 4

Husbands and Wives, Parents and Children in Puritan Society

As Robert Feke's 1741 painting Isaac Royal & Family reveals, pride in family, status, and possessions was quite apparent in mid-18th-century New England.

In sharp contrast to the privatism and individualism that marked seventeenth-century Virginia, a deep sense of cooperative commitment to building a new Zion characterized the society established in the Massachusetts Bay Colony. Nowhere was the notion of communal responsibility more fully developed or more clearly illustrated than in the Puritan family. As you read the essay "The Godly Family of Colonial Massachusetts," by Steven Mintz and Susan Kellogg, note the innumerable ways in which Puritan family life affected and was affected by the larger social, political, and economic community. How would you compare the role of the family in Massachusetts with that in Virginia during the same period?

Although few today would find Puritan notions regarding marriage and relations between the genders appealing, Mintz and Kellogg remind us that these people were not as devoid of warmth and feeling as the term *Puritan* often implies. As evidence, the authors refer to sentiments expressed in the poems of Anne Bradstreet, the first important woman writer in the colonies. The document that follows the essay presents two of Bradstreet's poems, "To My Dear and Loving Husband" and "Before the Birth of One of Her Children"—works that evoke a sense of deep and abiding love in a Puritan marriage. The poet's husband, Simon Bradstreet, served two terms as colonial governor of Massachusetts (1679–1686, 1689–1692).

As the essay reveals, the Puritans considered the proper upbringing of children and the maintenance of a sound moral climate cardinal family responsibilities. They also believed that the state had a vital role to play in ensuring that families fulfill these obligations. The second document, an act passed by the colonial Massachusetts legislature, orders parents to educate their children. Such a legal step was highly unusual in the English-speaking world of the seventeenth century. Take note of all the items included under the term "good education" and the penalties imposed on parents who neglected their duties. The legislation in the third document describes the kinds of behavior deemed improper and the kinds of action deemed necessary to safeguard public morality. After reading these two documents, you should notice that the idea of a separation between church and state was totally absent from Puritan Massachusetts.

The final document is an excerpt from Eleazer Moody's *The School of Good Manners,* a well-known book of eighteenth-century children's literature. Which of the forty-two dicta that Moody lists might today's parents consider valid? Which, if any, would they likely reject? What conclusions can you draw regarding differences in attitudes toward children's behavior today and in colonial New England?

ESSAY

The Godly Family of Colonial Massachusetts

Steven Mintz and Susan Kellogg

The roughly twenty thousand Puritan men, women, and children who sailed to Massachusetts between 1629 and 1640 carried with them ideas about the family utterly foreign to Americans today. The Puritans never thought of the family as purely a private unit, rigorously separated from the surrounding community. To them it was an integral part of the larger political and social world; it was "the Mother Hive, out of which both those swarms of State and Church, issued forth." Its boundaries were elastic and

SOURCE: Reprinted with permission of The Free Press, a Division of Simon & Schuster Adult Publisher Group, from *Domestic Revolutions: A Social History of American Life,* by Steven Mintz and Susan Kellogg. Copyright © 1988 by The Free Press. All rights reserved.

inclusive, and it assumed responsibilities that have since been assigned to public institutions.

Although most Puritan families were nuclear in structure, a significant proportion of the population spent part of their lives in other families' homes, serving as apprentices, hired laborers, or servants. At any one time, as many as a third of all Puritan households took in servants. Convicts, the children of the poor, single men and women, and recent immigrants were compelled by selectmen to live within existing "well Governed families" so that "disorders may bee prevented and ill weeds nipt."

For the Puritans, family ties and community ties tended to blur. In many communities, individual family members were related by birth or marriage to a large number of their neighbors. In one community, Chatham, Massachusetts, the town's 155 families bore just thirty-four surnames; and in Andover, Massachusetts, the descendants of one settler, George Abbott I, had by 1750 intermarried into a dozen local families. The small size of the seventeenth-century communities, combined with high rates of marriage and remarriage, created kinship networks of astonishing complexity. In-laws and other distant kin were generally referred to as brothers, sisters, aunts, uncles, mothers, fathers, and cousins.

Today spousal ties are emphasized, and obligations to kin are voluntary and selective. Three centuries ago the kin group was of great importance to the social, economic, and political life of the community. Kinship ties played a critical role in the development of commercial trading networks and the capitalizing of large-scale investments. In the absence of secure methods of communication and reliable safeguards against dishonesty, prominent New England families, such as the Hutchinsons and Winthrops, relied on relatives in England and the West Indies to achieve success in commerce. Partnerships among family members also played an important role in the ownership of oceangoing vessels. Among merchant and artisan families, apprenticeships were often given exclusively to their own sons or nephews, keeping craft skills within the kinship group.

Intermarriage was also used to cement local political alliances and economic partnerships. Marriages between first cousins or between sets of brothers and sisters helped to bond elite, politically active and powerful families together. Among the families of artisans, marriages between a son and an uncle's daughter reinforced kinship ties.

In political affairs the importance of the kin group persisted until the American Revolution. By the early eighteenth century, small groups of interrelated families dominated the clerical, economic, military, and political leadership of New England. In Connecticut and Massachusetts, the most powerful of these kinship groups was made up of seven interrelated families. The "River Gods," as they were known, led regional associations of ministers, controlled the county courts, commanded the local militia, and represented their region in the Massachusetts General Court and Governor's Council. Following the Revolution, most states adopted specific reforms designed to reduce the power of kin groups in politics by barring nepotism, establishing the principle of rotation in office, prohibiting multiple officeholding, providing for the election of justices of the peace, and requiring officeholders to reside in the jurisdiction they served.

Unlike the contemporary American family, which is distinguished by its isolation from the world of work and the surrounding society, the Puritan family was deeply embedded in public life. The household—not the individual—was the fundamental unit of society. The political order was not an agglomeration of detached individuals; it was an organic unity composed of families. This was the reason that Puritan households received only a single vote in town meetings. Customarily it was the father, as head of the household, who represented his family at the polls. But if he was absent, his wife assumed his prerogative to vote. The Puritans also took it for granted that the church was composed of families and not of isolated individuals. Family membership—not an individual's abilities or attainments—determined a person's position in society. Where one sat in church or in the local meetinghouse or even one's rank at Harvard College was determined not by one's accomplishments but by one's family identity.

The Puritan family was the main unit of production in the economic system. Each family member was expected to be economically useful. Older children were unquestionably economic assets; they worked at family industries, tended gardens, herded animals, spun wool, and cared for younger brothers and sisters. Wives not only raised children and cared for the home but also cut clothes, supervised servants and apprentices, kept financial accounts, cultivated crops, and marketed surplus goods.

In addition to performing a host of productive functions, the Puritan family was a primary educational and religious unit. A 1642 Massachusetts statute required heads of households to lead their households in prayers and scriptural readings; to teach their children, servants, and apprentices to read; and to catechize household members in the principles of religion and law. The family was also an agency for vocational training, assigned the duty of instructing servants and apprentices in methods of farming, housekeeping, and craft skills. And finally the Puritan family was a welfare institution that carried primary responsibility for the care of orphans, the infirm, or the elderly.

Given the family's importance, the Puritans believed that the larger community had a compelling duty to ensure that families performed their functions properly. The Puritans did not believe that individual households should be assured freedom from outside criticism or interference. The Puritan community felt that it had a responsibility not only to punish misconduct but also to intervene within households to guide and direct behavior. To this end, in the 1670s, the Massachusetts General Court directed towns to appoint "tithingmen" to oversee every ten or twelve households in order to ensure that marital relationships were harmonious and that parents properly disciplined unruly children. Puritan churches censured, admonished, and excommunicated men and women who failed to maintain properly peaceful households, since, as minister Samuel Willard put it, "When husband and wife neglect their duties they not only wrong each other, but they provoke God by breaking his law." In cases in which parents failed properly to govern "rude, stubborn, and unruly" children, Puritan law permitted local authorities to remove juveniles from their families "and place them with some master for years . . . and force them to submit unto government." Men who neglected or failed to support their wives or children were subject to judicial penalties. In instances in which spouses seriously violated fundamental duties—such as cases of adultery, desertion, prolonged absence, or nonsupport—divorces were granted. In cases of fornication outside marriage, courts sentenced offenders to a fine or whipping; for adultery, offenders were punished by fines, whippings, brandings, wearing of the letter *A*, and in at least three cases, the death penalty.

The disciplined Puritan family of the New World was quite different from the English family of the sixteenth and seventeenth centuries that had been left behind. In fact, it represented an effort to re-create an older ideal of the family that no longer existed in England itself.

English family life in the era of New World colonization was quite unstable. Because of high mortality rates, three-generational households containing grandparents, parents, and children tended to be rare. The duration of marriages tended to be quite brief—half of all marriages were cut short by the death of a spouse after just seventeen to nineteen years. And the number of children per marriage was surprisingly small. Late marriage, a relatively long interval between births, and high rates of infant and child mortality meant that just two, three, or four children survived past adolescence. Despite today's mythical vision of stability and rootedness in the preindustrial world, mobility was rampant. Most Englishmen could expect to move from one village to another during their adult lives, and it was rare for an English family to remain in a single community for as long as fifty years. Indeed, a significant proportion of the English population was denied the opportunity to *have* a family life. Servants, apprentices, and university lecturers were forbidden from marrying, and most other young men had to wait to marry until they received an inheritance on their father's death.

The English migrants who ventured to New England sought to avoid the disorder of English family life through a structured and disciplined family. They possessed a firm idea of a godly family, and they sought to establish it despite the novelty of American circumstances. Puritan religion had a particularly strong appeal to these men and women who were most sensitive to the disruptive forces transforming England during the sixteenth and seventeenth centuries—such forces as an alarming increase in population, a rapid rise in prices, the enclosure of traditional common lands, and the sudden appearances of a large class of propertyless men and women who flocked to the growing cities or took to the woods. To the Puritans, whose spiritual community was threatened by these developments, establishment of a holy commonwealth in New England represented a desperate effort to restore order and discipline to social behavior. And it was the family through which order could most effectively be created.

Migration to the New World wilderness intensified the Puritan fear of moral and political chaos and encouraged their focus on order and discipline. In the realm of economics, Puritan authorities strove to regulate prices, limit the rate of interest, and fix the maximum wages—at precisely the moment that such notions were breaking down in England. And in the realm of family life, the Puritans, drawing on the Old Testament and classical political theory, sought to reestablish an older ideal of the family in which the father was endowed with patriarchal authority as head of his household. Their religion taught that family roles were part of a continuous chain of hierarchical and delegated authority descending from God, and it was within the family matrix that all larger, external conceptions of authority, duty, and discipline were defined.

Puritans organized their family around the unquestioned principle of patriarchy. Fathers represented their households in the public realms of politics and social leadership; they owned the bulk of personal property; and law and church doctrine made it the duty of wives, children, and servants to submit to the father's authority. The colonies of Connecticut, Massachusetts, and New Hampshire went so far as to enact statutes calling for the death of children who cursed or struck their fathers.

Patriarchal authority in the Puritan family ultimately rested on the father's control of landed property or craft skills. Puritan children were dependent upon their father's support in order to marry and set up independent households. Since Puritan fathers were permitted wide discretion in how they would distribute their property, it was important that children show a degree of deference to their father's wishes. The timing and manner in which fathers conveyed property to the next generation exerted a profound influence upon where children decided to live and when and whom they decided to marry. In many cases fathers settled sons on plots surrounding the parental homestead, with title not to be surrendered until after their deaths. In other instances fathers conveyed land or other property when their sons became adults or were married. Not uncommonly such wills or deeds contained carefully worded provisions ensuring that the son would guarantee the parent lifetime support. One deed, for example, provided that a son would lose his inheritance if his parents could not walk freely through the house to go outdoors.

Such practices kept children economically dependent for years, delayed marriage, and encouraged sons to remain near their fathers during their lifetimes. In Andover, Massachusetts, only a quarter of the second-generation sons actually owned the land they farmed before their fathers died. Not until the fourth generation in mid-eighteenth-century Andover had this pattern noticeably disappeared. In Plymouth, Massachusetts, and Windsor, Connecticut, fathers gave land to children on marriage. Among Quaker families in Pennsylvania, fathers who were unable to locate land for sons in the same town bought land in nearby communities. In order to replicate their parents' style of life, sons had to wait to inherit property from their fathers. In most cases ownership and control of land reinforced the authority of fathers over their children.

A corollary to the Puritan assumption of patriarchy was a commitment to female submission within the home. Even by the conservative standards of the time, the roles assigned to women by Puritan theology were narrowly circumscribed. The premise guiding Puritan theory was given pointed expression by the poet Milton: "God's universal law gave to man despotic power/Over his female in due awe." Women were not permitted to vote or prophesy or question church doctrine. The ideal woman was a figure of "modesty" and "delicacy," kept ignorant of the financial affairs of her family. Her social roles were limited to wife, mother, mistress of the household, seamstress, wet nurse, and midwife. Although there was no doubt that she was legally subordinate to her husband, she had limited legal rights and protections.

Puritan doctrine did provide wives with certain safeguards. Husbands who refused to support or cohabit with their wives were subject to legal penalties. Wives, in theory, could sue for separation or divorce on grounds of a husband's impotence, cruelty, abandonment, bigamy, adultery, or failure to provide, but divorce was generally unavailable, and desertion was such a risky venture that only the most desperate women took it as an option. Colonial statutes also prohibited a husband from striking his wife, "unless it be in his own defense." Before marriage single women had the right to conduct business, own property, and represent themselves in court. Upon marriage, however, the basic legal assumption was that of "coverture"—that a woman's legal identity was absorbed in her husband's. Spouses were nevertheless allowed to establish antenuptial or postnuptial agreements, permitting a wife to retain control over her property.

For both Puritan women and men, marriage stood out as one of the central events in life. Despite their reputation as sexually repressed, pleasure-hating bigots, the Puritans did not believe that celibacy was a condition morally superior to marriage. The only thing that Saint Paul might have said in favor of marriage was that it is "better to marry than to burn," but the Puritans extolled marriage as a sacrament and a social duty. John Cotton put the point bluntly: "They are a sort of Blasphemers then who dispise and decry" [women as a necessary evil,] "for they are a necessary Good; such as it was not good that man should be without."

For the Puritans love was not a prerequisite for marriage. They believed that the choice of a marriage partner should be guided by rational considerations of property, religious piety, and family interest, not by physical attraction, personal feelings, or romantic love. Affection, in their view, would develop after marriage. This attitude reflected a recognition of the essential economic functions of the colonial family. Marriage was a partnership to which both bride and groom were expected to bring skills and resources. A prospective bride was expected to contribute a dowry (usually in the form of money or household goods) worth half of what the bridegroom brought to the marriage. Artisans tended to choose wives from families that practiced the same trade precisely because these women would be best able to assist them in their work. In New England the overwhelming majority of men and women married—and many remarried rapidly after the death of a spouse—because it was physically and economically difficult to live alone.

According to Puritan doctrine, a wife was to be her husband's helpmate, not his equal. Her role was "to guid the house &c. not guid the Husband." The Puritans believed that a wife should be submissive to her husband's commands and should exhibit toward him an attitude of "reverence," by which they meant a proper mixture of fear and awe; not "a slavish Fear, which is nourished with hatred or aversion; but a noble and generous Fear, which proceeds from Love."

The actual relations between Puritan spouses were more complicated than religious dogma would suggest. It was not unusual to find mutual love and tenderness in Puritan marriages. In their letters Puritan husbands and wives frequently referred to each other in terms suggesting profound love for each other, such as "my good wife . . . my sweet wife" or "my most sweet Husband." Similarly, the poems of Anne Bradstreet refer to a love toward her husband that seems deeply romantic: "To My Dear and Loving Husband/I prize thy love more than whole Mines of gold." It is also not difficult, however, to find evidence of marriages that failed to live up to the Puritan ideal of domestic harmony and wifely submissiveness. In 1686, a Boston spinster, Comfort Wilkins, publicly spoke out about the "Tears, and Jars, and Discontents, and Jealousies" that marred many Puritan marriages.

Puritan court records further reveal that wife abuse is not a recent development. Between 1630 and 1699, at least 128 men were tried for abusing their wives. In one case a resident of Maine kicked and beat his wife with a club when she refused to feed a pig; in another case an Ipswich man poured poison into his wife's broth in an attempt to kill her. The punishments for wife abuse were mild, usually amounting only to a fine, a lashing, a public admonition, or supervision by a town-appointed guardian. Two colonists, however, did lose their lives for murdering their wives.

Even in cases of abuse, Puritan authorities commanded wives to be submissive and obedient. They were told not to resist or strike their husbands but to try to reform their spouses' behavior. Some women refused to conform to this rigid standard. At least thirty-two seventeenth-century Puritan women deserted their husbands and set up separate residences, despite such risks as loss of their dower rights and possible criminal charges of adultery or theft. Another eight women were brought to court for refusing to have sexual relations with their husbands over extended periods. Seventy-six New England women petitioned for divorce or separation, usually on grounds of desertion, adultery, or bigamy.

Women who refused to obey Puritan injunctions about wifely obedience were subject to harsh punishment. Two hundred seventy-eight New England women were brought to court for heaping abuse on their husbands, which was punishable by fines or whippings. Joan Miller of Taunton, Massachusetts, was punished "for beating and reviling her husband and egging her children to healp her, biding them knock him in the head." One wife was punished for striking her husband with a pot of cider, another for scratching and kicking her spouse, and a third for insulting her husband by claiming he was "no man." How widespread these deviations from Puritan ideals were, we do not know.

Within marriage, a woman assumed a wide range of responsibilities and duties. As a housewife she was expected to cook, wash, sew, milk, spin, clean, and garden. These domestic activities included brewing beer, churning butter, harvesting fruit, keeping chickens, spinning wool, building fires, baking bread, making cheese, boiling laundry, and stitching shirts, petticoats, and other garments. She participated in trade—exchanging surplus fruit, meat, cheese, or butter for tea, candles, coats, or sheets—and manufacturing—salting, pickling, and preserving vegetables, fruit, and meat and making clothing and soap—in addition to other domestic tasks. As a "deputy husband," she was responsible for assuming her husband's responsibilities whenever he was absent from home—when, for example, he was on militia duty. Under such circumstances she took on his tasks of planting corn or operating the loom or keeping accounts. As a mistress she was responsible for training, supervising, feeding, and clothing girls who were placed in her house as servants.

Marriage also brought another equally tangible change to women's lives: frequent childbirth. Childlessness within marriage was an extreme rarity in colonial New England, with just one woman in twelve bearing no children. Most women could expect to bear at least six children and delivered children at fairly regular intervals averaging every twenty to thirty months, often having the last child after the age of forty. The process of delivery was largely in the hands of women and took place within the home. Labor was typically attended by a large number of observers. When one of Samuel Sewall's daughters gave birth in January 1701, at least sixteen women were in attendance in the lying-in room to offer encouragement and give advice. Often a midwife would intervene actively in the birth process by breaking the amniotic sac surrounding the infant in the uterus, steering the infant through the birth canal, and later removing the placenta.

Death in childbirth was frequent enough to provoke fear in many women. It appears that almost one delivery in thirty resulted in the death of the mother. Among the complications of pregnancy that could lead to maternal death were protracted labor, unusual presentation of the infant (such as a breech presentation), hemorrhages and convulsions, and infection after delivery. The sense of foreboding that was felt is apparent in the words of a Massachusetts woman, Sarah Stearns, who wrote in her diary, "Perhaps this is the last time I shall be permitted to join with my earthly friends."

After childbirth, infants were commonly breast-fed for about a year and were kept largely under their mother's care. Not until a child reached the age of two or three is there evidence that fathers took a more active role in child rearing.

Unlike marriages in contemporary England—where a late age of marriage and short life expectancy combined to make the average duration of marriage quite short—colonial unions tended to be long-lived, even by modern standards. A detailed study of one New England town found that an average marriage lasted almost twenty-four years. The extended duration of New England marriages gave such unions a sense of permanence that contrasted sharply with the transience characteristic of English marriages. In contrast to the pattern found today, however, the death of a spouse did not usually lead to the creation of households composed of a widow or widower living alone. Single adults of any age living alone were very unusual, and lifelong bachelors and spinsters were a rarity. Remarriage after the death of a spouse was common, particularly among wealthier men, and even individuals of very advanced ages (into their seventies or eighties) often remarried. Among those least likely to remarry were wealthy widows. If these women did remarry, they generally made an antenuptial agreement allowing them to manage their own property. The remarriage of a spouse often led to the rearrangement of families; the fostering out of children from an earlier marriage was not uncommon.

The experience of widowhood did give a small number of colonial women a taste of economic independence. Legally, a widow in seventeenth-century New England was entitled to at least a third of her husband's household goods along with income from his real estate until she remarried or died. Actual control of the house and fields—and even pots and beds—usually fell to a grown son or executor. But, in a number of cases, widows inherited land or businesses and continued to operate them on their own, assuming such jobs as blacksmith, silversmith, tinsmith, beer maker, tavern-keeper, shoemaker, shipwright, printer, barber, grocer, butcher, and shopkeeper—occupations and crafts usually monopolized by men.

Of all the differences that distinguish the seventeenth-century family from its present-day counterpart, perhaps the most striking involves the social experience of children. Three centuries ago, childhood was a much less secure and shorter stage of life than it is today. In recent years it has become fashionable to complain about the "disappearance of childhood," but historical perspective reminds us that—despite high divorce rates—childhood is more stable than it was during the colonial era. For a child to die during infancy was a common occurrence in colonial New England; more deaths occurred among young children than in any other age group. In Plymouth, Andover, or Ipswich, Massachusetts, a family could anticipate an infant death rate of one out of ten; in less-healthy towns such as Salem or Boston, three of every ten children died in infancy. It cannot be emphasized too strongly that high infant death rates did not necessarily make parents indifferent toward their young children. Cotton Mather, who lost eight of his fifteen children before they reached their second birthdays, suggests the depth of feeling of parents: "We have our children taken from us; the Desire of our Eyes taken away with a stroke."

Not only were children more likely to die in infancy or to be orphaned than today, they were raised quite differently. In certain respects young children were treated, by our standards, in a casual way. Child rearing was not the family's main function; the care and nurture of children were subordinate to other family interests. In colonial New England newborn infants of well-to-do families were sometimes "put out" to wet nurses who were responsible for breast-feeding, freeing mothers to devote their time to their household duties. As in Europe, new babies were sometimes named for recently deceased infants. In contrast to Europeans, however, New Englanders did not wrap infants in tightly confining swaddling clothes, and carelessly supervised children sometimes crawled into fires or fell into wells.

The moral upbringing of Puritan children was never treated casually. The Puritan religion taught that even newborn infants were embodiments of guilt and sin (traceable to Adam's transgression in Eden), who, unless saved by God, were doomed to writhe in Satan's clutches for eternity. This belief in infant depravity and original sin exerted a powerful influence on methods of child rearing. In their view the primary task of child rearing was to break down a child's sinful will and internalize respect for divinely instituted authority through weekly catechisms, repeated admonitions, physical beatings, and intense psychological pressure. "Better whipt, than damned," was Cotton Mather's advice to parents.

Although Calvinists could be indulgent with very small children, among many parents their religious faith led to an insistence that, after the age of two, any assertion of a child's will be broken. A Pilgrim pastor eloquently defined a parent's responsibility to combat the inherent evil of a child's nature: "Surely," he affirmed, "there is in all children (though not alike) a stubbernes and stoutnes of minde arising from naturall pride which must in the first place be broken and beaten down so the foundation of their education being layd in humilitie and tractablenes other virtues may in turne be built thereon." A child's willfulness could be suppressed through fierce physical beatings, exhibition of corpses, and tales of castration and abandonment—techniques designed to drive out "the old Adam" and produce traits of tractableness and peaceableness highly valued by Calvinists. The Puritans would strongly have rejected the twentieth-century "progressive" child rearing advice that the goal of parents should be to draw out their children's innate potentialities.

Without a doubt the most striking difference between seventeenth-century child rearing and practices today was the widespread custom of sending children to live with another family at the age of fourteen or earlier, so that a child would receive the proper discipline its natural parents could not be expected to administer. Children of all social classes and both sexes were frequently fostered out for long periods in order to learn a trade, to work as servants, or to attend a school. Since the family was a place of work and its labor needs and its financial resources often failed to match its size and composition, servants or apprentices might temporarily be taken in or children bound out.

If childhood is defined as a protected state, a carefree period of freedom from adulthood responsibilities, then a Puritan childhood was quite brief. Childhood came to an end abruptly around the age of seven when boys adopted adult clothing (prior to this both boys and girls wore frocks or petticoats) and were prevented from sleeping any longer with their sisters or female servants. By their teens most children were largely under the care and tutelage of adults other than their own parents. They were fostered out as indentured servants or apprentices or, in rare cases, sent to boarding schools.

While childhood ended early and abruptly, adulthood did not begin right away. Around the age of seven, young Puritans entered into a prolonged intermediate stage of "semi-dependency" during which they were expected to begin to assume a variety of productive roles. Young boys wove garters and suspenders on small looms, weeded flax fields and vegetable gardens, combed wool and wound spools of thread, and were taught to be blacksmiths, coopers, cordwainers (shoemakers), tanners, weavers, or shipwrights. Teenage girls received quite different training from their brothers. They were taught "housewifery" or spinning, carding, sewing, and knitting. Girls customarily helped their mothers or another mistress by hoeing gardens, spinning flax and cotton, tending orchards, caring for domestic animals, and by making clothing, lye, soap, and candles. Like their mothers, teenage girls might also assist their fathers in the fields or in a workshop.

For both young men and women, marriage, economic independence, and establishment of an independent household would come much later. For young men, the transition to full adulthood only occurred after they had received a bequest of property from their father. Marriage took place relatively late. The average age of marriage for men was over twenty-five years, and few women married before the age of twenty.

For New Englanders, migration across the Atlantic gave the family a significance and strength it had lacked in the mother country. In the healthful environment of New England, family ties grew tighter than they had ever been in the Old World. The first settlers lived much longer than their contemporaries in England and were much more likely to live to see their grandchildren. Marriages lasted far longer than they did in contemporary England, and infant mortality rates quickly declined to levels far below those in the old country. Migration to the New World did not weaken paternal authority; it strengthened it by increasing paternal control over land and property.

Even when individuals did move around in New England, they almost always migrated as part of a family group. Few sons moved farther than sixteen miles from their paternal home during their father's lifetime. Contrary to an older view that the New World environment dissolved extended family ties, it now seems clear that the family in early-seventeenth-century New England was a more stable, disciplined, and cohesive unit than its English counterpart in the Old World.

DOCUMENTS

Two Poems, 1678

To My Dear and Loving Husband

If ever two were one, then surely we;
If ever man were loved by wife, then thee;
If ever wife was happy in a man,
Compare with me, ye women, if you can.
I prize thy love more than whole mines of gold,
Or all the riches that the East doth hold.

My love is such that rivers cannot quench,
Nor aught but love from thee give recompense.
Thy love is such I can no way repay;
The heavens reward thee manifold, I pray.
Then while we live in love let's so persevere
That when we live no more we may live ever.

SOURCE: Anne Bradstreet, *Poems of Mrs. Anne Bradstreet* (Boston, 1758).

Before the Birth of One of Her Children

All things within this fading world have end.
Adversity doth still our joys attend;
No ties so strong, no friends so dear and sweet,
But with death's parting blow are sure to meet.
The sentence passed is most irrevocable,
A common thing, yet, oh, inevitable.
How soon, my dear, death may my steps attend,
How soon it may be thy lot to lose thy friend,
We both are ignorant; yet love bids me
These farewell lines to recommend to thee,
That when the knot's untied that made us one
I may seem thine who in effect am none.
And if I see not half my days that are due,
What nature would God grant to yours and you.
The many faults that well you know I have
Let be interred in my oblivion's grave;
If any worth or virtue were in me,
Let that live freshly in thy memory,
And when thou feelest no grief, as I no harms,
Yet love thy dead, who long lay in thine arms;
And when thy loss shall be repaid with gains
Look to my little babes, my dear remains,
And if thou love thyself, or lovedst me,
These oh protect from stepdam's injury.
And if chance to thine eyes shall bring this verse,
With some sad sighs honor my absent hearse;
And kiss this paper for thy love's dear sake,
Who with salt tears this last farewell did take.

A Law for "the good education of children," 1642

Forasmuch as the good education of children is of singular behoof and benefit to any commonwealth, and whereas many parents and masters are too indulgent and negligent of their duty in that kind:

It is ordered, that the selectmen of every town, in the several precincts and quarters where they dwell, shall have a vigilant eye over their brethren and neighbours, to see, first that none of them shall suffer so much barbarism in any of their families, as not to endeavour to teach, by themselves or others, their children and apprentices, so much learning, as may enable

SOURCE: *The Charter and General Laws of the Colony and Province of Massachusetts Bay* (Boston: T. B. Waite and Co., 1814), 73–74.

them perfectly to read the English tongue, and knowledge of the capital laws: upon penalty of twenty shillings for each neglect therein.

Also that all masters of families do once a week (at the least) catechise their children and servants in the grounds and principles of religion; and if any be unable to do so much, that then at the least they procure such children and apprentices to learn some short orthodox catechism without book, that they may be able to answer unto the questions that shall be propounded to them out of such catechism, by their parents or masters, or any of the selectmen when they shall call them to a trial, of what they have learned in that kind.

And farther that all parents and masters do breed and bring up their children and apprentices in some honest lawful calling, labour or employment, either in husbandry or some other trade, profitable for themselves and the commonwealth, if they will not or cannot train them up in learning, to fit them for higher employments.

And if any of the selectmen, after admonition by them given to such masters of families, shall find them still negligent of their duty in the particulars aforementioned, whereby children and servants become rude, stubborn, and unruly: the said selectmen with the help of two magistrates, or the next county court for that shire, shall take such children or apprentices from them, and place them with some masters for years, (boys till they come to twenty-one, and girls eighteen years of age complete) which will more strictly look unto, and force them to submit unto government, according to the rules of this order, if by fair means and former instructions they will not be drawn unto it. [May 1642]

Monitoring Style and Behavior in Puritan Massachusetts, 1675

Whereas there is manifest pride openly appearing amongst us in that long hair, like women's hair, is worn by some men, either their own or others hair made into periwigs, and by some women wearing borders of hair, and their cutting, curling, and immodest laying out their hair, which practise doth prevail and increase, especially among the younger sort:

This Court* doth declare against this ill custom as offensive to them, and divers sober Christians among us, and therefore do hereby exhort and advise all persons to use moderation in this respect; and further, do empower all grand juries to present to the County Court such persons, whether male or female, whom they shall judge to exceed in the premises; and the County Courts are hereby authorized to proceed against such delinquents either by admonition, fine, or correction, according to their good discretion. . . .

SOURCE: Nathaniel B. Shurtleff, ed., *Records of the Governor and Company of Massachusetts Bay, 1628–1686* (Boston, 1853–1854), 5: 60–61.

*"Court" refers to the General Court, the legislature of colonial Massachusetts. (Eds.)

Whereas there is much disorder and rudeness in youth in many congregations in time of the worship of God, whereby sin and profaneness is greatly increased, for reformation whereof:

It is ordered by this Court, that the selectmen do appoint such place or places in the meeting house for children or youth to sit in where they may be most together and in public view, and that the officers of the churches, or selectmen, do appoint some grave and sober person or persons to take a particular care of and inspection over them, who are hereby required to present a list of the names of such who, by their own observance or the information of others, shall be found delinquent, to the next magistrate or Court, who are empowered for the first offense to admonish them, for the second offense to impose a fine of five shillings on their parents or governors, or order the children to be whipped, and if incorrigible, to be whipped with ten stripes or sent to the house of correction for three days.

Good Manners for Colonial Children, 1772

When at Home

1. Make a bow always when you come home, and be immediately uncovered.
2. Be never covered at home, especially before thy parents or strangers.
3. Never sit in the presence of thy parents without bidding, tho' no stranger be present.
4. If thou passest by thy parents, and any place where thou seest them, when either by themselves or with company, bow towards them.
5. If thou art going to speak to thy parents, and see them engaged in discourse with company, draw back and leave thy business until afterwards; but if thou must speak, be sure to whisper.
6. Never speak to thy parents without some title of respect, viz., Sir, Madam, &c.
7. Approach near thy parents at no time without a bow.
8. Dispute not, nor delay to obey thy parents commands.
9. Go not out of doors without thy parents leave, and return within the time by them limited.
10. Come not into the room where thy parents are with strangers, unless thou art called, and then decently; and at bidding go out; or if strangers come in while thou art with them, it is manners, with a bow to withdraw.

SOURCE: Eleazer Moody, *The School of Good Manners. Composed for the Help of Parents in Teaching Their Children How to Carry It in Their Places During Their Minority* (Boston: Fleets, 1772), 17–19.

11. Use respectful and courteous but not insulting or domineering carriage or language toward the servants.
12. Quarrel not nor contend with thy brethren or sisters, but live in love, peace, and unity.
13. Grumble not nor be discontented at anything thy parents appoint, speak, or do.
14. Bear with meekness and patience, and without murmuring or sullenness, thy parents reproofs or corrections: Nay, tho' it should so happen that they be causeless or undeserved.

In Their Discourse

1. Among superiors speak not till thou art spoken to, and bid to speak.
2. Hold not thine hand, nor any thing else, before thy mouth when thou speakest.
3. Come not over-near to the person thou speakest to.
4. If thy superior speak to thee while thou sittest, stand up before thou givest any answer.
5. Sit not down till thy superior bid thee.
6. Speak neither very loud, nor too low.
7. Speak clear, not stammering, stumbling nor drawling.
8. Answer not one that is speaking to thee until he hath done.
9. Loll not when thou art speaking to a superior or spoken to by him.
10. Speak not without, Sir, or some other title of respect.
11. Strive not with superiors in argument or discourse; but easily submit thine opinion to their assertions.
12. If thy superior speak any thing wherein thou knowest he is mistaken, correct not nor contradict him, nor grin at the hearing of it; but pass over the error without notice or interruption.
13. Mention not frivolous or little things among grave persons or superiors.
14. If thy superior drawl or hesitate in his words, pretend not to help him out, or to prompt him.
15. Come not too near two that are whispering or speaking in secret, much less may'st thou ask about what they confer.
16. When thy parent or master speak to any person, speak not thou, nor hearken to them.
17. If thy superior be relating a story, say not, "I have heard it before," but attend to it as though it were altogether new. Seem not to question the truth of it. If he tell it not right, snigger not, nor endeavor to help him out, or add to his relation.
18. If any immodest or obscene thing be spoken in thy hearing, smile not, but settle thy countenance as though thou did'st not hear it.
19. Boast not in discourse of thine own wit or doings.
20. Beware thou utter not any thing hard to be believed.

21. Interrupt not any one that speaks, though thou be his familiar.
22. Coming into company, whilst any topic is discoursed on, ask not what was the preceding talk but hearken to the remainder.
23. Speaking of any distant person, it is rude and unmannerly to point at him.
24. Laugh not in, or at thy own story, wit or jest.
25. Use not any contemptuous or reproachful language to any person, though very mean or inferior.
26. Be not over earnest in talking to justify and avouch thy own sayings.
27. Let thy words be modest about those things which only concern thee.
28. Repeat not over again the words of a superior that asketh thee a question or talketh to thee.

Chapter 5

Eighteenth-Century Religion: Progress and Piety

George Whitefield, preacher of the Great Awakening.

Religion pervaded the lives of American colonists. Indeed, the New England colonies, Pennsylvania, and Maryland were established by founders with religious purposes in mind. In the other colonies, as well, religion played a central role.

Eighteenth-century immigration, much of it non-English in origin, intensified and diversified the religious climate. German Mennonites, Dunkers, and Moravians established settlements in Pennsylvania. Lutherans from Scandinavia and Germany, by the time of the Revolution, had built some 130 churches throughout the middle and southern colonies. Scots-Irish settlers brought their Presbyterian faith with them as they settled the western regions of Pennsylvania and moved south along the Appalachian mountain chain. English Baptists established a strong foothold in Philadelphia and eventually spread throughout the colonies, gaining particular strength in the South during the latter half of the century.

Alan Taylor's essay from his book *American Colonies* reviews religious developments in the American colonies during the seventeenth century, including religious motives for emigration, established religion, and the status of religious toleration. What is apparent to the reader was the wide diversity in matters religious among the several colonies. What are some of the reasons for this? Though not all the colonies were able to maintain a strong, single established religion, the author states that most founders of colonies desired religious uniformity. What benefits did they believe would accrue from establishment?

The major focus of the essay is on eighteenth-century religious movements, most notably on the spectacular series of evangelical revivals known as the Great Awakening. Starting in the middle colonies in the mid-1730s, the Great Awakening spread up and down the coast during the following decade. Revivalist preachers found responsive audiences at first in the more settled northern areas, where many had grown weary of the highly intellectual preaching of their ministers. In colorful, emotional sermons, the Great Awakening leaders preached a religion of the heart, emphasizing a personal relationship with God and the individual's responsibility for his or her own salvation. Saving grace, they insisted, was available through repentance and rejection of sin, prayer, moral behavior, and, most essential, a spiritual conversion, or being "born again."

The legacy of the Great Awakening went beyond religious practices and beliefs. What evidence does the essay offer that it impacted upon such things as intercolonial ties, religious toleration, and the social order? How does the author explain Virginia governor William Gooch's support of "liberty of conscience" on the one hand and his dread of "freedom of speech" on the other?

Seventeenth- and eighteenth-century colonial leaders viewed religion as an essential safeguard to an orderly society. Even the baptizing of slaves was considered to contribute to that end. Phillis Wheatley was a widely read African-born poet who spent most of her life as a slave in Boston. Encouraged by her owners, she converted to Christianity. The first document presents her poem "On the Death of the Rev. Mr. George Whitefield, 1770." What words of the poem provide a clue about why slaves were often quite receptive to conversion efforts?

The excitement engendered by the traveling ministers of the Great Awakening is described in the second document. In it Nathan Cole tells of events surrounding the appearance of evangelist George Whitefield in Middletown, Connecticut, on October 23, 1740.

To win the attention of potential converts, revivalist preachers usually painted vivid verbal pictures of the Hell that awaited sinners, as well as the Heaven promised to those "born again." The most famous "hellfire" sermon of the Great Awakening was delivered by Jonathan Edwards to his Enfield, Connecticut, congregation in 1741. The final document is taken from this sermon, which Edwards entitled "Sinners in the Hands of an Angry God."

As Taylor reveals, not everyone, particularly not the more traditional "old light" ministers, approved of the techniques of the revivalist or "new light" preachers. After reading the essay and documents, what do you think led many people to embrace the Great Awakening, and others to condemn it strongly?

Can you identify trends in modern religious life reminiscent of the eighteenth-century division between "new lights" and "old lights"?

ESSAY

Awakenings

Alan Taylor

During the mid-eighteenth century, British colonial America experienced a dramatic and sweeping set of religious revivals collectively known as the Great Awakening (or the First Great Awakening). After noting significant lags and regional exceptions, we find a dramatic, widespread, and increasingly synchronized outburst of revival religion that astonished and polarized the colonists. The evangelical revivalists undermined the traditional convictions that society must be stratified and corporate. They promoted a more pluralistic, egalitarian, and voluntaristic social order by defending the free flow of itinerant preachers and their converts across community and denominational lines. The revivalists also imagined an enlarged society: an intercolonial and transatlantic network of congregations united by a shared spirituality communicated over long distances by itinerants and print. That imagination rested upon a persistent hope that the revivals would spread around the globe to initiate Christ's triumphant millennial return to earth.

By no means did all colonists become evangelicals, but the latter were sufficiently numerous and interconnected to influence the entire culture and society. Evangelical revivals also brought Protestant conversion, for the first time, to thousands of Indians and enslaved Africans. In the evangelical emphasis on the individual encounter with the Holy Spirit, the poor and the marginal found a divine license for their own preachers, who adapted Christianity to assert the dignity and the rights of all people.

Establishments

Myth insists that the seventh-century English colonists fled from religious persecution into a land of religious freedom. In addition to omitting economic considerations, the myth grossly simplifies the diverse religious motives for emigration. Not all colonists had felt persecuted at home, and few wanted to live in a society that tolerated a plurality of religions. Perfectly

SOURCE: Alan Taylor, *American Colonies* (New York: Viking, 2001), 339–362. Copyright © 2001 by Alan Taylor. Used by permission of Viking Penguin, a division of Penguin Group (USA) Inc.

content with the official Anglican faith of the homeland, many colonists sought to replicate it in the colonies. And although some English dissenters, principally the Quakers, did seek in America a general religious freedom, many more emigrants wanted their own denomination to dominate, to the prejudice of all others. Indeed, at the end of the seventeenth century, most colonies offered *less* religious toleration than did the mother country.

Most colonies' founders believed that public morality, political harmony, and social order required religious uniformity. On pain of fines, jail, and whipping, they required the colonists to attend, and pay taxes for, one "established" church. The establishment varied by colony, depending upon the faith of the founders. The Puritan colonies of Plymouth, Massachusetts, and Connecticut established their Congregational Church. The Dutch Reformed Church enjoyed legal primacy in New Netherland. The Church of England also enjoyed official favor in Virginia, Barbados, Jamaica, and the Leeward Islands. Because the establishment varied from colony to colony, so did religious dissent. Where Anglicans held the establishment, Congregationalists ranked among the dissenters. New England reversed that relationship, putting the Anglicans there in the unusual and uncomfortable position of championing minority rights.

Between 1660 and 1690, establishments seemed to be waning, reduced by the founding of New Jersey, Pennsylvania, and Carolina and by the English conquest of New York. That trend, however, reversed between 1690 and 1720, with the creation of new Anglican establishments in Maryland (1692), the southern New York counties (1693), South Carolina (1706), and North Carolina (1715). The prime movers were ambitious royal governors and leading colonists who sought favor in England and political advantage in their colony over non-Anglican rivals. The proponents both exploited and contributed to the increased colonial integration into a transatlantic empire. In 1693, Governor Benjamin Fletcher pointedly reminded the New York assembly, "There are none of you but what are big with the privilege of Englishmen and Magna Charta, which is your right; and the same law doth provide for the religion of the church of England."

Congregationalists sustained an especially impressive establishment in New England, except for Rhode Island. Thanks to compact settlement by towns and laws mandating churches, few inhabitants lived more than six miles from a meetinghouse. And unlike other colonial regions, New England had plenty of official clergymen to fill the many pulpits. Most were graduates of Harvard (founded in 1636) or Yale (1701). Indeed, New England struck visitors as the most conspicuously devout and religiously homogeneous region in British North America. The New English towns enforced a Sabbath that restricted activity to the home and church, imposing arrests and fines on people who worked, played, or traveled on Sunday. An English visitor found the New England Sabbath "the strictest kept that ever I saw."

A mixed blessing, entanglement in an establishment meant clerical dependence upon selectmen and town meetings that proved both meddlesome and stingy. During the early eighteenth century, most towns refused to increase church taxes, although inflation cut the real value of ministers' fixed salaries, leading to protracted and divisive debates. In the poorer rustic towns, the Congregational ministers had to supplement their eroding salaries by running a farm or by doubling as country doctors. Clerical resentments bred counterresentments by laypeople, who grumbled that their minister cared more about money than souls.

The establishment also imposed a growing tension between the inclusion and exclusion of parishioners. As an established church dependent upon taxation, the church needed to be inclusive to justify town support and to provide universal moral instruction and supervision. As an established church in the world, Congregationalism also accepted and reflected social inequalities, arranging the pews in the meetinghouse to reflect the local hierarchy of family wealth and status. On the other hand, that inclusion and hierarchy contradicted the traditional Puritan goal of a "gathered church" limited to the "visible saints"* by excluding the unworthy, regardless of their worldly status. During the later seventeenth century, the Puritans had compromised by adopting a two-tier system of membership: "halfway" for the baptized and full for those who proceeded on to spiritual "conversion" and communion. Because that tenuous compromise dissatisfied both the purists and the pragmatists, New England Congregationalism sat on a fault line that would shake the establishment during the Great Awakening of the 1740s.

Beyond New England, establishments were far weaker because official ministers were so few. The Anglican and Dutch Reformed churches demanded expensive ministries by relatively prestigious and learned men, who rarely left the comforts of England or the Netherlands for the instability, hardships, and uncertainties of the early colonies. In addition, beyond Congregational New England, the colonists were slow to found the colleges needed to train ministers. Not until 1693 did Anglicans found the College of William and Mary in Virginia, and it remained small, weak, and underfunded. Because an Anglican minister required ordination by a bishop and the colonies had no bishops, aspiring pastors faced the considerable expense and trouble of a transatlantic voyage for ordination in London. Consequently, the limited supply of Anglican pastors lagged behind the growing population and frontier expansion. In 1724, Virginia had 120,000 inhabitants but only twenty-eight Anglican pastors. Farther south the Anglican situation was even worse. In 1729, North Carolina had twelve Anglican parishes but no resident ministers.

*In Puritan society, a visible saint was one whose deeds and obedience to religious laws were attributed to having received faith and consequently salvation from God. (Eds.)

Access to religious services was also difficult because the sprawling pattern of settlement stretched southern parishes, often beyond one hundred square miles (compared with an average of twenty-five in England). The horrendous state of southern roads and bridges compounded the difficulties of distance, often discouraging travel by ministers and attendance by parishioners. Studded with roots, stumps, and rocks, the roads were dust traps in summer and mud pits the rest of the year. Ice and sleet hindered passage in winter; a torrid sun and voracious mosquitoes afflicted travelers in summer. Periodic Indian wars added deadly dangers to the discomforts.

In Maryland and Virginia, the establishment proved a mixed blessing for Anglican clergymen, who depended financially upon vestries dominated by great planters. Anglican pastors complained of chronic meddling, disrespectful treatment, and insufficient pay from contemptuous vestrymen. In 1747 in Virginia, the Reverend William Kay preached a sermon against pride, which Colonel Landon Carter, a great planter, took personally. When Carter complained, Kay worsened matters by replying "that I was glad he applied it, for it was against everyone that was proud." Carter dominated the parish vestry, which promptly ousted the pastor and locked up his church. As Kay so unpleasantly learned, an establishment tended to increase the power of colonial elites over the church rather than the power of the church over the colonists.

In the middle colonies, ethnic and religious diversity precluded any church establishment and obliged every denomination to rely on voluntary attendance and contributions. Unparalleled in Europe or any other colonial region, the competition shocked orthodox ministers, who wished that their own denomination commanded a majority and enjoyed an establishment. With characteristic hyperbole, an Anglican minister denounced the middle colonies as a "soul destroying whirlpool of apostasy." In fact, despite the greater difficulties of supporting churches in the region, the middle colonists established more than their share. By 1750 the middle colonies sustained one congregation for every 470 colonists, compared with one per 600 in New England and one per 1,050 in the south. The denser network of middle colony churches reflected the ethnic and cultural diversity and their rivalries. Almost every denominational cluster of settlers sought its own local church to preserve its distinct identity.

In the middle colonies, prosperous farmers and artisans took the lead as governing elders who organized, funded, and supervised the local congregations. Lacking a sufficient supply of ministers, the elders annually hired devout schoolteachers to preach. During the 1730s and 1740s, however, educated ministers began to arrive in significant numbers from Scotland and Germany. They found that the leading colonial laymen had grown accustomed to governing their congregations and resented the air of command brought by the new clergymen used to the more hierarchical conditions of Europe.

Growth and Limits

Despite the difficult conditions, every colonial region developed an extensive and conspicuous array of churches. In 1750 the mainland colonies sustained approximately 1,500 local congregations, each averaging about ninety families attending, which suggests that at least two-thirds of colonial adults were "churched" in the broad sense of affiliation. The Congregationalists composed the largest single denomination, with 450 churches, almost all in New England. The Anglicans ranked second, sustaining 300 parishes, primarily in the South, followed by the Quakers with 250 meetings and the Presbyterians with about 160 churches, most in the middle colonies. They competed with Baptists (100), Lutherans (95), Dutch Reformed (78), and German Reformed (51), all principally based in the middle colonies. Although overwhelmingly a Protestant society, the colonies also hosted a few Catholic churches (especially in Maryland) as well as Jewish synagogues in Newport, New York City, and Charles Town.

In a land of dispersed farms and plantations, church services filled a hunger for social gatherings and for information from the wider world. Church buildings also provided a forum for reading government proclamations, posting new laws, and holding elections to the assembly. Prior to 1750, most books published in the colonies (or imported from Britain) were religious tracts and sermons. Accepting and reflecting the inequalities of colonial society, every denomination included all social ranks but reserved lay leadership as vestrymen, deacons, and elders for the wealthiest and most prestigious men within each congregation.

Despite the impressive extensive growth in religion, many ministers complained that only a declining minority of adults qualified for full church membership and communion. The decline was especially conspicuous among Congregational men, who increasingly remained only halfway members. In most churches, full membership required an applicant to describe his spiritual experiences—a process that dismayed growing numbers of men, who preferred to keep their emotions private. Female full membership did not decline, because women remained more at ease discussing their spiritual feelings. By 1740, in most Congregational churches, the female full members exceeded men by more than two to one.

Despite the decline in full church membership, church attendance remained high, even in the rural south, the least "churched" region in the colonies. In 1724, Anglican ministers in Maryland, Virginia, and South Carolina reported that about 60 percent of the adults in their counties regularly attended Anglican services, although only 15 percent took communion. Many in the remaining 40 percent must have attended rival Presbyterian,

Baptist, and Quaker churches, suggesting that at least two-thirds of the southern colonies participated in religious services.

Common people cherished preaching and access to the sacrament of baptism. Contrary to the teachings of their ministers, the common people regarded baptism as possessed of a magical power to fend off sickness and to invite God's saving grace. On the other hand, full membership stagnated because laypeople regarded communion more fearfully, from a conviction that God cursed hasty people who took it before they had been truly converted by grace. Devereux Jarratt, an Anglican, reported that most Virginians considered communion "a dangerous thing to meddle with." Even some vestrymen and deacons balked at full membership because of scrupulous doubts about their own spiritual readiness.

In addition to the many denominational divisions, colonial churches were developing an internal rift between evangelicals and rationalists. Evangelical clergy discounted formal, ceremonial, and sacramental worship in favor of cultivating a spontaneous, direct, and individual religious experience, which they called "experimental religion." Noting the dwindling full membership, evangelicals complained that worship had lost its former intensity, declining into empty formalism or utter indifference. They blamed the growing influence of Christian rationalism, especially among the colonial elite, including most Anglican and some Congregational, Presbyterian, and Dutch Reformed clergymen.

Favoring critical and empirical inquiry, the rationalists slighted the traditional foundations of Christian faith: scriptural revelation and spiritual experience. The rationalists instead found guidance in the science that depicted nature as the orderly and predictable operation of fundamental and discernible "laws," such as Isaac Newton's explication of gravity. Christian rationalism held that God created the natural universe and thereafter never interfered with its laws. God seemed less terrifying as learned people reinterpreted epidemics, earthquakes, and thunderbolts as "natural" rather than as direct interventions of divine anger. The Reverend Andrew Eliot, a New England Congregationalist, explained, "There is nothing in Christianity that is contrary to reason. God never did, He never can, authorize a religion opposite to it, because this would be to contradict himself."

The rationalists rejected the supernatural mysteries and overt emotionalism of evangelical worship. John Tillotson, the archbishop of Canterbury, argued that God asked "nothing but what is easy to be understood, and as easy to be practiced by an honest and willing mind." But the rationalists contradicted themselves by urging parishioners passively to accept instruction by a learned clergy who alone knew best. The Reverend Jonathan Mayhew, a Congregationalist, explained, "Those of the lower class can go but a little way with their inquiries into the moral constitution of the world."

Discarding the Calvinist notion of an arbitrary and punishing God, the rationalists worshiped a benign, predictable, forgiving, and consistent deity who rewarded good behavior with salvation, but who expected common people to defer to the learned and authoritative men at the top of the social hierarchy. The rationalist concept of God appalled the evangelicals as cold, distant, and irrelevant, for they sought direct, individual, and transforming contact with the Holy Spirit. They suspected that rationalists trumpeted their learning and prestige to mask their lack of conversion and to claim undue power over true believers. The latent conflict between the rational and evangelical emphases became manifest in the revivals of the 1730s and early 1740s.

Revivals

During the early eighteenth century, most Congregational and Presbyterian congregations had evangelical traditions that nurtured periodic "revivals": surges in fervor and new members. For example, the Congregational parish of Northampton in Massachusetts experienced six distinct revivals during the sixty-year pastorate of the Reverend Solomon Stoddard: in 1679, 1683, 1696, 1712, 1718, and 1727, with intervening lulls. Unpredictable, irregularly spaced, and of varying intensity, the Northampton revivals did not coincide in timing and velocity with their counterparts in other towns. Indeed, because Stoddard was an especially vigorous, evangelical, and effective preacher, Northampton experienced larger and more frequent revivals than did communities with less zealous ministers.

Revivals emphasized the emotional process of conversion that transformed sinners into saints who warranted eternal salvation. Committed to a Calvinist theology, the colonial evangelicals rejected the rationalists' suggestion that anyone could earn salvation by behaving well. On the contrary, the evangelicals insisted that God's grace alone could save and that he bestowed that grace as his free and arbitrary gift only upon some of those who accepted their own utter helplessness to save themselves. Yet the revivalists subtly contradicted their Calvinism by exhorting listeners to seek out evangelical preaching and to reform their conduct, as if such actions would help draw down God's saving grace.

To stimulate revivals, energetic ministers preached "soul-searching" sermons meant to shock their listeners into recognizing their impending and eternal sentence in hell. But the evangelicals balanced their images of terror with equally vivid depictions of eternal joy in heaven. These "awakening" sermons primarily appealed to the emotions, especially fear and hope, rather than to reason. A master of this style, Stoddard taught his grandson and successor the Reverend Jonathan Edwards, who explained, "Our people do not so much need to have their heads stored, as to have their hearts touched." A witness described hearing Edwards preach "a most awakening sermon, and before sermon was done there was a great moaning and crying through the whole house—What shall I do to be saved—oh, I am going to Hell—oh, what shall I do for Christ, etc., etc., so that the minister was obliged to desist—the shrieks and cries were piercing and amazing."

Evangelical preaching provoked conversion experiences that pulled a seeker through despair to an ecstatic experience of divine grace. In the first step, people had to forsake their false sense of security in their own good behavior and instead recognize their utter worthlessness and helplessness without God. Seekers then fell into a profound sense of despair, doubting that God would ever save them. Those who completed the process ultimately surrendered to God and felt an exhilarating and liberating infusion of saving grace called the New Birth. In 1741, Hannah Heaton, a Connecticut farm woman, recalled:

> The power of God came down. My knees smote together. . . . It seem[e]d to me I was a sinking down to hell. I tho[ugh]t the floor I stood on gave way and I was just a going, but then I began to resign and, as I resigned, my distress began to go off till I was perfectly easy, quiet, and calm. . . . It seem[e]d as if I had a new soul & body both.

Like Heaton, some evangelicals described their New Birth as so sudden and complete that they could identify the day and hour. Others experienced a more gradual and traditional ripening, over several weeks or months.

The cultivation of despair, however, was a dangerous business that imperiled the lives of the melancholy. Some seekers broke through to the New Birth, while others fell back into their worldly ways, but a few became trapped in despair and sought to escape through suicide. Unable to win any assurance in life, they sought immediately to face God and know their sentence. Such suicides dissipated the enthusiasm that sustained a revival, bringing the zeal and the conversions to a halt.

Congregational and Presbyterian revivals remained localized and episodic until the 1730s and early 1740s, when they began to interact and escalate as evangelical ministers cooperated over long distance as never before. The escalation of local into intercolonial revivalism began in the Raritan Valley of eastern New Jersey. Led by Theodore Frelinghuysen, a Dutch Reformed minister, and the Presbyterian brothers Gilbert and John Tennent and William Tennent, Jr., the Raritan evangelical crossed denominational lines to cooperate in the face of opposition from more conservative ministers in their own churches.

In animated letters, Gilbert Tennent reported their success to his Congregational correspondents in New England, which inspired emulation especially by Jonathan Edwards. In turn, his success encouraged other ministers and devout laypeople throughout the Connecticut Valley, affecting at least thirty-two other towns by 1735. As the most extensive and synchronized set of revivals in colonial experience, the Connecticut Valley revivals seemed a miraculous outpouring of divine grace rather than anything wrought by humans. In mid-1735, however, the revivals ground to a halt after the shocking suicide of Joseph Hawley, Northampton's richest merchant and an uncle to Jonathan Edwards. Longing for, but despairing of, salvation, Hawley cut his throat.

Whitefield

After fading in the Connecticut Valley, the revival assumed a new power and range by breaking into print. In London in 1737 and Boston in 1738, Edwards published a vivid account entitled *A Faithful Narrative of the Surprizing Work of God.* Linking the Connecticut Valley and Raritan Valley revivals, Edwards depicted God acting throughout the colonies, and perhaps the entire Protestant world. Widely and avidly read in Britain and the colonies, *A Faithful Narrative* provided models of preaching and conversion that guided subsequent revivals, imparting a greater similarity that evangelicals interpreted as a sure sign of God's uniform power, rather than as evidence of Edwards's influential account.

The English readers of *A Faithful Narrative* included George Whitefield, a young Anglican minister who developed an evangelical style at odds with the dominant rationalism of the Church of England. Inspired by God and Edwards, in 1739 Whitefield developed an innovative career as a tireless itinerant, touring England and Wales, seeking out the poor and laboring people usually ignored by Anglicans. Drawing immense crowds too large for churches and consisting of people uncomfortable in them, Whitefield preached conversion to thousands in the streets, fields, and parks, provoking outbursts of emotion. A charismatic and moving speaker, Whitefield directly engaged his audience by preaching without notes. Although short, slight, and cross-eyed, Whitefield compelled attention by his fluid and dramatic movements and by a magnificent voice that he modulated like a fine instrument. The contrast between Whitefield's insignificant appearance and commanding performance encouraged the impression that God inspired his preaching. A masterful promoter, Whitefield also exploited the marketing techniques of a commercial society, employing advance men, handbills, and newspaper notices to build his celebrity and audience expectation.

Edwards's words had crossed the Atlantic into London print to inspire Whitefield. In turn, London newsprint passed in ships to the colonies to convey vivid accounts of Whitefield's sensational impact in England. News of his immense crowds in London assured Whitefield of an eager audience in the colonies, for the colonists paid cultural deference to the great metropolis as the arbiter of all fashions. The more they read, the more the colonists longed to hear and see Whitefield preach.

In 1739, Whitefield crossed the Atlantic to tour the colonies, ostensibly to raise funds for an orphanage in Georgia but fundamentally to export his form of evangelical theater to new audiences. His American tour reflected the transatlantic integration of the British empire into an increasingly common market of goods and ideas. Whitefield exploited the proliferation of shipping and newspapers, the improved network of roads, and the greater density of settlement, which promised larger crowds, especially in the northern colonies. During his 1739–41 tour from Maine to Georgia,

Whitefield furthered transatlantic and intercolonial integration by becoming the first celebrity seen and heard by a majority of the colonists.

In late 1739, Whitefield arrived in Philadelphia, which became his base for the next fourteen months spent in the colonies. In Philadelphia, Whitefield found an important friend and collaborator in Benjamin Franklin, the leading writer, publisher, and social reformer in the colonies. They made an odd couple, for Franklin was a confirmed rationalist who resisted Whitefield's evangelical message. But Franklin admired Whitefield as a shrewd entrepreneur and dazzling performer. Armed with skepticism, Franklin attended one of Whitefield's Philadelphia services determined to give nothing to the collection.

> I had in my Pocket a Handful of Copper Money, three or four silver Dollars, and five Pistoles in Gold. As he proceeded, I began to soften, and concluded to give the Coppers. Another Stroke of his Oratory made me ashamed of that, and determined me to give the Silver; and he finished so admirably, that I emptied my Pocket wholly into the Collector's Dish, Gold and all.

Above all, Franklin applauded Whitefield for improving the morals of the common people in Philadelphia. Whitefield also benefited Franklin's printing business by creating a sensation that sold newspapers and by commissioning Franklin to publish his sermons and journals. Profitable to Franklin, the joint venture served Whitefield by spreading his words far beyond the reach of his voice.

With Franklin's help, Whitefield escalated the print revolution in the colonies. Items featuring the great evangelist appeared in three-quarters of the issues of Benjamin Franklin's *Pennsylvania Gazette* published during the evangelist's fourteen-month stay in America. From 1738 to 1741, the number of colonial imprints increased 85 percent, primarily owing to works by or about Whitefield. He wrote brief, plain, and often autobiographical tracts accessible to common people who lacked the leisure and training to decipher long and learned treatises. Between 1739 and 1745, American printers produced at least eighty thousand copies of Whitefield's publications, or about one for every eleven colonists. A Bostonian marveled: "The Press here never had so full employ before, nor were people ever so busy in reading."

During 1740, Whitefield preached throughout the colonies, from Georgia to Maine. Although nominally an Anglican, Whitefield was primarily sponsored by Presbyterians and some Dutch Reformed in the middle colonies and by Congregationalists in New England. Sharing his evangelical Calvinism, they hoped that Whitefield's sensational preaching would provoke a renewed wave of conversions—and they were not disappointed.

Whitefield, however, evoked a relatively tepid response beyond the evangelical Calvinists. Because most Anglicans distrusted his emotional preaching and ecumenical support, Whitefield made little impact in the southern colonies, which also lacked the dense settlement and many printing presses so critical to his celebrity in the north. In Anglican Virginia, Colonel Landon Carter boasted that "Whit[e]field did but hum and buzz, and die away like the Insect of the Day." Even excepting the south, however, Whitefield did conduct the most dramatic, extensive, and controversial religious phenomenon ever to affect the British colonies.

Whitefield especially affected audiences in New England, where almost all adults were literate, newspapers and religious tracts were most abundant, and a dense network of ministers prepared for his sensational arrival. The combination drew unprecedented crowds primed with an electric anticipation. A Connecticut farmer, Nathan Cole, recalled:

> When I saw Mr. Whitefield come upon the Scaffold he Lookt almost angelical; a young, Slim, slender, youth before some thousands of people with a bold, undaunted Countenance, and my hearing how God was with him every where as he came along, it Solemnized my mind; and put me into a trembling fear before he began to preach; for he looked as if he was Clothed with authority from the Great God; *and a sweet sollome solemnity sat upon his brow.* And my hearing him preach, gave me a heart wound; by God's blessing: my old Foundation was broken up.

In Boston, a leading minister marveled, "The Grand Subject of Conversation was Mr. Whitefield, and the whole Business of the Town [was] to run, from Place to Place, to hear him preach." On October 12, Whitefield's farewell sermon in Boston drew about twenty thousand, more than the seaport's population, as hundreds of country people flocked in to see the great evangelist.

In addition to drawing unprecedented crowds and making a sensational impression, Whitefield stirred controversy by blaming rationalist ministers for neglecting their duty to seek, experience, and preach conversion. He charged, "The generality of preachers talk of an unknown and unfelt Christ. *The reason why congregations have been dead is, because they had dead men preaching to them.*" Such rebukes divided the ministry, inspiring some to adopt Whitefield's spontaneous, impassioned, evangelical style while hardening others in opposition.

In early 1741, Whitefield returned to England, leaving his American admirers and critics to cope with the upheaval he had expanded. Evangelical ministers worked to sustain Whitefield's sensational impact by effecting many local revivals, collectively called a Great Awakening. In Connecticut in 1741–42 the local churches added an average of sixty-six new members, compared with just sixteen biennially during the preceding decade. The evangelicals hoped that the revivals would expand exponentially and, in Edwards's words, "make New England a kind of heaven upon earth."

The conversions seemed especially impressive and divine because they included so many men and young people, the colonists ordinarily under-represented in full church membership. In Massachusetts, the Reverend Peter Thacher reported:

> In the *ordinary* Excitations of Grace before this Time, there were more *Females* added than *Males*, . . . but in this *extraordinary* Season, the Grace of GOD has surprisingly seized and subdued the hardiest *Men*, and more *Males* have been added here than of the tenderer sex.

He added that the young people were "crying and wringing their hands, and bewailing their Frolicking and Dancing." During the early 1740s, the re-vivals temporarily corrected the skew in Congregational Church member-ship toward women and the elderly by drawing men and young people into the fold.

To highlight the universal and indiscriminate power of God, the re-vivalists emphasized the dramatic conversions of obscure, common people, the more marginal and previously sinful the better. In his *Faithful Narrative,* Jonathan Edwards set the pattern by featuring the emotional conversions of a four-year-old girl and a dying young woman—people ordinarily little noticed or heeded. The revivals offered a stage for otherwise obscure people to claim attention and even authority as channels for God's will and recipi-ents of his saving grace.

Itinerating evangelicals generated increasing controversy. At White-field's special request, the Reverend Gilbert Tennent left New Jersey to tour New England during the winter of 1740–41. Partisan and confrontational, Tennent became celebrated among evangelicals and detested by their critics for his 1740 sermon *The Danger of an Unconverted Ministry.* In this evangeli-cal manifesto, Tennent charged that rationalists lacked the evangelical expe-rience with Christ that was a prerequisite for truly Christian preaching. Doomed to hell, the rationalist ministers covertly menaced souls by offering a dull and easy religion that distracted congregants from the hard, emo-tional work of seeking the New Birth: "They have not the Courage, or Hon-esty, to thrust the Nail of Terror into sleeping Souls." Tennent urged parishioners to desert such ministers who preached only a "dead" formal-ism and who opposed the revivals.

Tennent, however, was tame compared with the Reverend James Dav-enport. Caught up in the fervor, Davenport neglected his own parish to itin-erate through Connecticut and Massachusetts. Denied access to most pulpits, Davenport gathered crowds in fields and streets to denounce their resident ministers as "unconverted hypocrites" and "the devil incarnate." During 1742, in Hartford and again in Boston, Davenport twice suffered arrest, trial, and verdicts of insanity from colonial courts. He culminated his itinerant career in March 1743 in New London, Connecticut, by gathering a throng around a bonfire to burn fashionable clothes and impious books, which, for Davenport, included religious tracts written by his many critics. Apparently burned out, a few weeks later Davenport publicly recanted his itinerant career "as enthusiastical and delusive."

Davenport's retreat did not stop the spread of evangelical preachers across the landscape and down the social ladder. Itineracy by well-educated and ordained ministers—such as Whitefield, Tennent, and Davenport— seemed bad enough to orthodox critics. Far worse were the poorly educated laypeople who itinerated as "exhorters." Finding a divine call to preach in their New Birth, they gathered audiences by testifying vociferously to their "experimental religion." Many exhorters claimed continuing communication with God in the form of trances, visions, and premonitions. Such certainty inspired common people to defy any minister or magistrate who opposed their preaching.

To the special horror of religious conservatives, some women became exhorters. Inspired by God's direct command, they felt obliged to defy the Biblical injunctions by the apostle Paul against female speaking in church. By claiming utter submission to God's command, and by speaking his words rather than their own, inspired women claimed a freedom from the social restraints placed on their gender. These women followed the precedent set by the Quakers, who had long recognized God's voice in their female preachers, known as Public Friends.

During the 1740s in western Massachusetts an inspired woman, Bathsheba Kingsley, defied her husband, stole a horse, and rode from town to town, preaching her "immediate revelations from heaven." Turning the tables, Kingsley rebuked men, including ministers, who commanded her to stop. When her husband resorted to "hard words and blows," she loudly and publicly prayed that he "might go quick to hell." Detecting a perversion of the revival, Jonathan Edwards denounced Kingsley as a "brawling Woman" who should "keep chiefly at home."

Sarah Haggar Osborne, a schoolteacher in Newport, Rhode Island, also felt too inspired to remain publicly silent. During the 1740s, she organized evening prayer meetings for younger women, a practice that did enjoy Biblical sanction. Later, during the mid-1760s, when another revival gripped Newport, Osborne expanded her de facto ministry to hundreds of seekers: boys and girls, men and women, slave and free. Defying her own minister, Osborne refused "to shut up my mouth and doors and creep into obscurity." In evangelical preaching, she found an exhilarating new avenue for public expression and influence.

Old Lights and New Lights

Whitefield's controversial tour and its divisive aftermath manifested the latent rupture between rationalists and evangelicals. At the same time, the revivals promoted greater cooperation, across denominational lines, between evangelicals in different churches. Whitefield (Anglican), Edwards (Congregationalist), the Tennents (Presbyterian), Frelinghuysen (Dutch Reformed), and Henry M. Muhlenberg (Lutheran) shared encouragement, information, and pulpits. In reaction, rationalists in the various churches recognized their own affinities and made temporary alliances against revivalism. The evangelicals became known as New Lights, because they believed in new dispensations of divine grace, while their foes were Old Lights, who defended venerable institutions and scriptural traditions. Launched in acrimonious publications, their battle spread into ministerial conventions and colonial politics. A Congregational minister sadly concluded, "The glorious work appears to me now as changed into a ruinous war."

The bitter controversy between New Lights and Old Lights split both the colonial elite and the common people. Both camps included some learned ministers, powerful magistrates, and wealthy merchants as well as numerous common farmers, artisans, and laborers. But initially more men of education, prestige, wealth, and influence lined up with the Old Lights than with the New, which gave a more populist tone to the revivalists. Among the clergy, the split was partly generational. Most Old Light ministers were older men, well established in their careers and set in their ways. They felt rattled by the ambitious zeal of New Light ministers, who were usually younger and quicker to embrace "new measures." Among the Presbyterian clergy, the generational split divided older men trained in British universities from the younger ministers educated in America, usually at an evangelical academy run by Gilbert Tennent's father, the Reverend William Tennent, at Neshaminy, Pennsylvania.

The Old Lights defended the traditional form of learned sermons: carefully written in advance and designed to persuade with precedents and reason. By contrast, the New Lights preached emotionally and spontaneously to channel their immediate sense of the Holy Spirit and to shock and inspire their listeners. Such unstructured preaching appalled the Old Lights as "full of Words, but very confused and inconsistent." Counterattacking, John Henry Goetschius (Dutch Reformed) charged the Old Lights with "impos[ing] on many people, against their will, their old, rotten, and stinking routine religion."

Used to a dispassionate style of worship, the Old Lights despised the emotional and physical outbursts evoked by the revivals: weeping, crying out, twitching, and falling down during worship. Jonathan Edwards conceded that the conversions of the early 1740s were louder and more emotional than anything he had seen before: "It was a very frequent thing to see an house full of outcries, faintings, convulsions, and such like, both with distress, and also with admiration and joy." The Old Lights called the outbursts "enthusiasm," then a pejorative term that meant human madness, at best, or Satan's manipulation, at worst. The Reverend Ezra Stiles commented that "multitudes were seriously, soberly and solemnly out of their wits."

The Old Lights especially distrusted the religious enthusiasm of children and women that so impressed revivalists. And where evangelicals celebrated the sudden conversions of conspicuous sinners, as proof of divine power, the critics countered that most unprepared converts promptly backslid into sin. For Old Lights, true grace ripened gradually and depended on patient study of the Bible, improved morality, and guidance by a learned and cautious minister.

Dismayed by evangelical itinerants, the Old Lights defended the traditional territorial parish that united all residents under the authority of an ordained and established minister who controlled public religious speech within his bounds. Because the New England establishment interwove church and state, the Congregational Old Lights charged that the invading itinerants were "endeavoring to overset the Government; to turn things *topsy, turvy*; and bring all into Convulsion." Another Old Light aptly noted that the itinerant evangelist "above all hates rules and good order, or *bounds and limits*." Where the New Lights championed the uninhibited and disruptive flow of divine grace by inspired itinerants, the Old Lights regarded Christianity as a stable faith that needed barricades against intrusive innovations.

Radicals

In addition to the fundamental divide between New and Old Lights, the evangelicals became subdivided into moderates and radicals. Both had a commitment to "experimental religion," but they differed over the implications for church and state institutions. Cherishing some measure of stability and security, the Congregational moderates clung to their establishment and its system of territorial parishes, which the radicals assailed as obstacles to the free flow of divine grace. The moderates asserted that church institutions necessarily belonged, in part, to this world and had to accommodate to its inequalities in wealth, status, and learning. The radicals, however, imagined otherworldly churches that brought heaven to earth during worship, temporarily dissolving the significance of all social distinctions.

The moderates embraced almost all of the professional clergy who supported the revivals, including Frelinghuysen, Muhlenberg, Whitefield, Edwards, and the Tennents. They favored evangelical preaching and conversions, but they also meant to preserve their own authority and privileges as educated and ordained ministers. In encouraging revivals, the moderates certainly had not bargained on unleashing poorly educated exhorters who urged parishioners to secede and found their own radical churches. The moderates felt caught between the Old Lights, who utterly rejected the revivals, and the radicals, who went too far. The moderates defended the revivals as the authentic work of God, but regretted the most emotional outbursts and censorious self-righteousness as unfortunate but incidental side effects. To vindicate the revivals from Old Light denunciation, the moderates felt compelled to denounce the radicals.

The radicals, however, rejected any church establishment as corrupting to both religion and government. They also gloried in the emotional and physical outbursts of the revivals as pure manifestations of God's overwhelming power. Regarding "experimental religion" as the only divine and true source of authority, they agued that no human institution of learning or government should interfere with God's commands felt in the souls of the converted. That conviction invited inspired common people of little education and low status to exhort and to denounce any officials who interfered. By emphasizing the overwhelming, miraculous, and fundamental power of God acting directly and indiscriminately upon souls, radical evangelicals weakened the social conventions of their hierarchical society.

In defying the established authority of minister and magistrate, the radical evangelicals championed individualism, a concept then considered divisive and anarchic. In matters of faith, a New Light minister asserted the "absolute Necessity for every Person to act singly . . . as if there was not another human Creature upon Earth." No matter how lowly in status or depressed by poverty, or how legally dependent upon another, everyone should choose how to find and worship Christ. A radical preacher insisted, "The common people claim as good [a] right to judge and act for themselves in matters of religion as civil rulers or the learned clergy."

Free choice had radical implications for a colonial society that demanded a social hierarchy in which husbands commanded wives, fathers dictated to sons, masters owned servants and slaves, and gentlemen claimed deference from common people. Although evangelicals avowed respect for all claims to service and deference in the secular world, they argued that no worldly authority could legitimately obstruct religious choice. Citing her husband's opposition, Relief Hooper, a Massachusetts woman, tried to excuse her long absence from her Baptist church, but her evangelical brothers and sisters replied, "When husbands' commands interfer[e]s with Christ's authority, we ought to obey God rather than man."

By distinguishing between worldly and spiritual duties, the evangelicals claimed to present no threat to the social order. But in an unequal society that interwove religious and social authority, the radical effort to separate the two alarmed men of prestige and property. Any elevation of individualism threatened elites, who felt that their authority depended upon the power to constrain the religious choices of their dependents.

Although the radicals invoked free choice to justify separations and itinerants, they were far from consistent in celebrating individualism. In summoning converts to desert their parish churches, the radicals urged them to defy all restaining bonds of family, neighborhood, and society. Then, however, the evangelicals formed their own, more demanding communities. The radical evangelicals considered themselves a spiritual family, calling one another "brother" and "sister." Old Light polemics charged that the radicals destroyed all moral restraints and wallowed in drink, contention, slander, and adultery. In fact, the radicals took great pains to supervise one another for strict morality and plain attire, for they knew that their enemies closely watched for any misdeed. The radicals rebuked or ousted anyone found wanting—a painful exclusion to those who had tasted the emotional intimacies of evangelical worship. Within the bounds of their own churches, the radicals meant to preserve the harmony of their worship from the individual assertion that had led them out of their former congregations.

The radical evangelicals sought to *include* every person in conversion, regardless of gender, race, and status, but they worked to *exclude* from church membership anyone they deemed unconverted by the New Birth. Impatient, the radicals demanded the immediate dismissal of ministers, and the ouster of all church members, whom they deemed unconverted hypocrites. A radical preacher exhorted, "O that the precious Seed might be preserved and *separated* from all gross Mixtures!" Of course, the radical attempts to distinguish and separate insulted and outraged those ministers and parishioners found wanting by the self-righteous. With good reason, the Old Lights and the moderate evangelicals worried that the divisive drive for purity would shatter the religious unity and establishment of Congregational New England.

When most Congregational churches balked at immediately adopting the higher standards of internal purity, the local radicals bolted to form their own "Separate" congregations or to join their fellow travelers the Baptists. A leading Separate announced his refusal 'to Sit under the Stupid and Deceiving performances of unconverted ministers." Sometimes the radicals seceded from staunch Old Light ministers and congregations utterly opposed to the revivals. More often, the radicals deserted congregations led by moderate New Lights who preached conversion but clung to the inclusive principles of the establishment.

The Separates and Baptists took seriously the spiritual equality of all awakened people (and their spiritual superiority to all unconverted hypocrites). The radicals ordained their own preachers: poorly educated but charismatic laypeople. They worshiped in open fields, private homes, and barns: settings that reinforced their break from the traditional practice of arranging church pews in a hierarchy of family status that reflected the earthly inequalities of the local community. The radicals suspended social distinctions during worship, mixing together as poor and prosperous; Indian, white, and black; men and women. The radicals even tended to include converted women in the government of their churches. Women helped to choose ministers, to accept or reject potential members, to administer church discipline, and to debate and decide controversial practices and ideas. The radicals even encouraged women to exhort in their local churches but stopped short of ordaining them as ministers.

Southern Revivals

Revivalism came relatively late to Virginia. In 1743, three years after White-field's brief and ineffective passage through Virginia, moderate evangelicals organized in a single county—Hanover—under the leadership of a local bricklayer assisted by occasional Presbyterian itinerants from the middle colonies. In 1748 the Hanover dissenters obtained a resident Presbyterian minister, Samuel Davies, who had studied at the evangelical seminary in Pennsylvania conducted by William Tennent, Gilbert's father.

To discourage itinerants, the Anglican-dominated government of Virginia required, and then denied, special licenses. Governor William Gooch denounced the itinerants for seeking "not liberty of conscience but freedom of speech." His distinction was important and revealing. Gooch and other elitists accepted "liberty of conscience" as the passive persistence of long-standing denominational loyalties, but they dreaded "freedom of speech" for inviting people to rethink their allegiances, which seemed likely to disrupt social harmony. By this reasoning, Presbyterian preachers should limit their preaching to their traditional constituencies in Scots and Scotch-Irish settlements, rather than roam into other parishes to recruit Anglican defectors.

An educated man with good manners, Samuel Davies evoked far less hostility than did the poorly educated Baptist preachers from New England, who began to itinerate in North Carolina and Virginia during the mid-1750s. Accepting a low standard of living and working as farmers and tradesmen when not preaching, the Baptist elders needed only small contributions from their audiences, who rarely could afford to give much. Consequently, the Baptists could more rapidly and cheaply expand their ministry, especially on the frontier, than could the more orthodox denominations that depended upon a limited supply of expensive and college-educated ministers.

In the settlements, the preachers recruited followers by tapping into independent local prayer groups of devout seekers. Hungry for preaching, the unaffiliated seekers welcomed and hosted a variety of itinerant preachers touring the settlements. Although numerous, such pious "independents" have been underestimated in standard religious histories, naturally drawn by better documentation to the institutionalized denominations. Although certain that they were not Anglicans, the pious independents rarely knew what they were until impressed by the Baptist itinerants. Despite their late start in Virginia, the Baptists grew rapidly from only seven congregations in 1769 to fifty-four by 1774, embracing at least a tenth of white Virginians.

Used to reading character from external appearances, the Virginia Anglicans regarded the Baptists as somber and melancholy people, for they wore dark and plain clothing, cut their hair short, and wove their faith into every conversation. But their external sobriety and austerity covered a more emotional, intimate, and supportive community for worship. Gathered together, they shared their despair and ecstasy in a manner discouraged by ridicule in the highly competitive and gentry-dominated society of Anglican Virginia. Addressing one another as "brother" and "sister," the Baptists conducted an egalitarian worship that contrasted with the hierarchical seating and service of the Anglican churches. The Baptists even welcomed slaves into their worship as "brothers" and "sisters," and encouraged some to become preachers. To break down worldly pride and build solidarity, Baptist services included extensive physical contact: laying on of hands, the exchange of the "kiss of charity," and ritual foot-washing. A visceral distaste for such intimate contact with ordinary people discouraged gentlemen and ladies from becoming Baptists. Appealing primarily to common planters and some slaves, the Baptists drew them together while drawing them away from the gentry.

By calling upon converts to desert their Anglican churches, the Baptists threatened a foundation of Virginia society: the expectation that everyone in a parish would worship together in the established church supervised by the county gentry. Baptists also discouraged the public amusements that had long demonstrated the gentry's leadership as the finest dancers and the owners of the best racehorses and gamecocks. Landon Carter bitterly complained that the Baptists were "quite destroying pleasure in the Country; for they encourage ardent Prayer; strong & constant faith, & an intire Banishment of *Gaming, Dancing,* & Sabbath-Day Diversions." The withdrawal of common evangelicals from public diversions and Anglican services implicitly rebuked the gentry and parsons for leading worldly lives.

Anglican pastors and gentlemen defended the traditional conviction that secular authority depended upon a religious establishment. Rigorously enforcing the laws against itineracy, Anglican magistrates whipped and jailed dozens of unlicensed preachers. Far from avoiding or resisting confrontation, the Baptists welcomed opportunities to endure persecution conspicuously for their faith. In 1771 a county sheriff and a posse of gentry tried to break up a Baptist meeting by pulling the preacher, John Waller, from the stage to inflict twenty lashes with a horsewhip. In Waller's words, the congregation gathered around the whipping to sing psalms "so that he Could Scarcely feel the Stripes." Released, Waller "Went Back singing praise to God, mounted the Stage & preached with a Great Deal of Liberty." For evangelicals, to preach with "Liberty" meant to channel the Holy Spirit spontaneously. Astonished and ashamed, the posse rode away discredited. By enduring, Waller turned his whipping into a Baptist victory that impressed onlookers and made the case for toleration. . . .

Legacies

Revivals were too emotionally demanding to last. As northern revivalism receded after 1743, the moderate evangelicals and most Old Light clergy regretted their animosities, which had weakened public respect for a learned clergy. Even Gilbert Tennent denounced "everything which tends to enthusiasm and division." Although still differing in their modes of preaching, the Old Lights and the moderate New Lights agreed to disagree without impugning each other's salvation and godliness. The New England Congregational clergy quietly reconciled during the late 1740s; the Presbyterians followed suit in 1758, and the Dutch Reformed in 1772. The clergies of all three denominations were brought together, first, by the clear victories of the moderates in attracting more listeners and in training the next generation of ministers. Second, both groups recognized their shared antipathy toward the radical evangelicals who championed lay exhorters, anti-intellectualism, latter-day visions, and church separations.

The educated clergy also worked to regain popular support by reaffirming the fundamental power of the laity to govern each local church. Most clergymen wisely paid a new tribute to the piety and wisdom of their congregants, especially their role in judging the authentic conversions of applicants for membership. By 1775 these concessions to popular authority and conversion religion eased the return of about half of the Separates to the Congregational fold. The remaining radicals took refuge in Baptist congregations, while the most hard-line rationalists found havens in Anglican churches. Indeed, Anglicanism experienced a modest boom in the northern colonies by welcoming Old Lights opposed to any compromise with evangelical ways.

The renewed consensus within the leading denominations failed to reverse the greatest change wrought by the Great Awakening: the popular enthusiasm for sampling an array of traveling preachers of remarkable social and theological diversity. In her diary for 1769, Mary Cooper of Long Island recorded attending a Quaker "woman preach[er] that lately came from England," a "New Light meeten to here a Black man preach," and two Indian preachers holding "verry happy meetens" as "grate numbers flocked to here them." Ecumenical seekers like Mary Cooper cherished their expanding religious choices. Such a free flow of itinerants and audiences— and the spiritual authority of some Africans and Indians over whites— would have been inconceivable thirty years earlier.

Multiple itinerants offered a perpetual source of religious fluidity and innovation, which, however, was counteracted by the tendency of evangelical groups eventually to institutionalize in search of greater stability and respectability. At their genesis in a revival, evangelical groups defied the social order in hopes of bringing heaven to earth, but as their own revivalism cooled and millennial hopes faded, evangelical groups either institutionalized or dissolved. The persistent affiliated with a denomination and compromised with the inequalities and conventions of their larger society. To finance their churches and to attain respectability, they recruited converts farther up the social ladder, abandoning radical practices that might offend. For example, at the end of the eighteenth century most Baptists forbade female exhorting and voting, restricted lay exhorting, reduced rituals of physical contact, founded colleges to educate their ministers, accepted slavery, and enhanced the authority and prestige of their clergy.

The changes made it easier for gentlemen and ladies to become Baptists. But the changes also alienated purists, who usually bolted into some emerging evangelical group that privileged spiritual spontaneity over institutional regularity. During the 1790s, for example, alienated Baptists found haven among the newer and more radical Freewill Baptists or the Methodists. In sum, the Great Awakening accelerated a religious dialectic that pulled seekers and their congregations between the spiritual hunger to transcend the world and the social longing for respect in it.

DOCUMENTS

On the Death of the Rev. Mr. George Whitefield, 1770

Hail, happy saint, on thine immortal throne,
Possessed of glory, life, and bliss unknown;
We hear no more the music of thy tongue,
Thy wonted auditories cease to throng
Thy sermons in unequaled accents flowed,
And every bosom with devotion glowed;
Thou didst in strains of eloquence refined
Inflame the heart, and captivate the mind.

He freely offered to the numerous throng,
That on his lips with listening pleasure hung.
Take Him, ye wretched, for your only good,
Take Him my dear Americans', he said;
'Ye thirsty, come to this life-giving stream,
Ye preachers, take Him for your joyful theme;
Take Him my dear Americans,' he said,
Be your complaints on His kind bosom laid:
Take Him, ye Africans, He longs for you,
Impartial Savior is His title due:
Washed in the foundation of redeeming blood,
You shall be son, and kings, and priests to God.'

Yet let us view him in the eternal skies,
Let every heart to this bright vision rise,
While the tomb safe retains its sacred trust,
Till life divine re-animates his dust.

SOURCE: Phillis Wheatley, *Poems on Various Subjects, Religious and Moral* (London: Printed for Archibald Bell and Sold in Boston by Cox and Berry, 1773).

The Great Awakening in Connecticut, 1740

Now it pleased God to send Mr. Whitefield into this land; and my hearing of his preaching at Philadelphia, like one of the old apostles, and many thousands flocking to hear him preach the Gospel, and great numbers were converted to Christ, I felt the Spirit of God drawing me by conviction; I longed to see and hear him and wished he would come this way. I heard he was come to New York and the Jerseys and great multitudes flocking after him under great concern for their souls which brought on my concern more and more, hoping soon to see him; but next I heard he was at Long Island, then at Boston, and next at Northampton. Then on a sudden, in the morning about 8 or 9 of the clock there came a messenger and said Mr. Whitefield preached at Hartford and Wethersfield yesterday and is to preach at Middletown this morning at ten of the clock. I was in my field at work. I dropped my tool that I had in my hand and ran home to my wife, telling her to make ready quickly to go and hear Mr. Whitefield preach at Middletown, then ran to my pasture for my horse with all my might, fearing that I should be too late. Having my horse, I with my wife soon mounted the horse and went forward as fast as I thought the horse could bear; and when my horse got much out of breath, I would get down and put my wife on the saddle and bid her ride as fast as she could and not stop or slack for me except I bade her, and so I would run until I was much out of breath and then mount my horse again, and so I did several times to favour my horse. We improved every moment to get along as if we were fleeing for our lives, all the while fearing we should be too late to hear the sermon, for we had twelve miles to ride double in little more than an hour and we went round by the upper housen parish. And when we came within about half a mile or a mile of the road that comes down from Hartford, Wethersfield, and Stepney to Middletown, on high land I saw before me a cloud of fog arising. I first thought it came from the great river, but as I came nearer the road I heard a noise of horses' feet coming down the road, and this cloud was a cloud of dust made by the horses' feet. It arose some rods into the air over the tops of hills and trees; and when I came within about 20 rods of the road, I could see men and horses slipping along in the cloud like shadows, and as I drew nearer it seemed like a steady stream of horses and their riders, scarcely a horse more than his length behind another, all of a lather and foam with sweat, their breath rolling out of their nostrils every jump. Every horse seemed to go with all his might to carry his rider to hear news from heaven for the saving of souls. It made me tremble to see the sight, how the world was in a struggle. I found a vacancy between two horses to slip in mine and my wife said "Law, our clothes will

SOURCE: Nathan Cole, ms. cited in Leonard W. Labaree, "George Whitefield Comes to Middletown," *William and Mary Quarterly*, 3d ser. 7 (1950): 590–591.

be all spoiled, see how they look," for they were so covered with dust that they looked almost all of a colour, coats, hats, shirts, and horse. We went down in the stream but heard no man speak a word all the way for 3 miles but every one pressing forward in great haste; and when we got to Middletown old meeting house, there was a great multitude, it was said to be 3 or 4,000 of people, assembled together. We dismounted and shook off our dust, and the ministers were then coming to the meeting house. I turned and looked towards the Great River and saw the ferry boats running swift backward and forward bringing over loads of people, and the oars rowed nimble and quick. Everything, men, horses, and boats seemed to be struggling for life. The land and banks over the river looked black with people and horses; all along the 12 miles I saw no man at work in his field, but all seemed to be gone. When I saw Mr. Whitefield come upon the scaffold, he looked almost angelical; a young, slim, slender youth, before some thousands of people with bold undaunted countenance. And my hearing how God was with him everywhere as he came along, it solemnized my mind and put me into a trembling fear before he began to preach; for he looked as if he was clothed with authority from the Great God, and a sweet solemn solemnity sat upon his brow, and my hearing him preach gave me a heart wound. By God's blessing, my old foundation was broken up, and I saw that my righteousness would not save me.

"Sinners in the Hands of an Angry God," 1741

The God that holds you over the pit of hell, much as one holds a spider or some loathsome insect over the fire, abhors you, and is dreadfully provoked. His wrath towards you burns like fire; he looks upon you as worthy of nothing else but to be cast into the fire. He is of purer eyes than to bear you in his sight; you are ten thousand times as abominable in his eyes as the most hateful, venomous serpent is in ours.

You have offended him infinitely more than ever a stubborn rebel did his prince, and yet it is nothing but his hand that holds you from falling into the fire every moment. It is to be ascribed to nothing else that you did not go to hell last night; that you were suffered to awake again in this world, after you closed your eyes to sleep. And there is no other reason to be given why you have not dropped into hell since you arose in the morning, but that God's hand has held you up. There is no other reason to be given why you have not gone to hell since you have sat here in the house of God provoking his pure eye by your sinful, wicked manner of attending his solemn worship. Yea, there is nothing else that is to be given as a reason why you do not this very moment drop down into hell.

SOURCE: Jonathan Edwards, *Works* (1840), 2:10–11.

O sinner! consider the fearful danger you are in! It is a great furnace of wrath, a wide and bottomless pit, full of the fire of wrath that you are held over in the hand of that God whose wrath is provoked and incensed as much against you as against many of the damned in hell. You hang by a slender thread, with the flames of Divine wrath flashing about it, and ready every moment to singe it and burn it asunder. . . .

It would be dreadful to suffer this fierceness and wrath of Almighty God one moment; but you must suffer it to all eternity. There will be no end to this exquisite, horrible misery. When you look forward, you shall see along forever a boundless duration before you, which will swallow up your thoughts, and amaze your soul. And you will absolutely despair of ever having any deliverance, any end, any mitigation, any rest at all. You will know certainly that you must wear out long ages, millions of millions of ages in wrestling and conflicting with this Almighty, merciless vengeance. And then when you have so done, when so many ages have actually been spent by you in this manner, you will know that all is but a point [dot] to what remains. So that your punishment will indeed be infinite.

Oh! who can express what the state of a soul in such circumstances is! All that we can possibly say about it gives but a very feeble, faint representation of it. It is inexpressible and inconceivable: for "who knows the power of God's anger"!

How dreadful is the state of those that are daily and hourly in danger of this great wrath and infinite misery! But this is the dismal case of every soul in this congregation that has not been born again, however moral and strict, sober and religious, they may otherwise be. Oh! that you would consider it, whether you be young or old!

There is reason to think that there are many in this congregation, now hearing this discourse, that will actually be the subjects of this very misery to all eternity. We know not who they are, or in what seats they sit, or what thoughts they now have. It may be they are now at ease, and hear all these things without much disturbance, and are now flattering themselves that they are not the persons, promising themselves that they shall escape.

If we knew that there was one person, and but one in the whole congregation, that was to be the subject of this misery, what an awful thing it would be to think of! If we knew who it was, what an awful sight would it be to see such a person! How might all the rest of the congregation lift up a lamentable and bitter cry over him!

But, alas! instead of one, how many is it likely will remember this discourse in hell! And it would be a wonder, if some that are now present should not be in hell in a very short time before this year is out. And it would be no wonder if some persons that now sit here in some seats of this meeting-house, in health, and quiet and secure, should be there before tomorrow morning!

Chapter 6

Urban Life in the Eighteenth Century

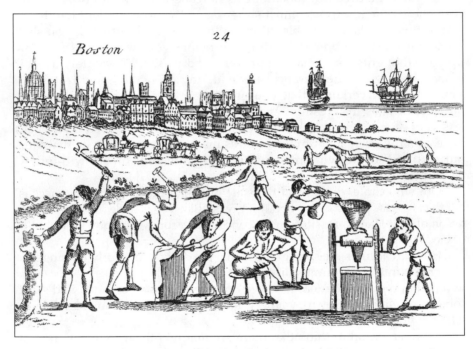

A 1766 drawing showing Boston's skyline in the background, while focusing on those who were essential to the town's economic wellbeing: artisans, merchants, tradesmen, farmers and seamen.

Colonial American society was overwhelmingly agrarian—throughout the eighteenth century, farmers and their families represented over 90 percent of the population—but cities also prospered during this period. The very success of agriculture ensured their growth, for the primary function of Boston, Newport, New York, Philadelphia, Baltimore, and Charleston was to gather for export the surplus products of the farms and forests and to import and market manufactured goods. As centers of commerce and political, social, and cultural life, cities played a crucial role in shaping the character of the emerging nation.

In her essay "Boston and New York in the Eighteenth Century," Pauline Maier discusses the functions and characteristics common to American colonial cities. She describes and explains what made New York and Boston unique and very different from one another by the end of the eighteenth century. As you read, observe how the different reasons for the founding of these two cities exerted a lasting influence on them. Notice in each case the impact of geography, war, social class, and political structure. How does Maier's essay help to explain why Boston, America's third city in population and prosperity by 1775, stood in the forefront of events leading to the Revolutionary War?

The documents following the essay provide a view of another colonial city. By the outbreak of the Revolution, Philadelphia had become colonial America's largest city and within the British Empire was second only to London in population and prestige. In cities as on the frontier, colonial Americans learned the value of cooperative effort; voluntary militias, barn raisings, and husking bees provide apt examples. One of the chief advocates of cooperative ventures in an urban setting was Benjamin Franklin. He is credited with organizing America's first cooperative lending library, the first adult self-improvement group (the Junto), and, described in the initial document, the first adult volunteer fire department.

Visitors to Philadelphia found qualities to admire other than the city's cooperative spirit. The second document gives the impressions of Swedish botanist Peter Kalm during his 1748 visit to Philadelphia. What factors did Kalm deem most significant in accounting for Philadelphia's rapid rise to prominence?

Philadelphia also illustrates a fact of early American urban life that often goes unnoticed. City dwellers had to overcome numerous hazards: fires, street crime, primitive sanitary facilities, and epidemics of cholera, malaria, and yellow fever. The third document describes the yellow-fever epidemic that struck Philadelphia in 1793, causing the deaths of more than 5,000 of the city's approximately 55,000 inhabitants. What does the document reveal about the state of medical knowledge in the late eighteenth century?

The English cities of the east coast were not the only ones experiencing growth during the eighteenth century. The future American city of New Orleans, then the capital of France's Louisiana colony, also impressed visitors. The final document is from a letter by a French naval officer, Jean-Bernard Bossu, who visited New Orleans in 1751. In what ways was Bossu's response to what he saw in New Orleans similar in tone to that of Peter Kalm's description of Philadelphia? Notice the diverse populations in both cities. Letters and memoirs by visitors like Kalm and Bossu often played a key role in encouraging Europeans to immigrate to America.

ESSAY

Boston and New York in the Eighteenth Century

Pauline Maier

My title was inspired by George Rudé's *Paris and London in the Eighteenth Century,* though my concerns were not his. In the course of working on urban politics in the Revolutionary period I became aware of how remarkably different were Boston and New York—different not just in their people and politics but in feeling, in character, in that wonderfully all-encompassing thing called culture. Their differences were neither incidental nor ephemeral: to a remarkable extent the distinctive traits each city had developed by the end of the eighteenth century survived into the nineteenth and even the twentieth century. And so I propose to consider those differences, how they began and persisted over time, and their more general importance in American history.

Any such exercise assumes that the subjects of inquiry were comparable, that is, that they had some essential identity in common upon which distinctions were grafted. The existence of such a common identity for two early American ports on the Atlantic seaboard is in part obvious. But there remains a problem relevant to their comparability that is worth beginning with, one that has troubled me and, I suppose, other students of the period since first encountering Carl Bridenbaugh's path-breaking books *Cities in the Wilderness* and *Cities in Revolt.* That is, by what right do we classify together Boston, New York, and similar communities as "cities" before 1800?

Consider the gulf between Rudé's subjects and mine. He wrote about two of the greatest cities in the Western world, population centers that no one hesitates to call urban. Paris already had over a half million people in 1700. It grew only modestly over the next century, while London expanded at a quick pace—from 575,000 people in 1750 to almost 900,000 fifty years later. By contrast Boston's population stood at 6,700, New York's nearer 5,000 when the eighteenth century began. One hundred years later New York had over 60,000 and Boston almost 25,000 people. It takes no very sophisticated statistical analysis to suggest that a "city" of 6,700 was something very different from one of a half million, that New York at its eighteenth-century peak was still in many ways distinct from London, whose population was some fifteen times greater. If "city" denotes a community's size, Boston and New York would not qualify.

SOURCE: Pauline Maier, "Boston and New York in the Eighteenth Century," *Proceedings of the American Antiquarian Society* 91, Part 2 (Oct. 21, 1981): 177–195.

The word "city" has not, however, distinguished places by size so much as by function. Historically it designated independent communities that served as centers for a surrounding countryside and as points of contact with the outside world. The word derives from the Latin word *civitas*, which the Romans used, as it happens, for a colonial situation—for the separate states or tribes of Gaul, and then for their most important towns. They were also *civitates* in Roman Britain, but the Angles and Saxons used instead the word *burh* or *borough,* adopting *city* in the thirteenth century for foreign or ancient cities, for large indigenous communities such as London, and later for the chief boroughs of a diocese, those that became cathedral towns.

Cities perform their centralizing function in many ways, most of which were exercised by Boston and New York. Like other major colonial cities, they were provincial capitals as well as important cultural centers where newspapers and pamphlets were published, discussed, and distributed. But above all they were commercial centers, Atlantic coastal ports where the produce of the countryside was collected and shipped to the West Indies, Africa, or Europe and exchanged for products or credits that could in turn be exchanged for goods of foreign origin needed by colonists in both city and country. Later cities became the merchandising centers for manufactures of either rural or urban origin, whose "reach" and therefore whose volume of business grew with the development of more advanced transportation systems; they became the homes of banks, of insurance companies, of stock exchanges. As they did so, they drew upon the efforts of increasing numbers of people. But it was not the size of their populations that made them cities so much as the functions Boston and New York shared with Paris and London even when their people were counted in thousands, not tens or hundreds of thousands.

From the beginning, moreover, colonial cities had a cosmopolitan character that distinguished them from more rural towns, of whose people it could be said, as [historian] George Homans wrote of thirteenth-century English villagers, that they "had upon the whole more contact with one another than they had with outsiders." While their ships traded at ports-of-call in the Caribbean and the larger Atlantic world, the cities played host to numbers of transients or "strangers," whether in the laboring force or among the more substantial persons of affairs who found business to transact at Boston or New York. Already in the seventeenth century Boston merchants found themselves in conflict with their colony's Puritan leaders, whose effort to isolate Massachusetts from Old World contamination proved incompatible with the demands of commerce. "The well-being of trade," [historian] Bernard Bailyn has observed, "demanded the free movement of people and goods." In the end the merchants won, but their victory was never such as made Boston altogether hospitable to new immigrants, particularly those of non-English origin. Only the French Huguenots—the

Faneuils, Bowdoins, Rivoires, and their like—found a welcome there and were easily assimilated.

New York's population was more diverse in origin, including persons of Dutch as well as of French and English origin along with lesser numbers of Germans, Irishmen, Jews, and other Europeans as well as substantial numbers of Africans. Manhattan and the nearby counties of Long Island had the largest concentration of blacks anywhere in North America above the plantation colonies. The city also absorbed substantial numbers of migrants from New England.

The diversity of New York's peoples has, however, often been exaggerated, for they were, like Boston's people, predominantly Northern European Calvinists who shared, out of diverse historical experiences, a militant hostility to "papism" and to Catholic Absolutism in France and Spain. Even Manhattan's Sephardic [of Spanish or Portuguese origin] Jews shared in some measure this "Protestant" culture, for they had suffered from the same forces that the Dutch [had] and fought in their long struggle for national independence—the Spanish monarchy and the Catholic Church. With people already so alike, the "melting pot" could melt: by the mid-eighteenth century . . . younger persons of Dutch descent, particularly on Manhattan, spoke mostly English, attended the English church, "and would even take it amiss if they were called Dutchmen and not Englishmen." French Huguenots [Protestants] who first arrived at New York in the seventeenth century also gradually became Anglicans, helping to make the city by the late eighteenth century far more culturally unified than it had been one hundred years earlier or would be a century later, when Italian Catholics, the Ashkenazic Jews of Eastern Europe, and other decidedly alien people were added in great numbers to the older "native stock."

In the course of the eighteenth century, Boston and New York also gave evidence of a new anonymity among their people that reflected the growth of their populations. That development was slow in coming. Certainly there remained much of the small town about Philadelphia, the largest of American cities in 1771 when Esther DeBerdt Reed reported to her father in London that "the people must either talk of their neighbors, of whom they know every particular of what they both do and say, or else of marketing. . . . We hardly dare tell one another our thoughts," she added, "lest it should spread all over town; so, if anybody asks you how we like Philadelphia, you must say very well." The newspapers published in colonial cities in their very dearth of local news also testify to the way eighteenth-century urban people knew their news without reading about it. There were, however, signs of change. [Historian] Thomas Bender cites the appearance of craftsmen's ads in New York newspapers of the 1750s as evidence that artisans were finding it necessary to announce their existence to townsmen who might in an earlier day have known of it without such formal notice. The publication of city directories at New York in 1786 and Boston in 1789 attests again to an increasing unfamiliarity of city people with each other. Soon thereafter authorities addressed themselves to the problem of locating people within the increasingly anonymous urban masses. In 1793 New York's Common Council ordered that buildings along the streets be numbered according to a prescribed method. From that regulation it was but a short step to the 1811 report of a New York commission that surveyed the island and planned the expanse of practical if monotonously regular numbered streets that would in time stretch from the old and irregular colonial city on the lower tip of Manhattan up toward the Harlem River, and which has been logically taken as the beginning of New York's emergence as a "modern" city.

In all these ways—in the functions that marked them as cities, in their relative cosmopolitanism and common Protestant culture, in the gradual development by the late eighteenth century of a social anonymity that has since become so much a part of urban life—Boston and New York were almost interchangeable. And yet they had acquired, like children, distinctive traits that they would carry with them into later life. The appearance of differences early in the cities' histories is striking, their persistence over time the more so. Both need to be explained. Their reasons lie, I suggest, in the ideals or purposes of the cities' founders, and in the peculiar, unpredictable way those early traditions were reinforced by eighteenth-century circumstances.

Boston's Puritan fathers came to America with a mission defined against the avarice and corruption of contemporary England. They sought to establish close-knit communities where love of God and concern for neighbor took precedence over selfish gain. Their ideology proved well suited to the business of colonizing. Because the Puritans sought to found permanent homes in America, whole families migrated, not the men alone. The population of New England therefore grew naturally at a far faster rate than elsewhere in seventeenth-century North America. The Puritans' commitment to their "callings" and their emphasis on industry also contributed to the cause of success in this world as much as in the next, and Boston became the premier city of British North America.

Its early achievement proved impossible to sustain, however, and as the eighteenth century proceeded Boston gradually yielded its leadership to Philadelphia and New York. It is commonplace to say that geography determined Boston's destiny: the proximity of the Appalachian mountains to the Atlantic coast in New England, the rocky quality of soil along the coastal belt, the course of its rivers, which too often ran on a north-south axis and so provided no ready path to the interior, all these limited the extent and the richness of that hinterland upon which Boston's importance depended. But its fate, we now know, is not so simply explained. An "almost biblical series of misfortunes" afflicted Boston in the mid-eighteenth century, most of which were related to the series of colonial wars [with France] that brought disaster to Boston even as they blessed with prosperity the artisans and merchants of New York and Philadelphia. The city contributed heavily to imperial armies, and therefore to the casualty lists, which cut deeply into its male population and so into its tax base. Meanwhile taxes rose to finance the expeditions to Canada and to support the widows and orphans left behind, making Boston (then as now) a particularly expensive place to live, even in comparison to neighboring towns. Its shipbuilding industry dispersed to Marblehead, Salem, and Newport, and fear of impressment [seizure of sailors for service in the British navy] disrupted its trade. The results could be read in Boston's population figures, which reached 17,000 in 1740, then dropped, and failed to recover completely until after independence; in the striking excess of white adult females to males among Bostonians of 1764 (3,612 to 2,941); in the dense occupancy of Boston's houses, which included about half again as many people as those of New York and Philadelphia at mid-century, a difference [historian] Gary Nash attributes to the practice of taking in boarders by hard-pressed Boston widows; in the emergence of poverty as a serious social problem well before it reached such importance in other colonial ports.

It is too much to say that Boston never recovered, but its record in the late colonial period was overall one of decline. And hard times served the cause of tradition, for the Spartan ideal of the founders could ennoble necessity by calling it virtue. New England's ministers continued to cite the first generation of settlers as a model of achievement, as they had done from the late seventeenth century, and to chastise the children for failing to take up their fathers' "Errand into the Wilderness," explaining the calamities that fell upon them as punishments for the sinful shortcomings of those who had inherited that New World Israel. The ideals of the fathers provided, in short, a way of understanding and of organizing experience, of ordering history, and so continued to influence the life of the region and of its major city.

New York was founded instead as an outpost of the Dutch West India Company in its search for profit. No greater mission brought the Dutch from Holland: indeed, the Dutch were on the whole unwilling to migrate, finding their homeland hospitable as the English Puritans did not. The Dutch West India Company therefore turned elsewhere for settlers—to the oppressed Protestants of France, to Africa—in the hope that they might help make New Netherland economically viable. The commitment to material gain that marked Company rule continued after the British conquest. The financial needs of the later Stuart kings, the hopes of greater fortunes that motivated the governors appointed by them and their successors, the ambitions of colonists who flattered royal officials in a quest for land grants, contracts, or lucrative appointments, all these only enhanced New York's materialistic bent. The city became a nest of those after profit however won—of pirates and privateers, of slave traders and smugglers—a community whose spokesmen on into the Revolutionary era emphasized interest while those of Boston cultivated virtue.

New Yorkers did well—and then did better. The city sat at the mouth of the great Hudson River, which, with the Mohawk, provided ready access to a rich and extensive market even before the canal era added the trans-Appalachian West to Manhattan's "back yard." It benefited also from wartime contracts and privateering returns, and except for occasional years of recession continued the ascent that would in time make it the foremost American city. The results there could be seen in a sense of widespread opportunity such as possessed the immigrant James Murray in 1737, when he advised a clergyman in his native Northern Ireland to "tell aw the poor Folk of your place, tha God has open'd a Door for their Deliverance." In New York there was "no Scant of Breed"; and it was, "in short, . . . a bonny Country" where a man could readily make a good life for himself. In his *History of the Province of New-York,* first published in 1757, a more established New Yorker, William Smith, Junior, made much the same point. "Every man of industry and integrity has it in his power to live well," he wrote, and many who arrived "distressed by their poverty . . . now enjoy easy and plentiful fortunes."

Smith also claimed that there was "not so great an inequality" of riches among New Yorkers "as is common in Boston and some other places," but there he was almost certainly incorrect. The rich of Manhattan combined mercantile wealth with great landed estates in the Hudson Valley in a way unknown among Bostonians. The city's people shared a sense of social distance that also distinguished it from its urban neighbor to the northeast. Some of the most memorable expressions of class consciousness that the Revolutionary era produced came from New York—as in Gouverneur Morris's arrogant description of local mechanics and seamen as "poor reptiles . . . struggling to cast off their winter slough" who "bask in the sunshine, and ere noon . . . will bite." As for Morris's "riotous mob," it was characterized by deferential habits such as shocked John Hancock when he visited New York on his way to the Continental Congress. On his arrival there Hancock learned that the city's people intended to remove the horses from his carriage and pull it through the streets themselves, a ritual common enough in the Old World. But Hancock, no modest man but a Bostonian nonetheless, "would not have had [that] taken place upon any Consideration, not being fond of such Parade." His efforts to dissuade the crowd were unsuccessful, and he was saved from that "disagreeable occurrence" only by the intercession of some local gentlemen whose wishes the people of New York were more accustomed to honoring.

Politics moderated the distance between rich and poor in Boston. There the governing town meeting brought together persons of different station and blessed men with power for their eloquence, reason, and character as well as their wealth. Boston had a board of selectmen and a series of other municipal officers who were chosen by the town meeting, and those who sought such preferment learned, if they did not instinctively know, that respect was a prerequisite of political support. New York was governed differently. By the terms of the Montgomery Charter of 1731, the governor and provincial council named the city's mayor, recorder, clerk, and the treasurer. Municipal ordinances were passed by a Common Council that consisted of the mayor and recorder along with the city's aldermen, who were elected by voice vote within the several wards into which New York had been divided. Qualified voters also chose a set of assistants, several minor officials, and the vestrymen who cared for the poor. But they had no continuing, direct voice in governing the city as in Boston, where "the meanest citizen ratable at £20 beside the poll, may deliver his sentiments and give his suffrage in very important matters, as freely as the greatest Lord in the Land," according to the reports of Dr. Thomas Young, a native of the Hudson Valley who migrated to Boston in the mid-1760s. Political opportunities compensated in some measure for Boston's unpromising economy: "elevated stations," Young claimed, were there open "to every one whose capacity, integrity and diligence in the affairs of his country attracts the public attention." Those avenues of advancement, he wrote correspondents in Manhattan, "I lament are shut to you. . . ."

The existence of a wealthy upper class with a taste for European ways had, however, some cultural advantages, for its patronage set eighteenth-century New York on its way toward becoming an American center for the performing arts. Manhattan claimed two playhouses in 1732; by the time of the Revolution it had as many as seven. Not that all New Yorkers were free from scruples born of their Protestant heritage. William Hallam's London Company of Comedians, which came to the city in 1753, was denied official permission to perform until after it issued assurances that its members were "not cast in the same Mould" as their "Theatrical Predecessors," that "in private Life" and "publick Occupation" they were of a different moral order. In retrospect, however, it seems more important that the company went to New York because people in Virginia predicted a "genteel and favourable Reception" in Manhattan, where "the Inhabitants were generous and polite, naturally fond of Diversions rational, particularly those of the Theatre," and that Hallam's company finally enjoyed a successful and profitable run in the city. New York also saw occasional musical performances, as in January 1737 when the *New-York Gazette* advertised a "consort . . . for the benefit of Mr. Pachebell, the harpsicord parts performed by himself." And two years later an advertisement announced "A New Pantomime Entertainment. . . . To which will be added an Optick," which was a primitive predecessor of motion pictures. Cock-fighting was also popular, as was horse-racing, with wagers part of the event—all of which remained far from Boston, a city less open to such forms of commercial entertainment. Indeed, theatre was introduced at Boston only during the 1790s, having been earlier outlawed by an act of 1750.

Boston was distinguished instead by its traditional respect for learning and for the printed word. Before the Puritan fathers were more than a decade in America they founded Harvard College and established a printing press in Cambridge. New York City was settled in 1626—four years before Boston—but had no press for almost seventy years, until William Bradford was lured to Manhattan in 1693. Even a casual survey of the Evans bibliography of early American imprints testifies to the immense and continuing superiority of eighteenth-century Boston as a place of publication. Few books and pamphlets came out of New York, and those were heavily weighted toward the official publications of the provincial government. As for newspapers, the first to be published on a continuous schedule in British North America was the *Boston News-Letter,* begun in 1704. And Boston had two other papers, the *Boston Gazette* (1719) and the *New-England Courant* (1721) before the *New-York Gazette* began publication in 1725.

New Yorkers' sense of a good education apparently differed from that of Bostonians: the City of New York was "so conveniently Situated for Trade and the Genius of the people so inclined to merchandise," wrote the Rev. John Sharpe in 1713 after some twelve years on Manhattan, "that they generally seek no other Education for their children than writing and Arithmetick. So that letters must be in a manner forced upon them not only without their seeking, but against their consent"—a proposal unlikely to meet with success. New Yorkers were in fact bizarrely innocent in the world of learning—or so James Murray suggested when he told of a fellow Scots-Irish immigrant who "now gets ane Hundred Punds for ane year for teechin a Letin Skulle, and God kens, little he is skilled in Learning, and yet they think him a high learned Man. Ye kin I had but sma Learning when I left ye," he added—and his primitive phonetic spelling suggests he had accumulated little thereafter. Yet Murray reported that he kept a "Skulle for wee Weans." Two decades later William Smith, Junior, concluded that New York's schools were of "the lowest order" and that their "instructors want instruction." "Through a long shameful neglect of all the arts and sciences," he added, "our common speech is extremely corrupt, and the evidences of a bad taste, both as to thought and language, are visible in all our proceedings, publick and private."

New York was, quite simply, a different kind of place than Boston, shaped by different values that were sustained by economic success. The "Art of getting money" preoccupied its people and served, according to Cadwallader Colden, as "the only principle of life propagated among the young People." New Yorkers of both town and country were "sober, industrious and hospitable," Smith noted, "though intent upon gain." The city's contemporary reputation reflected those traits. "Our Neighbours have told us in an insulting Tone, that the Art of getting money is the highest Improvement we can pretend to," wrote a pamphleteer arguing in 1749 for "Erecting a College in the Province of New-York." They say "that the wisest Man among us without a Fortune, is neglected and despised; and the greatest Blockhead with one, caress'd and honour'd: That, for this Reason, a poor

Man of the most shining Accomplishments, can never emerge out of his Obscurity; while every wealthy Dunce is loaded with Honours, and bears down all before him." Such accusations were made, he thought, out of envy over "the flourishing Circumstances of this City," and could be easily refuted. "But that Learning hath not been encourag'd as it ought, admits of no Controversy."

These distinctions were reflected in John Adams's perceptions of New York, which he visited on the way to the Continental Congress in Philadelphia, as did Hancock, with eyes fully open and with Boston as a constant standard of comparison. Like all travellers, Adams was impressed by New York's beauty, for it was in ways long since lost a garden city whose clean and spacious streets were lined with trees, and where the noise of frogs, especially on hot nights when rain was expected, provided a major annoyance. He remarked on the striking views or "prospects" the city offered of the Hudson and East Rivers, of Long Island and what he called the "Sound River," and of New Jersey. He found New York's streets "vastly more regular and elegant than those in Boston, and the houses are more grand, as well as neat." New Yorkers were as hospitable as Smith—and Madam Sarah Knight before him—indicated they would be, and Adams was struck, too, by the evidence of wealth, as in the costly accoutrements of John Morin Scott's breakfast table, which he inventoried lovingly ("rich plate, a very large silver coffee-pot, a very large silver tea-pot, napkins of the very finest materials"), or the "rich furniture" at the home of Isaac Low. Still, the continuous socializing he found "very disagreeable on some accounts." It seems never to have crossed the New Yorkers' minds that a Bostonian might be more anxious to see the twenty-year-old King's College, or the city's churches, printers' offices, and bookshops. And "with all the opulence and splendor of this city," Adams reported that there was "very little good breeding to be found. . . . I have not seen one real gentleman, one well-bred man, since I came to town." There was, moreover, "no conversation that is agreeable" at their "entertainments": there was "no modesty, no attention to one another," for the New Yorkers of that still-pastoral island had already acquired the conversational style of the modern metropolis. "They talk very loud, very fast, and altogether," Adams observed. "If they ask you a question, before you can utter three words of your answer, they will break out upon you again, and talk away."

There are in these observations testimony not merely to style, but to the pace, the bewildering restlessness that already possessed New Yorkers long before the nineteenth century. Even the sleighs they rode in the winter to friends' homes out of town or to "Houses of entertainment at a place called the Bowery . . . fly with great swiftness," Madam Knight noted on her visit there in 1704, "and some are so furious that they'll turn out of the path for none except a Loaden Cart." What was the hurry? And why were New Yorkers always building, tearing down, rearranging, reconstructing their city, leaving not even the bones of their ancestors in peace? They seem forever to have done things with what struck outsiders as excess: convinced that "merchandizing" was a good employment, they went into trade in such numbers, reported the visitor John Miller in 1695, "that whosoever looks on their shops would wonder"—like a modern stroller down Madison Avenue—"where there are so many to sell, there should be any to buy." The monumental energy of colonial New Yorkers prefigured that of later Americans, who within a century of winning independence built from thirteen modest colonies a nation whose western boundary had pushed from the Appalachians to the Pacific. The enterprise of New Yorkers contributed generously to that development. Indeed, the very physical circumstances of New Yorkers identified them with the nation in 1776: they were concentrated within the lowest mile of a thirteen-and-a-half-mile-long island much as their countrymen were settled along the eastern edge of a vast continent whose expanses of empty land invited and even demanded expansion. People such as these had no time to celebrate the past. They were too engrossed with inventing the future.

How different the situation of the Bostonians, housed on a modest peninsula already fully settled by the time of the Revolution, suffering from a generation of decline, a people convinced that the model of their future lay in the past. In fact, nineteenth-century Boston, true to its colonial origins, became the literary capital of the new nation and also a financial center whose importance yielded to New York only in the 1840s. Meanwhile New Englanders, fleeing the rural poverty of their native region, settled and populated much of the West. There remains considerable irony nonetheless in the fact that Boston served for the generation of 1776 as a model for the new republic. Its democratic politics, tradition of disinterested public service, and modest style, inculcated by Puritanism and continued through hardship, coincided neatly with the demands of classical republicanism—so much so that Samuel Adams could see in the United States a final realization of New England's historic mission. New York played a far more ambiguous role in the politics of the Revolution than did Boston, and the city never took on a similar symbolic importance—perhaps because infinite possibilities are more difficult to comprehend than the limited values of an established and well-defined historical tradition. New York has in fact remained difficult to grasp, to summarize. "By preference, but also in some degree by necessity," Nathan Glazer and Daniel Patrick Moynihan observed in *Beyond the Melting Pot*, "America has turned elsewhere for its images and traditions. Colonial America is preserved for us in terms of the Doric simplicity of New England, or the pastoral symmetry of the Virginia countryside. Even Philadelphia is manageable. But who can summon an image of eighteenth-century New York that will *hold still in the mind*?" And yet the importance of openness, optimism, opportunity, and energy, even of materialism and of visual over literary entertainments to the nation that emerged from the American eighteenth century is undeniable. . . .

DOCUMENTS

Benjamin Franklin's Union Fire Company, 1738

About this time I wrote a paper . . . on the different accidents and carelessnesses by which houses were set on fire, with cautions against them and means proposed of avoiding them. This was much spoken of as a useful piece, and gave rise to a project which soon followed it of forming a company for the more ready extinguishing of fires, and mutual assistance in removing and securing of goods when in danger. Associates in this scheme were presently found amounting to thirty. Our articles of agreement obliged every member to keep always in good order and fit for use a certain number of leather buckets with strong bags and baskets (for packing and transporting of goods) which were to be brought to every fire; and we agreed to meet once a month and spend a social evening together in discoursing and communicating such ideas as occurred to us upon the subject of fires as might be useful in our conduct on such occasions. The utility of this institution soon appeared, and many more desiring to be admitted than we thought convenient for one company, they were advised to form another, which was accordingly done. And this went on, one new company being formed after another till they became so numerous as to include most of the inhabitants who were men of property; and now at the time of my writing this [1788], tho' upwards of fifty years since its establishment, that which I first formed, called the Union Fire Company, still subsists and flourishes, tho' the first members are all deceased but myself and one, who is older by a year than I am. The small fines that have been paid by members for absence at the monthly meetings have been applied to the purchase of fire engines, ladders, firehooks, and other useful implements for each company, so that I question whether there is a city in the world better provided with the means of putting a stop to beginning conflagrations; and in fact since those institutions, the city has never lost by fire more than one or two houses at a time, and the flames have often been extinguished before the house in which they began has been half consumed.

SOURCE: John Bigelow, ed., *Works of Benjamin Franklin* (New York: G. P. Putnam's Sons, 1877), 1: 204–205.

Philadelphia, 1748

All the streets except two which are nearest to the river, run in a straight line, and make right angles at the intersections. Some are paved, others are not; and it seems less necessary, since the ground is sandy, and therefore soon absorbs the wet. But in most of the streets is a pavement of flags, a fathom or more broad, laid before the houses, and posts put on the outside three or four fathom asunder. Under the roofs are gutters which are carefully connected with pipes, and by this means, those who walk under them, when it rains, or when the snow melts, need not fear being wet by the dropping from the roofs.

The houses make a good appearance, are frequently several stories high, and built either of bricks or of stone; but the former are more commonly used, since bricks are made before the town, and are well burnt. The stone which has been employed in the building of other houses, is a mixture of black or grey *glimmer*, running in undulated veins, and of a loose, and quite small grained *limestone*, which runs scattered between the bendings of the other veins, and are of a grey colour, excepting here and there some single grains of sand, of a paler hue. The glimmer makes the greatest part of the stone; but the mixture is sometimes of another kind. This stone is now got in great quantities in the country, is easily cut, and has the good quality of not attracting the moisture in a wet season. Very good lime is burnt every where hereabouts, for masonry.

Characteristics of Philadelphians

The town is now quite filled with inhabitants, which in regard to their country, religion, and trade, are very different from each other. You meet with excellent masters in all trades, and many things are made here full as well as in *England*. Yet no manufactures, especially for making fine cloth, are established. Perhaps the reason is, that it can be got with so little difficulty from *England*, and that the breed of sheep which is brought over, degenerates in process of time, and affords but a coarse wool.

Here is great plenty of provisions, and their prices are very moderate. There are no examples of an extraordinary dearth.

Every one who acknowledges God to be the Creator, preserver, and ruler of all things, and teaches or undertakes nothing against the state, or against the common peace, is at liberty to settle, stay, and carry on his trade here, be his religious principles ever so strange. No one is here molested on account of the erroneous principles of the doctrine which he follows, if he does not exceed the above-mentioned bounds. And he is so well secured by

SOURCE: Peter Kalm, *Travels in North America 1,* translated into English by John Reinhold Forester (London: Printed for editor, 1770), 34–45, 58–60.

the laws in his person and property, and enjoys such liberties, that a citizen of *Phildelphia* may in a manner be said to live in his house like a king.

On a careful consideration of what I have already said, it will be easy to conceive how this city should rise so suddenly from nothing, into such grandeur and perfection, without supposing any powerful monarch's contributing to it, either by punishing the wicked, or by giving great supplies in money. And yet its fine appearance, good regulations, agreeable situation, natural advantages, trade, riches and power, are by no means inferior to those of any, even of the most ancient towns in *Europe*. It has not been necessary to force people to come and settle here; on the contrary, foreigners of different languages have left their country, houses, property, and relations, and ventured over wide and stormy seas, in order to come hither. Other countries, which have been peopled for a long space of time, complain of the small number of their inhabitants. But *Pennsylvania*, which was no better than a desert in the year 1681, and hardly contained five hundred people, now vies with several kingdoms in *Europe* in number of inhabitants. It has received numbers of people, which other countries, to their infinite loss, have either neglected or expelled.

The Scourge of Yellow Fever, Philadelphia, 1793

On the origin of the disorder [yellow fever], there prevails a very good diversity of opinion. Dr. Hutchinson maintained that it was not imported, and stated, in a letter which he wrote on the subject to Captain Falconer, the health officer of the port of Philadelphia, that "the general opinion was, that the disorder originated from some damaged coffee, or other putrified vegetable and animal matters." . . .

Several persons were swept away before any great alarm was excited. . . . About this time began the removals from the city, which were for some weeks so general, that almost every hour in the day, carts, wagons, coaches, and chairs, were to be seen transporting families and furniture to the country in every direction. Business then became extremely dull. Mechanics and artists were unemployed; and the streets wore the appearance of gloom and melancholy.

The first official notice taken of the disorder, was on the 22d of August, on which day, the mayor of Philadelphia, Matthew Clarkson, esq., wrote to the city commissioners, and after acquainting them with the state of the city, gave them the most peremptory orders, to have the streets properly cleansed and purified by the scavengers, and all the filth immediately hawled away. These orders were repeated on the 27th, and similar ones

SOURCE: Matthew Carey, *A Short Account of the Malignant Fever Lately Prevalent in Philadelphia* (Philadelphia, 1793), 16–17, 20–23, 60–63.

given to the clerks of the market. [On the] 29th the governor of the state, in his address to the legislature, acquainted them, that a contagious disorder existed in the city; and that he had taken every proper measure to ascertain the origin, nature, and extent of it. He likewise assured them that the health officer and physician of the port, would take every precaution to allay and remove the public inquietude.

The 26th of the same month, the college of physicians had a meeting, at which they took into consideration the nature of the disorder, and the means of prevention and of cure. They published an address to the citizens, signed by the president and secretary, recommending to avoid all unnecessary intercourse with the infected; to place marks on the doors or windows where they were; to pay great attention to cleanliness and airing the rooms of the sick; to provide a large and airy hospital in the neighbourhood of the city for their reception; to put a stop to the tolling of the bells; to bury those who died of the disorder in carriages and as privately as possible; to keep the streets and wharves clean; to avoid all fatigue of body and mind, and standing or sitting in the sun, or in the open air; to accommodate the dress to the weather, and to exceed rather in warm than in cool clothing; and to avoid intemperance, but to use fermented liquors, such as wine, beer, and cider, with moderation. They likewise declared their opinion, that fires in the streets were very dangerous, if not ineffectual means of stopping the progress of the fever, and that they placed more dependence on the burning of gunpowder. The benefits of vinegar and camphor, they added, were confined chiefly to infected rooms, and could not be too often used on handkerchiefs, or in smelling bottles, by persons who attended the sick.

In consequence of this address, the bells were immediately stopped from tolling, which was a measure very expedient; as they had before been kept pretty constantly going the whole day, so as to terrify those in health, and drive the sick, as far as the influence of imagination could produce that effect, to their graves. An idea had gone abroad, that the burning of fires in the streets, would have a tendency to purify the air, and arrest the progress of the disorder. The people had, therefore, almost every night large fires lighted at the corners of the streets. [On the] 29th, the mayor published a proclamation, forbidding this practice. As a substitute, many had recourse to the firing of guns, which they imagined was a certain preventative of the disorder. This was carried so far, and attended with such danger, that it was forbidden by the mayor's order, of the 4th of September. . . .

On the 16th, the managers of Bushhill [hospital], after personal inspection of the state of affairs there, made report of its situation, which was truly deplorable. It exhibited as wretched a picture of human misery as ever existed. A profligate, abandoned set of nurses and attendants (hardly any of good character could at that time be procured,) rioted on the provisions and comforts, prepared for the sick, who (unless at the hours when the doctors attended) were left almost entirely destitute of every assistance. The dying and dead were indiscriminately mingled together. The ordure and other evacuations of the sick, were allowed to remain in the most offensive state imaginable. Not the smallest appearance of order or regularity existed. It was, in fact, a great human slaughter house, where numerous victims were immolated at the altar of riot and intemperance. No wonder, then, that a general dread of the place prevailed through the city, and that a removal to it was considered as the seal of death. In consequence, there were various instances of sick persons locking their rooms, and resisting every attempt to carry them away. At length, the poor were so much afraid of being sent to Bushhill, that they would not acknowledge their illness, until it was no longer possible to conceal it. For it is to be observed, that the fear of the contagion was so prevalent, that as soon as any one was taken sick, an alarm was spread among the neighbours, and every effort was used to have the sick person hurried off to Bushhill, to avoid spreading the disorder. The cases of the persons forced in this way to that hospital, though labouring under only common colds, and common fall fevers, are numerous and afflicting. There were not wanting instances of persons, only slightly ill, being sent to Bushhill, by their panic-struck neighbours, and embracing the first opportunity of running back to Philadelphia. But the case was soon altered under the direction of the two managers, Girard and Helm. They introduced such order and regularity, and had the patients treated with so much care and tenderness, that they retrieved the character of the hospital; and in the course of a week or two, numbers of sick people, who had not at home proper persons to nurse them, applied to be sent to Bushhill. Indeed, in the end, so many people, who were afflicted with other disorders, procured admittance there, that it become necessary to pass a resolve, that before an order of admission should be granted, a certificate must be produced from a physician, that the patient laboured under the malignant fever.

The committee sat daily at the city hall, and engaged a number of carts to convey the dead to a place of interment, and the sick to the hospital. From their organization to the present time, they have most unremittingly attended to the discharge of the trust reposed in them. Neither the regular increase of deaths till towards the middle of October, nor the afflicting loss of four very active members, in quick succession, appalled them. That the mortality would have been incomparably greater, but for their active interposition, is beyond doubt; as most of those who went to Bushhill, and died there, would have otherwise died in the city, and spread the contagion: and the dead bodies would have remained putrifying in deserted houses in every part of the city, and operated as dreadfully as the plague itself. In fact, at the time they entered on the execution of the dangerous office they undertook, there were found several bodies that had lain in this state for two, three, and four days.

New Orleans, 1751

. . . I shall describe the capital of Louisiana, but I do not think that it is necessary to speak of the city at length, since you are doubtless familiar with most of the maps and articles published on it. I simply want to call to your attention that New Orleans, with its well-laid-out streets, is bigger and more heavily populated today than formerly. There are four types of inhabitants: Europeans, Indians, Africans or Negroes, and half bloods, born of Europeans and savages native to the country.

Those born of French fathers and French, or European, mothers are called Creoles. They are generally very brave, tall, and well built and have a natural inclination toward the arts and sciences. Since these studies cannot be pursued very well because of the shortage of good teachers, rich and well-intentioned fathers send their children to France, the best school for all things.

As for the fair sex, whose only duty is to please, they are already born with that advantage here and do not have to go to Europe to acquire it artificially.

New Orleans and Mobile are the only cities where there is no patois; the French spoken here is good.

Negroes are brought over from Africa to clear the land, which is excellent for growing indigo, tobacco, rice, corn, and sugar cane; there are sugar plantations which are already doing very well. This country offers a delightful life to the merchants, artisans, and foreigners who inhabit it because of its healthful climate, its fertile soil, and its beautiful site. The city is situated on the banks of the Mississippi, one of the biggest rivers in the world, which flows through 800 leagues of explored country. Its pure and delicious waters flow forty leagues among numerous plantations, which offer a delightful scene on both banks of the river, where there is a great deal of hunting, fishing, and other pleasures of life.

SOURCE: Jean-Bernard Bossu, *Travels in the Interior of North America, 1751–1762,* ed. and trans. Seymour Feiler (Norman, Okla:, 1962), 21–24.

Chapter 7

People at War: Soldiers and Civilians During the American Revolution

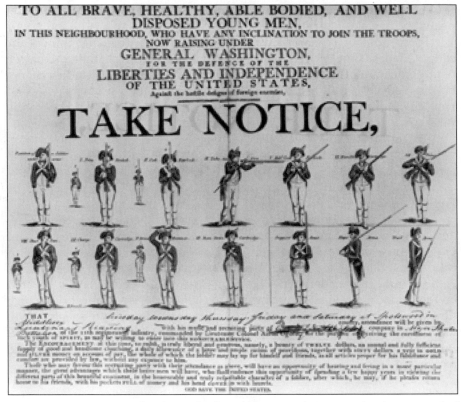

A 1775 recruiting poster for the newly formed Continental Army under the command of George Washington.

The American Revolution marked the end of the colonial epoch and the beginning of nationhood. Most Americans are well aware of the momentous events of the Revolutionary era and their historical significance. What is less well known and appreciated are the roles played by ordinary citizens in the drama and the conflict's impact on their lives. In the essay that follows from Gary B. Nash's *The Unknown American Revolution*, we are given a vivid view of those who served the patriot cause as soldiers, particularly those in the Continental forces. We learn who they were, their reasons for serving, and the conditions they had to endure. How does the author account for the fact that the poor, unmarried, and young made the most effective soldiers in this war? What motivated enslaved blacks to enlist in the American cause?

During the early days of the war, English officers and their Hessian allies frequently described the American forces as a ragtag, undisciplined mob. However, after Washington's victory at Trenton and Gates's defeat of Burgoyne at Saratoga, opinions began to change. In the first document, a German officer who fought with the British at Saratoga presented his views of the American officers and men. What did he think of their "military appearance," their "military talent," and their treatment of the defeated enemy?

The American Revolution was by no means a one-gender event. Before the outbreak of fighting, women were active in the attempts to pressure Parliament by boycotting imports from England. Their willingness to do without is illustrated in the second document, a rather humorous poem written by a woman who had joined the boycott of what she termed "this pernicious tea." During the war some women joined their soldier husbands on campaigns, doing their cooking and laundering and nursing the wounded. Those who remained at home often had to assume tasks normally the province of their husbands and fathers. Women also experienced suffering brought on by war. The third document is a letter written by Catherine Van Cortland, one of 80,000 loyalists who would ultimately flee the country under pressure. At the time of the writing, she was traveling with her children to join her husband in British-occupied New York. A safe-passage permit enabled her journey through patriot lines but not without considerable physical and emotional suffering. What evidence is offered in the letter to support the view that the American Revolution had elements of a civil war as well as a struggle for independence? Note that those who fought for independence referred to themselves as Patriots while their opponents termed them Rebels. In like manner, those opposed to the cause of independence preferred to be called Loyalists, but their enemies branded them Tories or worse.

ESSAY

Foot Soldiers of the Revolutionary Army

Gary B. Nash

State militias as well as the Continental army would have to fight in the Revolution, and the militia system seemed to promise a truly broad blood sacrifice because a large proportion of men were subject to militia duty in the late colonial period, usually from age sixteen to sixty. Probably a majority

SOURCE: "The Dual Revolution," from *The Unknown American Revolution* by Gary B. Nash. Copyright © 2005 by Gary B. Nash, pp. 217-30. Used by permission of Viking Penguin, a division of Penguin Group (USA) Inc.

of white male adults served at least one short militia term—often just a few months—during the prolonged military contest. But as the Continental Congress, Washington, and all his generals knew, the war could not be won without long-term soldiers marching in a regular army. One of the main problems of the war was how to fill the thirty-eight regular regiments, which at full strength consisted of some eight thousand men (not even half the soldiers the British fielded throughout the war). Upon inspection, most of these soldiers turn out to be those with pinched lives, often fresh from Ireland or Germany, recently released from jail, or downright desperate. In fact, only a small sliver of white American males of fighting age served in the Continental army under Washington and his generals. The people celebrated as citizen-soldiers "got tired of serving, and they got tired of contributing." Louis Duportail, who came from France to become the chief engineer of the Continental army, reported to his government at home in 1777 that "There is a hundred times more enthusiasm for this Revolution in any Paris café than in all the colonies together."

In recent years, historians have combed muster lists, town records, and military pension applications to come up with a composite picture of Washington's Continental army. How men were lured or dragooned into service varied according to the quotas set by the Continental Congress. What the men had in common, regardless of their place of enlistment, was their youth, their poverty, and their tenuous attachment to any particular community. The town of Concord, where the shot heard round the world was fired, is a good example of recruiting New Englanders. After the initial blush of patriotism, Concord found it difficult to induce its citizen-farmers to enlist as part of the town's quota, even though Massachusetts was peerless in glorifying its citizen-warriors for generations of fighting against Indians and the French. So Concord scoured the countryside for free blacks and other footloose men who could be bought up as substitutes for those who had lost their fire for military service. Ezekiel Brown, who apparently heard the first shots at North Bridge from the town's jail, where he languished as a debtor, was typical. "With little or nothing to lose," as he later related, he joined up. Landless and voteless, he had drifted around eastern Massachusetts for several years before the Revolution, a foot soldier in the army of "strolling poor." Half of the sixteen men who signed up from Concord in the first five years of the war were much like Ezekiel Brown, without "any known connection to the town," according to historian Robert Gross.

So it went from town to town. To be sure, at the beginning of the war in 1775 and soon after that, when the British army hovered nearby, towns such as Peterborough, New Hampshire, engaged in a cross-class people's war rather than fighting a poor man's war. When General John Burgoyne invaded New York in 1777, many of the townsmen saw action. But thereafter, few men with land and voting privileges stepped forward to enlist.

According to the town's historian of the revolutionary experience, most of the soldiers for the remainder of the war were "an unusually poor, obscure group of men, even by the rustic standards of Peterborough."

Even those who served far more than a few months were not necessarily fired by ideological rage toward English policies and practices. "Long Bill" Scott (so named to distinguish him from his cousin "Short Bill" Scott) was typical of this group. He did not spring to arms out of patriotic fervor after Lexington and Concord; rather, he was a shoemaker who "got my living by my labor." He saw the chance to better himself—"the only motives for my entering into the service," he related after the British captured him at Bunker Hill. "As to the dispute between Great Britain and the colonies," he told his British interrogator, "I knew nothing of it; neither am I capable of judging whether it is right or wrong." Scott was atypical only in that he was a bit better off than most of his townsmen who enlisted for service, for the majority of them served short terms, were poor when they enlisted, came home to remain obscure for the rest of their lives, or became transients looking somewhere else for something better.

In the mid-Atlantic states, as in New England, the yeoman farmer of revolutionary lore, shouldering his weapon and bidding his family good-bye, was mostly a myth. Mostly landless, drawn from unskilled laborers or lower artisans (such as shoemakers), and overwhelmingly drawn into service by bounties provided by those wanting to avoid Continental service, they differed from the dispossessed New Englanders only in one respect: The majority were foreign-born, and most of them had only recently arrived in North America. Fortuitously for middle-state recruiters, about 127,000 immigrants had poured into the colonies between 1760 and 1775. Most hailed from Scotland, Ireland, and England, but about 20,000 came from Germany. The majority of them settled in the mid-Atlantic region. Henry Lee, later to become famous as "Lighthorse Harry" Lee, called the Pennsylvania battalions "the Line of Ireland," but he might just as well have called them "the Line of Germany."

In the southern states the recruiting process was much the same. Maryland's Continental soldiers, who froze at Valley Forge in the winter of 1777–78, were mostly young, poor, landless, voteless, and, in about half the cases, immigrants. Maryland was unusual only in trying to take choice out of the hands of the dispossessed. By legislative decree, any local court could require a person considered a vagrant to serve at least nine months in the Continental army. Prime candidates for this kind of conscription were the thousands of convicts transported by the British to Maryland and Virginia—some 24,000 from 1746 to 1775—in order to sweep clean the jails of England. Once in the field in American uniforms, they stood a good chance of fighting against men from their own impoverished villages in Ireland, Scotland, and England, where the British rounded up jailbirds who were "chained to ringbolts and fed with bread and water" until they agreed to head into the War of Independence in British uniforms. In Virginia, substantial bounties lured lower-class youths, some as young as fourteen, into the regular army. By the end of 1776, looking for more men, the Virginia government followed Maryland by authorizing the impressment of "rogues and vagabonds"—a vagabond being described as any man neglecting to pay his county and parish taxes or any man with no visible estate. Looking over this army of the dispossessed, Charles Lee called them "riff raff—dirty, mutinous and disaffected."

Washington's officers had no illusions about the human material they had to shape into fighting units. "Food for Worms . . . , miserable sharp looking caitiffs, hungry lean faced Villains," Anthony Wayne labeled them. Tench Tilghman, Washington's aide-de-camp, called the recruits from New York City "mostly old disbanded Regulars and . . . foreigners." Other officers called them "the sweepings of the York [England] streets," or "a wretched motley Crew." Indeed they were. Many had arrived in North America like one numbed London weaver who landed in Virginia in 1758 in the company of indentured servants: "They all was set in a row, near a hundred men and women and the planters come down [from] the country to buy [them]. . . . I never see such passels of poor wretches in my life," wrote the weaver, "some almost starved by the ill usage in their passage by the captain, for they are used no better than so many negro slaves that are brought in here and sold in the same manner as horses or cows in our market or fair."

Notwithstanding all these unpleasant comments, Continental army officers could not do without such men. Absent such human material, the war would have quickly ended with a British victory. What is more, it was these down-and-outers who were most likely to endure the awful conditions of camp life and battlefield gore. Washington knew this. "Men just dragged from the tender scenes of domestic life; [and] unaccustomed to the din of arms" were almost worthless, he wrote. The fabled minuteman who left his farm to shoulder arms was also difficult to discipline and difficult to restrain from deserting. "Men accustomed to unbounded freedom, and no control," he concluded, "cannot brook the restraint which is indispensably necessary to the good order and government of an army; without which, licentiousness, and every kind of disorder triumphantly reign." It was only the poor, particularly the unmarried and young, who could stand up against England's professional army. The poor man's fight was the only fight that the Americans could wage.

For all his obscurity, the foot soldier was, in fact, one of the main reasons that the Americans were able to sustain a series of disheartening defeats in the first two years of the war and still continue the fight. Washington and his generals relied on the poor unsung youth—the guerrilla fighter whose capacity to survive in horrendous conditions proved crucial. Washington understood what would later become a famous dictum of war, one that also applied in Vietnam two centuries after the American Revolution: The standing army that does not win, loses; the guerrilla army that does not lose, wins. Private Joseph Plumb Martin, an out-of-work farm laborer who joined the Eighth Connecticut Regiment, was the kind of young, penniless soldier who made all the difference. In plainspoken but penetrating prose, inscribed in a diary kept through several enlistments, the seventeen-year-old Martin, born in the tiny farming village of Becket in western Massachusetts, showed what the common soldier faced, endured, and—sometimes—survived. "We had nothing to eat for two or three days previous, except what the trees of the fields and forests afforded us," he wrote in mid-December 1777, as Washington's army marched along a rutted road from Gulph Mills, on the Schuylkill River west of Philadelphia, to the Valley Forge encampment where they would spend the winter. "But we must now have what Congress said," Martin recalled, "a sumptuous Thanksgiving to close the year of high living we had now nearly seen brought to a close." Congress had indeed called for a day of thanksgiving on December 18, a day of wind and freezing rain, to remind Americans that their tattered army still survived. "Our country, ever mindful of its suffering army, opened her sympathizing heart so wide upon this occasion as to give us something to make the world stare. And what do you think it was, reader?" wrote Martin sardonically. "Guess. You cannot guess, be you as much of a Yankee as you will. I will tell you: It gave each and every man *half a gill of rice* and a *tablespoonful* of vinegar!" With four ounces of rice, "this extraordinary superabundant donation," Martin continued, "we were ordered out to attend a meeting and hear a sermon delivered upon the happy occasion. . . . The army was now not only starved but naked. The greatest part were not only shirtless and barefoot but destitute of all other clothing, especially blankets. I procured a small piece of raw cowhide and made myself a pair of moccasins, which kept my feet (while they lasted) from the frozen ground." Though the hard edges of the moccasins "galled my ankles," this was better than going barefoot, "as hundreds of my companions had to, till they might be tracked by their blood upon the rough frozen ground."

Martin recounted the sermon the men were obliged to hear. The minister urged the soldiers to fulfill their obligations honorably. He added that the preacher might also have told the freezing soldiers to be "content with your wages. But that would not do, it would be too apropos; however, he heard it as soon as the service was over, it was shouted from a hundred tongues." But despite the misery and the soldiers' resentment at Congress's pitiful ration for the day of thanksgiving, Martin showed his true colors. "Our prospect was indeed dreary. . . . However, there was no remedy, no alternative but this or dispersion [desertion]; but dispersion, I believe, was not thought of—at least I did not think of it. We had engaged in the defense of our injured country and were willing nay, we were determined, to persevere as long as such hardships were not altogether intolerable."

Martin reenlisted in 1777 for the duration of the war—which made him one of a small stouthearted minority determined to stick it out. Year in, year out, life in the army improved little. Benjamin Rush, appointed physician general of the military hospitals in spring 1777, found "scenes of distress shocking to humanity and disgraceful to a civilized country . . . , sons of our yeomanry . . . shivering with cold upon bare floors without a blanket to cover them, calling for fire, for water, for suitable food, and for medicines— and calling in vain." A year later, when he could not get support for cleaning up the filthy, military field hospitals, often barren of medicine, Rush resigned in disgust.

Though humble in origin and humble in status, the rank-and-file soldiers were anything but humble in their conception of their rights, either as Continental soldiers or state militiamen. Prompt payment of wages, adequate food and clothing, medical attention when wounded, and support for their families in need were the most important issues that aroused them. In April 1776, one of Washington's generals was warned that a mass of disaffected men promised to "go home in a Body" if not given their clothing allotment and pay. The counterthreat of the "severest Punishment" had some effect, but many of the soldiers deserted anyway. Desertion, from that point forward, was the bane of the commander in chief and his generals. More than four of every ten New Jersey troops in 1777 deserted. In New York, about one of every three privates deserted. Even in Washington's handpicked Life Guard, eight soldiers deserted during the war. Nearly desperate to keep troop levels up, Washington considered invading Vermont's Green Mountains, which had become "an asylum to all deserters" from the Continental army; but he gave up on trying to capture deserters, concluding that his soldiers could not be convinced "to imbue their hands in the blood of their Brethren."

For most Continental army soldiers, deserting was disgraceful. Like Private Joseph Plumb Martin, they endured bouts of homesickness, depression, disillusionment, boredom, and stark fear; yet the majority stood in place while contending for their rights. From the beginning of enlistment, the soldier's struggle was for food, clothing, medical attention, effective weapons, brave and just officers, and the pay they were promised. . . .

Fighting to Be Free

If any group within America's diversified people came close to answering John Adams's plea that "we must all be soldiers," it was black Americans. No part of revolutionary society responded to the call for arms with anywhere near the enthusiasm of those who were black. Proportionate to their number, African American males—and some females—were more likely to join the fray than white Americans. But, as we will see, Adams should have been careful about what he wished for, because the "spirit of '76" manifested among enslaved and free blacks mainly took the form of fighting *against* the side that proclaimed all men were born free, equal, and endowed with certain unalienable rights.

Those who fought at Lexington and Concord in April 1775 must have noticed the dusky Lemuel Haynes among the contingent of militiamen from Granville, Massachusetts, who rushed to the scene. Born in West Hartford, Connecticut, Haynes was twenty-two at the time. He was the son of a full-blooded African and a young white woman. After his mother gave him up when he was just five months of age, the town's selectmen indentured Haynes out to a farmer and Congregational church deacon in Granville, Massachusetts. There on the frontier he learned to plough, chop wood, and read. "I could vie with almost any of my age," he wrote many years later in telling of his love for books.

Full of martial ardor, Haynes joined the local militia in Granville in 1774. He marched with Captain Lebbeus Ball's militia company to arrive on the scene just a few days after the firefight between the minutemen and the redcoats at Concord and Lexington. Haynes then became part of the siege of Boston and the Battle of Bunker Hill. Fresh from this battle, his unit marched to secure Fort Ticonderoga. He mustered out after several weeks, reenlisted in October 1776, and was sent home with typhus a month later.

Haynes fought with his quill as well as his rifle; but the target of his quill was not the British but his fellow colonial Americans who practiced slavery. Now twenty-three, Haynes stole time in camp to work out "Liberty Further Extended: Or Free Thoughts on the Illegality of Slave-keeping." The only known essay by an African American of the revolutionary era, it drew from Anthony Benezet's *Some Historical Account of Guinea*, a pamphlet published in Philadelphia in 1771 to prod the Americans to cleanse themselves of slave trading and slave keeping. Haynes pointed to how the monster tyranny was "lurking in our own bosom" and argued that "an African . . . has an undeniable right to his Liberty." Quoting the book of Acts in the Old Testament, he wrote that "It hath pleased God to make of one blood all nations of men, for to dwell upon the face of the Earth." "What is precious to one man," Haynes proposed, "is precious to another, and what is irksome, or intolerable to one man, is so to another. . . . Those privileges that are granted to us by the Divine Being," he continued, "no one has the least right to take them from us without our consent."

Haynes never published his essay. Perhaps he could find no publisher for it. But he carried his message with him after laying down his weapon to take up the ministry. For many years, he pastored white congregations in different parts of New England, preaching some five thousand sermons and becoming, in the words of his first biographer, "a sanctified genius." Marrying a white woman, he became the first black minister to white Congregational churches in New England. His life's work, his biographer reasoned in 1837, could "hardly fail to mitigate the unreasonable prejudices against the Africans in our land."

Among enlisted men, Haynes was unusual, indeed nearly unique, for fighting with words as well as bullets. But he was by no means the only free African American who joined the patriot cause in the early years of the war. Crispus Attucks, half African and half Wampanoag, had already shed blood in the Boston Massacre of 1770. "The first to defy, and the first to die," wrote a Boston poet a century later of the muscular Attucks, who had charged the British soldiers with a stout cordwood stick. At Lexington and Concord, Prince Easterbrooks was one of the first wounded patriots. After this, many more black New Englanders joined up, including one of Venture Smith's sons. Some of them were free but many were slaves, fighting alongside or in place of their masters. White Americans were fighting to protect their liberty; enslaved Americans fought to attain it.

Those who fought as slaves held the hope that their masters would reward them with freedom. Sometimes they were actually promised it. Peter Salem signed up in the village of Framingham with his master's pledge of granting his freedom. Salem served at Lexington and a few weeks later at Bunker Hill, where he killed Major John Pitcairn of the British marines, who led the attack on the patriots' fortifications. Salem later fought at Stony Point, Monmouth, and Saratoga, survived the war, and built a cabin in Leicester, Massachusetts. In another case, Salem Poor fought alongside his master, Lieutenant Thomas Grosvenor, at Bunker Hill. So honorable was Poor's performance that fourteen Massachusetts officers petitioned the Continental Congress to award freedom to this "brave and gallant soldier." Poor went on to fight with Washington's army at White Plains, New York, in 1776, and endured the trying winter of 1777–78 at Valley Forge. He became a small property owner after the war. In still another case, Prince Whipple, the slave of a New Hampshire officer, pulled the stroke oar on a small boat carrying George Washington across the Delaware River in a piercing snow and sleet storm on Christmas night in 1776.

Peter Salem, Salem Poor, and Prince Whipple were the kind of men celebrated by William C. Nell, the first African American historian of the black revolutionary experience. Writing in the 1850s, while he worked to integrate Boston's public schools, Nell hoped to further the abolitionist crusade by pointing to the blood shed by black Americans for the "glorious cause." Nell meant to stimulate racial pride while countering the white Negrophobia that had spread rapidly throughout the North in the early nineteenth century. Rather than reaching for a broad understanding of how those of African descent reacted to the revolutionary tumult, Nell focused on specific black contributions to the struggle for independence. Harriet Beecher Stowe hoped Nell's *The Colored Patriots of the American Revolution* would "redeem the character of the [Negro] race," and abolitionist orator Wendell Phillips similarly wished that Nell's efforts would "stem the tide of prejudice against the colored race."

Intent on showcasing black patriots, Nell waxed cloquent about figures such as James Forten, the fourteen-year-old Philadelphia son of a free black sailmaker. Five years into the war, Forten enlisted on Stephen Decatur's privateer as a powder boy and soon "found himself amid the roar of cannon, the smoke of blood, the dying, and the dead" in a naval duel between Decatur's *Royal Louis* and the British *Lawrence*. When the British captured Decatur's ship after another battle at sea, the young Forten wore the colors of patriotism nobly, refusing the offer of the British captain to transport him to England to stay with his son, who had befriended the black American lad aboard the British ship. "NO, NO!" exclaimed Forten, according to Nell, who based his account on oral recollections, "I am here a prisoner for the liberties of my country. I never, NEVER, shall prove a traitor to her interests." Noble as it was, this was far from a typical story.

Nell's attempt to show that black Americans partook of the "spirit of '76" was unbalanced, ignoring entirely the large number of African Americans who fought on the British side. This is understandable and likely was intentional. What would Nell, the historian-activist, have done in the 1850s with evidence of the tens of thousands of slaves who sought freedom by fighting against the Americans? Probably he concluded it was best to bury this chapter of history because publicizing the general belief among slaves that life, liberty, and the pursuit of happiness were best pursued with the British would have crippled the abolitionist cause. William Lloyd Garrison felt the same publishing his *Loyalty and Devotion of Colored Americans in the Revolution and War of 1812* on the eve of the Civil War with the same basic narrative.

For black Americans who wanted to serve on the side of the Americans, the first battle was to acquire the right to fight. At first, free black men such as Cash Africa, from Litchfield, Connecticut, were welcomed into Washington's Continental army. Nearly 150 served at Bunker Hill (along with six Native Americans). But pressure from white southern leaders to purge the army of African Americans led to Washington's general order on November 12, 1775 (just five days, ironically, after Virginia's Governor Dunmore had offered freedom to slaves reaching his encampment), to exclude them all, whether enslaved or free. Within six weeks, Washington partially reversed his general order; with congressional approval, he reopened the Continental army to free blacks, though not to slaves. Cash Africa was back in the army by 1777 and served for the remainder of the war. By one estimate, some five hundred Massachusetts free blacks served in the war, roughly one half of all free black men of military age in the state. A Hessian officer fighting with the British observed in 1777 "that the Negro can take the field instead of his master; and, therefore, no regiment is seen in which there are not Negroes in abundance, and among them there are able-bodied, strong and brave fellows."

By the winter of 1777–78 Washington further amended his policy on black troops. Struggling to regroup his manpower-starved army, he accepted the plea of Brigadier General James Mitchell Varnum to raise a regiment of black soldiers from Rhode Island. The state's legislature quickly endorsed the idea with lofty language: "History affords us frequent precedents of the wisest, the freest, and bravest nations having liberated their slaves and enlisted them as soldiers to fight in defense of their country." But at heart, the motives were less lofty. In deeming the proposal "inspired by stark necessity," historian Lorenzo Greene is surely right. Rhode Island's First and Second Regiments, created at the beginning of the war, were composed mostly of poor white men, with a sprinkling of free blacks. By early 1778, the regiments were close to disintegration, their pay in arrears, uniforms tattered, and ranks thinned by disease, absenteeism, and desertion. One of its colonels described the First Regiment as "scandalous in its appearance in the view of everyone—as a result of their appearance townspeople provoke them with epithets of the Ragged Lousey Naked Regiment." If this was not enough, the term of enlistment for most men was up, and few were ready to reenlist under the three-year terms that had now been made the norm for Continental army service. Moreover, the British occupied much of Rhode Island, leaving the state's economy tottering.

In these dire straits, Rhode Island's considerable slave population—about 3,700—proved to be a godsend. In February 1778, desperate to fill the thinned ranks of its regiments, the state offered freedom to "every able-bodied Negro, Mulatto, or Indian Man slave in this state . . . to serve during the continuance of the present war with Great Britain." Every black enlistee would be "immediately discharged from the service of his master or mistress, and be absolutely free, as if he had never been encumbered with any kind of servitude or slavery." Slaves could not simply walk away from their masters and enlist; this had to be done with the consent of their owners. But many of Rhode Island's slave owners found this proposal too good to turn down. Releasing their slaves relieved them of army duty themselves and promised to fill the state's quota for Washington's army. In addition, they would receive compensation for their lost slave property from the state legislature at the market price. However, many slave owners vehemently opposed the plan, since they would lose their strongest, most valuable slaves.

Roughly one of every four able-bodied male slaves in Rhode Island obtained his master's consent to enlist. The First Regiment (dubbed the Black Regiment many years later), where almost all of them served, became almost entirely black and Indian below the rank of corporal. Leading the regiment was Colonel Christopher Greene, an entrepreneurial Quaker from Warwick who had given up pacifism in 1775 to lead white Rhode Island troops. African and Indian names roll off the muster lists, which can still be viewed today at the Rhode Island Historical Society: Bristol Prime, George Sambo, Quam Cook, Quacko Wanton, Thomas Sachems, Narragansett Perry, Peter Mohawk, Aaron Sucknesh, and dozens more. About two hundred slaves enlisted to fight as free men in the Continental army. Their masters were promised about £120 each, equivalent today to about $2,400.

The newly liberated slaves had to learn the manual of arms in a hurry. Luckily, Christopher Greene, their white commander, was a hardened veteran. He had been captured during the assault on Quebec on New Year's

Day in 1776, returned in a prisoner exchange, and dispatched southward in November 1777 to defend Fort Mercer, a Delaware River fort guarding Philadelphia. Now in the summer of 1778, after a few months' training under his command, Green threw his black recruits into the breach in the Battle of Newport, where a large American army, supported by a French fleet, sought to dislodge the British forces occupying Newport and southern Rhode Island. Assigned to a hot sector, the Black Regiment repulsed three assaults of Hessian mercenaries, inflicting heavy casualties and minimizing patriot losses in what became an American fiasco. From there, Rhode Island's First Regiment moved on to defend a post on the Croton River in New York, where an American Loyalist unit, in a surprise attack, killed Colonel Christopher Greene. The story passed down to William Nell, the Boston historian of *The Colored Patriots*, has it that Greene was "cut down and mortally wounded; but the sabres of the enemy only reached him through the bodies of his faithful guard of blacks, who hovered over him to protect him, and every one of whom was killed."

Sent south a few months later with Stephen Olney as their new white commander, the black Rhode Islanders fought at Yorktown in September 1781. There, they found no black southerners under arms. . . . The French officer François Jean Marquis de Chastellux described the First Regiment as three-quarters black and, of all the regiments in Washington's army, "the most neatly dressed, the best under arms, and the most precise in its maneuvers" he had seen. Knowing of its previous exploits, Lafayette and Washington hand-picked the Rhode Island regiment to participate in the assault on Redoubts 9 and 10, the strongholds that held the key to victory. Remembering the night of October 14, when he led the Black Regiment forward to storm the moated and heavily fortified redoubts, Colonel Olney recorded how "the column marched in silence . . . many no doubt thinking that less than one quarter of a mile would finish the journey of life with them." By the time they mustered out in late 1783, after nearly five years of fighting, only one third of the former slaves survived to taste freedom as civilians.* . . .

DOCUMENTS

A German Officer's View of American Soldiers, 1777

We passed the enemy's encampment, in front of which all their regiments, as well as the artillery, were standing under arms. Not a man of them was regularly equipped. Each one had on the clothes which he was accustomed

SOURCE: Albert Bushnell Hart, ed., with Mabel Hill, *Camps and Firesides of the Revolution* (Washington, D. C.: Regency Publishing Company, 1901), 253–255.

*The British, with considerable success, also used the promise of freedom to entice slaves to run away and join their forces. (Eds.)

to wear in the field, the tavern, the church and in everyday life. No fault, however, could be found with their military appearance, for they stood in an erect and a soldierly attitude.

All their muskets had bayonets attached to them, and their riflemen had rifles. They remained so perfectly quiet that we were utterly astounded. Not one of them made any attempt to speak to the man at his side; and all the men who stood in array before us were so slender, fine-looking, and sinewy, that it was a pleasure to look at them.

Nor could we but wonder that Dame Nature had created such a handsome race! As to their height, dear brother, the men averaged from five feet six to five feet seven inches, according to Prussian measurement; and I assure you I am not telling an untruth when I state that men five feet eight to ten inches high were oftener to be seen than those of only five feet five inches; and men of larger height were to be found in all the companies.

I am perfectly serious when I state that the men of English America are far ahead of those in the greater portion of Europe both as respects their beauty and stature. In regard to the gentler sex, I will give you some details of them also when I arrive at Kinderhook; and now for a space devoted to American WIGS!

Few of the officers in General Gates's army wore uniforms, and those that were worn were evidently of home manufacture and of all colors. For example, brown coats with sea-green facings, white linings, and silver dragons, and gray coats with yellow buttons and straw-colored facings, were to be seen in plenty.

The brigadiers and generals had, however, uniforms to distinguish them from the rest of the officers, and wore a band around the waist to designate their respective rank. On the other hand, most of the colonels and other officers wore their every-day clothes. They carried their muskets (to which a bayonet was attached) in their hands; their pouches or powder-horns were slung over their backs, and their left hand hung down by their side, while the right foot was slightly put forward.

In one place could be seen men with white wigs, from beneath which long and thick hair escaped thick lambs' tails hanging down from the back; in another, the glistening black wig of an abbé surmounting some red and copper-colored face; while in still another, white and gray clerical-looking wigs made of horse and goat hair, and piled up in successive rolls.

In looking at a man thus adorned one would imagine that he had entire sheep under his hat, with its tail dangling around his neck. A great deal of respect is entertained for these wigs, not only because they are supposed to give the wearer a learned appearance, but because they are worn by all the gentlemen composing the committees and those who are renowned for wisdom.

The gentlemen who wear these different kind of wigs are mostly between fifty and sixty years of age; and having but recently begun to wear them, you can imagine what a comical appearance they cut as soldiers. The determination which caused them to grasp a musket and powder-horn can be seen in their faces, as well as the fact that they are not to be fooled with, especially in skirmishes in the woods.

Seriously speaking, this entire nation has great natural military talent. There were many regiments of Continentals in the enemy's army who had not been properly equipped, owing to the lack of time and scarcity of cloth. They have flags with all kinds of emblems and mottoes.

It must also be said to the credit of the enemy's regiments, that not a man among them ridiculed or insulted us; and none of them evinced the least sign of hate or malicious joy as we marched by. On the contrary, it seemed rather as though they desired to do us honor. As we filed by the tent of General Gates, he invited the brigadiers and commanders of our regiments to enter, and when they had done so he placed all kinds of refreshments before them.

A Lady's Adieu to Her Tea-Table, 1774

FAREWELL the Tea-board with your gaudy attire,
Ye cups and ye saucers that I did admire;
To my cream pot and tongs I now bid adieu;
That pleasure's all fled that I once found in you.
Farewell pretty chest that so lately did shine,
With hyson and congo and best double fine;
Many a sweet moment by you I have sat,
Hearing girls and old maids to tattle and chat;
And the spruce coxcomb laugh at nothing at all,
Only some silly work that might happen to fall.
No more shall my teapot so generous be
In filling the cups with this pernicious tea,
For I'll fill it with water and drink out the same,
Before I'll lose LIBERTY that dearest name,
Because I am taught (and believe it is fact)
That our ruin is aimed at in the late act,
Of imposing a duty on all foreign Teas,
Which detestable stuff we can quit when we please.
LIBERTY'S The Goddess that I do adore,
And I'll maintain her right until my last hour,
Before she shall part I will die in the cause,
For I'll never be govern'd by tyranny's laws

SOURCE: http://www.foodreferece.com/html/a-ladys-adieu-to-her-tea-table.html

Travails of a Loyalist Wife and Mother, 1777

TO PHILLIP VAN CORTLANDT   FEBRUARY 19TH, 1777

My beloved husband,

Doctor Bond succeeded and with orders for my removal brought me General Washington's pass which I now enclose.*

To describe the scene at parting with our few though sincere friends, the destruction of our property, the insulting looks and behaviour of those who had been accessory to our ruin, the situation of our beloved children and faithful servants on the day we were turned off from our once peaceful and happy cottage, in a cold snow storm, with my feelings on the occasion, is more than I dare attempt. At four in the afternoon, a cold, disagreeable day, we bid *adieu* to our home to make room for the sick of General Washington's Army and, after an unpleasant and fatiguing journey, arrived at twelve o'clock at night at the Fork of the Rivers Rockaway, Pompton and Haakinsack. A Young Woman, whose father and brother were both in the Rebel service, was much affected with my Situation and endeavoured to remove me into another room. The next evening, after a most distressing ride through snow and rain with much difficulty in changing Carriages for ourselves and baggage, we arrived at Campbell's Tavern at Haakinsack, the mistress of which refused me admittance when she was informed whose family it was, alleging as an excuse that she expected a number of Officers, and notwithstanding my earnest entreaties only to permit me to have shelter in one of her empty rooms for myself and children from the inclemency of the weather, as I could make use of my own beds though wet.

The town was filled with Soldiers and the night advancing. Whilst reflecting on my situation, a person came up to me, looked me in the face, and asked me to accompany him to his Uncle's house with my whole family. I did not thank him, though I attempted more than once; he read my gratitude in my countenance. On entering a room with a large fire, it had an effect on the children, whose stomachs had been empty the greatest part of the day, that caused instant puking, and was near proving fatal to them.

The next morning early, we again set off in a most uncomfortable sleet and snow, and rode until ten o'clock, when our youngest children could not

---

SOURCE: H.O.H. Vernon-Jackson, ed., "A Loyalist Wife: Letters of Mrs. Philip Van Cortlandt, December 1776–February 1777," *History Today* 14 (1964): 580.

General Washington's pass to Mrs. Philip Van Cortlandt: Mrs. Catharine Cortlandt, wife of Philip Cortlandt, Esq., now in New York or Long Island and to carry with her, her Servants, Furniture and Apparel.

Given under my Hand at Head Quarters at Morris town this 15th day of February 1777.

                                                                G. Washington.

pass a farm yard where they were milking cows without wishing for some. My little Willing was almost in agonies, springing in my Arms and calling for milk. I therefore rode up and requested the good man to let me have some from one of his palis. He partly advanced. My dear boy reached out his arms. The man stopped, asked who we were and, upon being informed by the driver, swore bitterly he would not give a drop to any Tory Bitch. I offered him money, my children screamed; and, as I could not prevail, I drove on.

On my arrival here, it was necessary for me to take some repose, after which my anxiety was considerable until the coming of the servants, who had been obliged to leave me soon after setting off from Haakinsack, on account of the baggage and the badness of the roads. About two hours ago, they come in and inform me that, crossing the river on the ice at the ferry, they were stopped and fired upon by a party of armed Rebels, nearly killing several of them (as a ball went through Old Sam's hat). Upon being shewn a copy of General Washington's pass, the original being with me, they damned the General 'for giving the mistress a pass,' and said they were sorry they had not come a little sooner as they would have stopped the whole, but swore they would make a prize of the three loads they had in their possession, and immediately fell to plundering chests, trunks, boxes, etc., throwing the heavy Articles into a hole in the ice, and breaking a barrel of old fashioned China into a thousand pieces. The Officers of this party are a Captain Dodd and Lieutenant Irvin. The former put on your new plaid Gown which he wore.

The small remains of our property is now here; and, after paying the drivers in hard money and expenses on the road, but little remains. With that little, let us now, my dear Philly, be content, and though fortune frowns we will still be happy, in each other. When we parted a few months ago, I was hearty and blooming; but be not surprised, my dear Pappa, if you see your Kitty altered. Indeed, I am much altered. But I know your heart, you will not love me less, but heal with redoubled affection and tenderness the wounds received in your behalf for those principles of loyalty which alone induced you to leave to the mercy of Rebels nine innocent children and your fond and ever affectionate Wife,

C.V.C

Suggestions for Further Reading

For the racial and ethnic mix of the colonial American population, consult Gary Nash, *Red, White and Black: The Peoples of Early America* (1974). Richard White, *The Middle Ground: Indians, Empires and Republicans in the Great Lakes Region, 1650–1815* (1991) deals with relations between Indians and white Americans throughout the colonial period and into the early years of the republic. A most thorough treatment of the Iroquois Confederation may be found in Francis Jennings, *The Ambiguous Iroquois Empire* (1984). On the Puritans and Indians, see Alden Vaughan, *New England Frontier: Puritans and Indians* (1965). Newer accounts include Karen Ordahl Kupperman, *Indians and English: Facing Off in Early America* (2000), and Daniel K. Richter, *Facing East from Indian Country: A Native History of Early America* (2000). On the relations between the Dutch and Indians, see Donna Merwick, *The Shame and the Sorrow: Dutch-Amerindian Encounters in New Netherland* (2006). Also informative are James Horn, *A Land as God Made It: Jamestown and the Birth of America* (2005) and James F. Brooks, *Slavery, Kinship, and Community in the Southwest Borderland* (2002).

On African Americans, four books are outstanding: Peter Wood, *Black Majority: Negroes in Colonial South Carolina from 1676 Through the Stono Rebellion* (1974); Gerald Mullin, *Slave Resistance in Eighteenth Century Virginia* (1972); Donald R. Wright, *African Americans in the Colonial Era: From African Origins Through the American Revolution* (1990); and Philip D. Morgan, *Slave Counterpoint: Slave Culture in the Eighteenth Century Chesapeake and Lowcountry* (1998). On white racism, Winthrop Jordan, *White over Black: American Attitudes Toward the Negro, 1550–1812* (1968), is a classic. For African Americans generally, see James Horton and Lois Horton, *Hard Road to Freedom: The Story of African America* (2001). The standard history of early slavery is Ira Berlin, *Many Thousands Gone: The First Two Centuries of Slavery in North America* (1998).

On immigration, see Thomas Archdeacon, *Becoming American: An Ethnic History* (1983), and Maldwyn Jones, *American Immigration* (1992). For the Southwest, see Ramon Gutierrez, *When Jesus Came the Cornmothers Went Away: Marriage, Sexuality, and Power in New Mexico, 1500–1846* (1991). For New York, consult Joyce Goodfriend, *Before the Melting Pot: Society and Culture in New York City, 1664–1730* (1992). David Galenson, *White Servitude in Colonial America* (1982), and A. R. Ekirch, *Bound for America* (1987), discuss indentured servitude and convict labor. For colonial Germans, see Aaron Spencer Fogelman, *Hopeful Journeys: German Immigration, Settlement, and Political Culture in Colonial America, 1717–1775* (1997). For the voyage to America for immigrants, see Marianne S. Wokeck, *Trade in Strangers: The Beginning of Mass Immigration to America* (1999). A new account of the Acadians is John Mack Faragher, *A Great and Noble Scheme: The Tragic Story of the Expulsion of French Acadians from Their Homeland* (2005).

Jack P. Greene, *Pursuit of Happiness: The Social Development of Early Modern British Colonies and the Formation of American Culture* (1988), provides an excellent one-volume synthesis of the colonial experience. David Hacker Fischer, *Albion's Seed: Four British Folkways in America* (1989), combines anthropology and history in a detailed study of the development of American colonial culture. On the northern colonies, there are a number of good books. Among them are John Demos, *A Little Commonwealth: Family Life in Plymouth Colony* (1970); Sumner Powell, *Puritan Village: The Formation of a New Town* (1963); Kenneth A. Lockridge, *A New England Town; The First Hundred Years, Dedham, Massachusetts, 1636–1736* (1970); and T. H. Breen, *From Puritans and Adventurers: Change and Persistence in Early America* (1980). Gloria Main, *Peoples of a Spacious Land: Families and Cultures in Colonial New England* (2001), also deals with New England. On New York City, see Russell Shorto, *The Island in the Center of the World: The Epic Story of Dutch Manhattan and the Forgotten Colony That Shaped America* (2004).

On the southern colonies, see two works by Wesley Frank Craven: *The Southern Colonics in the Seventeenth Century, 1607–1689* (1949) and *White, Red, and Black: The Seventeenth Century Virginian* (1971). Edmund S. Morgan, *American Slavery, American Freedom: The Ordeal of Colonial Virginia* (1975), provides an exciting, readable treatment of developments in seventeenth-century Virginia. Also recommended are Clarence L. Ver Steeg, *Origin of the Southern Mosaic* (1975), and Carl Bridenbaugh, *Jamestown, 1544–1699* (1980).

On society in the eighteenth century, useful works are Richard Hofstadter, *America at 1750: A Social Portrait* (1971); Michael Zuckerman, *Peaceable Kingdoms: New England Towns in the Eighteenth Century* (1970); Gary Nash, *The Urban Crucible: Social Change, Political Consciousness, and the Origins of the American Revolution* (1979); Alan Kulikoff, *Tobacco and Slaves* (1986); and T. H. Breen, *Tobacco Culture* (1987).

A good general discussion of religion during the colonial period is found in George M. Marsden, *Religion in American Culture* (1990). On religious developments in the eighteenth century, refer to Carl Bridenbaugh, *Mitre and Sceptre: Trans-Atlantic Faiths, Ideas, Personalities, and Politics, 1689–1775* (1962). J. M. Bumstead and John E. Van de Wetering, *What Must I Do to Be Saved? The Great Awakening in Colonial America* (1976), provides an excellent introduction to the great revival movement of the colonial period. For the impact of the Great Awakening in Virginia, see Rhys Isaac, *The Transformation of Virginia, 1740–1790* (1982). See also Jon Butler, *Awash in a Sea of Faith: Christianizing the American People* (1990).

On women, see Laurel Ulrich, *A Midwife's Tale: The Life of Martha Ballard, Based on Her Diary* (1990). For the colonial period, information about women can be found in Edmund Morgan, *The Puritan Family: Religion and Domestic Relations in Seventeenth-Century New England* (1966), and John Demos, *A Little Commonwealth: Family Life in Plymouth Colony* (1970). On attitudes toward children, see Phillip Greven, *The Protestant Temperament: Patterns of Child-Rearing, Religious Experience and the Self in Early America* (1977). A general history of African American women is Darlene Clark Hine and Kathleen Thompson, *A Shining Thread of Home: The History of Black Women in America* (1998). See also Carol Berkin, *First Generations: Women in Colonial America* (1998), and Mary Beth Norton, *Founding Mothers and Fathers: Gendered Power and the Forming of American Society* (1996). See also Mary Beth Norton, *In the Devil's Snare: The Salem Witchcraft Crisis of 1692* (2002) and Stephanie Coontz, *Marriage: A History from Obedience to Intimacy, or How Love Conquered Marriage* (2005).

A number of books explore the social history of the American Revolution. See the new approach in Gary B. Nash, *The Unknown American Revolution: The Unruly Birth of Democracy and the Struggle to Create America* (2005). For a view that the Revolution was radical, see Gordon Wood, *The Radicalism of the American Revolution* (1991). For women, see Mary Beth Norton, *Liberty's Daughters: The Revolutionary Experience of American Women, 1750–1800* (1980), Linda Kerber, *Women of the Republic: Intellect and Ideology in Revolutionary America* (1980). Among studies of the Loyalist side of the conflict are Bernard Bailyn, *The Ordeal of Thomas Hutchinson* (1975); Robert M. Calhoon, *The Loyalists in Revolutionary America, 1760–1781* (1973); and William H. Nelson, *The American Tory* (1961). Regional studies of the war include Robert Gross, *The Minutemen and Their World* (1976), and Robert J. Taylor, *Western Masschusetts in the Revolution* (1954). For the middle colonies, Eric Foner, *Tom Paine and Revolutionary America* (1976), is useful. For a view of the war through the eyes of those who fought, see George F. Scheer and Hugh F. Rankin, *Rebels and Redcoats* (1957). The Revolution's impact on religion is the subject of John G. West, Jr., *The Politics of Revolution and Reason: Religion and Civil Life in the New Nation* (1996). Joyce Appleby, *Inheriting the Revolution: The First Generation of Americans* (1999), covers the generation after the Revolution.

PART II

Social Life in a New Nation
1784–1877

Chapter 8

The Onset of Industry: The Lowell Venture

The Industrial Revolution comes to America.

Urban centers in the new nation experienced dramatic growth and change during the first half of the nineteenth century. Established cities boomed and new ones sprang up, with industry and commerce the focus of endeavor. Canals, railroads, and steamboats linked city to city and town to countryside, facilitating the movement of people, products, and ideas within the United States as well as between the young nation and foreign lands.

The textile mill town of Lowell, Massachusetts, symbolized an evolving industrial order central to the dynamic new century. Its population of 200 in 1820 rose to 6,477 in 1830, 21,000 in 1840, and more than 33,000 by 1850. Most of the increase of these decades derived from an expanded work force of predominantly young, single women drawn to Lowell from their rural farm homes. Mill owners energetically sought such workers, for Lowell's founders wanted not only to build factories but also to establish a model, ordered community under their benevolent control and direction.

Thomas Dublin's essay "Women, Work, and Protest in the Early Lowell Mills" describes the life and labor of Lowell's female operatives during the 1830s and 1840s. It details the emergence of a close-knit community of workers that not only rejected the subservient role envisioned by the founders but that, first through strikes and later through political action, protested against employer policies and working conditions. What does Dublin identify as the key factors contributing to a sense of community among the operatives? What does the author mean when he states that "The Lowell mills both exploited and liberated women in ways unknown to the pre-industrial economy"?

As a young girl, Harriet Hanson Robinson had worked in a Lowell mill. In 1898 she looked back over more than sixty years and told of her experiences in a book that she titled *Loom and Spindle*. The first document contains an excerpt from this work in which she recalls her role in the mill workers' strike of 1836. How do you account for her pride, even after so many years, in having been associated with the action? Her reference to "the right of suffrage" should provide a clue to the answer.

Regulations governing employees of the Hamilton Manufacturing Company of Lowell are set forth in the second document. In what ways do these rules reflect the social outlook of the owners?

As competition in the textile industry grew heated, working conditions deteriorated. During the 1840s, the mill workers turned to the government for redress. The final document, from testimony before a Massachusetts legislative committee investigating workers' grievances, reveals those conditions and helps explain why the mills were losing their appeal for American farm women by the late 1840s and increasingly being staffed by immigrants.

ESSAY

Women, Work, and Protest in the Early Lowell Mills
Thomas Dublin

In the years before 1850 the textile mills of Lowell, Massachusetts, were a celebrated economic and cultural attraction. Foreign visitors invariably included them on their American tours. Interest was prompted by the massive scale of the mills, the astonishing productivity of the power-driven machinery, and the fact that women comprised most of the workforce. Visitors were struck by the newness of both mills and city as well as by the culture of the female operatives. The scene stood in sharp contrast to the gloomy mill towns of the English Industrial Revolution.

SOURCE: From "Women, Work, and Protest in the Early Lowell Mills," by Thomas Dublin, *Labor History*, Taylor & Francis Ltd., 1975, Vol. 16, No. 1, pp. 99–112, 115–116. Reprinted with permission of the publisher, Taylor & Francis Ltd., http://www.informaworld.com.

Lowell, was, in fact, an impressive accomplishment. In 1820, there had been no city at all—only a dozen family farms along the Merrimack River in East Chelmsford. In 1821, however, a group of Boston capitalists purchased land and water rights along the river and a nearby canal, and began to build a major textile manufacturing center. Opening two years later, the first factory employed Yankee women recruited from the nearby countryside. Additional mills were constructed until, by 1840, ten textile corporations with thirty-two mills valued at more than ten million dollars lined the banks of the river and nearby canals. Adjacent to the mills were rows of company boarding houses and tenements which accommodated most of the eight thousand factory operatives.

As Lowell expanded and became the nation's largest textile manufacturing center, the experiences of women operatives changed as well. The increasing number of firms in Lowell and in the other mill towns brought the pressure of competition. Overproduction became a problem, and the prices of finished cloth decreased. The high profits of the early years declined and so, too did conditions for the mill operatives. Wages were reduced and the pace of work within the mills was stepped up. Women operatives did not accept these changes without protest. In 1834 and 1836 they went on strike to protest wage cuts, and between 1843 and 1848 they mounted petition campaigns aimed at reducing the hours of labor in the mills.

These labor protests in early Lowell contribute to our understanding of the response of workers to the growth of industrial capitalism in the first half of the nineteenth century. They indicate the importance of values and attitudes dating back to an earlier period and also the transformation of these values in a new setting.

The major factor in the rise of a new consciousness among operatives in Lowell was the development of a close-knit community among women working in the mills. The structure of work and the nature of housing contributed to the growth of this community. The existence of community among women, in turn, was an important element in the repeated labor protests of the period. . . .

The mutual dependence among women in early Lowell was rooted in the structure of mill work itself. Newcomers to the mills were particularly dependent on their fellow operatives, but even experienced hands relied on one another for considerable support.

New operatives generally found their first experiences difficult, even harrowing, though they may have already done considerable hand-spinning and weaving in their own homes. The initiation of one of them is described in fiction in the *Lowell Offering*.*

---

*A publication produced by the mill workers with financial support from management. (Eds.)

> The next morning she went into the Mill; and at first the sight of so many bands, and wheels, and springs in constant motion, was very frightful. She felt afraid to touch the loom, and she was almost sure she could never learn to weave . . . the shuttle flew out, and made a new bump on her head; and the first time she tried to spring the lathe, she broke out a quarter of the treads.

While other accounts present a somewhat less difficult picture, most indicate that women only became proficient and felt satisfaction in their work after several months at the mills.

The textile corporations made provisions to ease the adjustment of new operatives. Newcomers were not immediately expected to fit into the mill's regular work routine. They were first assigned work as sparehands and were paid a daily wage independent of the quantity of work they turned out. As a sparehand, the newcomer worked with an experienced hand who instructed her in the intricacies of the job. The sparehand spelled her partner for short stretches of time, and occasionally took the place of an absentee. One woman described the learning process in a letter reprinted in the *Offering:*

> Well, I went into the mill, and was put to learn with a very patient girl. . . . You cannot think how odd everything seems. . . . They set me to threading shuttles, and tying weaver's knots, and such things, and now I have improved so that I can take care of one loom. I could take care of two if only I had eyes in the back part of my head. . . .

After the passage of some weeks or months, when she could handle the normal complement of machinery—two looms for weavers during the 1830s—and when a regular operative departed, leaving an opening, the sparehand moved into a regular job.

Through this system of job training, the textile corporations contributed to the development of community among female operatives. During the most difficult period in an operative's career, the first months in the mill, she relied upon other women workers for training and support. And for every sparehand whose adjustment to mill work was aided in this process, there was an experienced operative whose work was also affected. Women were relating to one another during the work process and not simply tending their machinery. Given the high rate of turnover in the mill workforce, a large proportion of women operatives worked in pairs. At the Hamilton Company in July 1836, for example, more than a fifth of all females on the Company payroll were sparehands. Consequently, over forty percent of the females employed there in this month worked with one another. Nor was this interaction surreptitious, carried out only when the overseer looked elsewhere; rather, it was formally organized and sanctioned by the textile corporations themselves.

In addition to the integration of sparehands, informal sharing of work often went on among regular operatives. A women would occasionally take off a half or full day from work either to enjoy a brief vacation or to recover from illness, and fellow operatives would each take an extra loom or side of spindles so that she might continue to earn wages during her absence. Women were generally paid on a piece rate basis, their wages being determined by the total output of the machinery they tended during the payroll period. With friends helping out during her absence, making sure that her looms kept running, an operative could earn almost a full wage even though she was not physically present. Such informal work-sharing was another way in which mutual dependence developed among women operatives during their working hours.

Living conditions also contributed to the development of community among female operatives. Most women working in the Lowell mills of these years were housed in company boarding houses. In July 1836, for example, more than 73 percent of females employed by the Hamilton Company resided in company housing adjacent to the mills. Almost three-fourths of them, therefore, lived and worked with each other. Furthermore, the work schedule was such that women had little opportunity to interact with those not living in company dwellings. They worked, in these years, an average of 73 hours a week. Their workday ended at 7:00 or 7:30 P.M., and in the hours between supper and the 10:00 curfew imposed by management on residents of company boarding houses, there was little time to spend with friends living "off the corporation."

Women in the boarding houses lived in close quarters, a factor that also played a role in the growth of community. A typical boarding house accommodated twenty-five young women, generally crowded four to eight in a bedroom. There was little possibility of privacy within the dwelling, and pressure to conform to group standards was very strong. The community of operatives which developed in the mills, it follows, carried over into life at home as well.

The boarding house became a central institution in the lives of Lowell's female operatives in these years, but it was particularly important in the initial integration of newcomers into urban industrial life. Upon first leaving her rural home for work in Lowell, a woman entered a setting very different from anything she had previously known. . . .

In the boarding house, the newcomer took the first steps in the process which transformed her from an "outsider" into an accepted member of the community of women operatives.

Recruitment of newcomers into the mills and their initial hiring was mediated through the boarding house system. Women generally did not travel to Lowell for the first time entirely on their own. They usually came because they knew someone—an older sister, cousin, or friend—who had already worked in Lowell. . . . The Hamilton Company Register Books indicate that numerous pairs of operatives, having the same surname and coming from the same town in northern New England, lived in the same boarding houses. If the newcomer was not accompanied by a friend or relative, she was usually directed to "Number 20, Hamilton Company," or to a similar address of one of the other corporations where her acquaintance lived. Her first contact with fellow operatives generally came in the boarding houses and not the mills. Given the personal nature of recruitment in this period, therefore, newcomers usually had the company and support of a friend or relative in their first adjustment to Lowell.

Like recruitment, the initial hiring was a personal process. Once settled in the boarding house a newcomer had to find a job. She would generally go to the mills with her friend or with the boarding house keeper who would introduce her to an overseer in one of the rooms. If he had an opening, she might start work immediately. More likely, the overseer would know of an opening elsewhere in the mill, or would suggest that something would probably develop within a few days. . . .

The boarding houses were the centers of social life for women operatives after their long days in the mills. There they ate their meals, rested, talked, sewed, wrote letters, read books and magazines. From among fellow workers and boarders they found friends who accompanied them to shops, to Lyceum lectures, to church and church-sponsored events. On Sundays or holidays, they often took walks along the canals or out into the nearby countryside. The community of women operatives, in sum, developed in a setting where women worked and lived together, twenty-four hours a day.

Given the all-pervasiveness of this community, one would expect it to exert strong pressures on those who did not conform to group standards. Such appears to have been the case. The community influenced newcomers to adopt its patterns of speech and dress. . . . In addition, it enforced an unwritten code of moral conduct. Henry Miles, a minister in Lowell, described the way in which the community pressured those who deviated from accepted moral conduct:

> A girl, suspected of immoralities, or serious improprieties, at once loses caste. Her fellow boarders will at once leave the house, if the keeper does not dismiss the offender. In self-protection, therefore, the patron is obliged to put the offender away. Nor will her former companions walk with her, or work with her; till at length, finding herself everywhere talked about, and pointed at, and shunned, she is obliged to relieve her fellow-operatives of a presence which they feel brings disgrace.

The power of the peer group described by Miles may seem extreme, but there is evidence in the writing of women operatives to corroborate his account. Such group pressure is illustrated by a story (in the *Offering*)—in which operatives in a company boarding house begin to harbor suspicions about a fellow boarder, Hannah, who received repeated evening visits from a man whom she does not introduce to the other residents. Two boarders declare that they will leave if she is allowed to remain in the household. The house keeper finally informed Hannah that she must either depart or not see the man again. She does not accept the ultimatum, but is promptly discharged after the overseer is informed, by one of the boarders, about her conduct. And, only one of Hannah's former friends continues to remain on cordial terms.

One should not conclude, however, that women always enforced a moral code agreeable to Lowell's clergy, or to the mill agents and overseers for that matter. After all, the kind of peer pressure imposed on Hannah could be brought to bear on women in 1834 and 1836 who on their own would not have protested wage cuts. It was much harder to go to work when one's roommates were marching about town, attending rallies, circulating strike petitions. Similarly, the ten-hour petitions of the 1840s were certainly aided by the fact of a tight-knit community of operatives living in a dense neighborhood of boarding houses. To the extent that women could not have completely private lives in the boarding houses, they probably had to conform to group norms, whether these involved speech, clothing, relations with men, or attitudes toward the ten-hour day. Group pressure to conform, so important to the community of women in early Lowell, played a significant role in the collective response of women to changing conditions in the mills.

In addition to the structure of work and housing in Lowell, a third factor, the homogeneity of the mill workforce, contributed to the development of community among female operatives. In this period the mill workforce was homogeneous in terms of sex, nativity, and age. Payroll and other records of the Hamilton Company reveal that more than 85 percent of those employed in July 1836, were women and that over 96 percent were native-born. Furthermore, over 80 percent of the female workforce was between the ages of 15 and 30 years old; and only 10 percent was under 15 or over 40.

Workforce homogeneity takes on particular significance in the context of work structure and the nature of worker housing. These three factors combined mean that women operatives had little interaction with men during their daily lives. Men and women did not perform the same work in the mills, and generally did not even labor in the same rooms. Men worked in the picking and initial carding processes, in the repair shop and on the watchforce, and filled all supervisory positions in the mills. Women held all sparehand and regular operative jobs in drawing, speeding, spinning, weaving and dressing. A typical room in the mill employed eighty women tending machinery, with two men overseeing the work and two boys assisting them. Women had little contact with men other than their supervisors in the course of the working day. After work, women returned to their boarding houses, where once again there were few men. Women, then, worked and lived in a predominantly female setting.

Ethnically the workforce was also homogeneous. Immigrants formed only 3.4 percent of those employed at Hamilton in July 1836. In addition, they comprised only 3 percent of residents in Hamilton Company housing. The community of women operatives was composed of women of New

England stock drawn from the hill-country farms surrounding Lowell. Consequently, when experienced hands made fun of the speech and dress of newcomers, it was understood that they, too, had been "rusty" or "rustic" upon first coming to Lowell. This common background was another element shared by women workers in early Lowell.

The work structure, the workers' housing, and workforce homogeneity were the major elements which contributed to the growth of community among Lowell's women operatives. To best understand the larger implications of community, it is necessary to examine the labor protests of this period. For in these struggles, the new values and attitudes which developed in the community of women operatives are most visible.

In February 1834, 800 of Lowell's women operatives "turned-out"— went on strike—to protest a proposed reduction in their wages. They marched to numerous mills in an effort to induce others to join them; and, at an outdoor rally, they petitioned others to "discontinue their labors until terms of reconciliation are made." Their petition concluded:

> Resolved, That we will not go back into the mills to work unless our wages are continued . . . as they have been.
> Resolved, That none of us will go back, unless they receive us all as one.
> Resolved, That if any have not money enough to carry them home, they shall be supplied.

The strike proved to be brief and failed to reverse the proposed wage reductions. Turning-out on a Friday, the striking women were paid their back wages on Saturday, and by the middle of the next week had returned to work or left town. Within a week of the turn-out, the mills were running near capacity.

This first strike in Lowell is important not because it failed or succeeded, but simply because it took place. In an era in which women had to overcome opposition simply to work in the mills, it is remarkable that they would further overstep the accepted middle-class bounds of female propriety by participating in a public protest. The agents of the textile mills certainly considered the turn-out unfeminine. William Austin, agent of the Lawrence Company, described the operatives' procession as an "amizonian [sic] display." He wrote further, in a letter to his company treasurer in Boston: "This afternoon we have paid off several of these Amazons & presume that they will leave town on Monday." The turn-out was particularly offensive to the agents because of the relationship they thought they had with their operatives. William Austin probably expressed the feelings of other agents when he wrote: " . . . notwithstanding the friendly and disinterested advice which has been on all proper occassions [sic] communicated to the girls of the Lawrence mills a spirit of evil omen . . . has prevailed, and overcome the judgement and discretion of too many, and this morning a general turn-out from most of the rooms has been the consequence."

Mill agents assumed an attitude of benevolent paternalism toward their female operatives, and found it particularly disturbing that the women paid such little heed to their advice. The strikers were not merely unfeminine, they were ungrateful as well.

Such attitudes notwithstanding, women chose to turn-out. They did so for two principal reasons. First, the wage cuts undermined the sense of dignity and social equality which was an important element in their Yankee heritage. Second, these wage cuts were seen as an attack on their economic independence.

Certainly a prime motive for the strike was outrage at the social implications of the wage cuts. In a statement of principles accompanying the petition which was circulated among operatives, women expressed well the sense of themselves which prompted the protest of these wage cuts:

Union is Power

Our present object is to have union and exertion, and we remain in possession of our unquestionable rights. We circulate this paper wishing to obtain the names of all who imbibe the spirit of our Patriotic Ancestors, who preferred privation to bondage, and parted with all that renders life desirable—and even life itself—to procure independence for their children. The oppressing hand of avarice would enslave us, and to gain their object, they gravely tell us of the pressure of the time, this we are already sensible of, and deplore it. If any are in want of assistance, the Ladies will be compassionate and assist them; but we prefer to have the disposing of our charities in our own hands; and as we are free, we would remain in possession of what kind Providence has bestowed upon us; and remain daughters of freemen still.

At several points in the proclamation the women drew on their Yankee heritage. Connecting their turn-out with the efforts of their "Patriotic Ancestors" to secure independence from England, they interpreted the wage cuts as an effort to "enslave" them—to deprive them of their independent status as "daughters of freemen." . . .

In point of fact, these Yankee operatives were subordinate in early Lowell's social and economic order, but they never consciously accepted this status. Their refusal to do so became evident whenever the mill owners attempted to exercise the power they possessed. This fundamental contradiction between the objective status of operatives and their consciousness of it was at the root of the 1834 turn-out and of subsequent labor protests in Lowell before 1850. The corporations could build mills, create thousands of jobs, and recruit women to fill them. Nevertheless, they bought only the workers' labor power, and then only for as long as these workers chose to stay. Women could always return to their rural homes, and they had a sense of their own worth and dignity, factors limiting the actions of management. . . .

While the women's traditional conception of themselves as independent daughters of freemen played a major role in the turn-out, this factor acting alone would not necessarily have triggered the 1834 strike. It would have led women as individuals to quit work and return to their rural homes. But the turn-out was a collective protest. When it was announced that wage reductions were being considered, women began to hold meetings in the mills during meal breaks in order to assess tactical possibilities. Their turn-out began at one mill when the agent discharged a woman who had presided at such a meeting. Their procession through the streets passed by other mills, expressing a conscious effort to enlist as much support as possible for their cause. At a mass meeting, the women drew up a resolution which insisted that none be discharged for their participation in the turn-out. This strike, then, was a collective response to the proposed wage cuts—made possible because women had come to form a "community" of operatives in the mill, rather than simply a group of individual workers. The existence of such a tight-knit community turned individual opposition of the wage cuts into a collective protest.

In October 1836, women again went on strike. This second turn-out was similar to the first in several respects. Its immediate cause was also a wage reduction; marches and a large outdoor rally were organized; again, like the earlier protest, the basic goal was not achieved; the corporations refused to restore wages; and operatives either left Lowell or returned to work at the new rates.

Despite these surface similarities between the turn-outs, there were some real differences. One involved scale: over 1500 operatives turned out in 1836, compared to only 800 earlier. Moreover, the second strike lasted much longer than the first. In 1834 operatives stayed out for only a few days; in 1836, the mills ran far below capacity for several months. . . .

Differences between the two turn-outs were not limited to the increased scale and duration of the later one. Women displayed a much higher degree of organization in 1836 than earlier. To co-ordinate strike activities, they formed a Factory Girls' Association. According to one historian, membership in the short-lived association reached 2,500 at its height. . . .

Now giving more thought than they had in 1834 to the specific tactics of the turn-out, the women made a deliberate effort to shut down the mills in order to win their demands. They attempted to persuade less committed operatives, concentrating on those in crucial departments within the mill. . . .

In their organization of a Factory Girls' Association and in their efforts to shut down the mills, the female operatives revealed that they had been changed by their industrial experience. Increasingly, they acted not simply as "daughters of freemen" offended by the impositions of the textile corporations, but also as industrial workers intent on improving their position within the mills.

There was a decline in protest among women in the Lowell mills following these early strike defeats. During the 1837–1843 depression, textile corporations twice reduced wages without evoking a collective response from operatives. Because of the frequency of production cutbacks and lay-offs in these years, workers probably accepted the mill agents' contention that they had to reduce wages or close entirely. But with the return of prosperity and the expansion of production in the mid-1840s, there were renewed labor protests among women. Their actions paralleled those of working men and reflected fluctuations in the business cycle. Prosperity itself did not prompt turn-outs, but it evidently facilitated collective actions by women operatives.

In contrast to the protests of the previous decade, the struggles now were primarily political. Women did not turn-out in the 1840s; rather, they mounted annual petition campaigns calling on the State legislature to limit the hours of labor within the mills. These campaigns reached their height in 1845 and 1846, when 2,000 and 5,000 operatives respectively signed petitions. Unable to curb the wage cuts, or the speed-up and stretch-out imposed by mill owners, operatives sought to mitigate the consequences of these changes by reducing the length of the working day. Having been defeated earlier in economic struggles, they now sought to achieve their new goal through political action. The Ten Hour Movement, seen in these terms, was a logical outgrowth of the unsuccessful turn-outs of the previous decade. Like the earlier struggles, the Ten Hour Movement was an assertion of the dignity of operatives and an attempt to maintain that dignity under the changing conditions of industrial capitalism. . . .

The women's Ten Hour Movement, like the earlier turn-outs, was based in part on the participants' sense of their own worth and dignity. . . . At the same time, however, [it] also indicted the growth of a new consciousness. It reflected a mounting feeling of community among women operatives and a realization that their interests and those of their employers were not identical, that they had to rely on themselves and not on corporate benevolence to achieve a reduction in the hours of labor. One woman, in an open letter to a State legislator, expressed this rejection of middle-class paternalism: "Bad as is the condition of so many women, it would be much worse if they had nothing but your boasted protection to rely upon; but they have at least learnt the lesson which a bitter experience teaches, that not to those who style themselves their 'natural protectors' are they to look for the needful help, but to the strong and resolute of their own sex." Such an attitude, underlying the self-organization of women in the ten-hour petition campaigns, was clearly the product of the industrial experience in Lowell.

Both the early turn-outs and the Ten Hour Movement were in large measure dependent upon the existence of a close-knit community of women operatives. Such a community was based on the work structure, the nature of worker housing, and workforce homogeneity. Women were drawn together by the initial job training of newcomers; by the informal work sharing among experienced hands, by living in company boarding houses, by sharing religious, educational, and social activities in their leisure hours. Working and living in a new and alien setting, they came to rely upon one another for friendship and support. Understandably, a community feeling developed among them.

This evolving community as well as the common cultural traditions which Yankee women carried into Lowell were major elements that governed their response to changing mill conditions. The pre-industrial tradition of independence and self-respect made them particularly sensitive to management labor policies. The sense of community enabled them to transform their individual opposition to wage cuts and to the increasing pace of work into public protest. In these labor struggles women operatives expressed a new consciousness of their rights both as workers and as women. Such a consciousness, like the community of women itself, was one product of Lowell's industrial revolution.

The experiences of Lowell women before 1850 present a fascinating picture of the contradictory impact of industrial capitalism. Repeated labor protests reveal that female operatives felt the demands of mill employment to be oppressive. At the same time, however, the mills provided women with work outside of the home and family, thereby offering them an unprecedented point of entry into the public realm. That they came to challenge employer paternalism was a direct consequence of the increasing opportunities offered them in these years. The Lowell mills both exploited and liberated women in ways unknown to the pre-industrial political economy.

DOCUMENTS

Recollections of a Strike (1836), 1898

One of the first strikes of cotton-factory operatives that ever took place in this country was that in Lowell, in October 1836. When it was announced that the wages were to be cut down, great indignation was felt, and it was decided to strike, *en masse*. This was done. The mills were shut down, and the girls went in procession from their several corporations to the "grove" on Chapel Hill, and listened to "incendiary" speeches from early labor reformers.

One of the girls stood on a pump, and gave vent to the feelings of her companions in a neat speech, declaring that it was their duty to resist all

SOURCE: Harriet Hanson Robinson, *Loom and Spindle or Life Among the Early Mill Girls* (New York: T. Y. Crowell, 1898), 51–53.

attempts at cutting down the wages. This was the first time a woman had spoken in public in Lowell, and the event caused surprise and consternation among her audience.

Cutting down the wages was not their only grievance, nor the only cause of this strike. Hitherto the corporations had paid twenty-five cents a week towards the board of each operative, and now it was their purpose to have the girls pay the sum; and this, in addition to the cut in wages, would make a difference of at least one dollar a week. It was estimated that as many as twelve or fifteen hundred girls turned out, and walked in procession through the streets. They had neither flags nor music, but sang songs, a favorite (but rather inappropriate) one being a parody on "I won't be a nun."

> "Oh! isn't it a pity, such a pretty girl as I—
>   Should be sent to the factory to pine away and die?
> Oh! I cannot be a slave,
>   I will not be a slave,
> For I'm so fond of liberty
>   That I cannot be a slave."

My own recollection of this first strike (or "turn out" as it was called) is very vivid.* I worked in a lower room, where I had heard the proposed strike fully, if not vehemently, discussed; I had been an ardent listener to what was said against this attempt at "oppression" on the part of the corporation, and naturally I took sides with the strikers. When the day came on which the girls were to turn out, those in the upper rooms started first, and so many of them left that our mill was at once shut down. Then, when the girls in my room stood irresolute, uncertain what to do, asking each other, "Would you?" or "Shall we turn out?" and not one of them having the courage to lead off, I, who began to think they would not go out, after all their talk, became impatient, and started on ahead, saying, with childish bravado, "I don't care what you do, *I* am going to turn out, whether any one else does or not;" and I marched out, and was followed by the others.**

As I looked back at the long line that followed me, I was more proud than I have ever been since at any success I may have achieved, and more proud than I shall ever be again until my own beloved State gives to its women citizens the right of suffrage.

The agent of the corporation where I then worked took some small revenges on the supposed ringleaders; on the principle of sending the weaker to the wall, my mother was turned away from her boarding-house, that functionary saying, "Mrs. Hanson, you could not prevent the older girls from turning out, but your daughter is a child, and *her* you could control."

---

*As the Dublin essay reveals, there actually was a brief earlier strike in 1834. (Eds.)
**She was then eleven years and eight months old.

"Regulations to Be Observed," Hamilton Manufacturing Company, 1848

Regulations to be observed by all persons employed in the factories of the Hamilton Manufacturing Company. The overseers are to be always in their rooms at the starting of the mill, and not absent unnecessarily during working hours. They are to see that all those employed in their rooms, are in their places in due season, and keep a correct account of their time and work. They may grant leave of absence to those employed under them, when they have spare hands to supply their places, and not otherwise, except in cases of absolute necessity.

All persons in the employ of the Hamilton Manufacturing Company, are to observe the regulations of the room where they are employed. They are not to be absent from their work without the consent of the overseer, except in cases of sickness, and then they are to send him word of the cause of their absence. They are to board in one of the houses of the company and give information at the counting room, where they board, when they begin, or, whenever they change their boarding place; and are to observe the regulations of their boarding-house.

Those intending to leave the employment of the company, are to give at least two weeks' notice thereof to their overseer.

All persons entering into the employment of the company, are considered as engaged for twelve months, and those who leave sooner, or do not comply with all these regulations, will not be entitled to a regular discharge.

The company will not employ any one who is habitually absent from public worship on the Sabbath, or known to be guilty of immorality.

A physician will attend once in every month at the counting-room, to vaccinate all who may need it, free of expense.

Any one who shall take from the mills or the yard, any yarn, cloth or other article belonging to the company, will be considered guilty of stealing and be liable to prosecution.

Payment will be made monthly, including board and wages. The accounts will be made up to the last Saturday but one in every month, and paid in the course of the following week.

These regulations are considered part of the contract, with which all persons entering into the employment of the Hamilton Manufacturing Company, engage to comply.

JOHN AVERY, AGENT.

SOURCE: John R. Commons, ed., *A Documentary History of American Industrial Society,* (Cleveland: Arthur H. Clark Co., 1910), 3:135–136.

A Mill Worker's Grievances, 1845

The first petitioner who testified was *Eliza R. Hemmingway.* She had worked 2 years and 9 months in the Lowell Factories, 2 years in the Middlesex, and 9 months in the Hamilton Corporations. Her employment is weaving,— works by the piece. The Hamilton Mill manufactures cotton fabrics. The Middlesex, woollen fabrics. She is now at work in the Middlesex Mills, and attends one loom. Her wages average from $16 to $23 a month exclusive of board. She complained of the hours for labor being too many, and the time for meals too limited. In the summer season, the work is commenced at 5 o'clock, A.M., and continued till 7 o'clock, P.M., with half an hour for breakfast and three quarters of an hour for dinner. During eight months of the year, but half an hour is allowed for dinner. The air in the room she considered not to be wholesome. There were 293 small lamps and 61 large lamps lighted in the room in which she worked, when evening work is required. These lamps are also lighted sometimes in the morning. —About 130 females, 11 men, and 12 children (between the ages of 11 and 14) work in the room with her. She thought the children enjoyed about as good health as children generally do. The children work but 9 months out of 12. The other 3 months they must attend school. Thinks that there is no day when there are less than six of the females out of the mill from sickness. Has known as many as thirty. She, herself, is out quite often, on account of sickness. There was more sickness in the Summer than in the Winter months: though in the Summer, lamps are not lighted.

SOURCE: Massachusetts House of Representatives, "Report on Hours of Labor, 1845," Doc. 50, in *Documents, 1845* (Boston, 1845), 2–3.

Chapter 9

The Cherokee Removal: An American Tragedy

Along the Trail of Tears.

Most people are aware of the fate of Native Americans as white settlement pushed ever westward. However, one episode in the history of white–Indian relations is in many ways unique and constitutes one of our nation's darkest moments: the forcible removal and transport in 1838–1839 of thousands of Cherokees from their ancestral homeland in the Southern uplands.

Ironically, no other Indian nation had responded so fully to Thomas Jefferson's urgings that they abandon their nomadic ways and pattern their lifestyle after that of the whites. Jefferson had told Congress in 1803, "In leading them [the Indians] thus to agriculture, to manufactures, and civilizations; in bringing together their and our sentiments, and in preparing them ultimately to participate in the benefits of our Government, I trust and believe we are acting for their greatest good." In 1806 Jefferson congratulated the Cherokee chiefs on the progress they had made in farming: "Go on, my children, in the same way and be assured the further you advance in it the happier and more respectable you will be. . . . "

Dee Brown's essay "The Trail of Tears" graphically describes the Cherokees' progress toward "civilization," and the betrayal by both state and federal governments of the assurances and promises made to the Cherokee nation by Jefferson and other national leaders. The Cherokees were not the only Native Americans removed forcibly from their ancestral lands, yet the large measure of sympathy and support on their behalf was atypical. How do you account for the apparent contradiction between the strong contemporary sentiment against the removal of the Cherokees and the failure to prevent it?

The three documents following the essay provide eloquent examples of the arguments presented on both sides of the removal controversy. The first is from the "Memorial of the Cherokee Nation" (July 1830), which sets forth the Cherokee view of the removal proposed by President Andrew Jackson. The second is from President Jackson's Second Annual Message to Congress (December 6, 1830). Contrast these two descriptions of the life awaiting the Indians in the new western territory. Whose argument do you find more convincing? How did Jackson respond to those who objected to white encroachment on Indian land?

Opposition to removal was particularly strong in the Northeast among the clergy and those engaged in causes of charity and moral uplift. Among them was Catherine Beecher, a well-known advocate for the education of women. The third document is from a circular she wrote and distributed that described the plight of the Cherokees and called upon women to take up their cause. Considering that women were denied the right to vote and hold political office, how did Beecher believe they could be an effective force in defeating the Indian Removal Act?

ESSAY

The Trail of Tears

Dee Brown

In the spring of 1838, Brigadier General Winfield Scott with a regiment of artillery, a regiment of infantry, and six companies of dragoons marched unopposed into the Cherokee country of northern Georgia. On May 10 at New Echota, the capital of what had been one of the greatest Indian nations in eastern America, Scott issued a proclamation:

> The President of the United States sent me with a powerful army to cause you, in obedience to the treaty of 1835, to join that part of your people who are already established in prosperity on the other side of the Mississippi. . . . The emigration must be commenced in haste. . . . The full moon of May is already on the wane, and before another shall have passed away every Cherokee man, woman and child . . . must be in motion to join their brethren

SOURCE: Dee Brown, "The Trail of Tears," *American History Illustrated* 7 (June 1972): 30–39. Reprinted through the courtesy of Cowles Magazines, publisher of *American History Illustrated*.

in the West. . . . My troops already occupy many positions . . . and thousands and thousands are approaching from every quarter to render resistance and escape alike hopeless. . . . Will you then by resistance compel us to resort to arms? Or will you by flight seek to hide yourselves in mountains and forests and thus oblige us to hunt you down? Remember that in pursuit it may be impossible to avoid conflicts. The blood of the white man or the blood of the red man may be spilt, and if spilt, however accidentally, it may be impossible for the discreet and humane among you, or among us, to prevent a general war and carnage.

For more than a century the Cherokees had been ceding their land, thousands of acres by thousands of acres. They had lost all of Kentucky and much of Tennessee, but after the last treaty of 1819 they still had remaining about 35,000 square miles of forested mountains, clean, swift-running rivers, and fine meadows. In this country which lay across parts of Georgia, North Carolina, and Tennessee, they cultivated fields, planted orchards, fenced pastures, and built roads, houses, and towns. Sequoya had invented a syllabary for the Cherokee language so that thousands of his tribesmen quickly learned to read and write. The Cherokees had adopted the white man's way—his clothing, his constitutional form of government, even his religion. But it had all been for nothing. Now these men who had come across the great ocean many years ago wanted all of the Cherokees' land. In exchange for their 35,000 square miles, the tribe was to receive five million dollars and another tract of land somewhere in the wilderness beyond the Mississippi River.

This was a crushing blow to a proud people. "They are extremely proud, despising the lower class of Europeans," said Henry Timberlake, who visited them before the Revolutionary War. William Bartram, the botanist, said the Cherokees were not only a handsome people, tall, graceful, and olive-skinned, but "their countenance and actions exhibit an air of magnanimity, superiority and independence."

Ever since the signing of the treaties of 1819, Major General Andrew Jackson, a man they once believed to be their friend, had been urging Cherokees to move beyond the Mississippi. Indians and white settlers, Jackson told them, could never get along together. Even if the government wanted to protect the Cherokees from harassment, he added, it would be unable to do so. "If you cannot protect us in Georgia," a chief retorted, "how can you protect us from similar evils in the West?"

During that period of polite urging, a few hundred Cherokee families did move west, but the tribe remained united and refused to give up any more territory. In fact, the council leaders passed a law forbidding any chief to sell or trade a single acre of Cherokee land on penalty of death.

In 1828, when Andrew Jackson was running for President, he knew that in order to win he must sweep the frontier states. Free land for the land-hungry settlers became Jackson's major policy. He hammered away at this theme especially hard in Georgia, where waves of settlers from the coastal lowlands were pushing into the highly desirable Cherokee country. He promised the Georgians that if they would help elect him President, he would lend his support to opening up the Cherokee lands for settlement. The Cherokees, of course, were not citizens and could not vote in opposition. To the Cherokees and their friends who protested this promise, Jackson justified his position by saying that the Cherokees had fought on the side of the British during the Revolutionary War. He conveniently forgot that the Cherokees had been his allies during the desperate War of 1812, and had saved the day for him in his decisive victory over the British-backed Creeks at Horseshoe Bend. (One of the Cherokee chiefs who aided Jackson was Junaluska. Said he afterward: "If I had known that Jackson would drive us from our homes I would have killed him that day at the Horseshoe.")

Three weeks after Jackson was elected President, the Georgia legislature passed a law annexing all the Cherokee country within that state's borders. As most of the Cherokee land was in Georgia and three-fourths of the tribe lived there, this meant an end to their independence as a nation. The Georgia legislature also abolished all Cherokee laws and customs and sent surveyors to map out land lots of 160 acres each. The 160-acre lots were to be distributed to white citizens of Georgia through public lotteries.

To add to the pressures on the Cherokees, gold was discovered near Dahlonega in the heart of their country. For many years the Cherokees had concealed the gold deposits, but now the secret was out and a rabble of gold-hungry prospectors descended upon them.

John Ross, the Cherokees' leader, hurried to Washington to protest the Georgia legislature's actions and to plead for justice. In that year Ross was 38 years old; he was well-educated and had been active in Cherokee government matters since he was 19. He was adjutant of the Cherokee regiment that served with Jackson at Horseshoe Bend. His father had been one of a group of Scottish emigrants who settled near the Cherokees and married into the tribe.

In Washington, Ross found sympathizers in Congress, but most of them were anti-Jackson men and the Cherokee case was thus drawn into the whirlpool of politics. When Ross called upon Andrew Jackson to request his aid, the President bluntly told him that "no protection could be afforded the Cherokees" unless they were willing to move west of the Mississippi.

While Ross was vainly seeking help in Washington, alarming messages reached him from Georgia. White citizens of that state were claiming the homes of Cherokees through the land lottery, seizing some of them by force. Joseph Vann, a hard-working half-breed, had carved out an 800-acre plantation at Spring Place and built a fine brick house for his residence. Two men arrived to claim it, dueled for it, and the winner drove Vann and his family into the hills. When John Ross rushed home he found that the same thing had happened to his family. A lottery claimant was living in his beautiful home on the Coosa River, and Ross had to turn north toward Tennessee to find his fleeing wife and children.

During all this turmoil, President Jackson and the governor of Georgia pressed the Cherokee leaders hard in attempts to persuade them to cede all their territory and move to the West. But the chiefs stood firm. Somehow they managed to hold the tribe together, and helped dispossessed families find new homes back in the wilderness areas. John Ross and his family lived in a one-room log cabin across the Tennessee line.

In 1834, the chiefs appealed to Congress with a memorial in which they stated that they would never voluntarily abandon their homeland, but proposed a compromise in which they agreed to cede the state of Georgia a part of their territory provided that they would be protected from invasion in the remainder. Furthermore, at the end of a definite period of years to be fixed by the United States, they would be willing to become citizens of the various states in which they resided.

"Cupidity has fastened its eye upon our lands and our homes," they said, "and is seeking by force and by every variety of oppression and wrong to expel us from our lands and our homes and to tear from us all that has become endeared to us. In our distress we have appealed to the judiciary of the United States, where our rights have been solemnly established. We have appealed to the Executive of the United States to protect those rights according to the obligation of treaties and the injunctions of the laws. But this appeal to the Executive has been made in vain."

This new petition to Congress was no more effectual than their appeals to President Jackson. Again they were told that their difficulties could be remedied only by their removal to the west of the Mississippi.

For the first time now, a serious split occurred among the Cherokees. A small group of subchiefs decided that further resistance to the demands of the Georgia and United States governments was futile. It would be better, they believed, to exchange their land and go west rather than risk bloodshed and the possible loss of everything. Leaders of this group were Major Ridge and Elias Boudinot. Ridge had adopted his first name after Andrew Jackson gave him that rank during the War of 1812. Boudinot was Ridge's nephew. Originally known as Buck Watie, he had taken the name of a New England philanthropist who sent him through a mission school in Connecticut. Stand Watie, who later became a Confederate general, was his brother. Upon Boudinot's return from school to Georgia, he founded the first tribal newspaper, the *Cherokee Phoenix,* in 1827, but during the turbulence following the Georgia land lotteries he was forced to suspend publication.

And so in February 1835 when John Ross journeyed to Washington to resume his campaign to save the Cherokee nation, a rival delegation headed by Ridge and Boudinot arrived there to seek terms for removal to the West. The pro-removal forces in the government leaped at this opportunity to bypass

Ross's authority, and within a few days drafted a preliminary treaty for the Ridge delegation. It was then announced that a council would be held later in the year at New Echota, Georgia, for the purpose of negotiating and agreeing upon final terms.

During the months that followed, bitterness increased between the two Cherokee factions. Ridge's group was a very small minority, but they had the full weight of the United States Government behind them, and threats and inducements were used to force a full attendance at the council which was set for December 22, 1835. Handbills were printed in Cherokee and distributed throughout the nation, informing the Indians that those who did not attend would be counted as assenting to any treaty that might be made.

During the seven days which followed the opening of the treaty council, fewer than five hundred Cherokees, or about 2 percent of the tribe, came to New Echota to participate in the discussions. Most of the other Cherokees were busy endorsing a petition to be sent to Congress stating their opposition to the treaty. But on December 29, Ridge, Boudinot and their followers signed away all the lands of the great Cherokee nation. Ironically, thirty years earlier Major Ridge had personally executed a Cherokee chief named Doublehead for committing one of the few capital crimes of the tribe. That crime was the signing of a treaty which gave away Cherokee lands.

Charges of bribery by the Ross forces were denied by government officials, but some years afterward it was discovered that the Secretary of War had sent secret agents into the Cherokee country with authority to expend money to bribe chiefs to support the treaty of cession and removal. And certainly the treaty signers were handsomely rewarded. In an era when a dollar would buy many times its worth today, Major Ridge was paid $30,000 and his followers received several thousand dollars each. Ostensibly they were being paid for their improved farmlands, but the amounts were far in excess of contemporary land values.

John Ross meanwhile completed gathering signatures of Cherokees who were opposed to the treaty. Early in the following spring, 1836, he took the petition to Washington. More than three-fourths of the tribe, 15,964, had signed in protest against the treaty.

When the governor of Georgia was informed of the overwhelming vote against the treaty, he replied: "Nineteen-twentieths of the Cherokees are too ignorant and depraved to entitle their opinions to any weight or consideration in such matters."

The Cherokees, however, did have friends in Congress. Representative Davy Crockett of Tennessee denounced the treatment of the Cherokees as unjust, dishonest, and cruel. He admitted that he represented a body of frontier constituents who would like to have the Cherokee lands opened for settlement, and he doubted if a single one of them would second what he was saying. Even though his support of the Cherokees might remove him from public life, he added, he could not do otherwise except at the expense of his honor and conscience. Daniel Webster, Henry Clay, Edward Everett, and other great orators of the Congress also spoke for the Cherokees.

When the treaty came to a final decision in the Senate, it passed by only one vote. On May 23, 1836, President Jackson signed the document. According to its terms, the Cherokees were allowed two years from that day in which to leave their homeland forever.

The few Cherokees who had favored the treaty now began making their final preparations for departure. About three hundred left during that year and then early in 1837 Major Ridge and 465 followers departed by boats for the new land in the West. About 17,000 others, ignoring the treaty, remained steadfast in their homeland with John Ross.

For a while it seemed that Ross might win his long fight, that perhaps the treaty might be declared void. After the Secretary of War, acting under instructions from President Jackson, sent Major William M. Davis to the Cherokee country to expedite removal to the West, Davis submitted a frank report: "That paper called a treaty is no treaty at all," he wrote, "because it is not sanctioned by the great body of the Cherokees and was made without their participation or assent. . . . The Cherokees are a peaceable, harmless people, but you may drive them to desperation, and this treaty cannot be carried into effect except by the strong arm of force."

In September 1836, Brigadier General Dunlap, who had been sent with a brigade of Tennessee volunteers to force the removal, indignantly disbanded his troops after making a strong speech in favor of the Indians: "I would never dishonor the Tennessee arms in a servile service by aiding to carry into execution at the point of the bayonet a treaty made by a lean minority against the will and authority of the Cherokee people."

Even Inspector General John E. Wool, commanding United States troops in the area, was impressed by the united Cherokee resistance, and warned the Secretary of War not to send any civilians who had any part in the making of the treaty back into the Cherokee country. During the summer of 1837, the Secretary of War sent a confidential agent, John Mason, Jr., to observe and report. "Opposition to the treaty is unanimous and irreconcilable," Mason wrote. "They say it cannot bind them because they did not make it; that it was made by a few unauthorized individuals; that the nation is not party to it."

The inexorable machinery of government was already in motion, however, and when the expiration date of the waiting period, May 23, 1838, came near, Winfield Scott was ordered in with his army to force compliance. As already stated, Scott issued his proclamation on May 10. His soldiers were already building thirteen stockaded forts—six in North Carolina, five in Georgia, one in Tennessee, and one in Alabama. At these points the Cherokees would be concentrated to await transportation to the West. Scott then ordered the roundup started, instructing his officers not to fire on the Cherokees except in case of resistance. "If we get possession of the women and children first," he said, "or first capture the men, the other members of the same family will readily come in."

James Mooney, an ethnologist who afterwards talked with Cherokees who endured this ordeal, said that squads of troops moved into the forested mountains to search out every small cabin and make prisoners of all the occupants however or wherever they might be found. "Families at dinner were startled by the sudden gleam of bayonets in the doorway and rose up to be driven with blows and oaths along the weary miles of trail that led to the stockades. Men were seized in their fields or going along the road, women were taken from their spinning wheels and children from their play. In many cases, on turning for one last look as they crossed a ridge, they saw their homes in flames, fired by the lawless rabble that followed on the heels of the soldiers to loot and pillage. So keen were these outlaws on the scent that in some instances they were driving off the cattle and other stock of the Indians almost before the soldiers had fairly started their owners in the other direction."

Long afterward one of the Georgia militiamen who participated in the roundup said: "I fought through the Civil War and have seen men shot to pieces and slaughtered by thousands, but the Cherokee removal was the cruelest work I ever knew."

Knowing that resistance was futile, most of the Cherokees surrendered quietly. Within a month, thousands were enclosed in the stockades. On June 6 at Ross's Landing near the site of present-day Chattanooga, the first of many departures began. Eight hundred Cherokees were forcibly crowded onto a flotilla of six flatboats lashed to the side of a steamboat. After surviving a passage over rough rapids which smashed the sides of the flatboats, they landed at Decatur, Alabama, boarded a railroad train (which was a new and terrifying experience for most of them), and after reaching Tuscumbia were crowded upon a Tennessee River steamboat again.

Throughout June and July similar shipments of several hundred Cherokees were transported by this long water route—north on the Tennessee River to the Ohio and then down the Mississippi and up the Arkansas to their new homeland. A few managed to escape and make their way back to the Cherokee country, but most of them were eventually recaptured. Along the route of travel of this forced migration, the summer was hot and dry. Drinking water and food were often contaminated. First the young children would die, then the older people, and sometimes as many as half the adults were stricken with dysentery and other ailments. On each boat deaths ran as high as five per day. On one of the first boats to reach Little Rock, Arkansas, at least a hundred had died. A compassionate lieutenant who was with the military escort recorded in his diary for August 1: "My blood chills as I write at the remembrance of the scenes I have gone through."

When John Ross and other Cherokee leaders back in the concentration camps learned of the high mortality among those who had gone ahead, they petitioned General Scott to postpone further departures until autumn. Although only three thousand Cherokees had been removed, Scott agreed to wait until the summer drought was broken, or no later than October. The Cherokees in turn agreed to organize and manage the migration themselves. After a lengthy council, they asked and received permission to travel overland in wagons, hoping that by camping along the way they would not suffer as many deaths as occurred among those who had gone on the river boats.

During this waiting period, Scott's soldiers continued their searches for more than a thousand Cherokees known to be still hiding out in the deep wildernesses of the Great Smoky Mountains. These Cherokees had organized themselves under the leadership of a chief named Utsala, and had developed warning systems to prevent captures by the bands of soldiers. Occasionally, however, some of the fugitives were caught and herded back to the nearest stockade.

One of the fugitive families was that of Tsali, an aging Cherokee. With his wife, his brother, three sons and their families, Tsali had built a hideout somewhere on the border between North Carolina and Tennessee. Soldiers surrounded their shelters one day, and the Cherokees surrendered without resistance. As they were being taken back toward Fort Cass (Calhoun, Tennessee), a soldier prodded Tsali's wife sharply with a bayonet, ordering her to walk faster. Angered by the brutality, Tsali grappled with the soldier, tore away his rifle, and bayoneted him to the ground. At the same time, Tsali's brother leaped upon another soldier and bayoneted him. Before the remainder of the military detachment could act, the Cherokees fled, vanishing back into the Smokies where they sought refuge with Chief Utsala. Both bayoneted soldiers died.

Upon learning of the incident, Scott immediately ordered that Tsali must be brought in and punished. Because some of his regiments were being transferred elsewhere for other duties, however, the general realized that his reduced force might be occupied for months in hunting down and capturing the escaped Cherokee. He would have to use guile to accomplish the capture of Tsali.

Scott therefore dispatched a messenger—a white man who had been adopted as a child by the Cherokees—to find Chief Utsala. The messenger was instructed to inform Utsala that if he would surrender Tsali to General Scott, the Army would withdraw from the Smokies and leave the remaining fugitives alone.

When Chief Utsala received the message, he was suspicious of Scott's sincerity, but he considered the general's offer as an opportunity to gain time. Perhaps with the passage of time, the few Cherokees remaining in the Smokies might be forgotten and left alone forever. Utsala put the proposition to Tsali: If he went in and surrendered, he would probably be put to death, but his death might insure the freedom of a thousand fugitive Cherokees.

Tsali did not hesitate. He announced that he would go and surrender to General Scott. To make certain that he was treated well, several members of Tsali's band went with him.

When the Cherokees reached Scott's headquarters, the general ordered Tsali, his brother, and three sons arrested, and then condemned them all to be shot to death. To impress upon the tribe their utter helplessness before the might of the government, Scott selected the firing squad from Cherokee prisoners in one of the stockades. At the last moment, the general spared Tsali's youngest son because he was only a child.

(By this sacrifice, however, Tsali and his family gave the Smoky Mountain Cherokees a chance at survival in their homeland. Time was on their side, as Chief Utsala had hoped, and that is why today there is a small Cherokee reservation on the North Carolina slope of the Great Smoky Mountains.)

With the ending of the drought of 1838, John Ross and the 13,000 stockaded Cherokees began preparing for their long overland journey to the West. They assembled several hundred wagons, filled them with blankets, cooking pots, their old people and small children, and moved out in separate contingents along a trail that followed the Hiwassee River. The first party of 1,103 started on October 1.

"At noon all was in readiness for moving," said an observer of the departure. "The teams were stretched out in a line along the road through a heavy forest, groups of persons formed about each wagon. The day was bright and beautiful, but a gloomy thoughtfulness was depicted in the lineaments of every face. In all the bustle of preparation there was a silence and stillness of the voice that betrayed the sadness of the heart. At length the word was given to move on. Going Snake, an aged and respected chief whose head eighty summers had whitened, mounted on his favorite pony and led the way in silence, followed by a number of younger men on horseback. At this very moment a low sound of distant thunder fell upon my ear . . . a voice of divine indignation for the wrong of my poor and unhappy countrymen, driven by brutal power from all they loved and cherished in the land of their fathers to gratify the cravings of avarice. The sun was unclouded—no rain fell—the thunder rolled away and seemed hushed in the distance."

Throughout October, eleven wagon trains departed and then on November 4, the last Cherokee exiles moved out for the West. The overland route for these endless lines of wagons, horsemen, and people on foot ran from the mouth of the Hiwassee in Tennessee across the Cumberland plateau to McMinnville and then north to Nashville where they crossed the Cumberland River. From there they followed an old trail to Hopkinsville, Kentucky, and continued northwestward to the Ohio River, crossing into southern

Illinois near the mouth of the Cumberland. Moving straight westward they passed through Jonesboro and crossed the Mississippi at Cape Girardeau, Missouri. Some of the first parties turned southward through Arkansas; the later ones continued westward through Springfield, Missouri, and on to Indian Territory.

A New Englander traveling eastward across Kentucky in November and December met several contingents, each a day apart from the others. "Many of the aged Indians were suffering extremely from the fatigue of the journey," he said, "and several were quite ill. Even aged females, apparently nearly ready to drop into the grave, were traveling with heavy burdens attached to their backs—on the sometimes frozen ground, and sometimes muddy streets, with no covering for the feet except what nature had given them. . . . We learned from the inhabitants on the road where the Indians passed, that they buried fourteen or fifteen at every stopping place, and they make a journey of ten miles per day only on an average. They will not travel on the Sabbath . . . they must stop, and not merely stop—they must worship the Great Spirit, too; for they had divine service on the Sabbath—a camp meeting in truth."

Autumn rains softened the roads, and the hundreds of wagons and horses cut them into morasses, slowing movement to a crawl. To add to their difficulties, tollgate operators overcharged them for passage. Their horses were stolen or seized on pretext of unpaid debts, and they had no recourse to the law. With the coming of cold damp weather, measles and whooping cough became epidemic. Supplies had to be dumped to make room for the sick in the jolting wagons.

By the time the last detachments reached the Mississippi at Cape Girardeau it was January, with the river running full of ice so that several thousand had to wait on the east bank almost a month before the channel cleared. James Mooney, who later heard the story from survivors, said that "the lapse of over half of century had not sufficed to wipe out the memory of the miseries of that halt beside the frozen river, with hundreds of sick and dying penned up in wagons or stretched upon the ground, with only a blanket overhead to keep out the January blast."

Meanwhile the parties that left early in October were beginning to reach Indian Territory. (The first arrived on January 4, 1839.) Each group had lost from thirty to forty members by death. The later detachments suffered much heavier losses, especially toward the end of their journey. Among the victims was the wife of John Ross.

Not until March 1839 did the last of the Cherokees reach their new home in the West. Counts were made of the survivors and balanced against the counts made at the beginning of the removal. As well as could be estimated, the Cherokees had lost about four thousand by deaths—or one out of every four members of the tribe—most of the deaths brought about as the direct result of the enforced removal. From that day to this the Cherokees remember it as "the trail where they cried," or the Trail of Tears.

DOCUMENTS

Memorial of the Cherokee Nation, 1830

We are aware, that some persons suppose it will be for our advantage to remove beyond the Mississippi. We think otherwise. Our people universally think otherwise. Thinking that it would be fatal to their interests, they have almost to a man sent their memorial to congress, deprecating the necessity of a removal. This question was distinctly before their minds when they signed their memorial. Not an adult person can be found, who has not an opinion on the subject, and if the people were to understand distinctly, that they could be protected against the laws of the neighboring states, there is probably not an adult person in the nation, who would think it best to remove; though possibly a few might emigrate individually. There are doubtless many, who would flee to an unknown country, however beset with dangers, privations and sufferings, rather than be sentenced to spend six years in a Georgia prison for advising one of their neighbors not to betray his country. And there are others who could not think of living as outlaws in their native land, exposed to numberless vexations, and excluded from being parties or witnesses in a court of justice. It is incredible that Georgia should ever have enacted the oppressive laws to which reference is here made, unless she had supposed that something extremely terrific in its character was necessary in order to make the Cherokees willing to remove. We are not willing to remove; and if we could be brought to this extremity, it would be not by argument, not because our judgment was satisfied, not because our condition will be improved; but only because we cannot endure to be deprived of our national and individual rights and subjected to a process of intolerable oppression.

We wish to remain on the land of our fathers. We have a perfect and original right to remain without interruption or molestation. The treaties with us, and laws of the United States made in pursuance of treaties, guaranty our residence and our privileges, and secure us against intruders. Our only request is, that these treaties may be fulfilled, and these laws executed.

But if we are compelled to leave our country, we see nothing but ruin before us. The country west of the Arkansas territory is unknown to us. From what we can learn of it, we have no prepossessions in its favor. All the inviting parts of it, as we believe, are preoccupied by various Indian nations, to which it has been assigned. They would regard us as intruders, and look upon us with an evil eye. The far greater part of that region is, beyond all controversy, badly supplied with wood and water; and no Indian tribe can live as agriculturists

SOURCE: *Nile's Weekly Register* 38 (August 21, 1830): 454–457.

without these articles. All our neighbors, in case of our removal, though crowded into our near vicinity, would speak a language totally different from ours, and practice different customs. The original possessors of that region are now wandering savages lurking for prey in the neighborhood. They have always been at war, and would be easily tempted to turn their arms against peaceful emigrants. Were the country to which we are urged much better than it is represented to be, and were it free from the objections which we have made to it, still it is not the land of our birth, nor of our affections. It contains neither the scenes of our childhood, nor the graves of our fathers.

The removal of families to a new country, even under the most favorable auspices, and when the spirits are sustained by pleasing visions of the future, is attended with much depression of mind and sinking of heart. This is the case, when the removal is a matter of decided preference, and when the persons concerned are in early youth or vigorous manhood. Judge, then, what must be the circumstances of a removal, when a whole community, embracing persons of all classes and every description, from the infant to the man of extreme old age, the sick, the blind, the lame, the improvident, the reckless, the desperate, as well as the prudent, the considerate, the industrious, are compelled to remove by odious and intolerable vexations and persecutions, brought upon them in the forms of law, when all will agree only in this, that they have been cruelly robbed of their country, in violation of the most solemn compacts, which it is possible for communities to form with each other; and that, if they should make themselves comfortable in their new residence, they have nothing to expect hereafter but to be the victims of a future legalized robbery!

Such we deem, and are absolutely certain, will be the feelings of the whole Cherokee people, if they are forcibly compelled, by the laws of Georgia, to remove; and with these feelings, how is it possible that we should pursue our present course of improvement, or avoid sinking into utter despondency? We have been called a poor, ignorant, and degraded people. We certainly are not rich; nor have we ever boasted of our knowledge, or our moral or intellectual elevation. But there is not a man within our limits so ignorant as not to know that he has a right to live on the land of his fathers, in the possession of his immemorial privileges, and that this right has been acknowledged and guaranteed by the United States; nor is there a man so degraded as not to feel a keen sense of injury, on being deprived of this right and driven into exile. . . .

Removal Defended, 1830

It gives me pleasure to announce to Congress that the benevolent policy of the Government, steadily pursued for nearly thirty years, in relation to the removal of the Indians beyond the white settlements is approaching to a happy consummation. Two important tribes [the Choctaws and the Chicka-saws] have accepted the provision made for their removal at the last session of Congress, and it is believed that their example will induce the remaining tribes also to seek the same obvious advantages.

The consequences of a speedy removal will be important to the United States, to individual States, and to the Indians themselves. The pecuniary advantages which it promises to the Government are the least of its recom-mendations. It puts an end to all possible danger of collision between the authorities of the General and State Governments on account of the Indians. It will place a dense and civilized population in large tracts of country now occupied by a few savage hunters. By opening the whole territory between Tennessee on the north and Louisiana on the south to the settlement of the whites, it will incalculably strengthen the southwestern frontier and render the adjacent States strong enough to repel future invasions without remote aid. It will relieve the whole State of Mississippi and the western part of Alabama of Indian occupancy, and enable those States to advance rapidly in population, wealth, and power. It will separate the Indians from immediate contact with settlements of whites; free them from the power of the States; enable them to pursue happiness in their own way and under their own rude institutions; will retard the progress of decay, which is lessening their numbers, and perhaps cause them gradually, under the protection of the Government and through the influence of good counsels, to cast off their savage habits and become an interesting, civilized, and Christian commu-nity. These consequences, some of them so certain and the rest so probable, make the complete execution of the plan sanctioned by Congress at their last session an object of much solicitude.

Toward the aborigines of the country no one can indulge a more friendly feeling than myself, or would go further in attempting to reclaim them from their wandering habits and make them a happy, prosperous people. I have endeavored to impress upon them my own solemn convictions of the duties and powers of the General Government in relation to the State authorities. For the justice of the laws passed by the States within the scope of their re-served powers, they are not responsible to this Government. As individuals we may entertain and express our opinions of their acts, but as a Govern-ment we have as little right to control them as we have to prescribe laws for other nations.

With a full understanding of the subject, the Choctaw and the Chickasaw tribes have with great unanimity determined to avail themselves of the liberal offers presented by the act of Congress, and have agreed to remove beyond the Mississippi River. Treaties have been made with them, which in due

SOURCE: Andrew Jackson, "Second Annual Message to Congress" (December 6, 1830), in J. D. Richardson, ed., *A Compilation of the Messages and Papers of the Presidents* (Washington, D.C.: Government Printing Office, 1896), 2:519–522.

season will be submitted for consideration. In negotiating these treaties they were made to understand their true condition, and they have preferred maintaining their independence in the Western forests to submitting to the laws of the States in which they now reside. These treaties, being probably the last which will ever be made with them, are characterized by great liberality on the part of the Government. They give the Indians a liberal sum in consideration of their removal, and comfortable subsistence on their arrival at their new homes. If it be their real interest to maintain a separate existence, they will there be at liberty to do so without the inconveniences and vexations to which they would unavoidably have been subject in Alabama and Mississippi.

Humanity has often wept over the fate of the aborigines of this country, and Philanthropy has been long busily employed in devising means to avert it, but its progress has never for a moment been arrested, and one by one have many powerful tribes disappeared from the earth. To follow to the tomb the last of his race and to tread on the graves of extinct nations excite melancholy reflections. But true Philanthropy reconciles the mind to these vicissitudes as it does to the extinction of one generation to make room for another. In the monuments and fortresses of an unknown people, spread over the extensive regions of the West, we behold the memorials of a once powerful race, which was exterminated or has disappeared to make room for the existing savage tribes. Nor is there anything in this which, upon a comprehensive view of the general interests of the human race, is to be regretted. Philanthropy could not wish to see this continent restored to the condition in which it was found by our forefathers. What good man would prefer a country covered with forests and ranged by a few thousand savages to our extensive Republic, studded with cities, towns, and prosperous farms, embellished with all the improvements which art can devise or industry execute, occupied by more than 12,000,000 happy people, and filled with all the blessings of liberty, civilization, and religion?

The present policy of the Government is but a continuation of the same progressive change by a milder process. The tribes which occupied the countries now constituting the Eastern States were annihilated or have melted away to make room for the whites. The waves of population and civilization are rolling to the westward, and we now propose to acquire the countries occupied by the red men of the South and West by a fair exchange, and, at the expense of the United States, to send them to a land where their existence may be prolonged and perhaps made perpetual. Doubtless it will be painful to leave the graves of their fathers; but what do they more than our ancestors did or than our children are now doing? To better their condition in an unknown land our forefathers left all that was dear in earthly objects. Our children by thousands yearly leave the land of their birth to seek new homes in distant regions. Does Humanity weep at these painful separations from everything, animate and inanimate, with which the young heart has become entwined? Far from it. It is rather a source of joy that our country affords scope where our young population may range unconstrained in body or in mind, developing the power and faculties of man in their highest perfection. These remove hundreds and almost thousands of miles at their own expense, purchase the lands they occupy, and support themselves at their new homes from the moment of their arrival. Can it be cruel in this Government when, by events which it can not control, the Indian is made discontented in his ancient home to purchase his lands, to give him a new and extensive territory, to pay the expense of his removal, and support him a year in his new abode? How many thousands of our own people would gladly embrace the opportunity of removing to the West on such conditions! If the offers made to the Indians were extended to them, they would be hailed with gratitude and joy.

And is it supposed that the wandering savage has a stronger attachment to his home than the settled, civilized Christian? Is it more afflicting to him to leave the graves of his fathers than it is to our brothers and children? Rightly considered, the policy of the General Government toward the red man is not only liberal, but generous. He is unwilling to submit to the laws of the States and mingle with their population. To save him from this alternative, or perhaps utter annihilation, the General Government kindly offers him a new home, and proposes to pay the whole expense of his removal and settlement.

In the consummation of a policy originating at an early period, and steadily pursued by every Administration within the present century—so just to the States and so generous to the Indians—the Executive feels it has a right to expect the cooperation of Congress and of all good and disinterested men. . . .

Catherine Beecher's Appeal, 1829

Circular
Addressed to Benevolent Ladies of the U. States, December 25, 1829

The present crisis in the affairs of the Indian nations in the United States demands the immediate and interested attention of all who make any claims to benevolence or humanity. The calamities now hanging over them threaten not only these relics of an interesting race, but, if there is a Being who avenges the wrongs of the oppressed, are causes of alarm to our whole country.

The following are the facts of the case:—This continent was once possessed only by the Indians, and earliest accounts represent them as a

SOURCE: *Christian Advocate and Journal, December 25, 1829*, cited in Theda Perdue and Michael D. Green, *The Cherokee Removal: A Brief History with Documents* (Boston: Bedford/St. Martin's, 2005), pp. 111–114.

race numerous, warlike, and powerful. When our forefathers sought refuge from oppression on these shores, this people supplied their necessities, and ministered to their comfort; and though some of them, when they saw the white man continually encroaching upon their land, fought bravely for their existence and their country, yet often, too, the Indian has shed his blood to protect and sustain our infant nation.

As we have risen in greatness and glory, the Indian nations have faded away. Their proud and powerful tribes have gone; their noble sachems* and mighty warriors are heard of no more; and it is said the Indian often comes to the borders of his limited retreat to gaze on the beautiful country no longer his own, and to cry with bitterness at the remembrance of past greatness and power.

Ever since the existence of this nation, our general government, pursuing the course alike of policy and benevolence, have acknowledged these people as free and independent nations, and has protected them in the quiet possession of their lands. In repeated treaties with the Indians, the United States, by the hands of the most distinguished statesmen, after purchasing the greater part of their best lands have *promised* them *"to continue the guarantee of the remainder of their country* FOR EVER." And so strictly has government guarded the Indian's right to his lands, that even to go on to their boundaries to survey the land, subjects to heavy fines and imprisonment.

Our government also, with parental care, has persuaded the Indians to forsake their savage life, and to adopt the habits and pursuits of civilized nations, while the charities of Christians and the labours of missionaries have sent to them the blessings of the gospel to purify and enlighten. The laws and regular forms of a civilized government are instituted; their simple and beautiful language, by the remarkable ingenuity of one of their race, has become a written language with its own peculiar alphabet, and, by the printing press, is sending forth among these people the principles of knowledge, and liberty, and religion. Their fields are beginning to smile with the labours of the husbandman; their villages are busy with the toils of the mechanic and the artisan; schools are rising in their hamlets, and the temple of the living God is seen among their forests.

Nor are we to think of these people only as naked and wandering savages. The various grades of intellect and refinement exist among them as among us; and those who visit their chieftains and families of the higher class, speak with wonder and admiration of their dignified propriety, nobleness of appearance, and refined characteristics as often exhibited in both sexes. Among them are men fitted by native talents to shine among the statesmen of any land, and who have received no inferior degree of cultivation. Among them, also, are those who, by honest industry, have assembled around them most of the comforts and many of the elegancies of life.

*Chiefs.

But the lands of this people are *claimed* to be embraced within the limits of some of our southern states, and as they are fertile and valuable, they are demanded by the whites as their own possessions, and efforts are making to dispossess the Indians of their native soil. And such is the singular state of concurring circumstances, that it has become almost a certainty that these people are to have their lands torn from them, and to be driven into western wilds and to final annihilation, unless the feelings of a humane and Christian nation shall be aroused to prevent the unhallowed sacrifice.

Unless our general government interfere to protect these nations, as by solemn and oft-repeated treaties they are bound to do, nothing can save them. The states which surround them are taking such measures as will speedily drive them from their country, and cause their final extinction. . . .

Have not then the females of this country some duties devolving upon them in relation to this helpless race?—They are protected from the blinding influence of party spirit, and the asperities of political violence. They have nothing to do with any struggle for power, nor any right to dictate the decisions of those that rule over them.—But they may *feel* for the distressed; they may stretch out the supplicating hand for them, and by their prayers strive to avert the calamities that are impending over them. It may be, that female petitioners can lawfully be heard, even by the highest rulers of our land. Why may we not approach and supplicate that we and our dearest friends may be saved from the awful curses denounced on all who oppress the poor and needy, by Him whose anger is to be dreaded more than the wrath of man; who can "blast us with the breath of his nostrils," and scatter our hopes like chaff before the storm. It may be this will be *forbidden*; yet still we remember the Jewish princess who, being sent to supplicate for a nation's life, was thus reproved for hesitating even when *death* stared her in the way: "If thou altogether hold thy peace at this time, then shall deliverance arise from another place; but thou and thy father's house shall be destroyed. And who knoweth whether thou art come to the kingdom for such a cause as this?"

To woman it is given to administer the sweet charities of life, and to *sway the empire of affection*; and to her it may also be said, "Who knoweth whether thou art come to the kingdom for such a cause as this?" . . .

You who gather the youthful group around your fireside, and rejoice in their future hopes and joys, will you forget that the poor Indian loves his children too, and would as bitterly mourn over all their blasted hopes? And, while surrounded by such treasured blessings, ponder with dread and awe these fearful words of Him, who thus forbids the violence, and records the malediction of those, who either as individuals, or as nations, shall oppress the needy and helpless. . . .

This communication was written and sent abroad solely by the female hand. Let every woman who peruses it, exert that influence in society which falls within her lawful province, and endeavour by every suitable expedient to interest the feelings of her friends, relatives, and acquaintances, in behalf of this people, that are ready to perish. *A few weeks* must decide this interesting and important question, and after that time sympathy and regret will all be in vain.

DECEMBER 1, 1829.

Chapter 10

Moving West

Oregon Trail emigrants traveling along the Sweetwater River in Wyoming.

The westward movement of American settlement, which spanned a large part of the nineteenth century, to this day continues to stir the imagination. Covered wagons by the hundreds have crossed motion picture and television screens and the dust jackets of books. Frontier heroes the likes of Daniel Boone, Kit Carson, and Buffalo Bill have become widely recognized names. Even so, the popular media have not revealed much about the personal dimension of the families in those wagons.

Those who made the decision to take the journey did so for a variety of reasons: the promise of new and fertile land to farm, like that which initially attracted settlers to California and Oregon; the search for a place to practice their religion without interference, such as led the Mormons to Utah; the dream of wealth, like that which drew thousands to the gold fields of California and the silver-rich Comstock Lode of Nevada. Whatever their motives and wherever their destination, they all shared the wrenching experience of leaving home, friends, and families as well as the drama and difficulties of the long journey west. In his book *The Oregon Trail: An American Saga*, David Dary draws upon letters, diaries, and journals to relate in vivid detail the story of those who made the 2,000-mile journey west on the Oregon Trail. In the essay that follows from his book we are able to view the experiences of people who traveled by wagon train from Missouri to California in 1846. It is a tale of both tragedy and triumph. What evidence does the author provide that Americans of this era were a people on the move? Take note of the number of states represented by the travelers on the trail. The essay concludes with the story of the tragic Donner party. What is your response to the author's view of the historical significance of that episode?

The first document is an excerpt from Frederick Law Olmstead's *A Journey Through Texas* (1857), in which the author describes caravans of emigrants heading for Texas. (Olmstead, a famous landscape architect, wrote a number of works describing his extensive travels through the South.) Note the difference between the makeup of the travelers to Texas and those on the Oregon Trail in terms of where they originally came from as well as ethnic variety and status.

The visions that inspired thousands to head west were shaped in large measure by accounts in travel journals, newspapers, and letters from those already arrived in the new territories. An example of such writing is found in the second document, a letter from an Oregon settler to a friend in Illinois. Identify the elements in the letter that would most likely attract potential emigrants.

Those gold seekers who flocked to California by land and sea beginning in the winter of 1848–1849 generally came alone. They anticipated either sending for wives and children or returning home after first striking it rich. Consequently, as evidenced in the third document, the appearance of a woman in a mining camp could cause quite a stir. The final document provides a picture of Virginia City, Nevada, the West's premier mining town, home of the Comstock Lode. It was written by Samuel Clemens, who, before he took the pen name Mark Twain, worked as a reporter for the Virginia City *Enterprise*. Between 1860 and 1890, silver mining added $901,160,660 to the nation's wealth, but, as the article makes clear, for most miners it was a matter of boom followed by bust.

ESSAY

On the Oregon Trail
David Dary

We know something of the experiences of the emigrants following the Oregon Trail in 1846 because some of them later wrote their recollections. More than a dozen wrote letters along the way that have survived and

SOURCE: From *The Oregon Trail: An American Saga* by David Dary, pp. 154–167. Copyright © 2004 by David Dary. Used by permission of Alfred A. Knopf, a division of Random House, Inc.

contain bits and pieces of information. At least six emigrants kept diaries and a few kept journals. One of the better diaries was kept by thirty-year-old Nicholas Carriger, who had been born and raised on a farm in Carter County, Tennessee. He served in the First Tennessee Mounted Volunteers in 1835 and 1836 during the Seminole War and then returned home to work in milling and distilling, and later joined his father in manufacturing iron and hardware. In 1840, Carriger moved to Missouri, where in 1842 he married Mary Ann Wardlow, a native of Highland County, Ohio. He and his wife had two children but decided to leave Missouri for Mississippi, where Carriger purchased 160 acres of land, built a house, fenced his land, and began raising hemp, tobacco, and cereals. Soon he heard talk about the fertility of California. Displeased with his farm and without consulting anyone, Carriger sold his farm for only $500, less than what he had spent building his house. In April 1846, Carriger, his wife, and their two children left Mississippi and returned to Missouri, determined to go west.

Carriger and family joined a company of emigrants that began crossing the Missouri River near Oregon, Missouri, in early May. It took several days for all of the wagons to be ferried across. Beginning on May 11, Carriger's diary reads:

> 11th set out across the bluffs into the Prairie about 3 miles where we again encamped and lay by the 12th.
> 12th our members have increased to 31 Waggons and are still Waiting for more to Cross.
> 13th and 14th this day Joseph Blanton died and his family went bak [back] set out with fifty Waggons from our Camp on Honey Creek and Travelled about 12 miles to a Water of the big Ome Haw [Great Nemaha River].
> 15th Travelled about 5 miles and encamped on Water of the Big Ome haw [Great Nemaha River].

It is obvious that Carriger spent little time making his diary entries, but they reflect the flavor and tempo of overland travel. Carriger's company blazed a new trail along the ridge between the Big and Little Nemaha rivers to a junction with the road from Independence and St. Joseph, where they met another company of emigrants with nine wagons belonging to the Reed and Donner families from Illinois. They traveled together, arriving at the Big Blue River only to find the stream swollen. That was on May 26 and the emigrants went into camp to wait for the water level to recede. The women took advantage of the break and washed clothes while some of the men went fishing. One man caught a catfish three feet long. That evening the leaders of the company held a meeting with everyone to discuss the preparation of a system of law so that order could be preserved. As the sun set, a new moon appeared above the treetops, and soon nearly everyone but the guards went to sleep. During the night there was a rainstorm, but at dawn the sky was clear and blue. A few men went in search of bee trees and eventually returned with several baskets of honey. The emigrants were still waiting for the river to recede on the morning of May 29. The day was beautiful, but there was a feeling of gloom throughout the camp. Early that morning Mrs. Sarah Keyes, age seventy, the mother-in-law of J. H. Reed from Illinois, died. She had been in poor health. Her son had emigrated to Oregon two or three years earlier, and she expected to meet him at Fort Hall. At two o'clock that afternoon Rev. Josephus Adamson Cornwall, a forty-eight-year-old Presbyterian minister from Georgia, performed the funeral service, and Sarah Keyes's body was laid to rest in a grave that today is marked and not far from Marysville, Kansas.

Two days later the company was able to cross the Blue River and move northwest toward the Platte River. When they reached a Pawnee Indian village on the Platte, the emigrants gave the Indians presents and an ox, which the Indians killed, cooked, and ate. In his diary, Carriger mentions that a woman fell under the wheel of a wagon and was badly hurt. Two days later, June 6, Carriger noted: "One boy [seven-year-old Enoch Garrison] fell and two wheels run over one leg and the other foot and ancle near cutting the leg off breaking the bone." The company went into camp and some of the emigrants did what they could for the boy. Two days later the company resumed travel with the injured boy carried in his family's wagon.

Within a few days the boy's condition worsened and three men were sent to locate a doctor in one of the other emigrant companies. They traveled back along the trail and apparently stopped at each emigrant company and asked if they had a doctor. After traveling about thirty miles without finding one, they came upon a large company in camp, captained by William H. Russell. When asked if they had a doctor, someone pointed to Edwin Bryant, who with two friends was heading for California. Bryant, former editor of the *Louisville* (Kentucky) *Courier*, was well educated and had treated some emigrants in his company as a "good Samaritan," but he was not a doctor. He told this to the three men, but they insisted he accompany them back to where their company was camped. What happened next is told in Bryant's own words:

> After a most fatiguing and exhausting ride, we reached the encampment to which I had been called about five o'clock, p.m. . . . When I reached the tent of the unfortunate family to which the boy belonged, I found him stretched out upon a bench made of planks, ready for the operation which I would perform. I soon learned, from the mother, that the accident had occurred nine days previously. That a person professing to be a "doctor," had wrapped some linen loosely about the leg, and made a sort of trough or plank

box, in which it had been confined. In this condition the child had remained, without any dressing of his wounded limb, until last night, when he called to his mother, and told her that he *could feel worms crawling in his leg*! This, at first, she supposed to be absurd; but an examination of the wound for the first time was made, and it was discovered that gangrene had taken place, and the limb of the child was swarming with maggots! They then immediately dispatched their messengers for me. I made an examination of the fractured limb, and ascertained that what the mother had stated was correct. The limb had been badly fractured, and had never been bandaged; and from neglect gangrene had supervened, and the child's leg, from his foot to the knee, was in a state of putrefaction. He was so much enfeebled by his sufferings that death was stamped upon his countenance, and I was satisfied that he could not live twenty-four hours, much less survive an operation. I so informed the mother, stating to her that to amputate the limb would only hasten the boy's death, and add to his pains while living; declining at the same time, peremptorily, all participation in a proceeding so useless and barbarous under the circumstances. She implored me, with tears and moans, not thus to give up her child without an effort. I told her again, that all efforts to save him would be useless, and only add to the anguish of which he was now dying.

But this could not satisfy a mother's affection. She could not thus yield her offspring to the cold embrace of death, and a tomb in the wilderness. A Canadian Frenchman, who belonged to this emigrating party, was present, and stated that he had formerly been an assistant to a surgeon in some hospital, and had seen many operations of this nature performed, and that he would amputate the child's limb, if I declined doing it, and the mother desired it. I could not repress an involuntary shudder when I heard this proposition, the consent of the weeping woman, and saw the preparations made for the butchery of the little boy. The instruments to be used were a common butcher-knife, a carpenter's handsaw, and a shoemaker's awl to take up the arteries. The man commenced by gashing the flesh to the bone around the calf of the leg, which was in a state of putrescence. He then made an incision just below the knee and commenced sawing; but before he had completed that amputation of the bone, he concluded that the operation should be performed above the knee. During these demonstrations the boy never uttered a groan or a complaint, but I saw from the change in his countenance, that he was dying. The operator, without noticing this, proceeded to sever the leg above the knee. A cord was drawn round the limb, above the spot where it was intended to sever it, so tight that it cut through the skin into the flesh. The knife and saw were then applied and the limb amputated. A few drops of blood only oozed from the stump; the child was dead—his miseries were over. The scene of weeping and distress which succeeded this tragedy cannot be described. The mother was frantic, and the brothers and sisters of the deceased boy were infected by the intense grief of their parent.

Bryant was then asked to visit the father of the dead child, who was lying prostrate in his tent suffering from inflammatory rheumatism. The man had been devouring his medicines like food, believing large quantities would produce a fast cure. Bryant advised him to cut back on the amount of medicine. Bryant was then invited to attend a wedding in the camp. It was performed by Rev. Josephus Cornwall of Russell's company, in the tent of the bride's father. Bryant recalled: "The wedding-cake was not frosted with sugar, nor illustrated with matrimonial devices, after the manner of confectioners in the 'settlements,' but cake was handed round to the whole party present. There was no music or dancing on the occasion. The company separated soon after the ceremony was performed, leaving the happy pair to the enjoyment of their connubial felicities."

It was dark when Bryant left the wedding. In the distance he saw the torches and lanterns of a funeral procession. From the wedding Reverend Cornwall had gone to the wagon of the dead boy to conduct a funeral service. Now the boy's remains were being taken to the spot where a grave had been dug near the trail. While watching the funeral procession, a man approached Bryant and told him that a woman in a nearby emigrant company had just given birth to a baby and both mother and child were doing well. Bryant walked away and later wrote: "I could not but reflect upon the singular concurrence of the events of the day. A death and funeral, a wedding and a birth, had occurred in this wilderness, within a diameter of two miles, and within two hours' time; and tomorrow, the places where these events had taken place, would be deserted and unmarked, except by the grave of the unfortunate boy deceased!"

The company Edwin Bryant was going with was the largest one traveling westward in 1846. It was led by Colonel William Henry Russell, a hard-drinking Kentuckian born in 1802. He became a lawyer and represented Nicholas County in the Kentucky legislature in 1830 and married Zanette Freeland of Baltimore, Maryland. Russell, who was a large man, boastful and bombastic in speech but with many substantial and endearing qualities, came to the attention of Henry Clay. For a time, Russell served as Clay's secretary. Russell moved to Missouri in 1831, served in the Black Hawk War, and in 1841 was appointed U.S. marshal for the District of Missouri. At some point he was given the courtesy title of "Colonel." The story goes that Russell one evening supposedly mistook a chorus of "tu-whoo's" from some owls as a challenge of "Who are you?" He supposedly thundered back, "Colonel William H. Russell, of Kentucky—a bosom friend of Henry Clay." Thereafter he was known as "Owl" Russell. Like Bryant, Russell was heading for California and was elected captain of the company of about 250 people that included Bryant; former Missouri Governor Liburn Boggs and his wife Panthea Grant Boone, a granddaughter of Daniel Boone; and another Boone relative, probably Albert G. Boone, a nephew. Some days later the nine wagons carrying thirty-one members of the James F. Reed and George and Jacob Donner families and their hired hands joined the company.

Colonel Russell had managed to keep cohesion among the emigrants as their company moved across what is now Nebraska, but disputes over firewood and water, petty grievances, and complaints about almost anything the mind can conceive, made it difficult for Russell to keep everyone happy. Near Fort Laramie, Russell resigned as captain. He said he was suffering from an attack of "bilious fever," something many other captains had complained about. Liburn Boggs was elected captain as the emigrants rested in the vicinity of Fort Laramie. On June 29, a twenty-two-year-old man from Boston visited the post and saw Colonel Russell "drunk as a pigeon." The Bostonian also saw emigrants purchasing supplies. The young man from Boston was none other than Francis Parkman, who had also traveled the trail from Missouri.

Parkman, the son of a well-known Unitarian minister in Boston, finished his education at Harvard and headed west in 1845 to find Indians and adventure and to regain his health after his studies. . . . Returning east, Parkman wrote an account of his four-month journey, which was published serially in *Knickerbocker* magazine between February 1847 and February 1849, and then was published as a book in 1849 titled *The California and Oregon Trail*. It became a classic and was reprinted many times and through the twentieth century was a perennial favorite of high school students.

From the beginning Edwin Bryant was bound for California. So were a few others in the party, including William H. Russell, whose company Bryant joined at Independence. By the time Russell resigned as captain, Russell, Bryant, and a few other men in the company were dissatisfied with the slow pace of the travel. In the vicinity of Fort Laramie, Bryant traded his wagon and oxen for mules with packsaddles and associated trappings. Others in the company apparently did the same, and the following day, June 28, a small party of nine men including Bryant and Russell set out. Some days later, on July 17, Bryant and the others arrived at Fort Bridger. Several emigrant companies arrived at the trading post with whom they could travel north west to Fort Hall. The following day Bryant's party decided to go with Benoni M. Hudspeth, who earlier in the summer had returned from California with Lansford W. Hastings to explore a new desert route.

Bryant wrote:

> Mr. Hudspeth—who with a small party . . . will start in advance of the emigrant companies which intend traveling by this route, for the purpose of making further explorations—has volunteered to guide us as far as the Salt Plain, a day's journey west of the [Salt] Lake. Although such was my own determination, I wrote several letters to my friends among the emigrant parties in the rear, advising them *not* to take this route, but to keep on the old trail, via Fort Hall. Our situation was different from theirs. We were mounted on mules, had no families, and could afford to hazard experiments, and make explorations. They could not.

Bryant and the eight other men in his party along with Hudspeth and three men from the emigrant parties set out on July 20. That same day Lansford Hastings, who had been waiting for late California-bound companies to arrive, decided to move on and took those who had gotten there and left. Bryant's group, led by Hudspeth, made better time since they had no wagons, but soon unseasonably cold weather set in, and a few days later Bryant and the others could see forest fires in the mountains. In late July they reached the Great Salt Lake, where Hudspeth and his party left to explore the area. Bryant's party made preparations to cross the Salt Desert, to the west of the Great Salt Lake. Early in August they started and soon

> entered upon the hard smooth plain . . . composed of bluish clay, incrusted in wavy lines, with a white saline substance, the first representing the body of the water, and the last the crests and froth of the mimic waves and surges. Beyond this we crossed what appeared to have been beds of several small lakes, the waters of which have evaporated, thickly incrusted with salt, and separated from each other by small mound-shaped elevations of a white, sandy, or ashy earth, so imponderous that it has been driven by the action of the winds into these heaps, which are constantly changing their positions and their shapes. Our mules waded through these ashy undulations, sometimes sinking to their knees, at others to their bellies, creating dust that rose above and hung over us like a dense fog.

Bryant's party pushed on as rapidly as they could, but travel became more difficult. The mules became so fatigued that Bryant and the others dismounted and walked, leading their animals. It took them about two days to cross the Salt Plain, which Bryant estimated was seventy-five miles across. Later, it was measured as sixty-five miles and not the forty miles Hastings had estimated. As they followed Hastings's directions, they soon reached the Humboldt River, where the party met one or both Applegate brothers and some other men from Oregon working out a new route between the Humboldt and the headwaters of the Willamette River in Oregon Country.

From the Humboldt, Bryant and the others followed the Truckee River over the Sierra Nevada and reached Johnson's Ranch on August 31 and Sutter's Fort the following day.

Bryant later calculated the following table of distances from Independence to Sutter's Fort by the route he traveled:

From Independence, Mo., to Fort Laramie	672 miles
From Fort Laramie to "Pacific Springs," (South Pass,)	311 "
From the "South Pass," (Pacific Springs,) to Fort Bridger	133 "
From Fort Bridger to Salt Lake,	106 "
From Salt Lake to Mary's river [Humboldt River],	315 "
Down Mary's river to the "Sink,"	274 "
From the "Sink" to Truckee Lake, [Donner Lake]	134 "
From Truckee Lake to Johnson's,	111 "
From Johnson's to Sutter's Fort,	35 "
Total distance from Independence, Mo., to Sutter's Fort in California,	2091 "
The distance from Sutter's Fort by land, to the town of San Francisco, (via the Pueblo of San Jose,) near the mouth of the Bay of S. F., and five miles from the Pacific Ocean, is	200 "
Total	2291 miles

Before leaving Fort Bridger, Bryant had sent letters to emigrant friends advising them not to follow the same route for the reasons already stated, but about eighty wagons of emigrants set out from Fort Bridger to follow Lansford Hastings's route. Before arriving at the fort, they and other emigrants met Wales B. Bonney, who was carrying an open letter from Hastings, whose *Emigrants' Guide to Oregon and California* was published in 1845. The *Guide* had inspired many of the emigrants to go west. Hastings's letter advised emigrants bound for California that he would wait for them at Fort Bridger to lead them over a newly explored cutoff route south of the Great Salt Lake. Hastings claimed the new route would reduce the distance by as much as three hundred miles, and cut the time it would take to reach California.

Exactly how many emigrants traveled by way of Fort Bridger is not known. Many who did continued on to Fort Hall and Oregon. But there were those who followed Lansford Hastings over his cutoff. By the time the Donner company arrived at Fort Bridger, Hastings had already left, leading those emigrants who had gotten there earlier. The eighty-seven emigrants now in the Donner company debated whether to follow the Hastings cutoff. After discussion they decided they would and apparently were given some directions by Jim Bridger or Louis Vasquez. The Donner company set out southwest, the last emigrants that summer to leave Fort Bridger for California. For several days they traveled without much difficulty. When they reached the Weber River near the head of Weber Canyon, they found a letter from Hastings stuck in the split of a stick addressed to any emigrants who might be following. Hastings wrote that the road down Weber Canyon was in terrible condition, and he indicated it was doubtful if wagons would be able to reach the plain below. Hastings urged all emigrants to avoid the canyon road, and to go over the mountains. In his letter he faintly outlined the directions emigrants should follow. . . .

It had taken the Donner company a month, instead of a week, to cover the distance from Fort Bridger to the Great Salt Lake. The emigrants and their oxen were fatigued and camped in a valley called Twenty Wells, where they found wells of pure and cold water. There they prepared for their journey across the Salt Plain. Once the party was ready, they started in the evening, traveled all night, all the next day, and the next night, suffering from piercing cold at night and thirst and heat during the day. Some families lost their oxen and had to leave their wagons. Some of their possessions were loaded on the remaining wagons and the rest were buried near their abandoned transport. When the company neared the end of the Salt Plain desert, the emigrants took an inventory of their provisions and realized they were not sufficient to reach California. That night there was a storm, and by morning the hilltops were covered with snow. Two members of the party, C. T. Stanton and William McCutchen, offered to go ahead to Sutter's Fort and get provisions. The two men left, and the rest of the party soon resumed its journey. Days later it reached Gravelly Ford on the Humboldt River and afterward the Truckee River. The spirits of the emigrants were raised when C. T. Stanton, returning with two Indian vaqueros sent to help by Captain Sutter, met the emigrants along the Truckee River. Stanton brought seven mules loaded with provisions. McCutchen had taken ill and remained at Sutter's Fort.

As the Donner company climbed the Sierra Nevada in late October, snow began falling. Winter was beginning a month early. Virginia Reed* recalled:

> When it was seen that the wagons could not be dragged through the snow, their goods and provisions were packed on oxen and another start was made, men and women walking in the snow up to their waists, carrying their children in their arms and trying to drive their cattle. The Indians said they could find no road, so a halt was called, and Stanton went ahead with the guides, and came back and reported that we could get across if we kept right on, but that it would be impossible if snow fell. He was in favor of a forced march until the other side of the summit should be reached, but some of our party were so tired and exhausted with the day's labor that they

*Virginia Reed was twelve years old in 1846. (Eds.)

declared they could not take another step; so the few who knew the danger that the night might bring yielded to the many, and we camped within three miles of the summit. That night came the dreaded snow. Around the campfires under the trees great feathery flakes came whirling down. The air was so full of them that one could see objects only a few feet away. . . . We children slept soundly on our cold bed of snow with a soft white mantle falling over us so thickly that every few moments my mother would have to shake the shawl—our only covering—to keep us from being buried alive. In the morning the snow lay deep on mountain and valley. With heavy hearts we turned back to a cabin that had been built by the Murphy-Schallenberger party two years before.

Some emigrants constructed tents out of wagon canvas and others built cabins. Many books have since been written about what happened to the stranded emigrants during the weeks that followed. There was cold, starvation, and death, and some of those who survived did so by living off the flesh of those who died. On February 19, 1847, the first of several rescue parties reached the area where the emigrants were located and began to take survivors to Johnson's Ranch. William O. Fallon, an old mountain man and member of the fourth relief party, kept a journal. He described what he found:

> Left Johnson's on the evening of April 13th, and arrived at the lower end of the Bear Valley on the 15th. Hung our saddles upon the trees, and sent the horses back, to be returned again in ten days, to bring us in again. Started on foot, with provisions for ten days, and traveled to the head of the valley and camped for the night, snow from 2 to 3 feet deep.
>
> 15th. Started early in the morning and traveled 23 miles, snow 10 feet deep.
>
> April, 17th. Reached the Cabins between 12 and 1 o'clock. Expected to find some of the sufferers alive, Mrs. Donner and Kiesburg in particular. Entered the cabins and a horrible scene presented itself,—human bodies terribly mutilated, legs, arms, and skulls scattered in every direction. One body, supposed to be that of Mrs. Eddy, lay near the entrance, the limbs severed off and a frightful gash in the skull. The flesh from the bones was nearly consumed and a painful stillness pervaded the place. The supposition was that all were dead, when a sudden shout revived our hopes, and we flew in the direction of the sound, three Indians [who] were hitherto concealed, started from the ground and fled at our approach, leaving behind their bows and arrows. We delayed two hours in searching the cabins, during which we were obliged to witness sights from which we would have fain turned away, and which are too dreadful to put on record.—We next started for "Donner's camp"

8 miles distant over the mountains. After traveling about half way, we came upon a track in the snow, which excited our suspicion, and we determined to pursue it. It brought us to the camp of Jacob Donner, where it had evidently been left that morning. There we found property of every description, books, calicoes, tea, coffee, shoes, percussion caps, household and kitchen furniture scattered in every direction, and mostly in the water. At the mouth of the tent stood a large iron kettle; filled with human flesh cut up, it was the body of Geo. Donner, the head had been split open and the brains extracted therefrom, and to the appearance, he had not been long dead, not over three or four days at the most. Near by the kettle stood a chair, and thereupon three legs of a bullock that had been shot down in the early part of the winter, and snowed under before it could be dressed. The meat was found sound and good, and with the exception of a small piece out of the shoulder, wholly un-touched. We gathered up some property and camped for the night.

April, 18. Commenced gathering the most valuable property, suitable for our packs, the greater portion requiring to be dried. We then made them up and camped for the night.

April 19. This morning, [William] Foster, [John] Rhodes, and J. Foster [Joseph Sels] started with small packs for the first cabins intending from thence to follow the trail of the person that had left the morning previous. The other three remained behind to cache and secure the goods necessarily left there. Knowing the Donners had a considerable sum of money, we search diligently but were unsuccessful. The party for the cabins were unable to keep the trail of the mysterious personage owing to the rapid melting of the snow, they therefore went direct for the cabins, and upon entering discovered Kiesburg lying down amidst the human bones and beside him a large pan full of fresh liver and lights. They asked him what had become of his companions, whether they were alive, and what had become of Mrs. Donner. He answered them by stating they were all dead; Mrs. Donner, he said, had in attempting to cross from one cabin to another, missing the trail, and slept out one night; that she came to his camp the next night very much fatigued, he made her a cup of coffee, placed her in bed and rolled her well in the blankets, but the next morning found her dead; he eat her body and found her flesh the best he had ever tasted! He further stated that he obtained from her body at least four pounds of fat! No traces of her person could be found, nor the body of Mrs. Murphy either.—

Of eighty-nine emigrants who had set out to follow the Hastings Cutoff from Fort Bridger, only forty-five survived. . . .

While the experience of the Donner party is only one page in the history of the Oregon Trail, the horrors of the cannibalism that occurred often make it seem more significant than it really was in the trail's broader history. Of far more importance is the fact that about 1,200 emigrants successfully reached Oregon and more than 1,400 reached California that year. As the late Bernard De Voto wrote in his classic book *The Year of Decision, 1846*, that year "best dramatizes personal experience as national experience. Most of the characters are ordinary people, unremarkable commoners of the young democracy."

DOCUMENTS

Emigrants to Texas, c. 1857

We overtook, several times in the course of each day, the slow emigrant trains, for which this road, though less frequented than years ago, is still a chief thoroughfare. Inexorable destiny it seems that drags or drives on, always Westward, these toil-worn people. Several families were frequently moving together, coming from the same district, or chance met and joined, for company, on the long road from Alabama, Georgia, or the Carolinas. Before you come upon them you hear, ringing through the woods, the fierce cries and blows with which they urge on their jaded cattle. Then the stragglers appear, lean dogs or fainting negroes, ragged and spiritless. An old granny, holding on, by the hand, a weak boy—too old to ride and too young to keep up. An old man, heavily loaded, with a rifle. Then the white covers of the wagons, jerking up and down as they mount over a root or plunge into a rut, disappearing, one after another, where the road descends. Then the active and cheery prime negroes, not yet exhausted, with a joke and a suggestion about tobacco. Then the black pickininnies, staring, in a confused heap, out at the back of the wagon, more and more of their eyes to be made out among the table legs and bedding as you get near; behind them, further in, the old people and young mothers, whose turn it is to ride. As you get by, the white mother and babies, and the tall, frequently ill-humored master, on horseback, or walking with his gun, urging up the black driver and his oxen. As a scout ahead is a brother, or an intelligent slave, with the best gun, on the look-out for a deer or a turkey. We passed in the day perhaps one hundred persons attached to these trains, probably an unusual number; but the immigration this year had been retarded and condensed by the fear of yellow fever, the last case of which, at Natchitoches, had indeed begun only the night before our arrival. Our chances of danger

SOURCE: Frederick Law Olmsted, *A Journey Through Texas* (New York: Dix, Edwards & Co., 1857), 55–57.

were considered small, however, as the hard frosts had already come. One of these trains was made up of three large wagons, loaded with furniture, babies, and invalids, two or three light wagons, and a gang of twenty able field hands. They travel ten or fifteen miles a day, stopping wherever night overtakes them. The masters are plainly dressed, often in home-spun, keeping their eyes about them, noticing the soil, sometimes making a remark on the crops by the roadside; but, generally, dogged, surly, and silent. The women are silent, too, frequently walking, to relieve the teams, and weary, haggard, mud-bedraggled, forlorn, and disconsolate, yet hopeful and careful. The negroes, mud-incrusted, wrapped in old blankets or gunny-bags, suffering from cold, plod on, aimless, hopeless, thoughtless, more indifferent than the oxen to all about them.

A Letter from Oregon Territory, 1847

APRIL 6, 1847

We arrived safe in Oregon City on the 12th of September last. We reached Fort Laramie in 42 days from Independence; Fort Hall in 33 days more; the Dalles in 37 days more; and Oregon City in 16 days more—making in all 128 days. Our journey was two weeks longer than necessary had we lost no time. We met with no serious obstructions on our journey. We had to raise the front of our wagon beds two or three inches in crossing the Larimie Fork to keep the water out; sometimes we had long drives to find a good place for camping, with water and grass. . . . No single man should come to this country. One third of the men in Oregon at this time are without wives. Nothing but men of families are wanted here to till the soil, to make this one of the greatest countries in the world. This country does not get so muddy as Illinois. There is no dust in summer here. The good land in this country is more extensive than I expected to find it. The hills are not so high as represented. From the Cascade mountains to the Pacific, the whole country can be cultivated. The natural soil of the country, especially in the bottoms, is a black loam, mixed with gravel and clay. We have good timber; but there appears to be a scarcity of good building rock. The small streams furnish us with trout the year round.

My wife to the old lady—Greeting; says she was never more satisfied with a move in her life before; that she is fast recovering her health; and she hopes you will come to Oregon, where you can enjoy what little time you have remaining in health.

The roads to Oregon are not as bad as represented. Hastings in his history speaks of the Falls of Columbia being 50 feet and roaring loud,

SOURCE: Letter from Richard R. Howard, dated April 6, 1847, and published in the [Springfield] *Illinois Journal*, November 11, 1847.

making the earth tremble, & c. The falls are about like that of a mill-dam. Everything in this country now is high, except molasses, sugar and salt; but when we raise our wheat crop to trade on, we will make them pay for their high charges. I think no place where a living is to be made out of the earth can be preferable to Oregon for that purpose—and let people say what they may—all agree that it is healthy. It is certainly the healthiest country in the world, disease is scarcely known here, except among the late emigrants, ninety-nine out of a hundred of them get well the first season. I have heard of only two deaths since I have been in Oregon; one of them was a man who came here diseased and in one year died; the other was a woman who it is said was near dead ten years before she came here.

RICHARD.R.HOWARD

A Most Welcome Guest, c. 1849

We knew that delays were dangerous, so shouldering our picks and shovels, pistols and rifles, and taking a bottle or two of *guardiente*, we marched to the new tent, in file, our leader whistling. "Come haste to the wedding," and gave three cheers and a discharge of firearms. The alarmed occupants rushed to the door to see what was up. Our captain mounted a rock, and addressed the amazed husband in something, like this strain:

"Stranger; we have been shut up here so long that we don't know what is going on in the world, and we have already forgotten what it is made of. We have understood that our mothers were women, but it is so long since we have seen them, that we have forgotten how woman looks, and being told that you have caught one, we are prospecting to get a glimpse." The man, a sensible fellow, by the way, entering into the humor of the joke, produced the *animal*, when the nine cheers, a drink all around, and a few good natured jokes, we quietly dispersed.

Flush Times* in Nevada, c. 1862

Six months after my entry into journalism that grand "flush times" of Silverland began, and they continued with unabated splendor for three years. All difficulty about filling up the "local department" ceased, and the only trouble

source: Alonzo Delano, *Pen Knife Sketches, or Chips of the Old Block: a Series of Original Illustrated Letters, Written By One of the California's Pioneer Miners* (San Francisco: Grabhorn Press, 1934; originally published in 1853).

source: Samuel L. Clemens, *Roughing It* (New York: Harper and Brothers, 1890), 2:11–13, 16–19.

*The term *flush times* refers to the silver and gold boom in Nevada in the 1860s. (Eds.)

now was how to make the lengthened columns hold the world of incidents and happening that came to our literary net every day. Virginia had grown to be the "livest" town, for its age and population, that America had ever produced. The sidewalks swarmed with people—to such an extent, indeed, that it was generally no easy matter to stem the human tide. The streets themselves were just as crowded with quartz-wagons, freight-teams, and other vehicles. The procession was endless. So great was the pack, that buggies frequently had to wait half an hour for an opportunity to cross the principal street. Joy sat on every countenance, and there was a glad, almost fierce, intensity in every eye, that told of the money-getting schemes that held sway in every heart. Money was as plenty as dust; every individual considered himself wealthy, and a melancholy countenance was nowhere to be seen. There were military companies, fire companies, brass bands, banks, hotels, theaters, "hurdy-gurdy houses,"** wide-open gambling-palaces, political pow-wows, civic processions, street-fights, murders, inquests, riots, a whiskeymill every fifteen steps, a Board of Aldermen, a Mayor, a City Surveyor, a City Engineer, a Chief of the Fire Department, with First, Second, and Third Assistants, a Chief of Police, City Marshal, and a large police force, two Boards of Mining Brokers, a dozen breweries, and a half dozen jails and station-houses in full operation, and some talk of building a church. The "flush times" were in magnificent flower! Large fireproof brick buildings were going up in the principal streets, and the wooden suburbs were spreading out in all directions. Town lots soared up to prices that were amazing.

The great "Comstock lode" stretched its opulent length straight through the town from north to south, and every mine on it was in diligent process of development. One of these mines alone employed six hundred and seventy-five men, and in the matter of elections the adage was, "as the 'Gould & Curry' [mine] goes, so goes the city." Laboring-men's wages were four and six dollars a day, and they worked in three "shifts" or gangs, and the blasting and picking and shoveling went on without ceasing, night and day.

The "city" of Virginia roosted royally midway up the steep side of Mount Davidson, seven thousand two hundred feet above the level of the sea, and in the clear Nevada atmosphere was visible from a distance of fifty miles! It claimed a population of fifteen thousand to eighteen thousand, and all day long half of this little army swarmed the streets like bees and the other half swarmed the drifts and tunnels of the "Comstock," hundreds of feet down in the earth directly under those same streets. . . .

My salary was increased to forty dollars a week. But I seldom drew it. I had plenty of other resources, and what were two broad twenty-dollar gold pieces to a man who had his pockets full of such and a cumbersome

---

***Hurdy-gurdy houses* is a slang term for dance halls. (Eds.)

abundance of bright half-dollars besides? (Paper money has never come into use on the Pacific coast.) Reporting was lucrative, and every man in the town was lavish with his money and his "feet."* The city and all the great mountainside were riddled with mining-shafts. There were more mines than miners. True, not ten of these mines were yielding rock worth hauling to a mill, but everybody said, "Wait till the shaft gets down where the ledge comes in solid, and then you will see!" So nobody was discouraged. These were nearly all "wildcat" mines, and wholly worthless, but nobody believed it then. The "Ophir," the "Gould Curry," the "Mexican," and other great mines on the Comstock lode in Virginia and Gold Hill were turning out huge piles of rich rock every day, and every man believed that his little wildcat claim was as good as any on the "main lead" and would infallibly be worth a thousand dollars a foot when he "got down where it came in solid." Poor fellow! he was blessedly blind to the fact that he would never see that day. So the thousand wildcat shafts burrowed deeper and deeper into the earth day by day, and all men were beside themselves with hope and happiness. How they labored, prophesied, exulted! Surely nothing like it was ever seen before since the world began. Every one of these wildcat mines—not mines, but holes in the ground over imaginary mines—was incorporated and had handsome engraved "stock" and the stock was salable, too. It was bought and sold with a feverish avidity on the boards every day. You could go up on the mountainside, scratch around and find a ledge (there was no lack of them), put up a "notice" with a grandiloquent name on it, start a shaft, get your stock printed, and with nothing whatever to prove that your mine was worth a straw, you could put your stock on the market and sell out for hundreds and even thousands of dollars. To make money, and make it fast, was as easy as it was to eat your dinner. Every man owned "feet" in fifty different wildcat mines and considered his fortune made. Think of a city with not one solitary poor man in it! One would suppose that when month after month went by and still not a wildcat mine (by wildcat I mean, in general terms, *any* claim not located on the mother vein, *i.e.*, the "Comstock") yielded a ton of rock worth crushing, the people would begin to wonder if they were not putting too much faith in their prospective riches; but there was not a thought of such a thing. They burrowed away, bought and sold, and were happy.

New claims were taken daily, and it was the friendly custom to run straight to the newspaper offices, give the reporter forty or fifty "feet" and get him to go and examine the mine and publish a notice of it. They did not care a fig what you said about the property so [long as] you said something. Consequently we generally said a word or two to the effect that the

---

*Shares of stock in wildcat mines were measured in feet. (Eds.)

"indications" were good, or that the ledge was "six feet wide," or that the rock "resembled the Comstock" (and so it did—but as a general thing the resemblance was not startling enough to knock you down!) . . .

There was *nothing* in the shape of a mining claim that was not salable. We received presents of "feet" every day. If we needed a hundred dollars or so, we sold some; if not we hoarded it away, satisfied that it would ultimately be worth a thousand dollars a foot. I had a trunk about half full of "stock." When a claim made a stir in the market and went up to a high figure, I searched through my pile to see if I had any of its stock—and generally found it.

Chapter 11

Paths to Salvation: Revivalism and Communitarianism

A Methodist camp meeting during the Second Great Awakening.

During the first decades of the nineteenth century, a wave of evangelical revivalism began in upstate New York, western New England, and frontier Kentucky and Tennessee. Ultimately, this Second Great Awakening swept the nation. Like its mid-eighteenth-century predecessor, the revival was initiated by clergymen concerned with what they perceived to be a climate of moral laxity and religious decline. America, as they viewed it, had paid a price for its rapid growth and expansion: rootlessness, Godlessness, and drunkenness, which too often afflicted both frontier settlements and urban centers. They believed that the intellectualism and mechanistic view of the universe spawned by the Enlightenment philosophy of the Revolutionary era had contributed to these conditions. What the country needed was a return to spiritual values, to faith in God's guiding hand.

In many respects similar in style to the first Great Awakening, the nineteenth-century revival was even less constrained by theological orthodoxy. Its clergy placed less emphasis on threats of damnation for sin, and more on preaching a message of God's love, which, if freely accepted, offered both a better life on earth and eternal salvation. Appealing to the emotions of their listeners, using words all could understand, revivalist preachers found enthusiastic audiences.

In this chapter's essay, from Sean Wilentz's *The Rise of American Democracy: Jefferson to Lincoln,* the beginning and development of what came to be known as the Second Great Awakening are described in vivid detail. What evidence does Wilentz provide to support his statement that the Second Great Awakening was a "diverse movement"? Compare the initial and later attitudes of the southern revivalists toward slavery and the slaveholders. How did the moral focus of the northern version of the Great Awakening differ from that of the South?

One of the most successful of the northern preachers was Charles Grandison Finney. His employment of highly emotional sermons was, as he reveals in the first document, the result of thoughtful planning. Indeed, as you read, note Finney's keen insight into patterns of human behavior decades before the rise of modern psychological study.

The revivalist preachers of the rural South often employed highly theatrical methods to whip their audience into a religious frenzy. In the second document Anne Royall, a noted travel writer, describes a revival meeting she attended in the Tennessee backcountry. Compare Royall's response to what she witnessed to that of the majority of the audience. What might account for the difference? Why do you think women were far more accepting than men of the preacher's appeals?

Some Americans of this period believed that they could create the ideal community only by removing themselves from society and building anew. Prominent among several religious communitarian sects were the Shakers. By 1830, they had gathered themselves into more than twenty communities throughout the East and Midwest to await what they believed would be Christ's imminent return and rule on earth. In anticipation of this event, they forsook private ownership of property and practiced celibacy. The third document provides a view of this sect by a Lowell mill girl who paid two visits to a New York Shaker community. Does your previous reading about Lowell suggest why this young woman initially found Shaker village life so appealing?

From the 1820s through the 1840s, a number of predominantly secular utopian experiments in communal living were initiated, with the goal of serving as models of nobler, purer ways of life. One of the most famous was the Brook Farm community established in West Roxbury, Massachusetts, under the leadership of George Ripley, a New England Transcendentalist. Its participants included some of the leading New England intellectuals, among them Nathaniel Hawthorne, Margaret Fuller, and Charles A. Dana. The final document is from a letter that Hawthorne wrote to his sister Louisa a few weeks after he arrived at Brook Farm in April 1841. How do you account for his enthusiasm for the agrarian, communitarian life? Despite his initial sentiments, six months later Hawthorne left the community after deciding that he could not be both farmer and writer. Other members made similar decisions. In 1847, after six years of existence, the Brook Farm experiment ended. The farm's short life was a fate shared by most other utopian communities.

ESSAY

The Second Great Awakening

Sean Wilentz

In 1771, when the Regulator country democrats of North Carolina squared off against the royal governor William Tryon, a backwoods Prebysterian minister, David Caldwell, tried unsuccessfully to mediate between his plebeian flock and the imperial British government. Caldwell became an active patriot in 1776 and, after independence, a leading participant in North Carolina politics. He left legacies in both politics and religious life. His grandson, John Caldwell Calhoun, would become one of the leading American nationalists—and then the leading southern sectionalist—of his day. And at the turn of the nineteenth century, several young ministers whom Caldwell had helped train headed west to sanctify the newly settled farmers and planters of Kentucky.

Among the most successful of Caldwell's students was a tall, awkward Pennsylvania-born minister of Scots-Irish extraction, James McGready. What McGready lacked in elegance he made up for with eloquence and homiletic fervor. In 1797 (and thereafter for three years running) his sermonizing sparked a remarkable excitement and religious revival in the still-raw settlements of Logan County, in southwestern Kentucky near the Tennessee border. Then, in August 1801, in a clutch of cabins called Cane Ridge in Bourbon County near Lexington, another of David Caldwell's pupils, Barton Stone, hosted an ecumenical three-day communion service that turned into a week-long explosion of ecstatic devotion, involving more than twenty preachers (Presbyterian and Methodist, white and black) and upwards of twenty thousand worshippers. The roar of raucous piety at Cane Ridge sounded like Niagara: "Sinners dropping down on every hand," one participating minister wrote, "shrieking, groaning, crying for mercy, convoluted; professors [of religion] praying, agonizing, fainting, falling down in distress, for sinners, or in raptures of joy!"

One year after Cane Ridge, hundreds of miles away in New Haven, Connecticut, a more sedate but still remarkable revival of religion gripped the undergraduates of Yale College. In 1795, Timothy Dwight, grandson of the great New England evangelist Jonathan Edwards, had ascended to the presidency of Yale in place of Thomas Jefferson's friend Ezra Stiles, hoping to rid the place of its reputation for irreligion and pro-French radical politics. Dwight's stern hand did not work immediate wonders—in 1800, there was only one church member in the college's graduating class—but in 1802, a revival hit the campus. "Wheresoever students were found," remarked one participant, the future minister Noah Porter "in their rooms, in the chapel, in the hall, in the college-yard, in their walks about the city—the reigning impression was, 'surely God is in this place!' The salvation of the soul was the greatest subject of conversation, of absorbing interest."

Fifteen more revivals would break out at Yale over the next forty years. Under Dwight's spur, Yale became the intellectual seedbed of the so-called New Haven Theology, formulated by Dwight's student, professor of theology Nathaniel W. Taylor, which recast and energized received Calvinist doctrine. And although "Pope" Dwight could not save the Connecticut Standing Order* (which finally collapsed one year after his death in 1817), his students, above all the great organizing cleric Lyman Beecher, spread revised versions of the New Haven revival out into the rest of New England, and then into upstate New York, Ohio, and points west—wherever New Englanders and their children settled in large numbers.

The concurrent events at Cane Ridge and Yale were in no way the result of a coordinated effort. Their differences—in denominational origins, liturgy, and social setting—outweighed their similarities. Likewise, the so-called Second Great Awakening—of which these revivals were harbingers, and which would last into the 1840s—was a diverse movement, generated by impulses too unruly and doctrines too contradictory to be contained by any one organization. It was a movement that, at its outermost edges, saw farmers and factory workers talk directly with Christ Jesus, angels appear in remote villages bearing wholly new dispensations and commandments from the Lord, and women of all ages and backgrounds commune with the spirits of the dead. Closer to its core, the Awakening saw rival denominations (especially Methodists and Baptists) denounce each others' beliefs and practices nearly as much as they denounced sin and Satan.

A few recurring and overriding themes are detectable through the furor. First, the sheer scale of religious conversions was astounding, in every part of the nation. Although the figures are sketchy, it appears that as few as one in ten Americans were active church members in the unsettled aftermath of the American Revolution. The evangelizing that ensued proceeded, at first, in fits and starts, but gathered tremendous momentum after 1825. By the 1840s, the preponderance of Americans—as many as eight in ten—were churched, chiefly as evangelizing Methodists or Baptists (in the South) or as so-called New School revivalist Presbyterians or Congregationalists (in the North). What was, in 1787, a nation of nominal Christians—its public culture shaped more by Enlightenment rationalism than Protestant piety—had turned, by the mid-1840s, into the most devoted evangelical Protestant nation on earth.

Second, although it is better understood as a movement of the heart and the spirit than of the mind, the Awakening asserted a hopeful, crisis-driven,

---

*Standing Order refers to the clergy of the Congregationalist Church, who had dominated the religious and political life of Connecticut since the seventeenth century and who were closely allied with the state's Federalist elite. (Eds.)

post-Calvinist theology. The awakeners' devotions contrasted sharply both with the hyper-Calvinism of the Edwardseans* and the Old School Presbyterians (with their strict belief in predestination and God's inscrutable will) and with the laxity about salvation promoted by well-heeled Unitarians and more plebeian Universalists. The degree of departure from Calvinist orthodoxy varied: whereas the Methodists and New School churches largely abandoned the central Calvinist doctrines of election and predestination, the Baptists, at least formally, retained them. (Some Baptists, objecting to what they perceived as even the slightest backsliding, formed their own more fiercely traditional Calvinist connections.) But in all of the largest denominations, there was a fresh emphasis placed on individual rejection of personal sin and on the struggle to attain God's merciful grace, through His Son, the Redeemer Jesus Christ—an intense process that culminated in a wrenching moment of spiritual rebirth.

Emotional display reached a deafening intensity in the camp-meeting style that prevailed in the South. Drawing heavily on the "new measures" of the Wesleyan Methodists, the camp-meeting phenomenon shattered the unity of the largely Presbyterian clergy of the southern and southwestern backcountry, prompting some church leaders to back off in disapproval and others (including the Cane Ridge preacher, Barton Stone) to reject their own Calvinist orthodoxy. The communal camp-meeting uproars (commonly attended, on their outskirts, by scoffers, drinkers, and prostitutes, drawn by the mere presence of a throng) in turn solidified the believers' faith that they truly had gained redemption and a holy discipline that set them apart from the rest of the world (not least from the sinners at the edges of the crowd). For the preachers, meanwhile, the camp meetings' aftermath helped institutionalize the revival, binding the fresh harvests of souls into local congregations that could be linked to other congregations, within regular, regionally organized denominations.

Socially and spiritually, the southern revivals paradoxically challenged and confirmed existing structures of authority. In contrast to the Episcopal and old-line Presbyterian connections, and the smaller but influential deistic** currents among the enlightened gentry, the revivals bred a devotional upsurge from the lower and middle strata of southern life that can only be described as democratic. In place of refined, highly trained ministers, young Methodist circuit riders and unschooled Baptist farmer-preachers became cynosures of religious life, preaching a gospel of holiness open to the most degraded and forlorn of God's children. Simplicity and directness in all things were signs of grace, in contrast to ornament and artifice. Among the truest believers, restraint in all but love of Christ was the only way to escape hellfire. "Therefore avoid the allurements of Voluptuousness," one self-reproving Methodist

*Refers to those who adhered to the theology as preached by Jonathan Edwards. (Eds.)
**Deism is the belief that God created a world subject to natural laws, which could be revealed not through prayer or God-sent miracles, but through man's employment of reason. (Eds.)

preacher wrote in his diary, "and fly every temptation that leads to her banquet as you would the devil himself."

Most unsettling of all, in the southern revival's opening stages, was the announced indifference of some evangelicals to race and their outright hostility to slavery. Methodist circuit riders were particularly aggressive in seeking out black converts, slave and free. In the 1780s, conferences of Methodists and Baptists condemned slaveholding as, in the words of one Methodist assembly, "contrary to the laws of God, man, and nature, and hurtful to society, contrary to the dictates of conscience and pure religion." (In 1784, the Methodists actually moved to excommunicate slaveholders, although they quickly retreated into less coercive methods of moral suasion.) At least one black minister preached to a separate throng of blacks at the Cane Ridge meeting in 1801. In the first wave of conversions, African Americans accounted for as much as one-third to one-quarter of the membership in individual evangelical churches. And into the 1820s, evangelical egalitarianism among whites helped make the mountainous areas of the upper southern states, notably Tennessee, home to the largest number of antislavery societies in the nation.

By 1830, however, the more egalitarian and antislavery implications of the southern revivals had adapted to the resurgent slaveholders' regime. Middling evangelical farmers who cashed in on the cotton boom and became small slaveholders had little use for imprecations against African bondage. Established planters mostly ignored antislavery preaching with a cold contempt—although, from time to time, they took firmer action, as in Charleston where, in 1800, authorities publicly burned Methodist antislavery pamphlets. In 1816, the Methodists formally gave up on trying to end slaveholding, while still pronouncing it "contrary to the principles of moral justice." Over the next thirty years, southern evangelicalism, among whites, transformed itself into a doctrine of Christian mastery, no longer troubled by human bondage but providing slaveholders with a set of religious and moral imperatives to treat the slaves, as they would all subordinates, on the highest moral level, in accord with scriptural injunctions. While instilling order and benevolence, the churches also reinforced the slaveholders' claims to supremacy. "We who own slaves," the well-known South Carolina Baptist clergyman James C. Furman wrote to a master suspected of wrongdoing, "honor God's law in the exercise of our authority."

More broadly, the southern evangelicals' spiritual egalitarianism centered increasingly on inculcating personal holiness to the exclusion of all else—an ethos of individual sanctification that precluded wider secular campaigns or benevolent reform. Older social distinctions between elite nonevangelicals and plebeian evangelicals blurred, as successful Methodists and Baptists began striving for their own sort of refinement, signaled by the building of several denominational academies and colleges, like the Virginia Baptist Education Society of Richmond, all across the region. Simultaneously, the color line grew darker, creating a southern revivalist piety that, among whites, fully accommodated itself to the slaveholders' regime. Slaveholders did spearhead the spread of Christian devotion in rural areas, especially in the 1830s and 1840s, but did so with an eye to provide their property with the kind of moral uplift that would make them better slaves (and make the masters better Christian stewards). Black evangelical churches, with their own preachers and proselytizers, held their own services, most conspicuously in seaboard cities like Charleston with large free black populations. But these segregated houses of worship came under close scrutiny from officials as possible breeding grounds of sedition—scrutiny that intensified following Charleston's allegedly church-based Denmark Vesey affair in 1822. Among the slaves as well as free blacks, despite their masters' intentions and surveillance, Christianity became what they made it, a source of communal solidarity, pride, and endurance, with a millennial edge of impending liberation. But among whites, slaveholder and nonslaveholders, the Second Great Awakening become a pillar of the reborn slaveholding order.

The northern awakening involved dramatic adaptations by the declining patrician Yankee establishment. Pressured on one side by the passing popularity of anticlerical "Jacobin" skeptics and, even more, by dissenting evangelicals and liberalizing Unitarians who opposed their political privileges, the old-line Calvinist clergy had embraced Federalism with unsurpassed fervor. The election of the deist and secularist Jefferson in 1801 and the rise of a viable northern Republican party further sapped the clerics' dominance. But Timothy Dwight's reclamation of Yale from the infidels energized the orthodox by borrowing the evangelicals' voluntarist organizing methods—above all, the formation of the Moral Society to effect and enforce what one of his acolytes called a "reformation" among students and faculty. When Dwight's student Nathaniel Taylor loosened Calvinist doctrine and argued that salvation was a matter of individual regeneration as well as God's will, fresh opportunities opened to expand the flock of the faithful. Looking back, Taylor's accomplice, Lyman Beecher, would even call the Connecticut Standing Order's destruction in 1818, paradoxically, *"the best thing that ever happened,"* because it forced the more complacent congregations to evangelize. "By voluntary efforts, societies, missions, and revivals," Beecher observed, "[ministers] exert a deeper influence than ever they could by queues and shoe buckles, and cocked hats and gold-headed canes."

Beecher was the most vigorous and ambitious of the Yankee missionaries. Born and raised in New Haven, well outside the local patriciate—both his father and his grandfather were blacksmiths—Beecher was an eminently practical and blunt man of God, more a polemicist and organizer than a theologian. Ordained a Presbyterian minister in 1799, he took up his first ministry in East Hampton, Long Island, where he gained notice in 1804 for a sermon, following Alexander Hamilton and Aaron Burr's fatal interview, that denounced dueling and its sinful code of "honor." In 1810, he moved to Litchfield, Connecticut, and burnished his reputation with Dwight-inspired sermons on the gloomy state of the nation's soul. Everywhere, Beecher charged, "[t]he name of God is blasphemed: the bible is denounced; the Sabbath is profaned; the worship of God is neglected; intemperance hath destroyed its thousands . . . while luxury, with its diversified evils, with a rapidity unparalleled, is spreading in every direction, and through every class."

Beecher's solution was to encourage circuit-riding ministers to spark revivals and establish local lay moral reform groups. In 1813, Beecher organized the Connecticut Society for the Promotion of Good Morals, which quickly boasted dozens of branches and several thousand members. Three years later, he helped launch the Domestic Missionary Society for Connecticut and Vicinity, sending young reformist Congregational and "New Side" Presbyterian ministers to convert the soaring numbers of Yankee migrants in upstate New York and northern New England. At about the same time, like-minded churchmen opened a branch of the New England Tract Society. By 1817, Beecher and his allies had established a mass-circulation religious magazine and, in Hartford, a charitable school for the deaf and dumb, the first of its kind in the country. Quicker than many of his colleagues, Beecher came to understand how the successful voluntarist innovations of the revivals had rendered formal state support unnecessary. "[T]ruly," he wrote, "we do not stand on the confines of destruction. The mass is changing. We are becoming another people."

Methodist circuit riders and Baptist exhorters also crisscrossed the North with growing success, but it was the allied front of evangelized Presbyterians and Congregationalists, the so-called Presbygationals, who left the strongest spiritual, cultural, and, in time, political mark in the northern states. The Presbygationals' influence redoubled in the 1820s when, backed by pious businessmen in the seaboard cities, they confederated various state and local efforts to form the American Sunday-School Union (claiming fifty thousand students), the American Tract Society, the American Home Missionary Society, and the American Society for the Promotion of Temperance (a special interest of Lyman Beecher's). And by the latter years of John Quincy Adams's presidency, Presbygationals were contemplating political efforts to shape public morality. Like their southern counterparts, Yankee evangelicals eschewed parties and formal electoral politics as profane and divisive. Yet far more than most southerners, the northerners believed that proper moral stewardship demanded direct participation in secular affairs, including the promotion of what the Philadelphia pastor Ezra Stiles Ely described in 1827, a bit rashly and vaguely, as a "Christian party in politics."

The first notable evangelical political campaign focused on ending desecration of the Sabbath. Despite local ordinances enforcing the restriction of commerce on Sundays, Sabbath breaking had increased across the country during the early years of the nineteenth century. Most egregiously, in the eyes of the pious, the Jeffersonian Congress, in 1810, had passed a postal regulation requiring postmasters to conduct business on Sunday whenever mail arrived on that day. Already perturbed by the Jeffersonians' adamant hostility to any merging of church and state, evangelicals saw the Sunday postal law as an assault, both real and symbolic, on proper Christian order. By compelling Sunday mail operations, the government not only forced thousands of postal workers to violate the Sabbath, but also invited townsmen and farmers from surrounding districts to defile the Lord's Day, which in turn invited local businessmen to do the same and encouraged local officials to ignore Sunday closing laws. That so many local postmasters (political appointees all) were also petty merchants and "greengrocers"— meaning that they sold liquor—only worsened the blasphemous rowdiness. Reestablishing the Sabbath was as "necessary to the health of the state," one evangelical observed, as enforcing "laws against murder and polygamy."

Sabbatarian efforts gained little notice until Lyman Beecher and his friends formed the General Union for Promoting the Observance of the Christian Sabbath in May 1828. Thanks to the financial backing of numerous, newly successful businessmen-converts with Yankee backgrounds— above all the flour merchant Josiah Bissell of Rochester, New York, and the silk merchant Lewis Tappan of Manhattan—the Union deployed all of the organizing and proselytizing techniques familiar to the northern revivalists, including tract distribution, public rallies, and prayer concerts. Bissell supplied the money to back a six-day, blue-law stagecoach service. A similar Sabbatarian boat line was established to travel (liquor-free) along the Erie Canal from Albany to Buffalo, but never on Sundays. Along with Tappan, Bissell toured the friendly Presbygational churches of the Northeast to drum up support for the cause. Over the summer and autumn of 1828, while most of the political nation was embroiled in a presidential campaign, the Sabbatarian machine promoted a national petition campaign directed at Congress. By year's end, Bissell was predicting imminent triumph, telling Tappan that the "petitions were flowing in well," and actually welcoming displays of anti-Sabbatarian opinion in the West as "just enough. . . to give a zest to the Sabbath measures."

With their new emphasis on inner sanctification, moral choice, and benevolent stewardship, the proponents of what came to be known as the New School transformed a staid New England Protestant devotionalism into a vital evangelizing creed, distinct from rationalist Unitarians and traditional Calvinists and from southern camp-meeting Methodists and Baptists. Agitation in turn created the institutional basis of what would become an entirely new kind of political power, democratic in tone and sophisticated in its organizational tactics, but very different from the main forms of democratic politics that had emerged since the Revolution. . . .

DOCUMENTS

Religious Excitability, 1835

A "Revival of Religion" presupposes a declension. Almost all the religion in the world has been produced by revivals. God has found it necessary to take advantage of the excitability there is in mankind, to produce powerful excitements among them, before he can lead them to obey. Men are so spiritually sluggish, there are so many things to lead their minds off from religion, and to oppose the influence of the Gospel, that it is necessary to raise an excitement among them, till the tide rises so high as to sweep away the opposing obstacles. They must be so excited that they will break over these counteracting influences, before they will obey God. Not that excited feeling is religion, for it is not; but it is excited desire, appetite and feeling that prevents religion. The will is, in a sense, enslaved by the carnal and worldly desires. Hence it is necessary to awaken men to a sense of guilt and danger, and thus produce an excitement of counter feeling and desire which will break the power of carnal and worldly desire and leave the will free to obey God. . . .

There is so little *principle* in the church, so little firmness and stability of purpose, that unless the religious feelings are awakened and kept excited, counter worldly feeling and excitement will prevail, and men will not obey God. They have so little knowledge, and their principles are so weak, that unless they are excited, they will go back from the path of duty, and do nothing to promote the glory of God. The state of the world is still such, and probably will be till the millennium is fully come, that religion must be mainly promoted by means of revivals. How long and how often has the experiment been tried, to bring the church to act steadily for God, without these periodical excitements? Many good men have supposed, and still suppose, that the best way to promote religion, is to go along *uniformly*, and gather in the ungodly gradually, and without excitement. But however sound such reasoning may appear in the abstract, *facts* demonstrate its futility. If the church were far enough advanced in knowledge, and had stability of principle enough to *keep awake*, such a course would do; but the church is so little enlightened, and there are so many counteracting causes, that she will not go steadily to work without a special interest being awakened. As the millennium advances, it is probable that these periodical excitements will be unknown. Then the church will be enlightened, and the counteracting causes removed, and the entire church will be in a state of habitual and steady obedience to God. The entire church will stand and take the infant

SOURCE: Charles G. Finney, *Lectures on Revivals of Religion* (New York: Fleming H. Revell Co., n.d.), 9–11.

mind, and cultivate it for God. Children will be trained up in the way they should go, and there will be no such torrents of worldliness, and fashion, and covetousness, to bear away the piety of the church, as soon as the excitement of a revival is withdrawn.

It is very desirable it should be so. It is very desirable that the church should go on steadily in a course of obedience without these excitements. Such excitements are liable to injure the health. Our nervous system is so strung that any powerful excitement, if long continued, injures our health and unfits us for duty. If religion is ever to have a pervading influence in the world, it cannot be so; this spasmodic religion must be done away. Then it will be uncalled for. . . . Then there will be no need that ministers should wear themselves out, and kill themselves, by their efforts to roll back the flood of worldly influence that sets in upon the church. But as yet the state of the Christian world is such, that to expect to promote religion without excitements is unphilosophical and absurd. The great political, and other-worldly excitements that agitate Christendom, are all unfriendly to religion, and divert the mind from the interests of the soul. Now these excitements can only be counteracted by *religious* excitements. And until there is religious principle in the world to put down irreligious excitements, it is vain to try to promote religion, except by counteracting excitements. This is true in philosophy, and it is a historical fact.

"This COUNTRY IS RUN MAD after Preaching," c. 1830

This country is run mad after preaching. Here is a new sect called Cumberland Presbyterians; and between these, the Baptists and Methodists, the woods resound. As they have no churches, they preach out-of-doors mostly. I have just returned from preaching, where I remained about two hours; and the parson, when I left him, appeared to be only about midway through his sermon. He ought to have a patent right, for he certainly has the strongest voice in the state. . . .

I placed myself in front of the preacher (a great, rough-looking man), and the congregation sat—some on fallen timber, some on benches carried there for the purpose, some sat flat on the ground, and many stood up—about 500 in all. His text was, "He that hath ears to hear, let him hear." The people must have been deaf indeed that could not have heard him. He neither made division or subdivision. He is one of the Cumberland Presbyterians. They are Calvinists, it is said, but do not deem education a necessary qualification to preach the Gospel.

But to the sermon. He began low but soon bawled to deafening. He spit in his hands, rubbed them against each other, and then would smite them

SOURCE: Anne Royall, *Letters from Alabama* (Washington, D.C.: 1830), 122–125.

together, till he made the woods ring. The people now began to covault and dance and shout, till they fairly drowned the speaker. Many of the people, however, burst out into a laugh. Seeing this, the preacher cried out, pointing to them with his finger, "Now look at them sinners there. You'll see how they will come tumbling down presently. I'll bring them down." He now re-doubled his strength; spit in his hands and smote them together, till he made the forest resound, and took a fresh start; and sure enough the sinners came tumbling down.

The scene that succeeded baffles description. Principally confined to women and children, the young women had carefully taken out their combs from their hair, and laid them and their bonnets in a place of safety, as though they were going to set in for a fight; and it was much like a battle. After tumbling on the ground and kicking sometime, the old women were employed in keeping their clothes civil, and the young men (never saw an old man go near them) would help them up; and taking them by each hand, by *their* assistance and their own agility, they would spring nearly a yard from the ground at every jump, one jump after another, crying out, "Glory, glory," as loud as their strength would admit. Others would be singing a lively tune to which they kept time; hundreds might be seen and heard going on in this manner at once.

Others, again, exhausted by this jumping, would fall down, and here they lay cross and pile, heads and points, yelling and screaming like wild beasts of the forest, rolling on the ground like hogs in a mire—very much like they do at camp meetings in our country, but more shameless. Their clothes were the color of the dirt; and, like those who attend the camp meetings, they were all of the lower class of the people. I saw no genteel person among them.

Are not people of education answerable for this degradation of society? It appears to me, since I have had opportunities of mixing with the world, that there are a certain class of citizens whose interest it is to keep their fel-lowmen in ignorance. I am very sure half a dozen words of common sense, well applied, would convince those infatuated young women that they were acting like fools. In fact, a fool is more rational. Not one of those but would think it a crying sin to dance.

The noise of the preacher was effectually drowned at length, and a uni-versal uproar succeeded louder than ever. While this was going on, I ob-served an old woman near me, sniveling and turning up the whites of her eyes (she was a widow—all the widows, old and young, covaulted), and often applying her handkerchief to her eyes, and throwing herself into con-tortions; but it would not do; she could not raise the steam.

I pointed to one young woman with a red scarf, who had tired down several young men and was still covaulting, and seeing she jumped higher than the rest, I asked who she might be. One of the gentlemen, a Mr. Gal-lagher, who was standing near, gave such an account of her (men know these things) as would shock a modest ear. "D——n her, she gets converted every meeting she goes to." How much better had she been at a ball (if they must dance) where they would be obliged to behave decent, and where vile characters dare not appear.

Shortly after they began to rear and covault, a daughter of Mr. B.'s began too. He walked up to her and led her off some distance, and sat her down at the root of a tree. When he returned, I inquired if she was sick. "No," he answered, "but she was beginning to go on as the rest, and I told her if she wished to worship God to do it there, and not to expose herself before faces."

The preacher, having spent all his ammunition, made a pause, and then called upon all the sinners to approach and be prayed for. Numbers went forward, all women and children (children of ten years old get religion!), and the priest began to pray, when a decent-looking man approached the stand and took a female by the arm and led her away. As he walked along, the preacher pointed to him and said, "God, strike that sinner down!" The man turned around, and in an angry tone said, "God has more sense than to mind such a d——d fool as you are!" and resumed his course. He was one of the brave Tennesseeans, and the lady was his wife.

Being tired of such an abominable scene, I proposed returning home; and, taking a near cut through a slip of woodland, we surprised the red-scarf lady in a manner that gave us no favorable opinion of her piety.

Visiting the Shakers, c. 1841

Sometime in the summer of 18—, I paid a visit to one of the Shaker villages in the State of New York. Previously to this, many times and oft had I (when tired of the noise and contention of the world, its erroneous opinions, and its wrong practices) longed for some retreat, where, with a few chosen friends, I could enjoy the present, forget the past, and be free from all anxiety respecting any future portion of time. And often had I pictured, in imagination, a state of happy society, where one common interest prevailed—where kindness and brotherly love were manifested in all of the every-day affairs of life—where liberty and equality would live, not in name, but in very deed—where idleness in no shape whatever would be tolerated—and where vice of every description would be banished, and neatness, with order, would be manifested in all things.

Actually to witness such a state of society, was a happiness which I never expected. I thought it to be only a thing among the airy castles which it has ever been my delight to build. But with this unostentatious and truly kind-hearted people, the Shakers, I found it; and the reality, in beauty and harmony, exceeded even the picturings of imagination.

SOURCE: "Visit to the Shakers," *Lowell Offering* (1841), 279–281, and "A Second Visit to the Shakers," *Lowell Offering* (1841), 337–340.

No unprejudiced mind could, for a single moment, resist the conviction that this singular people, with regard to their worldly possessions, lived in strict conformity to the teachings of Jesus of Nazareth. There were men in this society who had added to the common stock thousands and tens of thousands of dollars; they nevertheless labored, dressed, and esteemed themselves as no better and fared in all respects, like those who had never owned, neither added to the society, any worldly goods whatever. The cheerfulness with which they bore one another's burdens, made even the temporal calamities, so unavoidable among the inhabitants of the earth, to be felt but lightly. . . .

In whatever light it may appear to others, to me it appears beautiful indeed, to see a just and an impartial equality reign, so that the rich and the poor may share an equal privilege, and have all their wants supplied. That the Shakers are in reality what they profess to be, I doubt not. Neither do I doubt that many, very many lessons of wisdom might be learned of them, by those who profess to be wiser. And to all who wish to know if "any good thing can come out of Nazareth," I would say, you had better "go and see."

I was so well pleased with the appearances of the Shakers, and the prospect of quietness and happiness among them, that I visited them a second time. I went with a determination to ascertain as much as I possibly could of their forms and customs of worship, the every-day duties devolving on the members, &c.; and having enjoyed excellent opportunities for acquiring the desired information, I wish to present a brief account of what "I verily do know" in relation to several particulars.

First of all, justice will not permit me to retract a word in relation to the industry, neatness, order, and general good behavior, in the Shaker settlement which I visited. In these respects, that singular people are worthy of all commendation—yea, they set an example for the imitation of Christians every-where. Justice requires me to say, also, that their hospitality is proverbial, and deservedly so. They received and entertained me kindly, and (hoping perhaps that I might be induced to join them) they extended extra-civilities to me. I have occasion to modify the expression of my gratitude in only one particular—and that is, one of the female elders made statements to me concerning the requisite confessions to be made, and the forms of admission to their society, which statements she afterwards denied, under circumstances that rendered her denial a most aggravated insult. Declining further notice of this matter, because of the indelicacy of the confessions alluded to, I pass to notice,

1st. The domestic arrangements of the Shakers. However strange the remark may seem, it is nevertheless true, that our factory population work fewer hours out of every twenty-four, than are required by the Shakers, whose bell to call them from their slumbers, and also to warn them that it is time to commence the labors of the day, rings much earlier than our factory bells; and its calls were obeyed, in the family where I was entertained, with more punctuality than I ever knew the greatest "workey" among my numerous acquaintances (during the fourteen years in which I have been employed in different manufacturing establishments) to obey the calls of the factory-bell. And not until nine o'clock in the evening were the labors of the day closed, and the people assembled at their religious meetings.

Whoever joins the Shakers with the expectation of relaxation from toil, will be greatly mistaken, since they deem it an indispensable duty to have every moment of time profitably employed. The little portions of leisure which the females have, are spent in knitting—each one having a basket of knitting-work for a constant companion.

Their habits of order are, in many things, carried to the extreme. The first bell for their meals rings for all to repair to their chambers, from which, at the ringing of the second bell, they descend to the eating-room. Here, all take their appropriate places at the tables, and after locking their hands on their breasts, they drop on their knees, close their eyes, and remain in this position about two minutes. Then they rise, seat themselves, and with all expedition swallow their food; then rise on their feet, again lock their hands, drop on their knees, close their eyes, and in about two minutes rise and retire. Their meals are taken in silence, conversation being prohibited.

Those whose chambers are in the fourth story of one building, and whose work-shops are in the third story of another building, have a daily task in climbing stairs, which is more oppressive than any of the rules of a manufacturing establishment.

2d. With all deference, I beg leave to introduce some of the religious views and ceremonies of the Shakers.

From the conversation of the elders, I learned that they considered it doing God service, to sever the sacred ties of husband and wife, parent and child—the relationship existing between them being contrary to their religious views—views which they believe were revealed from heaven to "Mother Ann Lee," the founder of their sect, and through whom they profess to have frequent revelations from the spiritual world. These communications, they say, are often written on gold leaves, and sent down from heaven to instruct the poor, simple Shakers in some new duty. They are copied, and perused, and preserved with great care. I one day heard quite a number of them read from a book, in which they were recorded, and the names of several of the brethren and sisters to whom they were given by the angels, were told me. One written on a gold leaf, was (as I was told) presented to Proctor Sampson by an angel, so late as the summer of 1841. These "revelations" are written partly in English, and partly in some unintelligible jargon, or unknown tongue, having a spiritual meaning, which can be understood only by those who possess the spirit in an eminent degree. They consist principally of songs, which they sing at their devotional meetings, and which are accompanied with dancing, and many unbecoming gestures and noises.

Often in the midst of a religious march, all stop, and with all their might set to stamping with both feet. And it is no uncommon thing for many of the worshipping assembly to crow like a parcel of young chanticleers, while other imitate the barking of dogs; and many of the young women set to whirling round and round—while the old men shake and clap their hands; the whole making a scene of noise and confusion, which can be better imagined than described. The elders seriously told me that these things were the outward manifestations of the spirit of God.

Apart from their religious meetings, the Shakers have what they call "union meetings." These are for social converse, and for the purpose of making the people acquainted with each other. During the day, the elders tell who may visit such and such chambers. A few minutes past nine, work is laid aside; the females change, or adjust, as best suits their fancy, their caps, handkerchiefs, and pinners, with a precision which indicates that they are not *altogether* free from vanity. The chairs, perhaps to the number of a dozen, are set in two rows, in such a manner that those who occupy them may face each other. At the ringing of a bell, each one goes to the chamber where either he or she has been directed by the elders, or remains at home to receive company, as the case may be. They enter the chambers *sans ceremonie*, and seat themselves—the men occupying one row of chairs, the women the other. Here, with their clean, checked, home-made pocket-handkerchiefs spread in their laps, and their spitboxes standing in a row between them, they converse about raising sheep and kine, herbs and vegetables, building wall and raising corn, heating the oven and paring apples, killing rats and gathering nuts, spinning tow and weaving sieves, making preserves and mending the brethren's clothes—in short, everything they do will afford some little conversation. But beyond their own little world, they do not appear to extend scarcely a thought. And why should they? Having so few sources of information, they know not what is passing beyond them. They however make the most of their own affairs, and seem to regret that they can converse no longer, when, after sitting together from half to three-quarters of an hour, the bell warns them that it is time to separate, which they do by rising up, locking their hands across their breasts, and bowing. Each one then goes silently to his own chamber.

It will readily be perceived, that they have no access to libraries, no books, excepting school-books, and a few relating to their own particular views; no periodicals, and attend no lectures, debates, Lyceums, &c. They have none of the many privileges of manufacturing districts—consequently their information is so very limited, that their conversation is, as a thing in course, quite insipid. The manner of their life seems to be a check to the march of mind and a desire for improvement; and while the moral and perceptive faculties are tolerably developed, the intellectual, with a very few exceptions, seem to be below the average.

A Letter from Brook Farm, 1841

As the weather precludes all possibility of ploughing, hoeing, sowing and other such operations, I bethink me that you may have no objection to hear something of my whereabout and whatabout. You are to know then, that I took up my abode here on the 12th ultimo, in the midst of a snowstorm, which kept us all idle for a day or two. At the first glimpse of fair weather, Mr. Ripley summoned us into the cowyard and introduced me to an instrument with four prongs, commonly called a dung-fork. With this tool, I have already assisted to load twenty or thirty carts of manure, and shall take part in loading nearly three hundred more. Besides, I have planted potatoes and peas, cut straw and hay for the cattle, and done various other mighty works. This very morning, I milked three cows; and I milk two or three every night and morning. The weather has been so unfavorable, that we have worked comparatively little in the fields; but, nevertheless, I have gained strength wonderfully—grown quite a giant, in fact—and can do a day's work without the slightest inconvenience. In short, I am transformed into a complete farmer.

This is one of the most beautiful places I ever saw in my life, and as secluded as if it were a hundred miles from any city or village. There are woods, in which we can ramble all day, without meeting anybody, or scarcely seeing a house. Our house stands apart from the main road; so that we are not troubled even with passengers looking at us. Once in a while, we have a transcendental visitor, such as Mr. [Bronson] Alcott; but, generally, we pass whole days without seeing a single face, save those of the brethren. At this present time, our effective force consists of Mr. Ripley, Mr. Farley (a farmer from the far west), Rev. Warren Burton (author of various celebrated works), three young men and boys, who are under Mr. Ripley's care, and William Allen, his hired man, who has the chief direction of our agricultural labors. In the female part of the establishment there is Mrs. Ripley and two women folks. The whole fraternity eat together; and such a delectable way of life has never been seen on earth, since the days of the early Christians. We get up at half-past four, breakfast at half-past six, dine at half-past twelve, and go to bed at nine.

The thin frock, which you made for me, is considered a most splendid article; and I should not wonder if it were to become the summer uniform of the community. I have a thick frock, likewise; but it is rather deficient in grace, though extremely warm and comfortable. I wear a tremendous pair of cow-hide boots, with soles two inches thick. Of course, when I come to see you, I shall wear my farmer's dress.

SOURCE: Nathaniel Hawthorne to Louisa Hawthorne, cited by Richard B.Morris and James Woodress, eds., *Voices from America's Past* (New York: E. P. Dutton & Co., 1961, 1962, 1963), 2:46–47.

We shall be very much occupied during most of this month, ploughing and planting; so that I doubt whether you will see me for two or three weeks. You have the portrait by this time, I suppose; so you can very well dispense with the original. When you write to me (which I beg you will do soon) direct your letter to West Roxbury, as there are two post offices in the town. I would write more; but William Allen is going to the village, and must have this letter; so good-bye.

NATH HAWTHORNE
PLOUGHMAN

Chapter 12

New People in a New Land

Five Points, New York City.

The influx of people from abroad played a central role in the story of
America's growth from the seventeenth century forward. In the 1830s,
1840s, and 1850s, this immigration reached massive proportions: more than
4.5 million people arrived from the Old World. They sought a better life and
escape from economic deprivation, religious persecution, and political oppression. The overwhelming majority of these newcomers were non-English in origin;
approximately one-third came from Germany, and 40 percent were Irish
Catholics. The Germans, like their predecessors in eighteenth-century Pennsylvania, met with some prejudice, but, as in the past, their ability to settle quickly and
prosper as farmers, merchants, and craftsmen helped to curtail nativist (antifor-
eign) attacks. The Irish experience was quite different; they were desperately
poor; they settled mostly in cities, although they were not accustomed to urban
living; and they were steadfastly Catholic in a land overwhelmingly Protestant. As
a result, they suffered as no prior immigrants had in the land of promise.

Tyler Anbinder's essay, "From Famine to Five Points," traces the experiences
of one particular group of Irish immigrants, the former tenants of the marquis of
Landsowne, as they fled abject poverty and life-threatening famine to settle in
Five Points, New York City's and the nation's worst slum. As one reads of the

miserable conditions in Five Points, the belief in America as a land of opportunity might be called into question. Yet by the end of the essay it becomes apparent that in a relatively short time the Landsowne Irish managed to gain a measure of economic well-being. What conditions in New York, lacking in Ireland, contributed to this achievement? How did the attitudes and practices of the immigrants also play a role in their rise? Keep in mind that New York in the 1850s lacked workmen's compensation insurance, unemployment benefits, strong labor unions, child labor laws, and laws governing housing standards.

Poverty was not the only obstacle to be overcome by the immigrants from Ireland. At mid-century some of America's leading figures were outspoken nativists and anti-Catholic bigots. Prominent among them was artist and inventor Samuel F. B. Morse. The first document is from his tract "Imminent Dangers to the United States Through Foreign Immigration." What was the basis of Morse's hostility toward the Irish? In what ways are the arguments of today's advocates of immigration restriction similar or different from those put forth in Morse's day?

Despite the spread of nativist sentiment, many Americans welcomed the increase in foreign immigration. Factory owners in the northeast, faced with a shortage of labor, were quite happy to employ the newly arrived. As illustrated in the second document, civic leaders in the territories and states of the agricultural Midwest competed to attract immigrants to fill their empty lands. Learning of the probability of a large immigration from Holland, a conference was convened in Detroit on January 22, 1847, for the purpose of encouraging these potential newcomers to settle in Michigan. Reading the resolves adopted at the conclusion of the conference, what characteristics assigned to the Dutch immigrants by the conferees made them appear to be ideal future citizens of the state? Extreme poverty was the motive force behind Irish immigration. According to the resolutions, what conditions in Holland encouraged emigration?

For immigrants, the act of coming to America by no means signaled a desire to break ties to their homelands. Letters crossing the Atlantic in both directions were frequent, reflecting a strong desire by both immigrants and those left behind to receive the latest news of friends and family. The final document is a letter home written by Martin Weitz, a German immigrant. It is in many respects typical of those written by thousands of newcomers, relating their experiences and expressing hopes and concerns for the future. What evidence does Weitz reveal that his ties to Germany and German culture remain strong?

ESSAY

From Famine to Five Points

Tyler Anbinder

As New Yorker Ellen Holland looked back over her first forty-seven years of life in 1860, she must have wondered whether she was blessed or cursed. "Nelly" had been born and raised in southwestern Ireland in the County Kerry parish of Kenmare. There she grew up surrounded by jagged mountain peaks and lush green hills that sloped dramatically to the wide, majestic Kenmare River. Nelly and her family were tenants of the marquis of Lansdowne, whose estate was home to 13,000 of the most impoverished residents of nineteenth-century Ireland. Visitors to the huge property commonly chose terms such as "wretched," "miserable," "half naked," and "half fed" to describe the poor farmers and laborers who dominated its population.

Observers invoked such descriptions of Nelly's birthplace even *before* 1845, when a mysterious potato blight began to wreak havoc on the meager food supply. By late 1846, Kenmare residents began to succumb to starvation and malnutrition-related diseases. As conditions continued to deteriorate in early 1847, the death toll multiplied. An Englishman who visited the town of Kenmare at this time wrote that "the sounds of woe and wailing resounded in the streets throughout the night." In the morning, nine corpses were found in the village streets. "The poor people came in from the rural districts" in such numbers, wrote this observer, "it was utterly impossible to meet their most urgent exigencies, and therefore they came in literally *to die.*" Tens of thousands fled Ireland in 1847, but most none of the Lansdowne tenants could afford to emigrate. Relatively few had journeyed from this isolated estate to America in the pre-famine years, so they did not receive the remittances from abroad that financed the voyages of many famine emigrants leaving other parts of Ireland.

Although an abatement of the potato fungus in 1848 led British officials to declare the emergency over, such decrees meant nothing to Holland and others suffering in Kenmare. Most of Lansdowne's tenants were too weak to work or plant and too destitute to buy seed potatoes. And what few tubers they did cultivate in 1849 were again ravaged by the dreaded fungus. Kenmare once more became the center of suffering in the region, with people "dying by the dozens in the streets." Those on the brink of death crowded into the village workhouse, where, in return for giving up all of their

SOURCE: Tyler Anbinder, "From Famine to Five Points: Lord Lansdowne's Irish Tenants Encounter North America's Most Notorious Slum," *The American Historical Review*, 107, no. 2, 351–353, 368–385. Reprinted with permission of American Historical Association and Tyler Anbinder.

worldly possessions, the starving received just barely enough food to keep them alive. By April 1849, the institution held 1,800 souls "in a house built for 500—without shoes, without clothes, in filth, rags and misery," wrote Kenmare's Roman Catholic archdeacon, John O'Sullivan. "The women squatted on the ground, on the bare cold clay floor and [were] so imprisoned for months . . . without as much as a stool to sit on." One of these poor souls was Ellen Holland. She and her three sons, thirteen-year-old James, nine-year-old Thomas, and four-year-old George, were almost certainly among the institution's inmates by that point. Her husband Richard remained outside the workhouse hoping to find employment. Or he may have been one of the hundreds of men authorities turned away, both for want of space and on the theory that men could more readily find paying work than women.

Securing one of the coveted places in the Kenmare workhouse did not ensure survival. Hundreds died there during the famine from diseases that spread rapidly in the crowded, unsanitary institution. The food supply was so meager that some inmates died of starvation-related illnesses just hours after leaving the facility. Holland likely remained in the workhouse throughout 1849 and 1850, wondering how her life might ever return to normal, or if she and her sons would also fall victim to the unending cycle of disease and death. Nelly must have been elated, then, when Lansdowne's estate agent announced in December 1850 that the marquis would finance the emigration of all his workhouse tenants who wished to depart. Holland and her sons were among the first to take advantage of the offer.

Her jubilation soon became tinged with despair, however, as the difficulties of the journey for such emaciated, ill-equipped voyagers became more apparent. Sailors were horrified when they first encountered the Lansdowne emigrants, reporting that in the half-decade since the onset of the famine they had never laid eyes on such wretched beings. The emigrants continued to suffer as they made their way across the Atlantic. The rags they wore provided woefully inadequate protection from the elements aboard a North Atlantic sailing ship in the dead of winter. Holland's vessel, the *Montezuma*, had to detour around an iceberg and huge swaths of "field ice" during its voyage, giving some indication of the frigid conditions she and her shipmates endured. And although Lansdowne's agent had paid for the emigrants' tickets, he did not supply his charges with the foodstuffs that the typical Irish emigrant brought on a transatlantic voyage. Subsisting on just one pound of flour or meal and thirteen ounces of water each day during thirty-nine days at sea compounded the suffering that Holland and her Lansdowne shipmates had already endured at home.

But Nelly was a strong woman, determined to build a better life for her family. Like most of the Lansdowne immigrants, she settled in New York's "Five Points" neighborhood, the most infamously decrepit slum in North America. There, surrounded by drunks, brothels, and other Irish immigrants, and living in one of the most squalid blocks of tenements in the world, Holland and her family set to work rebuilding their lives. After years of unemployment, they must have been eager and delighted to take even the lowly jobs available to them. Her husband Richard found work as a menial day laborer. Ellen became a washerwoman. The boys undoubtedly pitched in as well, for when Ellen opened an account at the Emigrant Savings Bank in September 1853, thirty months after her arrival in New York, she was able to deposit a substantial sum, $110, equivalent to about $2,350 today.

Despite having accrued this significant nest egg in a relatively short period, Holland's struggles continued. By July 1855, both her husband and eldest son were dead. One might have expected her to dip into her savings to help make ends meet during such trying times, but Nelly did no such thing. In fact, despite losing her family's two primary breadwinners, by 1860 she had increased her bank balance to $201.20 (more than $4,200 today), a real feat for a widow who, just eight years earlier, had been on the brink of starvation and had lived the first thirty-eight years of her life in a land of chronic underemployment and hunger. More surprising still, among the hundreds of Lansdowne immigrants who came to New York—most, like Holland, arriving utterly destitute—such relative financial success was not all that unusual. . . .

Why the Lansdowne emigrants chose to concentrate in Five Points is not known. No longstanding Kerry enclave attracted these immigrants to the neighborhood. Kerry natives may have chosen to live there because, as the most destitute of immigrants (even by Irish famine standards), they gravitated to the cheapest housing in the city, much of which was in Five Points. Whatever their impetus for settling there, by 1860 about one in seven Five Points Irish Catholics was a Kerry native. More than 75 percent of these Kerry immigrants had once lived on the Lansdowne estate. Given that about two-thirds of the neighborhood's 14,000 residents in 1855 were Irish natives or their children, one can estimate that roughly 1,000 Five Points inhabitants were former Lansdowne tenants or their offspring. This sizable population resulted not merely from the massive emigration program of 1851 but also from the subsequent immigration underwritten by friends and relatives in New York, as well as occasional passages financed by Lansdowne after 1851. Of the 1,000 or so Lansdowne immigrants living in Five Points in 1855, approximately 500 had arrived in New York as part of the main Lansdowne flotilla in early 1851, while most of the remainder had emigrated later.

Neither the first Lansdowne immigrants nor those who joined them later chose haphazardly where within Five Points to reside. Each of the dominant Irish subgroups in the neighborhood—those from counties Sligo, Cork, and Kerry—created enclaves to some degree. But the Kerry immigrants were by far the most clannish of the three, with 84 percent of them crowded into just two of the neighborhood's twenty or so blocks. . . .

We know from various newspaper exposés and legislative investigations that the tenements in which the Lansdowne immigrants clustered were Five Points' very worst. The northernmost address in the Lansdowne enclave, for instance, was 39 Orange Street. Less than two years before the Lansdowne immigrants arrived, 106 hogs had been kept at this address along with the human inhabitants. In 1856, investigators sent by the state legislature found no more swine, but they were still astounded by the filth and crowding. As was the case at most of the addresses in this part of Five Points, each lot held both a front and rear tenement. Rear tenements were the most notorious abodes in the neighborhood. These small, ramshackle buildings were usually trapped in perpetual shadow as the larger surrounding structures blocked virtually all direct sunlight. In most cases, the only windows on rear tenement buildings faced the noxious outhouses in the yard between the front and rear structures, meaning that the stench from the privies permeated the rear buildings.

At 39 Orange, the alley leading from the street to the rear tenement measured only nineteen inches wide in some places, and only two feet at its widest. Squeezing through to the rear building, the legislative committee discovered fifteen people living in a single room measuring fifteen by fourteen feet. This was probably the household of Tuosist* native Barbara Sullivan. A year earlier, the 1855 state census enumerator had found the widowed fifty-year-old living there with her six children (ranging in age from four to sixteen) and six lodgers. Sullivan had arrived in New York in September 1851 just after the main Lansdowne flotilla. At the time of the census taker's visit, Sullivan lodged a forty-year-old widowed rag picker and her fifteen-year-old newsboy son, as well as a forty-year-old widowed "hawker" and her three children, the eldest of whom worked as a household servant. Ellen Holland also lived at this address from at least 1853 through 1855, though whether in the front or rear tenement is not known. While the legislators made no other comments about this residence, its inclusion in their report indicates that it must have been one of the worst in this miserable district.

As one moved south from 39 Orange toward the Five Points intersection, the frightful living conditions continued. Next door, 37½ Orange was also dominated by Lansdowne immigrants. The legislative inspectors found that as in most other parts of the neighborhood, the vast majority of the inhabitants spent the night in "sleeping closets," tiny windowless bedrooms that rarely measured more than six by eight feet. Among the residents at this address, one widowed "old dame of sixty" and her two daughters "supported themselves by picking curled hair sixteen hours a day, the three earning five dollars per week." The "old dame" was probably Honora Moriarty, who the 1855 census taker had found at this address along with twenty-year-old

---

*Tuosist was a parish adjacent to Kenmare, also within Lord Lansdowne's estate. (Eds.)

Margaret and sixteen-year-old Mary Moriarty. These three women and a fourth lodger shared an apartment with Denis Shea, his two young children, and his wife Mary and her brother Michael. Mary and Michael were themselves Moriartys, though not directly related to the boarders. Such arrangements indicated the continuing strength of "clanship" noted by Tuosist's Father McCarthy. Lansdowne immigrants took in far more boarders than the typical Five Points family. The majority of Five Points households did not take in any lodgers at all, and those that did typically took in only one or two. The Lansdowne immigrants' propensity to take in large numbers of boarders in 1855, four years after most had arrived in the United States, indicates that they were still anxious to supplement their work-related income.

While most Lansdowne immigrants rented space in their own homes to a few lodgers, some became full-time boardinghouse keepers, outfitting a basement or series of apartments with bunks to accommodate as many lodgers as possible. Such was the case at 35 Orange Street, another Lansdowne-dominated building, whose basement boarding establishment was referred to sarcastically by the *New York Illustrated News* as "Mrs. Sandy Sullivan's Genteel Lodging-House," operated by Lansdowne immigrants Sandy and Kate Sullivan from Tuosist. The Sullivans had arrived in New York with the main Lansdowne flotilla in March 1851. A *Times* reporter, stopping at their boardinghouse during a tour of Five Points in 1859, called it "one of the filthiest, blackest holes we had yet seen." The proprietor of this "damp and filthy cellar . . . with much loquacity, assured [us] that the bed-clothes were all 'clane and dacent sure,' that they were washed 'onst a week,' every Thursday, and that the place was quite sweet." Around the main room, the reporters saw

> a number of wretched bunks, similar to those on shipboard, only not half as convenient, ranged around an apartment about ten feet square. Nearly every one of the half-dozen beds was occupied by one or more persons. No regard was paid to age or sex; but man, woman, and child were huddled up in one undistinguishable mass. . . . The most fetid odors were emitted, and the floor and the walls were damp with pestiferous exhalations. But this was not all. There were two inner apartments, each of which was crowded to the same capacity as the outer one. Not the slightest breath of air reached these infernal holes, which were absolutely stifling with heat.

Inquiring about two small children sleeping soundly in one of the "hideous beds," the manager told the reporters that their older sister, who cared for them, "was out begging, even at this hour." Hard as it may be to believe, this lodging house must have been superior to many others in the neighborhood—to stay there cost six cents a night, far more than the worst dives. Sandy Sullivan told the *Times* that he "lodged none under any circumstances but honest hardworking people—which statement the police received with smiles and without contradiction." "To do them justice," agreed an *Express* reporter accompanying the journalist from the *Times*, "such as were awake seemed to be quite sober."

Genteel Americans wondered how and why immigrants tolerated such miserable conditions. Compared to their Irish cabins, however, Five Pointers may have perceived their tenements, at least initially, as somewhat pleasant. Five Pointers had wooden instead of dirt floors, typically with "bits of carpits" on them. Immigrants also undoubtedly preferred their plaster ceilings to the insect-filled thatch roofs that they had known in Kerry, and in winter a tenement's warm stove was far preferable to the open fire typically found in smoke-filled Irish cabins. Two large windows per dwelling did not seem like many to American natives, but to an Irish immigrant whose home had never before held more than a tiny pane or two, Five Points apartments must have seemed almost bright. And given that they had generally lived in Ireland in a single ten-by-thirteen-foot room, the typical two-room, 225-square-foot Five Points apartment might have seemed spacious, at least to those who did not take in many boarders. So while conditions in the Lansdowne immigrants' tenements were bad, they were really no worse, and in some ways were actually much better, than their living conditions in Ireland. This undoubtedly explains why even Five Points immigrants could write glowing, boastful letters to loved ones back in Ireland.

One would imagine that Lansdowne immigrants chose to live in such dilapidated, overcrowded tenements because they could afford nothing else. In fact, male Lansdowne immigrants did hold the city's lowest-paying, least desirable jobs. Lansdowne immigrants were much more likely than the typical Irish Five Pointer to toil as a menial day laborer, the job held by the overwhelming majority of the neighborhood's unskilled workers. Conversely, natives of the Lansdowne estate were significantly less likely to own their own businesses or hold lower-status "white-collar" jobs and were ten times less likely than the typical Five Pointers to work as skilled artisans.

Frustratingly little is known about the lives of nineteenth-century America's day laborers. Construction jobs probably provided most of such workers' employment. Day laborers could dig foundations, carry heavy hods full of bricks and mortar to the masons, and haul away the work-related debris. Municipal projects also employed many laborers, especially to dig sewer lines and pave streets. When outdoor work slowed in mid-summer, a laborer might find a job along the waterfront, loading or unloading sacks and crates from the hundreds of ships that plied New York City's waterways each week. Laborers' work was often very dangerous, and newspapers overflowed with reports of hod carriers killed in falls from ladders, longshoremen crushed by cargo, and laborers buried by the collapsing walls of unfinished buildings. A fair share of these work-related fatalities must have befallen Lansdowne families.

Dangerous as a laborer's work might be, his greatest fear was probably not death but unemployment. On days too cold or wet to work, the laborer did not get paid. Some might find steady employment at a single construction site; others had to look for a new position each day. Sudden sickness or a job-related injury could also throw one out of work at any time, since no position was held open for a laborer while he recuperated. Even in perfect health, observed the *New York Tribune* at this time, only "an energetic and lucky man . . . can make more than two hundred and fifty days' work as an out-door laborer in the course of a year, while the larger number will not average two hundred." During recessions, many laborers could not secure more than one or two days of paid work in a week. Such unemployment wreaked havoc on family finances. "A month's idleness, or a fortnight's sickness, and what misery!" observed an Irish journalist. Some Lansdowne immigrants left New York City permanently to search for steadier work. Upstate New York, Massachusetts, Ohio, and (to a lesser extent) Virginia were their favorite destinations. Many others undoubtedly made seasonal journeys to seek employment, especially in the winter, when there was little work for the city's laborers, a practice the Lansdowne immigrants would have found familiar. The laborer's life was thus one of the hardest, most dangerous, and most financially precarious in Five Points, and for at least his first few years in New York, nearly every adult male Lansdowne immigrant found himself forced to take such work.

Children contributed significantly to the family coffers in the Lansdowne enclave, either to supplement their parents' unreliable incomes or to replace it in the case of households headed by widows. Many youngsters worked as newsboys. Tim Sullivan, the son of Lansdowne emigrants Daniel Sullivan and Catherine Connelly, lived at 25 Baxter (formerly Orange) Street in 1870 when at age seven he began hawking newspapers. The other trade most popular with Five Points boys was shoe shining. Sullivan, in fact, had shined shoes outside a police stationhouse before peddling newspapers. Bootblacks typically ranged in age from ten to sixteen, although some (such as Sullivan) started work much younger. Other boys earned money in more unusual ways. Many Five Points saloons featured bowling alleys, where Charles Dickens observed that young lads "wait upon the players, setting up the pins, returning the balls, fetching a light for their segars, supplying them with liquor when thirsty," and receiving in return a small wage from the saloonkeeper and tips from the bowlers. One such "pin boy" was Timothy Harrington, a Lansdowne immigrant who had left Kerry in the summer of 1851 with a brother and three sisters. When the fourteen-year-old opened a savings account in 1853 with an initial deposit of $30 (about $640 today), he was living with his seventeen-year-old brother John in the heart of the Lansdowne enclave at 155 Anthony Street. Girls had fewer opportunities to earn cash than did their brothers. Some made significant sums sweeping the mud away from street corners on rainy days, receiving tips in return from passersby. In the late summer and early fall, they might sell hot corn from steaming buckets. But girls were more likely to contribute to the family economy in other ways, especially scavenging coal or kindling from waterfront docks. Such work sustained many an impoverished Five Points family.

Lansdowne women also contributed to their families' incomes, and in the cases of widows and unmarried women sometimes supported their dependents single-handedly. The employment figures for Lansdowne women, however, are somewhat misleading. Most Lansdowne immigrants earned extra income taking in boarders, an enterprise usually supervised by the female head of household, yet of the twenty-nine Lansdowne women who listed occupations when they opened bank accounts, none described themselves as boardinghouse keepers. Perhaps taking in boarders was so common in the Lansdowne enclave that neither the Lansdowne women nor the bank secretary considered it an "occupation." Nor do the bank records reflect the full range of work Lansdowne women engaged in outside the home, for we know from other sources that some of them (usually widows or their children) turned to one of the most degrading of nineteenth-century occupations—ragpicking. Ragpickers scavenged the city's ash bins and rubbish barrels looking for rags, bones, scrap meat, and metal or glass that could be sold to paper producers, fat renderers, candle and soap makers, and other manufacturers.

One can only speculate on the extent to which Lansdowne women participated in the female trade most associated with Five Points—prostitution. Writing in 1849, just before the Lansdowne immigrants arrived, New York journalist George Foster said of Five Points that "nearly every house and cellar is a groggery below and a brothel above." A minister who worked with the neighborhood's most impoverished residents remembered that on his arrival there in 1850 "every house was a brothel, and every brothel a hell."

Could such accounts of the ubiquity of Five Points prostitution have been true, or were they merely the exaggerated fantasies of imaginative or bigoted writers? At first glance, the claim that "every house was a brothel" seems ridiculous. Yet a review of the New York district attorney's indictment records reveals that for the two blocks that composed the Lansdowne enclave, such allegations were essentially accurate. Twenty of the twenty-five dwellings on Anthony Street between Centre and Orange housed prostitutes at some point during the 1850s. Brothel proprietors were likewise prosecuted in thirteen of the seventeen residences on Orange Street just north of the Five Points intersection in the same period. Five Points policemen were actually renowned for ignoring the neighborhood vice trade. Prosecutions usually ensued only when neighbors repeatedly complained about persistently raucous behavior. Thus it seems likely that brothels were found in most Lansdowne tenement buildings during the early 1850s. . . .

. . . [W]hile some Lansdowne immigrants may have worked as prostitutes, the evidence suggests that most lived among the neighborhood's brothels rather than working in them. Most Irish-American women who resorted to prostitution lived by themselves—most had emigrated on their own to work as domestics and had no family members to turn to for help when their financial circumstances became dire. Because almost all the Lansdowne immigrants had arrived in the United States with other family members, they had friends or kinsmen who could assist them in desperate times and were therefore less likely than other Five Pointers to become prostitutes. The Lansdowne immigrants, especially those with children, must have nevertheless found it embarrassing and humiliating to have to live in tenements where the sex trade was so brazenly and noisily carried on.

From all appearances, then, the Lansdowne immigrants must have been some of the most impoverished residents of Five Points, a neighborhood renowned for its destitution. After all, the Lansdowne men were especially likely to be lowly paid menial laborers, and they lived with their families in the district's most rundown tenements. The Lansdowne immigrants' propensity to open accounts at the Emigrant Savings Bank makes it possible to compare these appearances with reality. Of the 12,500 accounts opened at the bank in its first six years of operation (from September 1850 to August 1856), 153 were opened by Five Points Lansdowne immigrants. Although it is difficult to determine what proportion of Lansdowne immigrants had accounts, it appears that about 50 percent of the Lansdowne families living in Five Points had opened one by mid-1855. These account holders are not necessarily a representative sample, of course. It may be that only those who had found financial success bothered to open them. Even so, the bank records provide a rare glimpse into the economic fortunes of a very significant number of the Lansdowne immigrants.

The bank ledgers suggest that, even while living in Five Points, the Lansdowne immigrants saved far more money than one would have imagined given their wretched surroundings and low-paying jobs. Take the case of the Tuosist natives who, on July 2, 1853, walked the half mile from Five Points to the bank's Chambers Street office to open accounts. The first, Honora Shea, had been one of the earliest Lansdowne-assisted immigrants to arrive in New York, disembarking from the *American Eagle* in mid-March 1851 with her daughter Ellen Harrington, who the bank secretary described as "an illegitimate child, aged 14 yrs." Although Honora apparently did not live with a male breadwinner, and rented quarters in the decrepit tenement at 35 Orange Street, she was able to open her account with an initial deposit of $160, the equivalent of more than $3,400 today. The next account was assigned to laborer Patrick Murphy and his wife Mary, who lived next door to Shea at 33 ½ Orange and had also arrived in New York from Tuosist in March 1851. They made an initial deposit of $250, a sum worth roughly $5,300 in contemporary terms. Bank officials gave the subsequent account to "washer" Barbara Sullivan, whose cramped apartment, filled with her six children, son-in-law, and six boarders, was described earlier. Sullivan, who at this point also lived at 33 ½ Orange but had arrived in New York in

September 1851, made the smallest opening deposit of the three, $135 (or about $2,900 today). Later in the day, a fourth Tuosist native, forty-two-year-old Judy O'Neill, opened a joint account with her nineteen-year-old daughter Catherine (Judy was either widowed or never married). The O'Neills lived at 33 ½ Orange as well and had arrived in New York at the end of the initial Lansdowne flotilla in May 1851. Judy told the bank secretary that she was not employed outside the home but that her daughter worked in a tobacco factory. They made an initial deposit of $148 (about $3,100 today). These four Lansdowne families, who had probably arrived in New York virtually penniless, had managed despite their meager incomes to squirrel away *very* substantial sums. . . .

It appears that most Lansdowne immigrants saw the bank as a place to safely keep (and draw interest on) nest eggs they had already managed to accumulate before opening their accounts. This would explain why so many Lansdowne immigrants did not add substantially to their initial deposits, even when they kept their accounts open for extended periods. Bonane native Mary Flynn, for example, was in her early sixties when she opened an account in August 1853. Although she was married, her husband was not listed as a joint account holder. Mary, who told the bank secretary that she had no occupation, opened her account with $45, and in less than a year she had doubled her money. During the recession winters of 1855 and 1858, she withdrew as much as half her savings but always worked her way back to the $90 level within a year. That was the balance, give or take five dollars, at which her account remained into the late 1860s. Flynn undoubtedly saw $90 as the appropriate size for her family's emergency fund. . . .

What explains the Lansdowne immigrants' surprising ability to save? Perhaps the privation they had experienced in County Kerry enabled them to limit expenditures to the bare minimum in the years immediately after their arrival. Living in Five Points, they could pay among the lowest rents in New York (from $4.50 to $6 per month for a two-room dwelling), and taking in their countrymen as lodgers enabled the Lansdowne immigrants to recoup a significant proportion of their housing expenses. Having so many of their kinsmen and former neighbors with them in New York also undoubtedly helped the immigrants. Virtually overnight, they created a large, intricate network that could be used to help find jobs, housing, and even spouses. And if someone through sickness, injury, or death became unable to work, there were plenty of relatives around to help out. . . . For widows with young children, life was particularly hard. But the noticeable absence of Lansdowne surnames in the relief records of the Five Points Mission (where hundreds of desperate Five Points Catholics turned for help despite the institution's Methodist affiliation) suggests that the Lansdowne immigrants took care of each other—helping widows find new mates and unemployed men and women new jobs.

But what explains the apparent anomaly of the Lansdowne immigrants' menial jobs and poor living conditions on the one hand and their substantial bank balances on the other? It appears that, once they got settled and found work, the Lansdowne immigrants focused all their energies on saving money to establish nest eggs for their families, choosing to stay in Five Points even after they could afford to move to more spacious apartments in cleaner and safer neighborhoods. Inasmuch as many of them were also sending money to loved ones in Ireland, either to help support aged parents or to pay for relatives' emigration, the typical Lansdowne immigrant's ability to squirrel away $100 or more in just a few years is truly remarkable. Some undoubtedly moved out of Five Points or to less squalid blocks within the neighborhood once they had established these competencies. But many, despite their substantial savings, decided to stay in the Lansdowne enclave, either because they enjoyed being surrounded by so many fellow Kerry natives, or because they sought to continue saving as much money as possible by paying low Five Points rents. That so many of the Lansdowne immigrants' account balances remained relatively constant indicates that once they reached their savings goal, they began to raise their standard of living by spending more of their income. Through a concerted scheme of self-sacrifice, then, most of the Lansdowne immigrants in Five Points managed to improve their lives significantly, from both the misery of County Kerry and the initial privations of Five Points.

Eventually, the Lansdowne immigrants did begin to move out of Five Points, but it is impossible to determine exactly how long they remained in the district or where they went once they left. There were simply too many Sheas and Sullivans (and even Ellen Hollands) in New York to allow the tracking of the Lansdowne immigrants after they moved out of the neighborhood. That young bootblack and newsboy Tim Sullivan was living in Five Points in 1870 demonstrates that some of them still resided there, but by then Italian immigrants occupied the vast majority of the apartments in the buildings that Lansdowne immigrants had once dominated. At that point, most Lansdowne immigrants had probably moved further uptown to other, more prosperous Irish enclaves.

DOCUMENTS

Imminent Dangers, 1835

I have shown what are the *Foreign materials* imported into the country, with which the Jesuits can work to accomplish their designs. Let us examine this point a little more minutely. These materials are the *varieties of Foreigners* of the same Creed, the Roman Catholic, over all of whom the Bishops or Vicars General hold, as a matter of course, ecclesiastical rule; and we well know what is the nature of Roman Catholic ecclesiastical rule,—it is the double refined

SOURCE: Samuel F. B. Morse, *Imminent Dangers to the United States Through Foreign Immigration.* Document from Bibliobase®, edited by Micheal Bellesiles. Copyright © Houghton Mifflin Company. Reprinted by permission.

spirit of despotism, which, after arrogating to itself the prerogatives of Deity, and so claiming to bind or loose the *soul* eternally, makes it, in the comparison, but a mere trifle to exercise absolute sway in all that relates to the body. The notorious ignorance in which the great mass of these emigrants have been all their lives sunk, until their minds are dead, makes them but senseless machines; they obey orders mechanically, for it is the habit of their education, in the despotic countries of their birth. And can it be for a moment supposed by any one that by the act of coming to this country, and being naturalized, their darkened intellects can suddenly be illuminated to discern the nice boundary where their *ecclesiastical obedience* to their priests *ends,* and their *civil independence* of them *begins?* The very supposition is absurd. They obey their priests as demigods, from the habit of their whole lives; they have been taught from infancy that their priests are infallible in the greatest matters, and can they, by mere importation to this country, be suddenly imbued with the knowledge that in civil matters their priests may err, and that they are not in these also their infallible guides? . . . Must not the priests, as a matter almost of *certainty,* control the opinions of their ignorant flock in civil as well as religious matters? and do they not do it? . . .

That a change of some kind in the Naturalization Laws is required, seems to be conceded on all sides, but the nature and extent of this change are strangely opposite in character. While some, and doubtless the greater part of the American population, would have them changed with the view of *discouraging* immigration, and of guarding our institutions from foreign interference, at the point where they are not only assailable, but where they are at this moment actually assailed and greatly endangered; others would have them changed so as to throw down all the barriers which protect us as an independent nation, and extend the right of suffrage, strange as it may seem, with such an unheard of universality of application, as no advocate of the proper and just principles of universal suffrage ever before ventured to dream of; to the extent, in fact, virtually of giving the administration of our government to any and all nations of the world, no matter how barbarous, who choose to take the trouble to exercise it. Instead of guarding with greater vigilance and care our institutions, when attacked, by new defences, these patriots would not only make no resistance, but would actually invite the enemy, by demolishing the fortresses already existing, and yield up the country into his uncontrolled possession.

Resolves of Welcome and Support, 1847

Resolved, That this meeting has heard with much interest of a large prospective emigration from Holland to this country, proceeding from a love of civil and religious liberty, and stimulated by the oppressive interference of that government with education and the exercise of religion, it commends itself to our

SOURCE: Gerrit Van Schelven, "Michigan and the Holland Immigration of 1847," *Michigan History Magazine* 1, 1917.

admiration and sympathy. We pledge ourselves to cooperate, as far as we can, with those who elsewhere may aid and sustain this movement; and, if these emigrants make their abiding place in Michigan we will extend to them the hand of fellowship and friendship. We admire the past history and character of the people of the Netherlands. For their faith and independence they struggled for more than thirty years against the powers of Spain and Germany. They stood side by side with our English ancestors in arduous conflicts for freedom in civil and religious matters. They gave an asylum to the persecuted Puritans. They aided in the settlement of our most important state. In their industry, their enterprise, their frugality, their integrity, their love of country, their devotedness to their faith and to freedom in their civil institutions, we recognize those qualities which entitle their descendants to our respect and welcome.

Resolved, That a committee of seven be appointed, who may associate with them such others as they deem expedient, and whose duty it shall be to aid, in every practicable way, the emigrants who may reach our limits, and to correspond with such associations or committees as may be found elsewhere; and, in other ways, to invite, encourage, and direct the settlement of these emigrants within our state.

Resolved, That we recommend the appointment of committees and associations for a similar purpose, at such other points as may be deemed desirable by the Rev. A. C. Van Raalte, the agent and pioneer of this movement, and whom we cheerfully recommend as a gentleman of energy, talent, piety, and disinterested zeal.

The resolutions were unanimously adopted. . . .

It was further resolved, that the proceedings of this meeting be published in the papers of this city, and that the country papers generally be requested to publish them.

Rev. Van Raalte, in a most touching and impressive manner, expressed his gratitude for the sympathy and aid proffered to his countrymen, and his gratification at having advanced thus far in the preparatory steps for the settlement in a land where labor would meet with its reward, and civil and religious freedom be secure.

A German Immigrant Writes Home, *1857*

Rockville, August 23rd, 1857.

Dear father, brother, sister-in-law and children,

I am very pleased that you set things up for me. I received the 2 letters from *Mister* Johannes Leining behind the pharmacy in August and I wrote a

SOURCE: *News From the Land of Freedom: German Immigrants Write Home,* Walter D. Kamphoefner, Wolfgang Helbich, and Ulrike Sommer, eds. (Ithaca, N.Y.: Cornell University Press, 1991), 357–359.

letter to Philippina Fey from Gedern who is now in service in Ludwigshafen. I wrote her all about my situation and explained everything. I don't know whether she will come now or not, I am waiting with the greatest longing for a letter from her. I want to send you and *Mister* Leining and all my friend my heartiest thanks and I wish and hope that it will work out because I have put all my trust in her. I met her earlier, I know she is a good woman. The time has now come when I want to and must, since I've gotten tired of this life, you can't get very far unless you're married because from what I pay for *Board* alone you can almost pay for 2, if you set things up right. If it doesn't work out with the girl from Gedern then I'll have to look around some more because I have already waited long enough. [Everything is expensive in Germany and in America] Since the spring I've been paying II dollars for *Board*, that is very expensive but I can't blame the *Boarding-*keeper for that, they don't make much at it either [. . .] that's why I want to be on my own then I'd have more chance to save something. *Mister* Leining has 14 *Boardinger,* that means 14 *Kostgänger,* who board with him. Dear father, this fall I want to send you something so you'll get it before Christmas. I would have sent you something already, but this summer cost me a lot of money. I bought a whole set of clothes, that cost me 30 dollars, and some other things, because when you're single you don't save so much, and when you decide to really save, it costs you even more. But when you're married then you settle down and if you stay healthy and work together then you can really save something. You ask me how Michel Bork is doing, that I will tell you. Michel Bork worked here in a *Fecktori*, and there was an *Eirichsbeu* or in other words an *Irländer Bub*, the fellow never left Michel Bork one day in peace, always harassed him, until finally his anger got the better of him and he threw a piece of iron at him. He was right, that's what everyone said here, if it'd been me I'd have knocked him down, with those people you can't put up with any nonsense. Then the Irish fellow took it to court, then old Bork thought he would be hanged and left Rockville. Now he's few miles away from us, he works for a farmer, he likes it very much. Therefore I'd like to ask you to find out who wrote that Michel Bork had been stealing here. We want to find out who the lowdown creature was so we can take him to court, because such a creature who writes such mean things to Germany should be strung up right away. And they aren't true, Michel Bork is a good man, and no one in Schotten can say anything against him. [. . .] Dear father I am so very pleased that you are in good health at your age [77], I thought of you on your birthday on August 9, it fell on a Sunday before the summer fair when I would so much have liked to have been in your midst. I would have enjoyed it so much, but nothing can be done, we should be content, we are too far apart. Dear father, I want to arrange it as soon as possible. We have founded a *Turnverein** which has been well

*Turnvereins are athletic clubs specializing in gymnastics. (Eds.)

received by the Americans, we're also getting a German church and school which is a good thing for the Germans here. It costs me money too, but for something like that I'll sacrifice everything so the young people and adults get some education, they need it badly. Dear father and brother send me 10 to 12 pounds of good camomile when you get the first good chance. I will tell you why, I have a good friend who was a military doctor in the Hussar Regiment in Prussia, now he's here and my roommate, he is a clever doctor, because I'm writing to you he asked me to write you that if you get the chance you should send it, but only good camomile. Whoever brings it will be paid. Otherwise we are all well, many greetings from the Leining and Bork families, Peter Glock is waiting desperately for his family, but he thought it strange that you didn't write anything about them. Write me as soon as possible about what decision the girl makes and what else is being said. Expecting a speedy reply.

My best to my little godson and be a good boy. Later when you're a big boy you can come over to me, and Grethgen has gotten a good job in service, but watch out that she doesn't do anything foolish, you know what I mean by that.

Chapter 13

The Age of Reform

Lucretia Mott, champion of reform.

Economic growth, territorial expansion, and a spirit of democracy characterized the second quarter of the nineteenth century, a time of great national optimism. Americans believed that their institutions, know-how, and values could overcome all problems. Revivalism and the founding of utopian communities were manifestations of this seemingly boundless perfectionist faith, and so too were the great reform movements that began to emerge after the War of 1812. These movements reached their peak during the 1830s and 1840s before gradually declining in the 1850s. Wherever people perceived problems, they organized to do battle. They formed societies to promote such ideas as temperance, world peace, the abolition of slavery, women's rights, and prison reform, as well as to support such public institutions as libraries, hospitals for the mentally ill, and schools.

The subject of Margaret Hope Bacon's essay "Lucretia Mott: Pioneer for Peace" was one of the foremost figures of the era, certainly one of the most courageous. Although the author calls particular attention to Mott's role in the peace movement and to her advocacy of nonviolent, direct action on behalf of reform, clearly she also involved herself in a variety of causes seeking to improve society, most notably antislavery and women's rights. What evidence can you find to illustrate that many of the reform movements were interrelated? Note that although reformers generally agreed as to ends, they often disagreed over means or tactics. Can you identify areas of disagreement that persist to our own day?

The four documents reflect the scope of causes promoted during the great era and the fervent dedication of their adherents. One of the most eloquent and courageous spokesmen for the cause of the abolition of slavery was Frederick Douglass, former slave, newspaper editor, and political activist. The first document, Douglass's 1852 Independence Day address, delivered in Rochester, New York, readily reveals his eloquence. Once you identify the theme of his address, the courage he displayed becomes apparent. This speech not only antagonized the foes of abolition but also shocked many of the supporters of the cause. Can you understand why?

The temperance movement, like all reform causes, blended concern with optimism. However, it outdistanced the others in longevity and wide appeal. Some idea of the fervor of the attacks on drunkenness is revealed in the second document, "Songs of the Temperance Movement." These tunes were included in *The Mountain Minstrel,* compiled and edited in 1847 by T. D. Bonner, an agent of the New Hampshire Temperance Society. What evils attributed to alcohol are revealed in the songs' lyrics?

Horace Mann, foremost leader of the movement for universal, free, public schools, had been a successful politician and reformer in Massachusetts before being appointed secretary of the Massachusetts Board of Education. He had also spoken out and legislated on behalf of temperance, civil rights for blacks, prison reform, the prevention of pauperism, and better care of the mentally ill. The third document is a selection from Mann's twelfth, and final, *Annual Report* as secretary. How does the document explain why Mann viewed public education as the hub of all reform?

As women were very much involved in the abolition and other reform movements, it was inevitable that many would become sensitized to the fact that law and custom denied their sex social, political, and economic rights and opportunities. As you will recall from the essay, it was as a result of an incident that occurred within the abolitionist movement that led Lucretia Mott to join with Elizabeth Cady Stanton to convene the historic Seneca Falls Convention on women's rights. The final document is an excerpt from an address delivered by Stanton before the New York state legislature on February 18, 1860. She was speaking on behalf of a bill to grant women the right of suffrage. As you read, note her biblical references and her allusions to other reform causes. What is your opinion of the tone of Stanton's speech and the logic of her arguments? Unfortunately, they were not effective enough to sway the majority of legislators who voted against the bill. It was not until 1917 that New York women finally achieved the right to vote.

ESSAY

Lucretia Mott: Pioneer for Peace

Margaret Hope Bacon

So much has been written about Lucretia Mott's contribution to the antislavery and women's rights movement of the nineteenth century that an equally significant aspect of her public career has been lost sight of. No other nineteenth century American woman did as much to forward the cause of peace, to involve women in the peace movement, and to establish the links between women's rights and nonresistance, as did this small but dynamic Quaker minister. . . .

Speaking at an 1860 meeting of the Pennsylvania Anti-Slavery Society she laid out her creed:

> Robert Purvis has said that I was "the most belligerent Non-Resistant" he ever saw. I accept the character he gives me; and I glory in it. I have no idea, because I am a Non-Resistant, of submitting tamely to injustice inflicted either on me or on the slave. I will oppose it with all the moral powers with which I am endowed. I am no advocate of passivity. Quakerism, as I understand it, does not mean quietism. The early Friends were agitators; disturbers of the peace; and were more obnoxious in their days to charges which are now so freely made than we are.

As a . . . Quaker, Lucretia had grown up believing that war was wrong. On Nantucket, where she was born, the largely Quaker populace had suffered hunger from blockades inflicted by both the British and the Americans because of the islanders' neutrality during the Revolutionary War. Again, during the War of 1812, Lucretia experienced war personally when the cotton mill run by James Mott's uncle, Richard Mott, was forced to close because of the British blockade, and James lost his job.

The Mott family into which Lucretia had married were, like the Coffins, strong pacifists. James Mott's brother, Richard, who was a printer for a short time in his career, and published an almanac, enclosed small peace pamphlets in each one he sold, a task at which Lucretia assisted.

SOURCE: Margaret Hope Bacon, "Lucretia Mott: Pioneer for Peace," *Quaker History* 82 (fall 1993): 63–78. Reprinted by permission of the Friends Historical Society.

It was, however, in a time of comparative peace that Lucretia and James Mott began to develop their concepts of nonresistance. When the American Anti-Slavery Society was formed in Philadelphia in 1833 they were pleased that the constitution pledged its members to work against slavery by moral means alone. The Philadelphia Female Anti-Slavery Society, organized by Lucretia and others four days later, echoed these sentiments. The Motts supported their friend and fellow abolitionist William Lloyd Garrison as he began to unfold his commitment to nonresistance in his paper *The Liberator.* And they supported another friend, Henry C. Wright, also an early advocate of turning the other cheek.

The Motts themselves had been for some time involved in the Free Produce movement: an effort to permit those who felt conscientious scruples against buying products grown by slave labor to obtain them in small Free Produce shops. The supporters of Free Produce did not explicitly see their movement as a form of boycott, or an effort to place the burden or moral suasion on the merchant of slave-made produce, as it would have been seen in 20th-century nonviolent theory, but rather as answering a Christian need to keep oneself free of complicity. James Mott ran such a shop in 1829, himself in transition from the trade of cotton merchant to that of wool merchant. He was also president of the Free Produce Society. Lucretia supported him in these moves, and she used free produce religiously. She often exhorted others to do the same, as at the 1837 Anti-Slavery Convention of American Women, when she introduced a resolution:

> That the support of the iniquitous system of slavery at the South is dependent on the co-operation of the North, by commerce and manufactures, as well as by the consumption of its products— therefore that, despising the gain of oppression we recommend to our friends, by a candid and prayerful examination of the subject, to ascertain if it be not a duty to cleanse our hands from this unrighteous participation, by no longer indulging in the luxuries which come through this polluted channel; and in the supply of the necessary articles of food and clothing, &., that we "provide things honest in the sight of all men," by giving preference to goods which come through requited labor.

In addition, Lucretia Mott began advocating nonresistance explicitly. In November of 1837 when an abolitionist editor in Alton, Illinois, Elijah Lovejoy, defended his presses by force when he was attacked by a proslavery mob, and was himself shot and killed, abolitionists were divided between those who viewed his action as heroic, and those who considered his resort to the use of force as weakening the moral principles of their position. Lucretia Mott felt the latter rather strongly. The Philadelphia Female Anti-Slavery Society, under her leadership, decided to hold a public meeting for the support of

Lovejoy's widow, but stated that they regretted that he took up arms, not "the proper means" to pursue the antislavery crusade.

At first antislavery sentiment was respectable in the North. In Philadelphia, a number of prominent citizens had joined to form in 1775 the Pennsylvania Society for Promoting the Abolition of Slavery; the Relief of Negroes Unlawfully Held in Bondage; and For Improving the Condition of the African Race. Reorganized in 1784, it lobbied diligently to persuade the infant Congress to ban slavery. But as the years passed and slavery became more deeply entrenched in the South after the invention of the cotton gin, Northern businessmen began to feel that the antislavery movement was a danger, threatening to interrupt business connections up and down the Eastern seaboard, while Northern white laborers, especially the newly arrived Irish immigrants, saw free black labor as possible competition for jobs. Antislavery spokespersons were frequently booed by angry mobs, and even the churches began to refuse the use of their buildings for antislavery meetings. Although the Society of Friends had a traditional concern against slavery, even the Quakers began to fear the secular antislavery movement as disruptive, and to bar such gatherings in the meeting houses.

After several years of frustration, the reformers in Philadelphia decided to raise money for a structure of their own in which to hold antislavery and related meetings. By selling shares at twenty dollars apiece to some 2000 sympathetic persons, they were able to raise a sum of $40,000. Both James and Lucretia Mott started working on fundraising in 1836. In the early months of 1838 a beautiful new building, Pennsylvania Hall, began to take shape on Sixth Street between Mulberry and Sassafras. It had the pillared facade of a Greek temple. Its first floor contained a small auditorium, committee rooms, and a free produce store; the second floor consisted of a large hall with galleries. The whole was lit with modern gas, and there were ventilators in the ceiling to permit a flow of fresh air, all new inventions. By early May it was ready for use.

The dedication ceremonies were set for May 14. There were many speeches and a special poem written by John Greenleaf Whittier for the occasion. On Tuesday the 15th, the Second Annual Meeting of the Anti-Slavery Convention of American Women opened its sessions in the new hall. The women agreed upon resolutions calling for the boycotting of slave produce and for an end to slavery in the District of Columbia. They could not, however, agree on the question of the right or duty of antislavery women to speak to mixed or promiscuous audiences. This issue, which had been brought to the fore by the speaking tour of Angelina and Sarah Grimke, was proving divisive in the Boston Female Anti-Slavery Society, where some women attached to Garrison, under the leadership of Maria Weston Chapman and her sisters, Caroline, Anne and Deborah Weston, were in favor of "promiscuous" speaking, and others, influenced by the more conservative, clerical wing of the movement, were opposed. Many of the

New York women were close to the clerical wing and therefore also opposed antislavery women speaking to mixed audiences, while the Philadelphia Female Antislavery Society . . . supported public speaking for women. It was finally decided that a meeting would be held on Wednesday evening not under the formal sponsorship of the Convention, at which those who believed in woman's duty to speak to a mixed audience might be heard.

A mob had formed around the Hall on May 14, and each day it had become larger and uglier. When it was discovered that blacks and whites, men and women, were going to meet together at the hall, public prejudice against racial "amalgamation" flared. Each day the crowd grew a little more threatening, and the feminist-abolitionists had to learn to walk through it, heads held high, in order to attend their meetings.

Word about the promiscuous meeting on Wednesday night had gotten out, and the mob which gathered was larger and uglier than at any time before. Much of the anger was directed against the black delegates. It was estimated that 10,000 persons, primarily men, surrounded Pennsylvania Hall, and threats to break in and stop proceedings were widespread. The few policemen present made no secret that their sympathies lay with the mob and made no effort to restrain it. When William Lloyd Garrison, the very symbol of antislavery, rose to speak, some of the men surged into the hall, shouting catcalls. Unperturbed, Maria Chapman made a ten-minute speech, followed by Angelina Grimke Weld. The day before, Grimke had married abolitionist Theodore Weld in a ceremony in which they pledged themselves to equality in marriage, and had asked black friends as well as white to witness their union. Word of this affair, with its aspect of "social amalgamation," had spread through the city and led to further fury. When Angelina Weld spoke, telling of her first-hand experience with slavery as a Southerner, the mob began to shout again and to throw brickbats. This incensed a young admirer, Abby Kelley of Worcester, Massachusetts, who made an impassioned maiden speech as an antislavery orator. Lucretia Mott closed the meeting, deploring the fact that the session had not been sponsored by the convention. "Let us hope that such false notions of delicacy and propriety will not long obtain in this enlightened country," she said.

That night someone posted notices in prominent places throughout Philadelphia, calling on all citizens with a due regard for property and the preservation of the Constitution to interfere "forcibly if they must," with the proceedings of the convention. The crowd that gathered Thursday outside the hall was huge and in an ugly mood. Daniel Neall, the president of Pennsylvania Hall, visited the mayor with a delegation and asked for protection. The mayor told them that the trouble was their own fault for holding an amalgamated convention in the first place. Unable to protect the delegates, Daniel Neall next asked Lucretia Mott to suggest that the black women stay away, since they seemed to be the most exposed to danger. Mott agreed to deliver the message Thursday afternoon, but said that she did not agree with it, and hoped that no one would act upon it, not be put off by a "little *appearance* of danger."

Undeterred, the delegates of the convention completed their regular business sessions throughout the day. When it was time to adjourn, the women went arm in arm, each white delegate protecting a black woman, maintaining their dignity despite the outrageous words shouted and stones thrown by the mob. This technique, which had first been tried in Boston, again worked, and with no armor other than their own sense of moral purpose the women passed through the angry mob unharmed.

As soon as the hall was emptied, the mayor stepped forward and locked the door, then made a speech in which he told the mob that they must serve as his police. As for himself, he proposed to go home. After he had left, members of the mob burst the doors down, collected all the books and benches, and started a huge fire, breaking the gas pipes to increase the conflagration. After a while fire companies arrived and played their hoses on the adjacent buildings, while the new hall burned to the ground.

William Lloyd Garrison, Maria Chapman and Anne Weston were staying at the Motts' house at 148 North Ninth Street, a few blocks from Pennsylvania Hall. When friends came by to report that the mob might attack the Motts' house after the hall was consumed, these visitors thought it prudent to leave town. Local abolitionists however gathered at the Motts, who themselves had decided that nonresistance principles demanded that they not flee. One friend moved some furniture and clothes to a neighbor's, while another volunteered to spend the evening next door at the home of Maria Davis, where two younger Mott daughters as well as Lucretia's mother, Anna Coffin, had taken refuge.

At the Mott house, Lucretia and James and their guests tried to talk as though nothing was happening, while young Thomas Mott ran in and out to find out what was going on. By nine o'clock they learned that Pennsylvania Hall was consumed, and shortly afterwards, that a leader of the mob had shouted "On to the Motts" and started up Race Street toward the house on Ninth. But a friend of the Motts intervened. Shouting "On to the Motts" he turned the mob south, not north at the corner of Ninth and Race. Their anger unquenched, the members of the mob next attacked and burned Mother Bethel Church, then the nearby Shelter for Colored Orphans.

Undeterred by the burning of Pennsylvania Hall, the feminist-abolitionists met the next morning at the school house of Sarah Pugh to complete their convention, condemned the brutal actions of racial violence, and pledged themselves to "*expand*, not contract their social relations with their colored friends." Speaking to her fellow delegates, Lucretia Mott confessed she had found the occasion "a searching time":

> I had often thought how I should sustain myself if called to pass such an ordeal. I hope I speak it not in the spirit of boasting when I

tell you, my sisters, I believe I was strengthened by God. I felt at the moment that I was willing to suffer whatever the cause required. My best feelings acquit me of shrinking back in the hour of danger. But the mob was not suffered to molest us, and I feel thankful that we slept a few hours in tranquility and peace.

The next year the Anti-Slavery Convention of American Women again planned to meet in Philadelphia. After the mob scenes around Pennsylvania Hall the year before, Philadelphian reformers were frightened about the approaching convention. Lucretia Mott requested space to hold the convention from all the Quaker meetings, including her own Cherry Street Meeting, and was refused. Only the small Universalist Church was willing, but their space was much too small. The convention was finally forced to meet in a stable, the hall of the Pennsylvania Riding School.

City officials were also frightened of the approaching convention. Several days before it was scheduled, Mayor Isaac Roach called on Mott at her home on North Ninth Street. He told her that he wanted to prevent the troubles that had occurred last year, and that he had some questions and some suggestions. Was the meeting to be confined only to women? He would suggest Clarkson Hall, the property of the Pennsylvania Abolition Society which was already guarded by his officers. If the women would not meet in the evening, if they would avoid "unnecessary walking with colored people," he thought he could guarantee to prevent mob violence.

Lucretia Mott was furious. She regarded Mayor Roach's suggestions as disrespectful to all women and especially demeaning to black women, and let him know of her displeasure. . . .

The Convention assembled on May 1, 1839. Soon, however, a messenger arrived from Mayor Roach and called Lucretia Mott out of the meeting. The mayor wanted to know what time the Convention would close, since he had several officers in waiting whom he would like to discharge. According to the account of this interchange she gave to the convention, she had replied "that she could not tell when our business would be finished, but that we had not asked, and, she presumed, did not wish his aid."

Whether because of the firmness of their principles, or whether because they were not meeting at night, the convention passed without incident. For Lucretia Mott and those around her, the experience cemented their belief that turning to the corrupt power of the state in the form of police protection to guard their meetings was inconsistent with the moral nature of their crusade, and ineffectual as well, since the police often had the point of view of the mob. Thereafter, at their antislavery fairs and the women's rights conventions which were held following the Seneca Falls meeting of 1848, they generally refused to turn to the police to deal with the mob.

On one occasion in 1853, when Lucretia Mott was chairing a women's rights meeting in New York City which was beset by a mob organized by Tammany Hall boss Isaiah Rynders, she vacated the chair so that Ernestine Rose, who did not share her scruples, could call for police protection. Before the police could arrive however, the mob burst into the hall, and Lucretia Mott organized her colleagues to walk two by two through the angry crowd, choosing Rynders himself as her escort. To everyone's amazement, he complied.

The experience of the women also fed into the developing nonresistance movement. Henry C. Wright, agent of the New England Non-Resistance Society, wrote about the 1839 Convention in the *Non-Resistant*:

> The Mayor of the city went to the Convention and proffered the power at his command, to protect them from the violence of those who might be disposed to molest them. But the women, as I am told, gave him to understand that their confidence was in a higher power, that they dared not put themselves under the protection of clubs, swords and guns, and that their quiet and safety would be too dearly purchased by the destruction of those who might wish to disturb them. Half a day was spent in discussing what notice of the Mayor's offered protection should be entered in the minutes of the Convention or whether any notice should be taken of it.

Lucretia Mott was not present when the New England Non-Resistance Society was formed in the fall of 1838, after the clergymen present at a Peace Convention called by Garrison walked out over the issue of women's right to serve on a committee. In the fall of 1839, however, she attended the First Annual Meeting of the new society September 25–27 in Boston and was elected to the business committee. In a debate over what views could be expressed at the meetings, she insisted on freedom of expression, "the right we cannot deny and ought to respect though the opinion may be such as we disapprove." When a resolution calling on members of the Society to apply the principles of nonresistance to family life [was discussed], Henry Wright said he thought some physical restraint might be necessary for infants incapable of reason. Lucretia Mott said she believed that in family life all penalties were ineffective:

> My conviction is that penalty is ineffectual, and that there is a readier and better way of securing a willing obedience than by resorting to it. Some little incident in our own family will often illustrate the truth to us, in a way nothing else could do. One of our little girls when told to go to bed felt disinclined to obey, and some time after she was discovered hid under the table, thinking it a good piece of fun. No notice was taken of it, and she took her own time. We had forgotten the affair, when she came running

downstairs with her little bare feet, saying "do mother forgive me!" It was abundantly more efficacious than the theory of penalty called into practice could have been. I would wish this resolution would pass if we are prepared for it.

In the discussion that followed, Stephen S. Foster suggested that in some extreme cases punishment might be necessary. Lucretia argued:

> The extreme cases which may be brought to demand corporal punishment are like the extreme cases brought to nullify so many other arguments. The reason why such extreme cases occur is, I believe, because parents are not prepared. They overlook the fact that a child, like all human beings, has inalienable rights. It is the master that is not prepared for emancipation, and it is the parent that is not prepared to give up punishment.

In the spring of 1840 Lucretia Mott traveled in Delaware with Daniel Neall, the chair of Pennsylvania Hall, and his new wife, a cousin of hers, Rebecca Bunker Neall. Word that some abolitionists were speaking in this border state spread to proslavery forces. Near Smyrna, Delaware, some men gathered to throw stones at their carriage. Rebecca Neall, who was new to antislavery actions, was frightened but Lucretia quieted her fears, and they went on to the home of a local antislavery Friend. They were just having tea when some of the proslavery mob men came to the door, and demanded that Daniel Neall be turned over to them. When the host refused, the men shoved him aside and forced their way into the house. Lucretia Mott described what happened next in a letter to Maria Chapman:

> I pled hard with them to take me as I was the offender if offense had been committed and give him up to his wife—but they declining said "you are a woman and we have nothing to do with you"— to which I answered, "I ask no courtesy at your hands on account of my sex."

The men took Neall away, intending to tar and feather him. Lucretia Mott followed the party, continuing to offer herself as victim in place of Neall. Discomfited by her pursuit, the men finally gave way, having first smeared a bit of tar on Neall, and attached a few feathers, before shamefacedly turning him over to her. This story became famous in antislavery and nonresistance circles. . . .

In 1840, Lucretia and James Mott went to England to attend the World's Anti-Slavery Convention. The British hosts of this gathering were not prepared to accept women as delegates, and Lucretia and several other American women were denied seats on the floor of the convention, an action which had historic consequences. Elizabeth Cady Stanton, attending not as delegate but as the bride of her delegate husband, Henry Stanton, was so moved by Lucretia's handling of herself in reaction to this snub that she determined to do something for women. The Seneca Falls Convention of 1848, called by Lucretia Mott and Elizabeth Stanton, was the result. . . .

Throughout the 1840s, James and Lucretia Mott were occasionally involved in a form of nonviolent direct action, that of moving escaped slaves from safe house to safe house which was known as the underground railroad. Their friend Miller McKim, clerk of the Pennsylvania Anti-Slavery Society, and his black colleague, William Still, were central to this effort in Pennsylvania, and they occasionally called upon the Motts for help, as in the cases of Henry "Box" Brown and Jane Johnson, both escaped slaves who were briefly sheltered at the Motts.

With the passage of the Fugitive Slave Law in 1851, in an effort on the part of the U.S. Government to prevent this movement, and some forceful actions on the part of antislavery groups to prevent the recapture of slaves, some members of the antislavery movement began to believe that force was necessary to protect the fleeing slaves. Ultimately the connection between antislavery and nonresistance was broken.

In the Pennsylvania Anti-Slavery Society the issue came to the surface in 1851 when debate arose over the actions of William Parker and several other blacks in the town of Christiana, in Lancaster County, who had organized a mutual-protection group against slave hunters. When a slave master came to Christiana looking for four escaped slaves, an armed conflict arose, and the slaveowner was killed and his son wounded. Parker escaped to Canada, but a large number of blacks were arrested and charged with treason. So were three white farmers who had driven up but had refused to obey the marshal's order to help capture the slaves.

Lucretia Mott and the Female Anti-Slavery Society made warm clothes for the prisoners, who had been captured in early September in the clothes they were wearing, and held until their trial in late November in unheated prison cells at Moyamensing Prison. The women also attended the trial, which ended in acquittal. Lucretia Mott, however, was not convinced that the bloodshed at Christiana had been necessary. In 1852, when a report of the affair was made to the Pennsylvania Anti-Slavery Society, claiming that the results of the Christiana riot had been good, Lucretia Mott responded that good could never come from evil means. When Charles Burleigh argued that Harriet Beecher Stowe had been moved by the Fugitive Slave Law to write *Uncle Tom's Cabin*, recently serialized in the *National Era*, Lucretia Mott objected:

> We should attribute all good to the Infinite Source of Good. The evils of the Fugitive Law are infinite. Ask the colored people, whom it has scattered like sheep upon the mountains, what can compensate them for their sufferings and terrors and losses. See how it has corrupted the Northern people and how easily men, at first shocked at it, have become reconciled to it. This speculation is incapable of

demonstration. It opens a controversy without end. Is it not better to speak of evil as evil, not deducing from it any consequences which do not strictly belong to it? Does it not tend to weaken our abhorrence of wrong? There is nothing easier than to quote texts of Scripture in favor of any theory, as every sect supports its faith by texts. I am not willing to admit that Harriet Beecher Stowe was moved to write *Uncle Tom's Cabin* by that law; if she says so, I think she mistakes the influences which have moved her. I believe, rather, that it has been the moral sentiments and truths promulgated by the *Liberator,* the *National Era,* and the public discussion of the subject, upon her pure mind, exciting it to feel for the oppressed. If you point to the progress of our cause, through persecution, as evidence that the efforts of its enemies have helped it on, I have as good a right to say that but for those impediments, Slavery would have been abolished before now.

Throughout the 1850s, as slave rescues increased, and the actions of John Brown in Kansas caused many persons in the antislavery movement to reconsider their commitment to nonresistance, Lucretia Mott remained steadfast in her belief that moral force alone could be relied on to resist slave catchers, and to bring an eventual end to slavery. When John Brown was hanged at Harper's Ferry, and became a martyr in the eyes of many, Lucretia Mott was still careful to make a distinction between Brown's work against slavery, and his resort to violence:

> For it is not John Brown the soldier we praise, it is John Brown the moral hero; John Brown the noble confessor and patient martyr we honor, and whom we think it proper to honor in this day when men are carried away by the corrupt and proslavery clamour against him. Our weapons are drawn only from the armory of Truth; they are those of faith and love. They were those of moral indignation, strongly expressed against any wrong.

It was in this same speech that Lucretia Mott called herself "no advocate of passivity." Her belief that moral weapons were the only effective means with which to change institutions such as slavery did not abate with the coming of the Civil War. She regarded the resort to arms as a tragic error in the march toward justice. She was quick to point out, however, that the nation had not been at peace before Fort Sumter was fired upon; that there had been for years an "unequal, cruel war on the rights and liberties of millions of our unoffending fellow beings, a war waged from generation to generation with all the physical force of our government and our commander-in-chief." She was pointing out the violence of the status quo, not to excuse the resort to war but to clarify what real peace might mean. . . .

Prior to the war James and Lucretia Mott had attended several meetings of a group called the Pennsylvania Peace Society, which met sporadically. After the war they took part in forming a new organization, the Universal Peace Union, with a revived Pennsylvania Peace Society as its local affiliate. James Mott became president of the latter organization, serving until his death in 1868; Lucretia Mott was then president from 1870 until 1880, when she died. She was also for many years vice president of the Universal Peace Union. Into both these organizations she poured the fire of her remaining decades. Her sermons, which had previously focused largely on slavery and sometimes women's rights, now were often on the subject of peace. "Even the woman question, as far as voting goes, does not take hold of my every feeling as does war," she wrote a friend.

Lucretia Mott never conceded that the Civil War should have been fought with arms. It was moral warfare that had led to the abolition of slavery. The resort to arms had been a breakdown of that moral campaign:

> I regard the abolition of slavery as being much more the result of this moral warfare which was waged against the great crime of our nation than coming from the battlefield. It is true the Government had not risen to the high moral point which was required to accomplish this great object and [felt] it must use the weapons it was accustomed to employ.

In the same vein, she argued that it was possible to advocate nonresistance in a world where not everyone was yet converted to the use of moral force. We do not need to wait until everyone is converted to pure nonresistance, she argued, any more than we had to wait until everyone was converted to antislavery principles. It was possible to banish war and oppression without waiting for universal conversion. As she put it, "We are not to wait until there is no disposition to take revenge, but to declare that revenge shall not be acted out in the barbarous ways of the present."

The issues which Lucretia Mott supported through the peace societies were manifold. She campaigned to get military training out of the public schools, and continued to advocate the use of persuasion rather than punishment in raising children. She objected to capital punishment and insisted on the sacredness of human life. She argued for the arbitration of international disputes and the rights of the Native Americans, who were being driven ever further from their homes as the European Americans expanded the frontier westward. . . .

As she grew older, Lucretia Mott made peace the cornerstone of more and more of her sermons. She said she felt that peace was the natural instinct of humans, and that little children in particular grew up seeking peace. To turn from this instinctive support of peace to support of war required a high degree of miseducation. Jesus had taught peace, and so had many of the Old Testament prophets. It was not enough for members of the Religious Society of Friends to refuse to bear arms; they must actively work for peace with the "firmness and combativeness that marked us in the antislavery warfare."

The faith and optimism that had carried her through so many years of campaigning against slavery and for women's rights now made Lucretia Mott sure that the efforts to obtain world peace would be successful:

> When we see that the great mountain of slavery is cast down, we have great reason to believe that war also will be removed, for there are none but have a natural love of peace.

Modern advocates of nonviolence may not have quite the same faith in the goodness of human beings or the inevitability of progress which sustained Lucretia Mott through her many decades of struggle. Nevertheless they will find in her understanding of what we call the violence of the status quo: the need to couple peace with justice, and the need to pursue peace with "combativeness," concepts which have a modern ring. . . .

DOCUMENTS

An Abolitionist's Fourth of July, 1852

Fellow-Citizens—Pardon me, and allow me to ask, why am I called upon to speak here to-day? What have I, or those I represent, to do with your national independence? Are the great principles of political freedom and of natural justice, embodied in that Declaration of Independence, extended to us? And am I, therefore, called upon to bring our humble offering to the national altar, and to confess the benefits, and express devout gratitude for the blessings, resulting from your independence, to us?

Would to God, both for your sakes and ours, that an affirmative answer could be truthfully returned to these questions! Then would my task be light, and my burden easy and delightful. For who is there so cold that a nation's sympathy could not warm him? Who so obdurate and dead to the claims of gratitude, that would not thankfully acknowledge such priceless benefits? Who so stolid and selfish, that would not give his voice to swell the hallelujahs of a nation's jubilee, when the chains of servitude had been torn from his limbs? I am not that man. In a case like that, the dumb might eloquently speak, and the "lame man leap as an hart."

But, such is not the state of the case. I say it with a sad sense of the disparity between us. I am not included within the pale of this glorious anniversary! Your high independence only reveals the immeasurable

SOURCE: Frederick Douglass, *My Bondage and My Freedom.* Document from Bibliobase®, edited by Micheal Bellesiles. Copyright © Houghton Mifflin Company. Reprinted by permission.

distance between us. The blessings in which you this day rejoice, are not enjoyed in common. The rich inheritance of justice, liberty, prosperity, and independence, bequeathed by your fathers, is shared by you, not by me. The sunlight that brought life and healing to you, has brought stripes and death to me. This Fourth of July is yours, not mine. You may rejoice, I must mourn. To drag a man in fetters into the grand illuminated temple of liberty, and call upon him to join you in joyous anthems, were inhuman mockery and sacrilegious irony. Do you mean, citizens, to mock me, by asking me to speak to-day? If so, there is a parallel to your conduct.

And let me warn you that it is dangerous to copy the example of a nation whose crimes, towering up to heaven, were thrown down by the breath of the Almighty, burying that nation in irrecoverable ruin! I can to-day take up the plaintive lament of a peeled and woe-smitten people.

"By the rivers of Babylon, there we sat down. Yea! we wept when we remembered Zion. We hanged our harps upon the willows in the midst thereof. For there, they that carried us away captive, required of us a song; and they who wasted us required of us mirth, saying, Sing us one of the songs of Zion. How can we sing the Lord's song in a strange land? If I forget thee, O Jerusalem, let my right hand forget her cunning. If I do not remember thee, let my tongue cleave to the roof of my mouth."

Fellow-citizens, above your national, tumultuous joy, I hear the mournful wail of millions, whose chains, heavy and grievous yesterday, are to-day rendered more intolerable by the jubilant shouts that reach them. If I do forget, if I do not faithfully remember those bleeding children of sorrow this day, "may my right hand forget her cunning, and may my tongue cleave to the roof of my mouth!" To forget them, to pass lightly over their wrongs, and to chime in with the popular theme, would be treason most scandalous and shocking, and would make me a reproach before God and the world. My subject, then, fellow-citizens, is AMERICAN SLAVERY. I shall see this day and its popular characteristics from the slave's point of view. Standing there, identified with the American bondman, making his wrongs mine, I do not hesitate to declare, with all my soul, that the character and conduct of this nation never looked blacker to me than on this Fourth of July. Whether we turn to the declarations of the past, or to the professions of the present, the conduct of the nation seems equally hideous and revolting. America is false to the past, false to the present, and solemnly binds herself to be false to the future. Standing with God and the crushed and bleeding slave on this occasion, I will, in the name of humanity which is outraged, in the name of liberty which is fettered, in the name of the constitution and the bible, which are disregarded and trampled upon, dare to call in question and to denounce, with all the emphasis I can command, everything that serves to perpetuate slavery—the great sin and shame of America! "I will not equivocate; I will not excuse"; I will use the severest language I can command; and yet not one word shall escape me that any man, whose judgment is not blinded by prejudice, or who is not at heart a slaveholder, shall not confess to be right and just.

But I fancy I hear some one of my audience say, it is just in this circumstance that you and your brother abolitionists fail to make a favorable impression on the public mind. Would you argue more, and denounce less, would you persuade more and rebuke less, your cause would be much more likely to succeed. But, I submit, where all is plain there is nothing to be argued. What point in the anti-slavery creed would you have me argue? On what branch of the subject do the people of this country need light? Must I undertake to prove that the slave is a man? That point is conceded already. Nobody doubts it. The slaveholders themselves acknowledge it in the enactment of laws for their government. They acknowledge it when they punish disobedience on the part of the slave. There are seventy-two crimes in the state of Virginia, which, if committed by a black man (no matter how ignorant he be), subject him to the punishment of death; while only two of these same crimes will subject a white man to the like punishment. What is this but the acknowledgment that the slave is a moral, intellectual, and responsible being. The manhood of the slave is conceded. It is admitted in the fact that southern statute books are covered with enactments forbidding, under severe fines and penalties, the teaching of the slave to read or write. When you can point to any such laws, in reference to the beasts of the field, then I may consent to argue the manhood of the slave. When the dogs in your streets, when the fowls of the air, when the cattle on your hills, when the fish of the sea, and the reptiles that crawl, shall be unable to distinguish the slave from a brute, then will I argue with you that the slave is a man!

For the present, it is enough to affirm the equal manhood of the Negro race. Is it not astonishing that, while we are plowing, planting, and reaping, using all kinds of mechanical tools, erecting houses, constructing bridges, building ships, working in metals of brass, iron, copper, silver, and gold; that, while we are reading, writing, and cyphering, acting as clerks, merchants, and secretaries, having among us lawyers, doctors, ministers, poets, authors, editors, orators, and teachers; that, while we are engaged in all manner of enterprises common to other men—digging gold in California, capturing the whale in the Pacific, feeding sheep and cattle on the hillside, living, moving, acting, thinking, planning, living in families as husbands, wives, and children, and above all, confessing and worshipping the Christian's God, and looking hopefully for life and immortality beyond the grave—we are called upon to prove that we are men! Would you have me argue that man is entitled to liberty? that he is the rightful owner of his own body? You have already declared it. Must I argue the wrongfulness of slavery? Is that a question for republicans? Is it to be settled by the rules of logic and argumentation, as a matter beset with great difficulty, involving a doubtful application of the principle of justice, hard to be understood? How should I look to-day in the presence of Americans, dividing and subdividing

241

a discourse, to show that men have a natural right to freedom, speaking of it relatively and positively, negatively and affirmatively? To do so, would be to make myself ridiculous, and to offer an insult to your understanding. There is not a man beneath the canopy of heaven that does not know that slavery is wrong for him.

What! Am I to argue that it is wrong to make men brutes, to rob them of their liberty, to work them without wages, to keep them ignorant of their relations to their fellow-men, to beat them with sticks, to flay their flesh with the lash, to load their limbs with irons, to hunt them with dogs, to sell them at auction, to sunder their families, to knock out their teeth, to burn their flesh, to starve them into obedience and submission to their masters? Must I argue that a system, thus marked with blood and stained with pollution, is wrong? No; I will not. I have better employment for my time and strength than such arguments would imply.

What, then, remains to be argued? Is it that slavery is not divine; that God did not establish it; that our doctors of divinity are mistaken? There is blasphemy in the thought. That which is inhuman cannot be divine. Who can reason on such a proposition! They that can, may! I cannot. The time for such argument is past. At a time like this, scorching irony, not convincing argument, is needed. Oh! Had I the ability, and could I reach the nation's ear, I would today pour out a fiery stream of biting ridicule, blasting reproach, withering sarcasm, and stern rebuke. For it is not light that is needed, but fire; it is not the gentle shower, but thunder. We need the storm, the whirlwind, and the earthquake. The feeling of the nation must be quickened; the conscience of the nation must be roused; the propriety of the nation must be startled; the hypocrisy of the nation must be exposed; and its crimes against God and man must be proclaimed and denounced.

What to the American slave is your Fourth of July? I answer, a day that reveals to him, more than all other days in the year, the gross injustice and cruelty to which he is the constant victim. To him, your celebration is a sham; your boasted liberty, an unholy license; your national greatness, swelling vanity; your sounds of rejoicing are empty and heartless; your denunciations of tyrants, brass-fronted impudence; your shouts of liberty and equality, hollow mockery; your prayers and hymns, your sermons and thanksgivings, with all your religious parade and solemnity, are to him mere bombast, fraud, deception, impiety, and hypocrisy—a thin veil to cover up crimes which would disgrace a nation of savages. There is not a nation on the earth guilty of practices more shocking and bloody, than are the people of these United States, at this very hour.

Go where you may, search where you will, roam through all the monarchies and despotisms of the old world, travel through South America, search out every abuse, and when you have found the last, lay your facts by the side of the every-day practices of this nation, and you will say with me, that, for revolting barbarity and shameless hypocrisy, America reigns without a rival.

Songs of the Temperance Movement, 1847

Take Courage

Tune—Calvary

From the mountain top and valley,
See! the banner streaming high!
While the sons of freedom rally
To the widow's lonely cry,
Sisters weeping,
Bid us to the rescue fly.

Could we hear the mother pleading,
Heaven relief will quickly send;
Can we see our country bleeding,
Still refuse our aid to lend?
No! dread monster,
Here thy triumph soon shall end.

Must we see the drunkard reeling
(Void of reason) to the grave?
Where's the heart so dead to feeling,
Who would not the wanderer save?
God of mercy,
'Tis thy blessing now we crave.

Dearest Savior, O, relieve us.
Unto thee we humbly bow,
Let that fiend no more deceive us,
Grant thy loving favor now;
While against him,
Here we pledge a sacred vow.

Now the trump of Temperance sounding,
Rouse! ye freemen! why delay?
Let your voices all resounding,
Welcome on the happy day,
When that tyrant
Must resign his cruel sway.

SOURCE: Willard Thorp, Merle Curti, Carlos Baker, eds., *American Issues* (Chicago: J. B. Lippincott Co., 1944), 1:475–476.

One Glass More

Stay, mortal, stay! nor heedless thus
 Thy sure destruction seal;
Within that cup there lurks a curse,
Which all who drink shall feel.
Disease and death forever nigh,
Stand ready at the door,
And eager wait to hear the cry—
"O give me one glass more!"

Go, view that prison's gloomy cells—
Their pallid tenants scan;
Gaze—gaze upon these earthly hells,
Ask when they began:
Had these a tongue—oh, man! thy cheek
Would burn with crimson o'er—
Had these a tongue they'd to thee speak,
Oh take not *one glass more.*"

Behold that wretched female form,
An outcast from her home;
Crushed by affliction's blighting storm,
And doom'd in want to roam:
Behold her! ask that prattler dear,
Why mother is so poor,
He'll whisper in thy startled ear,
'Twas father's *one glass more.*"

Stay, mortal stay, repent, return!
Reflect upon thy fate;
The poisonous draught indignant spurn,
Spurn—spurn it ere too late.
Oh, fly thee ale-house's horrid din,
Nor linger at the door,
Lest thou perchance, should sip again
The treacherous *one glass more.*"

The "Reformatory and Elevating Influences" of the Public Schools, 1848

Under the Providence of God, our means of education are the grand machinery by which the "raw material" of human nature can be worked up into inventors and discoverers, into skilled artisans and scientific farmers, into scholars and jurists, into the founders of benevolent institutions, and the great expounders of ethical and theological science. By means of early education, those embryos of talent may be quickened, which will solve the difficult problems of political and economical law; and by them, too, the genius may be kindled which will blaze forth in the Poets of Humanity. Our schools, far more than they have done, may supply the Presidents and Professors of Colleges, and Superintendents of Public Instruction, all over the land; and send, not only into our sister states, but across the Atlantic, the men of practical science, to superintend the construction of the great works of art. Here, too, may those judicial powers be developed and invigorated, which will make legal principles so clear and convincing as to prevent appeals to force; and, should the clouds of war ever lower over our country, some hero may be found,—the nursling of our schools, and ready to become the leader of our armies,—the best of all heroes, who will secure the glories of a peace, unstained by the magnificent murders of the battle-field. . . .

Without undervaluing any other human agency, it may be safely affirmed that the Common School, improved and energized, as it can easily be, may become the most effective and benignant of all the forces of civilization. Two reasons sustain this position. In the first place, there is a universality in its operation, which can be affirmed of no other institution whatever. If administered in the spirit of justice and conciliation, all the rising generation may be brought within the circle of its reformatory and elevating influences. And, in the second place, the materials upon which it operates are so pliant and ductile as to be susceptible of assuming a greater variety of forms than any other earthly work of the Creator. The inflexibility and ruggedness of the oak, when compared with the lithe sapling or the tender germ, are but feeble emblems to typify the docility of childhood, when contrasted with the obduracy and intractableness of man. It is these inherent advantages of the Common School, which, in our own State, have produced results so striking, from a system so imperfect, and an administration so feeble. In teaching the blind, and the deaf and dumb, in kindling the latent spark of intelligence that lurks in an idiot's mind, and in the more holy work of reforming abandoned and outcast children, education has proved what it can do, by glorious experiments.

SOURCE: [Horace Mann], Massachusetts Board of Education, *Twelfth Annual Report of . . . the Secretary of the Board* (Boston, 1849), 32, 37.

These wonders, it has done in its infancy, and with the lights of a limited experience; but, when its faculties shall be fully developed, when it shall be trained to wield its mighty energies for the protection of society against the giant vices which now invade and torment it;—against intemperance, avarice, war, slavery, bigotry, the woes of want and the wickedness of waste,—then, there will not be a height to which these enemies of the race can escape, which it will not scale, nor a Titan among them all, whom it will not slay.

Elizabeth Cady Stanton: On Women's Rights, 1860

If the object of government is to protect the weak against the strong, how unwise to place the power wholly in the hands of the strong. Yet that is the history of all governments, even the model republic of these United States. You who have read the history of nations from Moses down to our last election, where have you ever seen one class looking after the interests of another? Any of you can readily see the defects in other governments and pronounce sentence against those who have sacrificed the masses to themselves; but when we come to our own case, we are blinded by custom and self-interest. Some of you who have no capital can see the injustice which the laborer suffers; some of you who have no slaves can see the cruelty of his oppression; but who of you appreciate the galling humiliation, the refinements of degradation to which women (the mothers, wives, sisters, and daughters of freemen) are subject in this last half of the 19th century? How many of you have ever read even the laws concerning them that now disgrace your statute books? In cruelty and tyranny they are not surpassed by any slaveholding code in the South. . . .

But, say you, we would not have woman exposed to the grossness and vulgarity of public life, or encounter what she must at the polls. When you talk, gentlemen, of sheltering woman from the rough winds and revolting scenes of real life, you must be either talking for effect or wholly ignorant of what the facts of life are. The man, whatever he is, is known to the woman. She is the companion, not only of the accomplished statesman, the orator, and the scholar; but the vile, vulgar, brutal man has his mother, his wife, his sister, his daughter. Yes, delicate, refined, educated women are in daily life with the drunkard, the gambler, the licentious man, the rogue, and the villain; and if man shows out what he is anywhere, it is at his own hearthstone. There are over 40,000 drunkards in this state. All these are bound by the ties of family to some woman. Allow but a mother and a wife to each, and you have over

SOURCE: Elizabeth Cady Stanton et al. (eds.), *History of Women's Suffrage*, vol. 1 (New York: 1881), 679–685.

80,000 women. All these have seen their fathers, brothers, husbands, sons in the lowest and most debased stages of obscenity and degradation. In your own circle of friends, do you not know refined women whose whole lives are darkened and saddened by gross and brutal associations?

Now, gentlemen, do you talk to woman of a rude jest or jostle at the polls where noble, virtuous men stand ready to protect her person and her rights, when alone in the darkness and solitude and gloom of night she has trembled on her own threshold awaiting the return of a husband from his midnight revels?—when stepping from her chamber she has beheld her royal monarch, her lord and master—her legal representative—the protector of her property, her home, her children, and her person, down on his hands and knees slowly crawling up the stairs? Behold him in her chamber—in her bed! The fairy tale of *Beauty and the Beast* is far too often realized in life. Gentlemen, such scenes as woman has witnessed at her own fireside where no eye save Omnipotence could pity, no strong arm could help, can never be realized at the polls, never equaled elsewhere this side the bottomless pit. No, woman has not hitherto lived in the clouds surrounded by an atmosphere of purity and peace; but she has been the companion of man in health, in sickness, and in death, in his highest and in his lowest moments. She has worshiped him as a saint and an orator, and pitied him as madman or a fool.

In paradise man and woman were placed together, and so they must ever be. They must sink or rise together. If man is low and wretched and vile, woman cannot escape the contagion, and any atmosphere that is unfit for woman to breathe is not fit for man. Verily, the sins of the fathers shall be visited upon the children to the third and fourth generation. You, by your unwise legislation, have crippled and dwarfed womanhood by closing to her all honorable and lucrative means of employment, have driven her into the garrets and dens of our cities where she now revenges herself on your innocent sons, sapping the very foundations of national virtue and strength. Alas! for the young men just coming on the stage of action who soon shall fill your vacant places, our future senators, our presidents, the expounders of our constitutional law! Terrible are the penalties we are now suffering for the ages of injustice done to woman.

Again it is said that the majority of women do not ask for any change in the laws; that it is time enough to give them the elective franchise when they as a class demand it.

Wise statesmen legislate for the best interests of the nation; the state, for the highest good of its citizens; the Christian, for the conversion of the world. Where would have been our railroads, our telegraphs, our ocean steamers, our canals and harbors, our arts and sciences if government had withheld the means from the far-seeing minority? This state established our present system of common schools, fully believing that educated men and women would make better citizens than ignorant ones. In making this provision for the education of its children, had they waited for a majority of the urchins of this state to petition for schools, how many, think you, would have asked to be transplanted from the street to the schoolhouse? Does the state wait for the criminal to ask for his prison house; the insane, the idiot, the deaf and dumb for his asylum? Does the Christian in his love to all mankind wait for the majority of the benighted heathen to ask him for the Gospel? No; unasked and unwelcomed, he crosses the trackless ocean, rolls off the mountain of superstition that oppresses the human mind, proclaims the immortality of the soul, the dignity of manhood, the right of all to be free and happy.

No, gentlemen, if there is but one woman in this state who feels the injustice of her position, she should not be denied her inalienable rights because the common household drudge and silly butterfly of fashion are ignorant of all laws, both human and divine. Because they know nothing of governments or rights and therefore ask nothing, shall my petitions be unheard? I stand before you, the rightful representative of woman, claiming a share in the halo of glory that has gathered round her in the ages; and by the wisdom of her past words and works, her peerless heroism and self-sacrifice, I challenge your admiration; and moreover claiming, as I do, a share in all her outrages and sufferings, in the cruel injustice, contempt, and ridicule now heaped upon her, in her deep degradation, hopeless wretchedness, by all that is helpless in her present condition, that is false in law and public sentiment, I urge your generous consideration; for as my heart swells with pride to behold woman in the highest walks of literature and art, it grows big enough to take in those who are bleeding in the dust.

Now do not think, gentlemen, we wish you to do a great many troublesome things for us. We do not ask our legislators to spend a whole session in fixing up a code of laws to satisfy a class of most unreasonable women. We ask no more than the poor devils in the Scripture asked, "Let us alone." In mercy, let us take care of ourselves, our property, our children, and our homes. True, we are not so strong, so wise, so crafty as you are, but if any kind friend leaves us a little money, or we can by great industry earn fifty cents a day, we would rather buy bread and clothes for our children than cigars and champagne for our legal protectors. . . .

Chapter 14

Plantation Society in the Antebellum South

African American families on an antebellum slave plantation.

By 1850 participants in a number of reform movements could point to some notable achievements. Throughout the Northeast and Midwest, public schools had sprung up in towns in which none had previously existed, while older systems were receiving substantially greater financial support. The public library movement enjoyed similar success, and the treatment of debtors, criminals, and the mentally ill improved. Despite these and other achievements, it is unlikely that any reform leader considered the goals of his or her movement attained by the beginning of the 1850s; much work remained. As the decade wore on, the spirit of perfectionism gradually gave way to the bitter divisiveness of sectionalism and slavery—issues that ultimately were resolved by neither moral suasion nor legislation, but by war.

During the American Revolution, a number of white Americans had seen the inconsistency of fighting Great Britain in the name of freedom while holding slaves in bondage. Virginia, North Carolina, and Maryland passed laws making it easier for masters to free their slaves. A few planters released their slaves outright, and some others, including George Washington, made provisions for manumission in their wills. Gradually the Northern states abolished slavery. With the expansion of the cotton kingdom, however, white Southerners became increasingly dependent on slave labor. Far from liberalizing their attitudes and practices toward slavery, after 1800 Southern legislatures passed new restrictions that made it extremely difficult for masters to emancipate their bondsmen. In response to abolitionist attacks, many Southerners shifted their public posture on slavery from defending it as a necessary evil to advocating it as a positive good. The first document, from a speech delivered before the South Carolina legislature by Governor George McDuffie in 1835, provides an example of the "slavery as a positive good" position as well as an example of a southern response to the abolition movement. Note his employment of religion in both instances. What were some of the other key arguments put forth by McDuffie as revealed in these excerpts? As you read this chapter's essay and remaining documents, keep in mind the governor's description of the slaves' response to their servitude.

In the eyes of the law, slaves were little more than property, with few legal rights. Yet their individual experiences could vary greatly. In recent years scholars have devoted considerable attention to how blacks survived and created their own distinctive culture within slavery. A vivid example of this is found in the essay "Culture, Conflict, and Community on an Antebellum Plantation," by Drew Gilpin Faust. As you read the story of Silver Bluff plantation, many of your previously held perceptions of the relationship between master and slaves will undoubtedly be challenged. Notice the limitations—not imposed by law but originating in the slaves' culture and society—on the master's ability to control his bondsmen totally, as well as the many factors contributing to a sense of community and autonomy among the slaves. How does the author explain the decision of the blacks of Silver Bluff to remain on the plantation at the close of the Civil War, even after their freedom was proclaimed?

Faust's essay provides numerous examples of how slaves asserted themselves as individuals and as a community. The spirituals that make up the second document display still another means by which blacks expressed their attitudes toward slavery and their aspirations for the future. Notice that the lyrics of each song have two levels of meaning, one telling a purely Biblical story or delivering a religious message, the other applying that story or message to the slaves' own lives. These songs should help to explain why James Hammond sought repeatedly to "break up negro preaching & negro churches."

A description of life on a single plantation cannot, of course, provide a complete picture of slavery. Conditions varied from plantation to plantation, from master to master. One factor was constant, however. Slaves were considered the property of their owners and treated as such. The final document provides only an inkling of the horrors endured by slaves at the mercy of a brutal master. Most slave narratives were written by men and, naturally, present a male perspective on plantation life. Harriet Jacobs's account, published shortly before the outbreak of the Civil War, enables us to see an aspect of slavery all too common yet rarely acknowledged at the time: the sexual abuse of female slaves by their owners. Note Jacobs's comments regarding the impact of the master's behavior on his wife's attitude toward the victims. In considering the descriptions of slavery in this chapter, bear in mind that slaves had no control over where and for whom they labored.

ESSAY

Culture, Conflict, and Community on an Antebellum Plantation
Drew Gilpin Faust

A dozen miles south of Augusta, Georgia, the Savannah River curves gently, creating two bends that were known to antebellum steamboat captains as Stingy Venus and Hog Crawl Round. Nearby, on the South Carolina shore, a cliff abruptly rises almost thirty feet above the water. Mineral deposits in the soil give the promontory a metallic tinge, and the bank and the plantation of which it was part came as early as colonial times to be called Silver Bluff.

In 1831, an opportune marriage placed this property in the hands of twenty-four-year-old James Henry Hammond. An upwardly mobile lawyer, erstwhile schoolmaster and newspaper editor, the young Carolinian had achieved through matrimony the status the Old South accorded to planters alone. When he arrived to take possession of his estate, he found and carefully listed in his diary 10,800 acres of land, a dwelling, assorted household effects, and 147 bondsmen. But along with these valued acquisitions, he was to receive a challenge he had not anticipated. As he sought to exert his mastery over the labor force on which the prosperity of his undertaking depended, he was to discover that his task entailed more than simply directing 147 individual lives. Hammond had to dominate a complex social order already in existence on the plantation and to struggle for the next three decades to control what he called a "system of roguery" amongst his slaves.

Hammond astutely recognized that black life on his plantation was structured and organized as a "system," the very existence of which seemed necessarily a challenge to his absolute control—and therefore, as he perceived it, a kind of "roguery." Because Hammond's mastery over his bondsmen depended upon his success at undermining slave society and culture, he established a carefully designed plan of physical and psychological domination in hopes of destroying the foundations of black solidarity. Until he relinquished management of the estate to his sons in the late 1850s,

SOURCE: Drew Gilpin Faust, "Culture, Conflict, and Community: The Meaning of Power on an Antebellum Plantation," *Journal of Social History* 14, no. 1 (fall 1980): 83–97. Reprinted by permission of *Journal of Social History*.

Hammond kept extraordinarily detailed records. Including daily entries concerning the treatment, work patterns, and vital statistics of his slaves, they reveal a striking portrait of slave culture and resistance and of the highly structured efforts Hammond took to overpower it. The existence of such data about one master and one community of slaves over a considerable period of time makes possible a tracing of the dialectic of their interaction as one not so much among individuals, but between two loci of power and two opposing systems of belief. While Hammond sought to assert both dominance and legitimacy, the slaves at Silver Bluff strove to maintain networks of communication and community as the bases of their personal and cultural autonomy. This struggle, which constantly tested the ingenuity and strength of both the owner and his slaves, touched everything from religion to work routines to health, and even determined the complex pattern of unauthorized absences from the plantation. . . .

When Hammond took possession of Silver Bluff, he assumed a role and entered a world largely unfamiliar to him. His father had owned a few slaves and even deeded two to young James Henry. But Hammond was entirely inexperienced in the management of large numbers of agricultural and domestic workers. The blacks at Silver Bluff, for their part, confronted a new situation as well, for they had become accustomed to living without a master in permanent residence. Hammond's wife's father, Christopher Fitzsimons, had been a prominent Charleston merchant who visited this upcountry property only intermittently. Upon his death in 1825, the plantation was left to his daughter Catherine, and came under the desultory management of Fitzsimons' sons, who had far less interest than would their future brother-in-law in making it a profitable enterprise. In 1831, therefore, both Hammond and his slaves faced new circumstances. But it was Hammond who was the outsider, moving into a world of established patterns of behavior and interaction in the community at Silver Bluff. Although by law all power rested with Hammond, in reality the situation was rather different.

As a novice at masterhood, Hammond received advice and encouragement from his friends. "Be kind to them. Make them feel an obligation," one acquaintance counselled, ". . . and by all means keep all other negroes away from the place, and make yours stay at home—and Raze their church to the ground—keep them from fanaticism for God's sake as well as for your own. . . ." Hammond took this exhortation to heart, seeking within a week of his arrival at the Bluff to enhance his power by extending control over the very souls of his slaves. "Intend to break up negro preaching & negro churches," he proclaimed in his diary. "Refused to allow Ben Shubrick to join the Negro Church . . . but promised to have him taken in the church . . . I attended. . . . Ordered night meetings on the plantation to be discontinued."

The desire to control black religious life led Hammond to endeavor to replace independent black worship with devotions entirely under white direction. At first he tried to compel slaves into white churches simply by making black ones unavailable, and even sought to prevent his neighbors from permitting black churches on their own lands. But soon he took positive steps to provide the kind of religious environment he deemed appropriate for his slaves. For a number of years he hired itinerant ministers for Sunday afternoon slave services. By 1845, however, Hammond had constructed a Methodist Church for his plantation and named it St. Catherine's after his wife.

The piety of the Hammond slaves became a source of admiration even to visitors. A house guest on the plantation in the 1860s found the services at St. Catherine's "solemn and impressive," a tribute, she felt, to Hammond's beneficent control over his slaves. "There was a little company of white people," she recalled, "the flower of centuries of civilization, among hundreds of blacks but yesterday . . . in savagery, now peaceful, contented, respectful and comprehending the worship of God. . . . By reason of Senator Hammond's wise discipline," the visitor assured her readers, there was no evidence of "religious excesses," the usual "mixture of hysteria and conversion" that she believed characterized most black religion. These slaves, it appeared to an outsider, had abandoned religious ecstasy for the reverential passivity prescribed for them by white cultural norms.

Hammond had taken great pains to establish just such white standards amongst his slaves, and the visitor's description of the behavior he succeeded in eliciting from his bondsmen would undoubtedly have pleased him. But even Hammond recognized that the decorous behavior of his slaves within the walls of St. Catherine's was but an outward compliance with his directives. He seemed unable to eradicate black religious expression, evidences of which appeared to him like tips of an iceberg indicating an underlying pattern of independent belief and worship that persisted among his slaves. Twenty years after his original decision to eliminate the slave church, Hammond recorded in his plantation diary, "Have ordered all church meetings to be broken up except at the Church with a white preacher." Hammond's slaves had over the preceding decades tested their master's initial resolve, quietly asserting their right to their own religious life in face of his attempt to deny it to them.

In the course of these years, they had re-established their church, forcing Hammond to accept a level of black religious autonomy and to permit the slaves to hold as many as four different prayer meetings in the quarters each week. Hammond returned to his original commitment to "break up negro preaching" only when the intensity of black religious fervor seemed to threaten that compromise level of moderation he and his slaves had come tacitly to accept. "Religious troubles among the negroes"—as in 1851 he described his sense of the growing disorder—revived his determination to control the very emotional and ideational sources of unruliness among his slaves. "They are running the thing into the ground," he remarked, "by

being allowed too much organization—too much power to the head men &
too much praying and Church meeting on the plantation." Black religious
life re-emerged as an insupportable threat when it assumed the characteristics
of a formal system, with, as Hammond explicitly recognized, organization
and leadership to challenge his own power. The recurrent need for Hammond to act against the expanding strength of the black church indicates his
failure either to eliminate this organization or to control his slaves' belief
and worship.

The struggle for power manifested in the conflict over religious autonomy
was paralleled in other areas of slave life on the Hammond domain. Just as
Hammond sought from the time of his arrival in 1831 to control religious behavior, so too he desired to supervise work patterns more closely. "When
I first began to plant," he later reminisced, "I found my people in very bad
subjection from the long want of a master and it required of me a year of severity which cost me infinite pain." The slaves, accustomed to a far less rigorous
system of management, resented his attempts and tried to undermine his
drive for efficiency. "The negroes are trying me," Hammond remarked in his
diary on more than one occasion during the early months of his tenure. In
response, he was firm, recording frequent floggings of slaves who refused to
comply with his will. When several bondsmen sought to extend the Christmas
holiday by declining to return to work as scheduled, Hammond was unyield-
ing, forcing them back to the fields and whipping them as well.

As the weeks passed, the instances of beatings and overt insubordination noted in plantation records diminished; a more subtle form of conflict
emerged. Over the next decade, this struggle over work patterns at Silver
Bluff fixed on the issue of task versus gang labor. The slaves clearly preferred the independent management of their time offered by the task system,
while Hammond feared the autonomy it provided the bondsmen. "They do
much more" in a gang, Hammond noted, and "are not so apt to strain themselves." Task work, he found, encouraged the blacks to complete required
chores too rapidly, with "no rest until 3 or 4 o'clock," and then gave them the
opportunity for hours of unsupervised recreation. But despite what owners
generally tended to see as its wholesomeness and security, gang work had
the significant disadvantage of displeasing the laborers, who at Silver Bluff
performed badly in a calculated effort to restore the task system. "Negroes
dissatisfied to work in a gang & doing badly," Hammond observed in 1838.
Almost exactly a year later he made a similar remark, noting that hoers were
leaving "all the weeds and bunches of grass" growing around the cotton
plants. "Evidently want to work task work which I will not do again."

Although at this time Hammond succeeded in establishing the gang as
the predominant form of labor at Silver Bluff, the victory was apparently
neither final nor total. Indeed, it may simply have served to regularize the
pattern of poorly performed work Hammond had viewed as a form of
resistance to the gang system. He continued to record hoeing that ignored

weeds, picking that passed over bulging cotton bolls, and cultivating that destroyed both mule and plough. But eventually the slaves here too won a compromise. By 1850, Hammond was referring once again in his correspondence and in his plantation diary to task work, although he complained bitterly about continuing poor performance and the frequent departure of many bondsmen from the fields as early as midafternoon.

Hammond seemed not so much to master as to manipulate his slaves, offering a system not just of punishments, but of positive inducements, ranging from picking contests to single out the most diligent hands, to occasional rituals of rewards for all, such as Christmas holidays; rations of sugar, tobacco and coffee; midsummer barbecues; or even the pipes sent all adult slaves from Europe when Hammond departed on the Grand Tour. The slaves were more than just passive recipients of these sporadic benefits; they in turn manipulated their master for those payments and privileges they had come to see as their due. Hammond complained that his bondsmen's demands led him against his will to countenance a slave force "too well fed & otherwise well treated," but he nevertheless could not entirely resist their claims. When after a particularly poor record of work by slaves in the fall of 1847 Hammond sought to shorten the usual Christmas holiday, he ruefully recorded on December 26 that he had been "persuaded out of my decision by the Negroes."

Hammond and his slaves arrived at a sort of accommodation on the issue of work. But in this process, Hammond had to adjust his desires and expectations as significantly as did his bondsmen. His abstract notions of order and absolute control were never to be fully realized. He and his slaves reached a truce that permitted a level of production acceptable to Hammond and a level of endeavor tolerable to his slaves.

Like his use of rewards and punishments, Hammond's more general instructions for plantation management reveal his understanding of the process of mastery as consisting in large measure of symbolic and psychological control. The necessity of resorting to physical punishment, he maintained, indicated a failure in ideal management. Hammond constantly tried to encourage the bondsmen to internalize their master's definition of their inferiority and thus willingly come to acknowledge his legitimacy. Yet Hammond recognized that to succeed in this aim, he had necessarily to mask his own dependence upon them. Hammond was well aware that the black driver Tom Kollock was a far more experienced agriculturist than his master or than the plantation overseers. "I wish you to consult him [Tom]," Hammond instructed a new overseer, "on all occasions & in all matters of doubt take his opinion wh. you will find supported by good reasons." But, he warned, Kollock must be kept "in ignorance of his influence. . . . I would not have Tom injured by the supposition that he was the head manager any more than I would have you mortified by such a state of things." Yet Kollock knew more than he showed, for Hammond found two decades later that the driver had long exploited the power of which the master had presumed him ignorant. While pretending to effective management of both crops and personnel, Kollock had instead worked to undermine productivity by demanding the minimum of his workers. Kollock had fooled Hammond, who in a fury of discovery proclaimed him a "humbug." "I now see," Hammond declared in 1854, "that in him rests the fault of my last . . . crops. He has trained his hands to do very little & that badly."

Unaware how transparent and easily manipulable he must have appeared to slaves, Hammond sought continually to refine and perfect his system of management. A devoted disciple of scientific agriculture and administration, he developed in the 1840s a formal set of rules for treatment and supervision of slaves, allocating carefully defined areas of responsibility to master, overseer, and driver.

Nearly every detail of these regulations indicates a conscious desire to impress the bondsmen with their total dependence upon their master, and, simultaneously, with the merciful beneficence of his absolute rule. Lest the overseer's power seem to diminish the master's own authority, Hammond defined the role of the black driver to serve as check upon him. Because he could only be whipped by the master, the driver was removed from the overseer's control and his status enhanced amongst his fellow slaves. In addition, the driver had the explicit right to by-pass the overseer and to appeal directly to the master with suggestions or complaints about plantation management—or the overseer's behavior. Hammond invested the driver with enough power to encourage the slaves to accept as their official voice the leader Hammond had chosen and, he hoped, co-opted. It was Hammond's specific intention, moreover, to use administrative arrangements to set the overseer and driver at odds and thus to limit the power of each in relation to his own. One of his greatest fears was that the two would co-operate to conspire against him.

Such divisions of authority were clearly designed to emphasize the master's power, but at the same time were meant to cast him as a somewhat distant arbiter of justice, one who did not involve himself in the sordidness of daily floggings. Instead, Hammond sought to portray himself as the dispenser of that mercy designed to win the grateful allegiance of the slave and to justify the plantation's social order. He constantly tried to make himself appear not so much the creator of rules—which of course in reality he was—but the grantor of exceptions and reprieves.

At Silver Bluff, the distribution of provisions was an occasion for Hammond to display this paternalistic conception. The event assumed the form and significance of a cultural ritual, a ceremony in which Hammond endeavored to present himself to his slaves as the source from whom all blessings flowed. Once a week, the bondsmen were required to put on clean clothes and appear before the master to receive their food allowance. "They should," he recorded in his plantation regulations, "be brought into that contact with the master at least once a week of receiving the means of subsistence from him." Although the overseer could perfectly well have executed such a task, the ceremonial importance of this moment demanded the master's direct participation. The special requirement for fresh apparel set the occasion off from the less sacred events of daily life, and underlined the symbolic character of this interaction between lord and bondsmen. The event illustrated Hammond's most idealized conception of the master-slave relationship and represented his effort to communicate this understanding to the slaves themselves, convincing them of his merciful generosity and of their own humble dependence and need. The interaction was a statement designed to help transform his power into legitimized authority.

But Hammond's slaves were not taken in by this ritual; they remained less dependent on his dispensations of food and far more active in procuring the necessary means of subsistence than their master cared to admit. Slaves tended their own garden plots and fished for the rich bounty of the Savannah River. And to Hammond's intense displeasure, they also stole delicacies out of his own larder. Pilfering of food and alcohol at Silver Bluff did not consist simply of a series of random acts by slaves seeking to alleviate hunger or compensate for deprivation. Instead, theft assumed the characteristics of a contest between master and slave. Indeed, the prospect of winning the competition may have provided the organized slaves with nearly as much satisfaction as did the actual material fruits of victory; it was clearly a battle over power as well as for the specific goods in question. Although Hammond began immediately in 1831 to try to reduce the level of depredations against his hogs, flogging suspected thieves made little impact. He could not prevent the disappearance of a sizeable portion of his pork or break what he saw as the "habit" of theft among his slaves. Over the years, his supply of livestock consequently diminished, and he found himself compelled to buy provisions to feed his slaves. Hammond recorded with grim satisfaction that the resulting reduction of the meat allowance would be just retribution for the slaves' conspiracy against his herds. Theirs would be, he consoled himself, a hollow victory. "The negroes," he noted in 1845, "have for years killed about half my shoats and must now suffer for it." But the impact of black theft was perhaps even greater on other plantation products. Hammond was resigned to never harvesting his potato crop at all, for the slaves stole the entire yield before it was even removed from the ground.

Alcohol, however, was the commodity that inspired the most carefully de-signed system of slave intrigue. When Hammond began to ferment wines from his own vineyards, slaves constantly tapped his bottles, then blamed the disap-pearance of the liquid on leaks due to miscorking. But the slave community's most elaborate assault on Hammond's supplies of alcohol went well beyond such crude tactics to call upon a unique conjunction of engineering skill with the power of voodoo. In 1835, Hammond found that several of his slaves had dug tunnels be-neath his wine cellar. Other house servants had provided aid, including necessary keys and information and some spiritual assistance as well. A female domestic,

Urana, Hammond recorded, used "'root work'" and thus "screened" the excavators by her "conjuration." Hammond determinedly "punished all who have had anything to do with the matter far or near." But his response could not replace the lost wine, nor compensate for the way the incident challenged the literal and figurative foundations of his plantation order. The force of voodoo lay entirely outside his system of domination and his efforts to establish cultural hegemony. The slaves were undermining his power as well as his house.

Folk beliefs flourished in other realms of slave life as well. Hammond's bondsmen succeeded in perpetuating African medical ideas and customs, even though their master's commitment to scientific plantation management necessarily included an effort to exercise close medical supervision over slave lives, in times of sickness and of health. The blacks of Silver Bluff may well have been encouraged in their resistance to Hammond's therapeutics by his record of dismal failure: he had great difficulty in achieving a slave population that reproduced itself. For the first twenty years of his management, slave deaths consistently exceeded slave births at the Bluff, despite Hammond's sincere and vigorous efforts to reverse these disheartening statistics. Hammond continually purchased new bondsmen, however, in order to offset a diminution in his labor supply probably caused as much by the low, damp and unhealthy location of much of his property as by any physical mistreatment or deprivation of his slaves.

In part, these difficulties arose from the shortcomings of medical knowledge in antebellum white America more generally. Initially, Hammond and the physicians he consulted employed a series of those heroic treatments that characterized accepted nineteenth-century medical practice—compelling the slaves to submit to disagreeable purges, bleedings and emetics. When these failed to cure, and seemed often to harm, Hammond gave up in disgust on conventional medicine and turned first to "Botanic Practice," then in 1854 to homeopathy, a medical fad that in its misguidedness at least had the virtue of advocating tiny dosages and thus minimizing the damage a practitioner might inflict.

Although Hammond never faltered in his certainty that Western science would eventually provide the solution to his dilemmas, his slaves retained an active skepticism, resisting his treatments by hiding illness and continuing to practice their own folk cures and remedies. In 1851, Hammond recognized that an entire alternative system of medical services thrived on his plantation. "Traced out the negro Doctors . . . who have been giving out medicine for years here & have killed I think most of those that have died. Punished them and also their patients very severely." Hammond was even able to use the existence of black medicine as a justification for the failures of his own methods. Although he did not refer to these doctors again, it seemed likely that he achieved no greater success in controlling them than in eliminating black preaching or voodoo.

For most of Hammond's slaves, insubordination served to establish cultural and personal autonomy within the framework of plantation demands. Resistance was a tool of negotiation, a means of extracting concessions from the master to reduce the extent of his claims over black bodies and souls. At Silver Bluff, such efforts often were directed more at securing necessary support for black community life than at totally overwhelming the master's power. Hammond learned that he could to a certain degree repress, but never eliminate black cultural patterns; his slaves in turn concealed much of their lives so as not to appear directly to challenge their master's hegemony.

For some Silver Bluff residents, however, there could be no such compromise. Instead of seeking indirectly to avoid the domination inherent to slavery, these individuals confronted it, turning to arson and escape as overt expressions of their rebelliousness. Throughout the period of his management, Hammond referred to mysterious fires that would break out in the gin house on one occasion, the mill house or the plantation hospital the next. While these depredations could not be linked to specific individuals and only minimally affected the operation of the plantation, running away offered the angry slave a potentially more effective means of immediate resistance to the master's control. Between 1831 and 1855, Hammond recorded fifty-three attempts at escape by his bondsmen. Because he was sometimes absent from the plantation for months at a time during these decades, serving in political office or travelling in Europe, it seems unlikely that this list is complete. Nevertheless, Hammond's slave records provide sufficient information about the personal attributes of the runaways, the circumstances of their departure, the length of their absence and the nature of their family ties to demonstrate the meaning and significance of the action within the wider context of plantation life.

The most striking—and depressing—fact about Silver Bluff's runaways is that Hammond records no instance of a successful escape. A total of thirty-seven different slaves were listed as endeavoring to leave the plantation. Thirty-five percent of these were repeaters, although no slave was recorded as making more than three attempts. Newly purchased slaves who made several efforts to escape were often sold; those with long-term ties to the Silver Bluff community eventually abandoned the endeavor.

Runaways were eighty-four percent male, averaged thirty-three years of age, and had been under Hammond's dominance for a median period of two years. Hammond's initial assumption of power precipitated a flurry of escapes, as did subsequent changes in management. When the owner departed for long summer holidays or for business elsewhere, notations of increased numbers of slave escapes appeared in plantation records. This pattern suggests that slavery was rendered minimally tolerable to its victims by the gradual negotiation between master and slave of the kinds of implicit compromises earlier discussed. A shift in responsibility from one master to another or from master to overseer threatened those understandings and therefore produced eruptions of overt rebelliousness.

While the decision to run away might appear to be a rejection of the ties of black community as well as the chains of bondage, the way in which escape functioned at Silver Bluff shows it usually to have operated somewhat differently. Because there were no runaways who achieved permanent freedom and because most escapees did not get far, they remained in a very real sense a part of the slave community they had seemingly fled. Forty-three percent of the runaways at the Bluff left with others. The small proportion—sixteen percent of the total—of females were almost without exception running with husbands or joining spouses who had already departed. Once slaves escaped, they succeeded in remaining at large an average of forty-nine days. Sixty-five percent were captured and the rest returned voluntarily. The distribution of compulsory and elective returns over the calendar year reveals that harsh weather was a significant factor in persuading slaves to give themselves up. Seventy-seven percent of those returning in the winter months did so voluntarily, while in the spring and summer eighty percent were brought back against their will. Weather and workload made summer the runaway season, and fifty-eight percent of all escape attempts occurred in June, July, and August.

While certain individuals—notably young males, particularly those without family ties—were most likely to become runaways, the slave community as a whole provided these individuals with assistance and support. Hammond himself recognized that runaways often went no farther than the nearby Savannah River swamps, where they survived on food provided by those remaining at home. The ties between the escapees and the community were sufficiently strong that Hammond endeavored to force runaways to return by disciplining the rest of the slave force. On at least one occasion Hammond determined to stop the meat allowance of the entire plantation until the runaways came in. In another instance, he severely flogged four slaves harboring two runaways, hoping thereby to break the personal and communal bonds that made prolonged absences possible.

In the isolation of Silver Bluff, real escape seemed all but hopeless. Some newly arrived slaves, perhaps with family from whom they had been separated, turned to flight as a rejection of these new surroundings and an effort permanently to escape them. Individuals of this sort were captured as far as a hundred miles away. The majority of runaways, however, were part of the established black community on Hammond's plantation. Recognizing the near certainty of failure to escape the chains of bondage forever, they ran either in pursuit of a brief respite from labor or in response to uncontrollable anger. One function of the black community was to support this outlet for frustration and rage by feeding and sheltering runaways either until they were captured or until they were once again able to operate within the system of compromise that provided the foundation for the survival of black culture and identity at Silver Bluff.

Two examples demonstrate the way runaways eventually became integrated into the plantation order. Cudjo was returned to the Bluff as a plough hand in 1833 after a year of being hired out in Augusta. Thirty-two years old, he perhaps missed urban life or had established personal relationships he could not bear to break. In any case, he began to run away soon after his return. He first succeeded in departing for two weeks, but was seized in Augusta and imprisoned. Hammond retrieved him and put him in irons, but within days he was off again with his fetters on. Captured soon on a nearby plantation, Cudjo tried again a few days later and remained at large for ten months. In March of 1834, Hammond recorded in his diary, "Cudjo came home. Just tired of running away." Although Cudjo was still on the plantation two decades later, there appeared no further mention of his attempting to escape.

Alonzo had been with Hammond only eight months when he first fled in 1843. Thirty-four years old, he had not yet developed settled family ties on the plantation, and he ran away alone. Captured in this first attempt, he escaped twice more within the year, disappearing, Hammond recorded, "without provocation." His second absence ended when he was caught in Savannah after thirty-two days and placed in irons. After less than two months at home, he was off again, but this time he returned voluntarily within two weeks. Reironed, Alonzo did not flee again. After 1851, Hammond recorded an ever-growing family born to Alonzo and another Silver Bluff slave named Abby. But while he stopped trying to run away and became increasingly tied to Silver Bluff, Alonzo was by no means broken of his independence. In 1864 he provoked Hammond with a final act of resistance, refusing to supply his master with any information about the pains that were to kill him within a month. "A hale hearty man," Hammond remarked with annoyance, "killed by the negro perversity."

In the initial part of his tenure at the Bluff, Hammond recorded efforts to round up runaway slaves by means of extensive searches through the swamps on horseback or with packs of dogs. After the first decade, however, he made little mention of such vigorous measures and seems for the most part simply to have waited for his escapees to be captured by neighbors, turn up in nearby jails, or return home. In order to encourage voluntary surrender, Hammond announced a policy of punishment for runaways that allotted ten lashes for each day absent to those recaptured by force and three lashes per day to those returning of their own will. The establishment of this standardized rule integrated the problem of runaways into the system of rewards and punishments at Silver Bluff and rendered it an aspect of the understanding existing between master and slaves. Since no one escaped permanently, such a rule served to set forth the cost of unauthorized absence and encouraged those who had left in irrational rage to return as soon as their tempers had cooled. When the respected fifty-three-year-old driver John Shubrick was flogged for drunkenness, he fled in fury and mortification, but within a week was back exercising his customary responsibility in plantation affairs.

For some, anger assumed a longer duration and significance. These individuals, like Alonzo or Cudjo, ran repeatedly until greater age or changed circumstances made life at home more bearable. Occasionally Hammond found himself confronted with a slave whose rage seemed so deep-rooted as to be incurable. When Hudson escaped soon after his purchase in 1844, he was not heard of for seven months. At last, Hammond was notified that the slave was in Barnwell, on trial for arson. To protect his investment, Hammond hired a lawyer to defend him. But when Hudson was acquitted, Hammond sold him immediately, determining that this individual was an insupportable menace to plantation life.

While runaways disrupted routine and challenged Hammond's system of management, his greatest anxieties about loss of control arose from the fear that slave dissatisfaction would be exploited by external forces to threaten the fine balance of concession and oppression he had established. From the beginning of his tenure at the Bluff, he sought to isolate his bondsmen from outside influences, prohibiting their trading in local stores, selling produce to neighbors, marrying off the plantation or interacting too closely with hands on the steamboats that refuelled at the Bluff landing. Despite such efforts, however, Hammond perceived during the 1840s and 1850s an ever-growing threat to his power arising from challenges levelled at the peculiar institution as a whole. To Hammond's horror, it seemed impossible to keep information about growing abolition sentiment from the slaves. Such knowledge, Hammond feared, might provide the bondsmen with additional bases for ideological autonomy and greater motivation to resist his control. In an 1844 letter to John C. Calhoun, Hammond declared himself "astonished and shocked to find that some of them are aware of the opinions of the Presidential candidates on the subject of slavery and doubtless most of what the abolitionists are doing & I am sure they know as little of what is done off my place as almost any set of Negroes in the State. I fancy . . . there is a growing spirit of insubordination among the slaves in this section. In the lower part of this district they have fired several houses recently. This is fearful— horrible. A quick and potent remedy must be applied. *Disunion* if *needs* be."

Yet when disunion came, it proved less a remedy than a further exacerbation of the problem. Both the possibility of emancipation by Union soldiers and the resort to slave impressment by the Confederates intervened to disrupt the established pattern of relationship between master and bondsmen. Hammond seemed almost as outraged by Southern as by Yankee challenges to his power. He actively endeavored to resist providing workers to the Confederate government and proclaimed the impressment system "wrong every way & odious."

At the beginning of the war, Hammond was uncertain about the sympathies of his slaves. In 1861, he noted that they appeared "anxious," but remarked "Can't tell which side." As the fighting grew closer, with the firing of large guns near the coast audible at Silver Bluff, Hammond began to sense growing disloyalty among his slaves, and to confront intensifying problems of control. "Negroes demoralized greatly. Stealing right and left," he recorded in 1863. By the middle of that year, it seemed certain that the slaves expected "some great change." Despite his efforts, they seemed at all times "well apprised" of war news, sinking into "heavy gloom" at any Union reverse. Hammond observed the appearance of "a peculiar furtive glance with which they regard me & a hanging off from me that I do not like." They seemed to "shut up their faces & cease their cheerful greetings." Hammond felt the war had rendered his control tenuous, and he believed that even though his slaves sought to appear "passive . . . the roar of a single cannon of the Federal's would make them frantic—savage cutthroats and incendiaries."

Hammond never witnessed the Union conquest of the South or the emancipation of his slaves, for he died in November of 1864. Despite his dire prophecies, however, the people of Silver Bluff did not rise in revolution against those who had oppressed them for so long. Unlike many slaves elsewhere who fled during the war itself, the Hammond bondsmen did not depart even when freedom was proclaimed. "We have not lost many negroes," Hammond's widow complained in September 1865 as she worried about having too many mouths to feed. "I wish we could get clear of many of the useless ones."

Given the turbulent nature of the interaction between Hammond and his slaves in the antebellum years, it would be misguided to regard the blacks' decision to remain on the plantation as evidence either of docility or of indifference about freedom. Instead, it might better be understood as final testimony to the importance of that solidarity we have seen among bondsmen on the Hammond estate. These blacks were more concerned to continue together as a group than to flee Hammond's domination. In the preoccupation with the undeniable importance of the master-slave relationship, historians may have failed fully to recognize how for many bondsmen, the positive meaning of the web of slave interrelationships was a more central influence than were the oppressive intrusions of the power of the master. Silver Bluff had been home to many of these slaves before Hammond ever arrived; the community had preceded him, and now it had outlived him. Its maintenance and autonomy were of the highest priority to its members, keeping them at Silver Bluff even when any single freedman's desire for personal liberty might have best been realized in flight. The values central to this cultural group were more closely associated with the forces of tradition and community than with an individualistic revolutionary romanticism.

On South Carolina's Sea Islands, blacks whose masters had fled perpetuated plantation boundaries as geographic definitions of black communal identity that have persisted to the present day. Although the ex-slaves at Silver Bluff never gained the land titles that would have served as the legal basis for such long-lived solidarity, they, like their Sea Island counterparts, chose in 1865 to remain on the plantation that in a powerful emotional way they had come to regard as their own. These freedmen saw themselves and their aspirations defined less by the oppressions of slavery than by the positive accomplishments of autonomous black community that they had achieved even under the domain of the peculiar institution.

DOCUMENTS

Attacking Abolitionists, Defending Slavery, 1835

Since your last adjournment, the public mind throughout the slaveholding states has been intensely, indignantly, and justly excited by the wanton, officious, and incendiary proceedings of certain societies and persons in some of the nonslaveholding states, who have been actively employed in attempting to circulate among us pamphlets, papers, and pictorial representations of the most offensive and inflammatory character, and eminently calculated to seduce our slaves from their fidelity and excite them to insurrection and massacre. These wicked monsters and deluded fanatics, overlooking the numerous objects in their own vicinity, who have a moral if not a legal claim upon their charitable regard, run abroad in the expansion of their hypocritical benevolence, muffled up in the saintly mantle of Christian meekness, to fulfill the fiendlike errand of mingling the blood of the master and the slave, to whose fate they are equally indifferent, with the smoldering ruins of our peaceful dwellings.

No principle of human action so utterly baffles all human calculation as that species of fanatical enthusiasm which is made of envy and ambition, assuming the guise of religious zeal and acting upon the known prejudices, religious or political, of an ignorant multitude. Under the influence of this species of voluntary madness, nothing is sacred that stands in the way of its purposes. Like all other religious impostures, it has power to consecrate every act, however atrocious, and every person, however covered with "multiplying villainies," that may promote its diabolical ends or worship at its infernal altars. . . .

For the institution of domestic slavery we hold ourselves responsible only to God, and it is utterly incompatible with the dignity and the safety of the state to permit any foreign authority to question our right to maintain it. It may nevertheless be appropriate, as a voluntary token of our respect for

SOURCE: Albert B. Hart and Edward Channing, eds., *American History Leaflets, Colonial and Constitutional*, No. 10, July 1893.

the opinions of our confederate brethren, to present some views to their consideration on this subject, calculated to disabuse their minds of false opinions and pernicious prejudices.

No human institution, in my opinion, is more manifestly consistent with the will of God than domestic slavery, and no one of His ordinances is written in more legible characters than that which consigns the African race to this condition, as more conducive to their own happiness, than any other of which they are susceptible. Whether we consult the sacred Scriptures or the lights of nature and reason, we shall find these truths as abundantly apparent as if written with a sunbeam in the heavens. Under both the Jewish and Christian dispensations of our religion, domestic slavery existed with the unequivocal sanction of its prophets, its apostles, and finally its great Author. The patriarchs themselves, those chosen instruments of God, were slaveholders. In fact, the divine sanction of this institution is so plainly written that "he who runs may read" it, and those overrighteous pretenders and Pharisees who affect to be scandalized by its existence among us would do well to inquire how much more nearly they walk in the ways of godliness than did Abraham, Isaac, and Jacob. . . .

If the benevolent friends of the black race would compare the condition of that portion of them which we hold in servitude with that which still remains in Africa, totally unblessed by the lights of civilization or Christianity and groaning under a savage despotism, as utterly destitute of hope as of happiness, they would be able to form some tolerable estimate of what our blacks have lost by slavery in America and what they have gained by freedom in Africa. Greatly as their condition has been improved by their subjection to an enlightened and Christian people—the only mode under heaven by which it could have been accomplished—they are yet wholly unprepared for anything like a rational system of self-government. Emancipation would be a positive curse, depriving them of a guardianship essential to their happiness, and they may well say in the language of the Spanish proverb, "Save us from our friends and we will take care of our enemies."

If emancipated, where would they live and what would be their condition? The idea of their remaining among us is utterly visionary. Amalgamation is abhorrent to every sentiment of nature; and if they remain as a separate caste, whether endowed with equal privileges or not, they will become our masters, or we must resume the mastery over them. This state of political amalgamation and conflict, which the Abolitionists evidently aim to produce, would be the most horrible condition imaginable and would furnish Dante or Milton with the type for another chapter illustrating the horrors of the infernal regions. The only disposition, therefore, that could be made of our emancipated slaves would be their transportation to Africa, to exterminate the natives or be exterminated by them; contingencies either of which may well serve to illustrate the wisdom, if not the philanthropy, of these superserviceable madmen who in the name of humanity would desolate the fairest region of the earth and destroy the most perfect system of social and political happiness that ever has existed.

It is perfectly evident that the destiny of the Negro race is either the worst possible form of political slavery or else domestic servitude as it exists in the slaveholding states. . . .

In all respects, the comforts of our slaves are greatly superior to those of the English operatives, or the Irish and continental peasantry, to say nothing of the millions of paupers crowded together in those loathsome receptacles of starving humanity, the public poorhouses. Besides the hardships of incessant toil, too much almost for human nature to endure, and the sufferings of actual want, driving them almost to despair, these miserable creatures are perpetually annoyed by the most distressing cares for the future condition of themselves and their children.

From this excess of labor, this actual want, and these distressing cares, our slaves are entirely exempted. They habitually labor from two to four hours a day less than the operatives in other countries; and it has been truly remarked, by some writer, that a Negro cannot be made to injure himself by excessive labor. It may be safely affirmed that they usually eat as much wholesome and substantial food in one day as English operatives or Irish peasants eat in two. And as it regards concern for the future, their condition may well be envied even by their masters. There is not upon the face of the earth any class of people, high or low, so perfectly free from care and anxiety. They know that their masters will provide for them, under all circumstances, and that in the extremity of old age, instead of being driven to beggary or to seek public charity in a poorhouse, they will be comfortably accommodated and kindly treated among their relatives and associates. . . .

In a word, our slaves are cheerful, contented, and happy, much beyond the general condition of the human race, except where those foreign intruders and fatal ministers of mischief, the emancipationists, like their arch-prototype in the Garden of Eden and actuated by no less envy, have tempted them to aspire above the condition to which they have been assigned in the order of Providence. . . .

Songs of Freedom, c. 1820–1860

Go Down, Moses

Go down, Moses
'Way down in Egypt land,
Tell ole Pharaoh,
To let my people go.

Go down, Moses,
'Way down in Egypt land,
Tell ole Pharaoh,
To let my people go.

When Israel was in Egypt land,
Let my people go,
Oppressed so hard they could not stand,
Let my people go,
Thus spoke the Lord, bold Moses said,
Let my people go,
If not I'll smite your first-born dead,
Let my people go.

Go down, Moses,
'Way down in Egypt land,
Tell ole Pharaoh,
To let my people go.

Steal Away to Jesus

Steal away, steal away, steal away to Jesus!
Steal away, steal away home,
I ain't got long to stay here.

My Lord, He calls me, He calls me by the thunder,
The trumpet sounds within-a my soul,
I ain't got long to stay here.

Steal away, steal away, steal away to Jesus!
Steal away, steal away home,
I ain't got long to stay here.

Green trees a-bending, po' sinner stand a-trembling,
The trumpet sounds within-a my soul,
I ain't got long to stay here.

SOURCE: Thomas R. Frazier, ed., *Afro-American History: Primary Sources* (New York: Harcourt, Brace, & World, Inc., 1970), 92–95.

Steal away, steal away, steal away to Jesus!
Steal away, steal away home,
I ain't got long to stay here.

Didn't My Lord Deliver Daniel

Didn't my Lord deliver Daniel,
deliver Daniel, deliver Daniel,
Didn't my Lord deliver Daniel,
An' why not every man.

He delivered Daniel from the lion's den,
Jonah from the belly of the whale,
An' the Hebrew chillun from the fiery furnace,
An' why not every man.

Didn't my Lord deliver Daniel,
deliver Daniel, deliver Daniel,
Didn't my Lord deliver Daniel,
An' why not every man.

The moon run down in a purple stream,
The sun forbear to shine,
An' every star disappear,
King Jesus shall-a be mine.

The win' blows eas' an' the win' blows wes',
It blows like the judg-a-ment day,
An' ev'ry po' soul that never did pray'll
Be glad to pray that day.

Didn't my Lord deliver Daniel,
deliver Daniel, deliver Daniel,
Didn't my Lord deliver Daniel,
An' why not every man.

A Sad Epoch in the Life of a Slave Girl, 1861

During the first years of my service in Dr. Flint's family, I was accustomed to share some indulgences with the children of my mistress. Though this seemed to me no more than right, I was grateful for it, and tried to merit the kindness by the faithful discharge of my duties. But I now entered on my

SOURCE: Harriet Jacobs with L. Maria Child, *Incidents in the Life of a Slave Girl*. Document from Bibliobase®, edited by Micheal Bellesiles. Copyright © Houghton Mifflin Company. Reprinted by permission.

fifteenth year—a sad epoch in the life of a slave girl. My master began to whisper foul words in my ear. Young as I was, I could not remain ignorant of their import.

I tried to treat them with indifference or contempt. The master's age, my extreme youth, and the fear that his conduct would be reported to my grandmother, made him bear this treatment for many months. He was a crafty man, and resorted to many means to accomplish his purposes. Sometimes he had stormy, terrific ways, that made his victims tremble; sometimes he assumed a gentleness that he thought must surely subdue. Of the two, I preferred his stormy moods, although they left me trembling. He tried his utmost to corrupt the pure principles my grandmother had instilled. He peopled my young mind with unclean images, such as only a vile monster could think of. I turned from him with disgust and hatred.

But he was my master. I was compelled to live under the same roof with him—where I saw a man forty years my senior daily violating the most sacred commandments of nature. He told me I was his property; that I must be subject to his will in all things. My soul revolted against the mean tyranny. But where could I turn for protection? No matter whether the slave girl be as black as ebony or as fair as her mistress. In either case, there is no shadow of law to protect her from insult, from violence, or even from death; all these are inflicted by fiends who bear the shape of men. The mistress, who ought to protect the helpless victim, has no other feelings towards her but those of jealousy and rage. The degradation, the wrongs, the vices, that grow out of slavery, are more than I can describe. They are greater than you would willingly believe. Surely, if you credited one half the truths that are told you concerning the helpless millions suffering in this cruel bondage, you at the north would not help to tighten the yoke. You surely would refuse to do for the master, on your own soil, the mean and cruel work which trained bloodhounds and the lowest class of whites do for him at the south.

Everywhere the years bring to all enough of sin and sorrow; but in slavery the very dawn of life is darkened by these shadows. Even the little child, who is accustomed to wait on her mistress and her children, will learn, before she is twelve years old, why it is that her mistress hates such and such a one among the slaves. Perhaps the child's own mother is among those hated ones. She listens to violent outbreaks of jealous passion, and cannot help understanding what is the cause. She will become prematurely knowing in evil things. Soon she will learn to tremble when she hears her master's footfall. She will be compelled to realize that she is no longer a child. If God has bestowed beauty upon her, it will prove her greatest curse. That which commands admiration in the white woman only hastens the degradation of the female slave. I know that some are too much brutalized by slavery to feel the humiliation of their position; but many slaves feel it most acutely, and shrink from the memory of it. I cannot tell how much I suffered in the presence of these wrongs, nor how I am still pained by the retrospect.

My master met me at every turn, reminding me that I belonged to him, and swearing by heaven and earth that he would compel me to submit to him. If I went out for a breath of fresh air, after a day of unwearied toil, his footsteps dogged me. If I knelt by my mother's grave, his dark shadow fell on me even there. The light heart which nature had given me became heavy with sad forebodings. The other slaves in my master's house noticed the change. Many of them pitied me; but none dared to ask the cause. They had no need to inquire. They knew too well the guilty practices under that roof; and they were aware that to speak of them was an offense that never went unpunished. . . .

O, what days and nights of fear and sorrow that man caused me! Reader, it is not to awaken sympathy for myself that I am telling you truthfully what I suffered in slavery. I do it to kindle a flame of compassion in your hearts for my sisters who are still in bondage, suffering as I once suffered.

I once saw two beautiful children playing together. One was a fair white child; the other was her slave, and also her sister. When I saw them embracing each other, and heard their joyous laughter, I turned sadly away from the lovely sight. I foresaw the inevitable blight that would fall on the little slave's heart. I knew how soon her laughter would be changed to sighs. The fair child grew up to be a still fairer woman. From childhood to womanhood her pathway was blooming with flowers, and overarched by a sunny sky. Scarcely one day of her life had been clouded when the sun rose on her happy bridal morning.

How had those years dealt with her slave sister, the little playmate of her childhood? She, also, was very beautiful; but the flowers and sunshine of love were not for her. She drank the cup of Sin, and shame, and misery, whereof her persecuted race are compelled to drink.

In view of these things, why are ye silent, ye free men and women of the north? Why do your tongues falter in maintenance of the right? Would that I had more ability! But my heart is so full, and my pen is so weak! There are noble men and women who plead for us, striving to help those who cannot help themselves. God bless them! God give them strength and courage to go on! God bless those, every where, who are laboring to advance the cause of humanity!

Chapter 15

The Soldiers' Civil War

Civil War encampment of the 31st Pennsylvania Infantry Regiment. Note the presence of women and children, who on occasion followed the armies and provided such services as laundering, cooking and general labor.

At its outset, the Civil War triggered romantic impulses. Colorful uniforms, martial and sentimental music, promises of adventure, and the certainty of quick victory stirred both sides of the conflict. Ultimately, however, the war produced death and destruction on a massive scale (about 1 million casualties including more than 600,000 dead), and its conclusion left a legacy of bitterness that lasted for generations.

James L. McDonough's essay "Glory Can Not Atone: Shiloh—April 6, 7, 1862" looks at battle from the perspective of the participants and considers examples of these romantic notions of war. Were there any significant differences between the Union and Confederate soldiers described in the essay in terms of their reasons for enlisting, their military skill, and their patriotism?

Blacks played more than a passive role in the Civil War; approximately 230,000 of them enlisted in the Union army and navy, and many others served the armed forces as laborers, nurses, scouts, cooks, and spies. The first document, a letter from Corporal James Henry Gooding of the Fifty-fourth Massachusetts Infantry Regiment to President Abraham Lincoln, reveals the intense patriotism of many black volunteers and the continuing injustices that they suffered. Gooding refers to the Confederacy's position that captured black soldiers would be treated as slaves rather than as prisoners of war, and to the Union's policy of paying black troops less than it paid whites. White privates were paid $13 per month; black soldiers, regardless of rank, received $10, the remaining $3 being deducted for clothing. Congress ultimately voted to equalize the pay of white and black soldiers in July 1864, by chance the month in which Corporal Gooding died of battle wounds. Why do you think such a discriminatory salary policy was established in the first place?

The prisoner-of-war status, denied to captured black soldiers by the Confederates, was by no means enviable. Conditions in the prison camps of both armies were generally dreadful, but among them one earned a lasting reputation as the most horrible: Andersonville in Georgia, a twenty-six-acre stockade where thousands of Union soldiers suffered and died. The second document is a description of Andersonville by one of its former inmates, Charles Ferren Hopkins of the First New Jersey Volunteers, captured at the Battle of the Wilderness in May 1864. He was twenty years old at the time, a three-year veteran of the war.

The final months of the conflict witnessed the armies of Grant and Lee engaged in siege warfare around the town of Petersburg, Virginia. One of the Confederate soldiers who endured the misery of those days leading up to Lee's surrender at Appomattox was R. J. Lightsey of Mississippi. In later years he recalled his wartime experiences for his children. In 1899, Lightsey's daughter Ada Christine Lightsey published his memoirs. The final document offers excerpts from this work describing events of February, March, and April 1865. Note that, even after defeat, a romantic note associated with the war persisted.

ESSAY

Glory Can Not Atone: Shiloh—April 6, 7, 1862

James L. McDonough

Will Pope was a young Confederate soldier who suffered a mortal wound at the Battle of Shiloh [Tennessee]. As his life was ebbing away he looked into the eyes of Johnnie Green, one of his comrades in arms from the border state of Kentucky, and earnestly asked the question: "Johnnie, if a boy dies for his country the glory is his forever isn't it?" Indeed it is manifest that the more than 600,000 who died in the most tragic of American wars, at least the most tragic until Viet Nam, have laid claim to a certain glory in the very heart of the America over whose fields and plains they fought, a glory which will endure as long as the annals of America herself shall last. The Battle of Shiloh, in which Will Pope lost his life, was a great part of that tragic war. And the stories of the Will Popes are an indispensable segment in the recounting of that Battle.

Confederate General Basil Duke, who fought at Shiloh, recalled the struggle some years later, and said that "Two great battles of the Civil War seem to command an especial interest denied the others. . . . There yet lingers a wish to hear all that may be told of Shiloh and Gettysburg. . . ." Otto Eisenchiml, newspaperman and Civil War scholar, after extensive study and visits to many of the battlefields of America, wrote of Shiloh: "No novelist could have packed into a space of two days more action, romance, and surprises than history did on that occasion. Of all the battlefields . . . I thought Shiloh the most intriguing."

Certainly Gettysburg has deservedly received widespread attention, but there is still much to be told about Shiloh. Somehow the Battle has been relegated in the literature of the present century to a second priority position. Even though it was the decisive engagement in the struggle for the Mississippi Valley, without which the Rebels could not realistically hope to win the war, and even though it was the biggest and bloodiest fight of the entire war west of the Appalachian Mountains, Shiloh has never received the attention which has often been accorded to lesser battles, some of which have had several books written about them. What has been written about Shiloh has usually dealt with the commanders such as Grant, Sherman, Johnston, Beauregard, etc. The blunders and the missed opportunities have been the focal points. But Shiloh is also intriguing because of the role played by some of the lesser known, even unknown figures; particularly by the common soldiers of both armies.

This article presents some of those little known, and sometimes previously unpublished, human interest occurrences. The Battle can only cease to seem like the movements on a chess board of war when one knows the tangible, flesh and blood characters, the common men of North and South, who fought, suffered, and died at Shiloh. To understand their emotions, and what happened to them, is a large part of understanding the Battle itself. Theirs are the stories which run the gauntlet of human emotions, from pathos to romance, but most of all reveal the tragedy of war.

SOURCE: James L. McDonough, "Glory Can Not Atone: Shiloh—April 6, 7, 1862," *Tennessee Historical Quarterly* 35 (fall 1976): 179–195. Reprinted by permission.

Many diverse elements composed the Southern army. From New Orleans came the heralded "Crescent Regiment," composed of men 18 to 35 years of age, many of whom regarded themselves as the Bluebloods of Louisiana. Nicknamed the "Kid Glove" regiment, the unit was a colorful, well-drilled outfit, including many members who were equipped with "servants," and enamored with the glory of war. The command impressed a resident of Corinth as one of the finest regiments he ever saw. The Crescents would fight gallantly and be badly cut up at Shiloh. On the other hand there were units like the Sixth Mississippi, which was a ragtag regiment whose men were dressed and equipped with little or no regard for uniformity.

Great numbers of the Southerners who assembled at Corinth were very young. Henry Morton Stanley of the Sixth Arkansas Infantry, the "Dixie Grays," who was nineteen years old, recalled going into battle at Shiloh beside Henry Parker, a boy seventeen. W. E. Yeatman, who fought at Shiloh with the "Cumberland Rifles," Company C., Second Tennessee Infantry (a regiment organized at Nashville which fought at Manassas and claimed to be the first to reenlist for the duration of the war) wrote that his company "mustered with a roll of 80 men, or boys rather, as much the largest number were youths from 16 to 18 years of age."

Willie Forrest, the son of Nathan Bedford Forrest, fought at Shiloh although he was only 15 years old. His father spent part of the night of April 6 searching for Willie among the casualties. The boy later turned up safe, along with two young companions and some Yankee stragglers the three had captured. Brigadier General James R. Chalmers commended two seventeen-year-old boys, in his official report of the battle, who acted as staff officers for him. He wrote that one of them, Sergeant-major William A. Rains, deserved special notice for carrying an order on Sunday evening "under the heaviest fire that occurred during the whole engagement." Major General B. F. Cheatham told of "a noble boy," John Campbell, who "while acting as my aide-de-camp, fell dead, his entire head having been carried away by a cannon shot."

A colonel of the Fifth Tennessee Infantry was amazed at the "coolness and bravery throughout the entire Shiloh fight" of a Private John Roberts who, although knocked down twice by spent balls, and his gun shattered to pieces, continued to push on with his advancing company. He was fifteen years old.

Not all of them were young, or even middle age, however. One man of about 60, who lived near Corinth, came to see his two sons who were in the army. He happened to arrive on the very day their unit was moving out to attack the enemy at Pittsburgh Landing. The father could not resist shouldering his musket and marching into the fight with his sons. He paid for his rashness with the loss of a leg.

A father and son, John C. Thompson, 70, and Flem, 13, enlisted in a north Mississippi company that fought at Shiloh. The old gentleman was a lawyer, who, when asked why he joined up, replied that he had talked and voted for secession and now felt that he ought to fight for the cause. Though wounded, he survived Shiloh only to fall at Chickamauga in the midst of a charge on Snodgrass Hill.

The Southerners were coming to fight for many reasons. Some were romantics. A Tennessean of Patrick Cleburne's command, George T. Blakemore, wrote that he "volunteered to fight in defense of the sunny South, the land of roses, . . . and for my Melissa, Ma and Sister, and all other fair women. . . ." Henry M. Doak described himself as a "soldier of fortune—eager for the fray. . . ." When he heard a great battle was expected near Corinth, so anxious was he for a fight that he arose from a sick bed and headed west on the first train in order not to miss it. He got to Shiloh in time—in time, after six years' instruction on the violin with German and French masters, for a rifle ball to shatter his left hand.

J. M. Lashlee came from Camden, Tennessee, to join the Confederates. He was a man opposed to slavery and to secession, who enlisted with the Rebels, as did many others, only because the Union army had invaded his state. For Lashlee the memory of the second day of the battle would hold an unlikely nostalgia—one all its own. For there on the battlefield, wounded, he would meet a young girl from near Iuka, Mississippi, by the name of Emma Dudley. And he would marry her.

Another soldier who reached Corinth in time to hear the guns of Shiloh but too late to take part in the fight was brief about his reasons for joining the Confederates. He said simply: "Our liberties are threatened, our rights endangered." He was perhaps echoing the Memphis *Daily Avalanche* which was calling forth every armed, able-bodied man to the "scenes of a great and decisive battle" in the struggle for "Southern Independence." The New Orleans *Daily Picayune* was likewise sounding the theme of a great "struggle for independence" without which there would be "nothing left . . . for which a free man would desire to live." The New Orleans paper was in fact running a series of articles under the heading "Chronicle of the Second American Revolution." Its editorials were also fervently declaring that the situation now facing the South was the "crisis of the Confederate cause." Governor Pettus of Mississippi proclaimed that the decision to be faced was "liberty or death."

Many Southerners, of course, fought to protect the "peculiar institution" [slavery]. . . . Some Confederates even took selected Negroes along with them as personal body servants when they went to war. A man who fought at Shiloh later recounted a gory but impressive occurrence he witnessed involving a young Rebel officer and his slave. As the officer rode into battle on the first day of the fight, a cannon shot decapitated the young man. The Negro servant almost immediately caught his master's horse, and put the lifeless body upon it. Then the Black man moved off the battlefield, going slowly to the rear with the remains in the saddle and he behind on the horse, steadying the animal while they made their way back toward Corinth. The witness was convinced that the slave was taking his dead master's body back home for burial.

Every type of man seemed to be represented among the soldiers gathering at Corinth. Like all armies the Confederates had their gamblers. Some had a mania for cockfighting, scouring the country for fighting cocks and whenever the opportunity offered, staging a contest and betting on the outcome. "There were five or six men, mostly officers, who were ring leaders in this sport," remembered James I. Hall, who was convinced that the Almighty took a dim view of their activities. "In the Battle of Shiloh," he wrote, "they were all killed and although I remained in the army three years after this, I do not remember ever seeing or hearing of another cock fight in our regiment. . . ."

Some of those who were coming to join the Rebels were in love. Confederate Captain Benjamin Vickers of Memphis, Tennessee, was no doubt thinking much of the time abut his fiancee, Sallie Houston, also of Memphis, as he marched to the defense of the South at the Battle of Shiloh. There in the midst of one of the many Rebel charges he suffered a mortal wound. The young lady, even though she knew he was about to die, insisted upon their marriage, which was solemnized ten days after the Battle, and a few days before his death.

There were men who came to pillage and plunder. Major General Braxton Bragg, commanding the Confederate Second Corps, was particularly disturbed by "the mobs we have, miscalled soldiers." He complained to General Beauregard that while there was "some discipline left" in those troops from the Gulf (Bragg's own command) there was "none whatever" in the rest of the army. He further stated that "the unrestrained habits of pillage and plunder" by Confederate soldiers about Corinth was making it difficult to get supplies, and, worse yet, reconciling the people to the approach of the Federals "who certainly do them less harm." The troops were even "monopolizing or plundering the eating and sleeping houses" on the railroads. The forty-five-year-old Bragg, with his lowering brow, haggard, austere, no-nonsense appearance, was determined to do something about the pillaging and he quickly gave substance to his growing reputation as a severe disciplinarian. One of the Rebel soldiers wrote that Bragg's name became a "terror to deserters and evil doers," claiming that "men were shot by scores." Another said he hanged sixteen men on a single tree.

The last two statements were, of course, wild exaggerations, but it was soon after the Shiloh campaign, on the retreat from Corinth, that an incident occurred which did much to stamp Bragg as a stern, unreasoning disciplinarian. Bragg gave orders that no gun be discharged lest the retreat route be given away, and set the penalty of death for disobedience. Subsequently a drunken soldier fired at a chicken and wounded a small Negro child. The soldier was tried by court martial, sentenced to be shot, Bragg approved, and the man was executed. Some of the facts of the actual event were soon twisted, or ignored, however, and the story circulated that because a Confederate soldier shot at a chicken Bragg had the soldier shot—a soldier for a chicken. Although he was falsely maligned as a result of this incident, there is no denying that many of the soldiers thought he was unreasonably strict. Even in the earlier Mexican War, where Zachary Taylor's statement at the Battle of Buena Vista had helped make Bragg famous ("Give them a little more grape, Captain Bragg"), somebody hated Bragg enough to attempt his destruction by planting a bomb under his tent. Bragg was undoubtedly right, however, about the Rebel army at Corinth being in need of more discipline.

Some of those gathering at Corinth were despondent. Jeremy Gilmer wrote of the "confusion and discomfort—dirty hotels, close rooms, hot weather—and many other disagreeable things." And no doubt many were thinking of the possibility of death. One man confided to his diary: "e'er I again write on these pages, I may be sleeping in the cold ground . . . as a battle is daily . . . anticipated."

Although they were a mixed lot, there was one quality shared by nearly everyone in the Confederate army and a sizeable part of the Union army also: they had little if any experience as soldiers. It has been stated that "probably 80 percent of each army had never heard a gun fired in hatred." The estimate may be about right for the Rebel army but not for the Union force. Three of the five Federal divisions which fought at Shiloh had also seen action at Forts Henry and Donelson. There was a smattering of men in the Confederate ranks who thought of themselves as veterans, usually because they had been in one battle or heavy skirmish, but most were green. And there would not be enough time or resources to train them properly. General Leonidas Polk, in his official report, stated that one company of artillery, because of "the scarcity of ammunition, had never heard the report of their own guns."

Many of the officers, elected by their soldiers, or appointed by state governors, were not better prepared than the men in the ranks. A Confederate brigadier general said later that before Shiloh he had never heard a lecture or read a book on the science of war, nor seen a gun fired. At least he could appreciate the necessity to learn, whereas among the enlisted men were many who could see no need for target practice; after all, they thought, they already knew how to shoot!

The top Rebel commanders were attempting to bring organization and discipline out of the chaos, but the necessity for haste in attacking the enemy came to seem imperative, finally overriding all other considerations.

Meanwhile, in the Union camp, although the new recruits and even some of the commands that fought at Forts Henry and Donelson were in need of better organization and discipline, most of those gathering in the Blue ranks at Pittsburgh Landing were not short on confidence. Excited by the recent victory at Fort Donelson, which had been climaxed with the surrender of nearly 15,000 soldiers in Gray, some of the Federals believed they were moving in for the *coup de grace*. A feeling of victory was in the air. That some of the Union soldiers coming up the Tennessee River to Pittsburgh Landing had not fought at Fort Donelson made little difference. The sense of pride in that triumph was contagious, and now the Union army "from private to commanding general" knew, in the words of a soldier in the Sixth Iowa Infantry, that a great battle was shaping up "for the mastery and military supremacy in the Mississippi Valley." With new Springfield muskets, good clothing, fine camp equipage, and wholesale rations, and inspired by music from "splendid bands and drum corps," the troops in his regiment were "happy and supremely confident," he said.

A Northerner in the Fifteenth Illinois agreed. "The weather was delightful," he wrote. "Spring had just begun to open. . . . We all knew that a battle was imminent" but the victory at Fort Donelson "had given us great confidence in ourselves. . . ." Alexander Downing of the Eleventh Iowa recorded in his diary: "The boys are getting anxious for a fight." Division Commander Major General Lew Wallace told his wife in a letter that the enemy was disorganized and demoralized and that the war, if pushed, could not last long. General Grant, writing to his wife and obviously misinterpreting the Southern will to resist, said the "'Sesesch' is . . . about on its last legs in Tennessee. A big fight" would soon occur which, "it appears to me, will be the last in the west." Many a man in the ranks, like William Skinner, was echoing the same sentiment. Skinner wrote his sister and brother on March 27, 1862: "I think the rebellion is getting nearly played out, and I expect we will be home soon." The same theme was found in the letters of some people who were writing to the soldiers. Mrs. James A. Garfield, wife of the thirty-two-year-old man then serving in Buell's army who would become the twentieth President of the United States, was telling her husband: "If our army accomplishes as much this month as during the past month it seems as though there will not be much left of the rebellion."

Some Union men were so confident that the Confederates were demoralized and giving up that they seemed to be looking for a sizeable number of Southerners to swell their ranks. A correspondent travelling with the army wrote, with evident satisfaction, of an alleged 150 or so men from Hardin County who joined the Federal army at Savannah. This does not seem particularly hard to believe since there was much Union sentiment in that county.

If the soldiers read the Northern newspapers, and many of them did (Chicago papers were available at the landing about a week after publication), they would have found it difficult to escape the conclusion that the war was about over. Through the latter part of February and March the headlines were continually recounting dramatic Union successes and some of the editorials were fervent in implying, and occasionally actually stating, that the war could not last much longer. A correspondent of the Chicago

Times who interviewed Confederate prisoners from Fort Donelson at Camp Douglas, reported that many of the Confederates were weary of war, that they declared the cause of the Confederacy was lost, and that it was useless to fight any longer. A few days later the same paper was reporting that the administration of Jefferson Davis was being bitterly denounced by even the Richmond newspapers.

The Cincinnati *Gazette*, on April 3, reported a great dissatisfaction in the Rebel ranks. Many Confederates, coming in from Corinth, Mississippi, were deserting to the Union army assembled at Pittsburgh Landing, the *Gazette* observed, and many more would desert if they could. The *New York Times* in big headlines was day after day heralding the triumphs of Union armies, noting that in London the capture of Fort Donelson had caused a change in British opinion and a rise in United States securities. Even the pro-Southern *London Times,* anticipating the demise of the Confederacy, was quoted as saying "There are symptoms that the Civil War can not be very long protracted."

Although Northern papers occasionally carried warnings that some signs indicated that the Confederate will to resist was still alive, such articles were often buried in the corner of a second or third page or else virtually obscured by the general optimism exuding from the continual accounting and recounting of Union triumphs.

Not only were some of the Union soldiers overconfident; there were also men gathering at Pittsburgh Landing who were so inexperienced and naive about war that they seemed to be enjoying a holiday. They banged away at flocks of wild geese from the steamboat decks as they came up the Tennessee River. It was all like "a gigantic picnic," one wrote. And some of them were getting wild, such as those men in the Twenty-First Missouri Infantry who were firing from the decks of their steamer as it moved up the river, aiming their guns at citizens on the river banks. Grant labelled the conduct "infamous" and preferred charges against the colonel of the regiment.

A correspondent from the *Chicago Times* traveling with the army thought that some of the soldiers had no respect for anything. He was appalled by their morbid curiosity, when, debarking at Pittsburgh Landing and finding some fresh and rather shallow graves—the evidence of a small skirmish early in March—some of the troops, with pointed sticks and now and then a spade, removed the scanty covering of earth, which in most cases was less than a foot deep, exposing the bodies of the dead, with remarks such as: "He keeps pretty well," and "By golly! What a red moustache this fellow had!"

The Union army, like the Confederate, had many very young soldiers in their ranks. A sixteen-year-old boy in the Union army would remember, sometime during the Battle of Shiloh, passing the corpse of a handsome Confederate, blond hair scattered about his face, with a hat lying beside him bearing the number of a Georgia regiment. Seeing the boy was about his own age, he broke down and cried.

A fourteen-year-old Yankee, Private David W. Camp, of the First Ohio Light Artillery, was said by his captain to deserve particular mention, having served "with the skill and bravery of an old soldier during the entire engagement." The captain further added, "I did not for a moment see him flinch."

Years later, Charles W. Hadley of the Fourteenth Iowa recalled one of the most affecting events of his war experience occurring in the area of prolonged and fierce fighting which became known as the "Hornet's Nest." He watched as a small boy, mounted on a fine horse, was suddenly lifted from the saddle by an exploding shell and dropped lifeless upon the ground.

The youngest of all usually were the drummer boys, among whom was Johnny Clem, ten years old, who went along with the Twenty-Second Wisconsin Infantry, and whose drum was smashed at Shiloh, the exploit winning him the name "Johnny Shiloh"; he later became still more famous as the drummer boy of Chickamauga and retired from the army in 1916 as a major general.

With the rapid concentration of so many men at Pittsburgh Landing it was inevitable that accidents would occur, some of them fatal. A soldier in the Fourteenth Iowa who had just come up the river on the steamer *Autocrat* watched as a soldier on the *Hiawatha* fell into the Tennessee close to Pittsburgh Landing and drowned before anyone could reach him. He was not the only one to suffer such a fate, for several drownings have been recorded. General Charles F. Smith, a crusty, square-shouldered, old officer who played a leading role at Fort Donelson as a division commander, and for a while afterward replaced Grant as the army's commander, slipped and fell while getting into a row boat and skinned his shin. Infection set in which forced him to relinquish his command while the buildup at Pittsburgh Landing was in process, and in about a month he was dead.

Many of the men in Blue who left records in letters, diaries, and memoirs revealing why they fought, said they did so for the Union. But of course, and again like the Confederates, the Federals had their share of soldiers seeking glory, adventure, and plunder. [Historian] Clement Eaton has suggested that it is "highly probable that the typical soldier, Northern or Southern, had no clear idea why he was fighting." It must have seemed to him, especially when he left for war as many did, with the hometown looking on, bands playing, girls waving, and small boys watching with awe and envy, that he fought for something splendid and glorious. The cheers told him so. And the realization assured him of his own individual worth and greatness; but, at the same time, he fought for something, whether "Southern Rights" or "the Union," that must also, at times, have seemed vague and intangible. Perhaps the most concrete thing for which the soldier fought, mentioned time and time again by the warriors on both sides, was "his country."

Regardless of why they were in the army, many of the Union troops, despite the recent successes and their confidence that more would soon follow, found that army life on the whole was dull, monotonous and unpleasant. When the exhilarating, but all too brief periods of interstate camaraderie through card playing, gambling, wrestling, joking and singing were over, the soldier still brooded, worried, got sick, and thought of loved ones back home. There was too much drill and routine, rain and mud. Sanitation was bad, with logs serving as latrines, and sickness and diarrhea (a correspondent remarked that no person could really claim to be a soldier who had not experienced the latter) were rampant at times.

Perhaps above all there was loneliness. An unknown soldier of "Co. C." of an unknown regiment was keeping a small, pocket-size diary, pathetic in its brief entries revealing utter boredom. Again and again, he set down such comments as: "Weather cold and unpleasant. Nothing of any importance"; "In camp . . . no drill. Nothing new"; "Drill today . . . boys sitting by fires." Toward the latter part of March, entries begin referring to "Beautiful morning," "Beautiful spring day," and "Weather pleasant," but the evidences of loneliness and boredom are still present. The pages are blank after March 29, except for one. There appears a final entry—in a different hand: "Killed in the evening by the exploding of a bombshell from the enemies battery." The entry is on the page for April 6.

One of the men who fought for "his country" at Shiloh and experienced something of the loneliness and sickness which was so common to all was forty-year-old Brigadier General William H. L. Wallace. Recently appointed as leader of the Second Division of the Union army, he was an Ohio-born, Illinois-educated lawyer who had served in the Mexican War as an adjutant. When the Civil War began he entered the service as a colonel of Illinois Volunteers. He fought at Fort Donelson, handled himself well, and was promoted to Brigadier General of Volunteers following that battle. Popular and respected by his men, he was a natural choice when Grant had to find a new division commander to replace the ailing General C. F. Smith.

On March 8, Wallace told his wife in a letter that he had been quite ill for several days and prayed for the "strength and wisdom to enable me to do my whole duty toward the country in this her hour of peril." In this and other letters he spoke often of his longing for the war to end, and how much he wanted to see his wife and all the family once more. Ann Dicky Wallace, twelve years younger than her husband, must have found his loneliness especially touching, for she decided to go south and visit him. Wallace had told her not to attempt the trip and friends and relatives warned that she would not be allowed to pass, that all civilians were being turned back. Ann was not easily persuaded to change her course once she had made up her mind.

The daughter of Judge T. Lyle Dicky, one of the most successful lawyers in Illinois, she may have thought her father's influence would help her get through. Most important in her decision, however, was her determination to see "Will" again. She had known her husband since she was just a small girl when Will, as a young lawyer, had visited many times in her father's home. Often he had taken an interest in the bright child, sometimes suggesting books for her to read, sometimes watching her ride her pet pony, or engage in some other sport, and on occasion just sitting and talking to her. When Will returned from the Mexican War he made the pleasant discovery that little Ann had become a charming young lady of fifteen. When she was sixteen he pledged his love and asked her to become his wife. Soon after her eighteenth birthday they were married.

Now, after all the years she had known him, it did not seem right to Ann for Will to be away, undergoing hardship, sickness, facing danger and possible death, while she remained passively at home. "Sometimes, Will, I can hardly restrain myself," she wrote on March 21. "I feel as if I must go to you, more so when I think of you sick. It seems wrong to enjoy every comfort of a good home and you sick in a tent. Is it indeed my duty to stay so far back and wait so anxiously?" Three days later she dispatched another letter in the same vein. And in a few more days she was on her way south.

On the morning of April 6 Ann Wallace was just arriving at Pittsburgh Landing on a steamboat—her coming still unknown to her husband. As she was putting on her hat and gloves, readying to walk from the boat to her husband's headquarters, she could hear a great deal of firing in the distance. It was first explained to her that this probably involved nothing more than the men on picket duty exchanging a few shots with some Rebel patrol. A captain in the Eleventh Illinois who was on board suggested that perhaps it would be better for him to first find out how far it was to General Wallace's headquarters, for it would be better for Mrs. Wallace to ride if the distance were great.

As she waited for the captain to return, the sounds of firing seemed to be growing more pronounced. In less than thirty minutes, she thought, the captain was back with news that it looked like a major battle was shaping up. Ann's husband had already taken his command to the front, and now it was too late for her to see him. There seemed to be nothing she could do except settle down on the steamboat and wait—disappointed, frustrated, fearful for Will's safety as well as for her other relatives who were in the army. In addition to her husband, Ann's father, two brothers, two of her husband's brothers, and several more distant relatives were all fighting on the field of Shiloh.

Late in the evening a man from back home in Illinois came up to her. She thought he looked worn and depressed. He had been wounded though not seriously. "This is an awful battle," he said. "Yes, but these fresh troops will yet win the day," she replied. He reminded her that she had many relatives in the battle and could not expect that all of them would come through safely. Ann's reply, as she remembered it, was that they had all come safely through the Battle of Fort Donelson, and her husband, now a division commander, should be in a comparatively safe position. The friend then repeated his earlier comment, "It is an awful battle," and then, looking at him carefully, she realized what he was trying to tell her. Her husband had been stricken down while making the defense at the "Hornet's Nest" which proved to be so vital to the salvation of the Union army.

About that time her brother Cyrus, who had been with her husband when he fell, came in and gave her some of the details. He explained how he and another man tried to bring the body back to the landing, but could not as the Rebels were closing in around them. In her grief Ann, who could not sleep, spent most of the night in helping care for the wounded who lay all about her.

About ten o'clock on Monday morning her spirit was wonderfully lifted as news came that Will had been found on the battlefield, still breathing. She had rushed to the adjoining boat where they had brought him. He was wet and cold, his face flushed, and the wound in his head was awful looking. Ann clasped his hand and, though those standing around doubted, was convinced that he immediately recognized her, if only for a moment. He was removed to Savannah where Ann stayed with him constantly. Her hopes for his recovery grew brighter for a while. But then it gradually became obvious that his condition was growing worse, and he was mortally wounded. He breathed his last on Thursday night. She later wrote how thankful she was that he had not died on the battlefield and that she was able to be with him during those final hours.

When the battle was over the Federal army was forming burial details and digging mass graves into which they were stacking the dead bodies in rows, one on top of another. The stench of the dead was sometimes almost unbearable, and the battlefield was filled with ghastly scenes, like in the Hornet's Nest where fire had taken hold in the leaves and grass, burning the flesh from around the set teeth of some of the dead, leaving them with a horrible grin. There were scenes of wonderment, like that of a big Northerner, still gripping his musket, and a young Southerner, revolver in hand, who lay up against one another in a death embrace, having shot each other at virtually point blank range, yet neither face showing any expression of pain or anger.

But unquestionably, there were feelings of bitterness which would not subside for generations. Among the relatives coming to claim the bodies of their dead kinfolk was Samuel Stokes Rembert, III. He drove a team of horses and a wagon from his farm in Shelby County, north of Memphis, to Shiloh and somehow found the body of his eldest son, Andrew Rembert, a private in the Confederate army. Andrew's body was brought back and buried on the homeplace. Some years later Andrew's brother Sam erected a monument to his memory. That monument, still a striking sight today, is in the form of a kneeling angel, and stands eleven or twelve feet in height. But more startling than the white angel suddenly looming up in the midst of the forested area, is the bitter epitaph, which reads: "Three generations of Remberts. To my dear parents and loving sisters and my noble, gentle, brilliant and brave brother, killed for defending home against the most envious lot of cut throats that ever cursed the face of this earth."

One of the men who was walking over the battlefield in those days immediately after Shiloh was James A. Garfield. Wandering out beyond the Union lines with his pickets he came upon a group of tents in which there were about thirty wounded Rebels, attended by a surgeon and a few soldiers. He found dead men lying right in among the living. Sight and smell, he said, were terrible. It was soon after this that he was moved to write, in a letter sent back home, "The horrible sights that I have witnessed on this field I can never describe. No blaze of glory, that flashes around the magnificent triumphs of war, can ever atone for the unwritten and unutterable horrors of the scene of carnage."

DOCUMENTS

A Black Soldier Writes to President Lincoln, 1863

MORRIS ISLAND, S. C.

YOUR EXCELLENCY ABRAHAM LINCOLN: SEPTEMBER 28, 1863

Your Excellency will pardon the presumption of an humble individual like myself, in addressing you, but the earnest solicitation of my comrades in arms besides the genuine interest felt by myself in the matter is my excuse, for placing before the Executive head of the Nation our Common Grievance.

On the 6th of the last Month, the Paymaster of the Department informed us, that if we would decide to receive the sum of $10 (ten dollars) per month, he would come and pay us that sum, but that, on the sitting of Congress, the Regt. [regiment] would, in his opinion, be allowed the other 3 (three). He did not give us any guarantee that this would be, as he hoped; certainly he had no authority for making any such guarantee, and we cannot suppose him acting in any way interested.

Now the main question is, are we Soldiers, or are we Laborers? We are fully armed, and equipped, have done all the various duties pertaining to a Soldier's life, have conducted ourselves to the complete satisfaction of

SOURCE: James Henry Gooding to Abraham Lincoln in Herbert Aptheker, ed., *A Documentary History of the Negro People in the U.S.* (New York: Citadel Press, 1951), 482–484.

General Officers, who were, if anything, prejudiced against us, but who now accord us all the encouragement and honors due us; have shared the perils and labor of reducing the first strong-hold that flaunted a Traitor Flag; and more, Mr. President, to-day the Anglo-Saxon Mother, Wife, or Sister are not alone in tears for departed Sons, Husbands and Brothers. The patient, trusting descendant of Afric's Clime have dyed the ground with blood, in defence of the Union, and Democracy. Men, too, your Excellency, who know in a measure the cruelties of the iron heel of oppression, which in years gone by, the very power their blood is now being spilled to maintain, ever ground them in the dust.

But when the war trumpet sounded o'er the land, when men knew not the Friend from the Traitor, the Black man laid his life at the altar of the Nation,—and he was refused. When the arms of the Union were beaten, in the first year of the war, and the Executive called for more food for its ravenous maw, again the black man begged the privilege of aiding his country in her need, to be again refused.

And now he is in the War, and how has he conducted himself? Let their dusky forms rise up, out of the mires of James Island, and give the answer. Let the rich mould around Wagner's parapets be upturned, and there will be found an eloquent answer. Obedient and patient and solid as a wall are they. All we lack is a paler hue and a better acquaintance with the alphabet.

Now your Excellency, we have done a Soldier's duty. Why can't we have a Soldier's pay? You caution the Rebel chieftain, that the United States knows no distinction in her soldiers. She insists on having all her soldiers of whatever creed or color, to be treated according to the usages of War. Now if the United States exacts uniformity of treatment of her soldiers from the insurgents, would it not be well and consistent to set the example herself by paying all her soldiers alike?

We of this Regt. were not enlisted under any "contraband"* act. But we do not wish to be understood as rating our service of more value to the Government than the service of the ex-slave. Their service is undoubtedly worth much to the Nation, but Congress made express provision touching their case, as slaves freed by military necessity, and assuming the Government to be their temporary Guardian. Not so with us. Freemen by birth and consequently having the advantage of thinking and acting for ourselves so far as the Laws would allow us, we do not consider ourselves fit subjects for the Contraband act.

We appeal to you, Sir, as the Executive of the Nation, to have us justly dealt with. The Regt. do pray that they be assured their service will be fairly appreciated by paying them as American Soldiers, not as menial hirelings. Black men, you may well know, are poor; three dollars per month, for a

*The term *contraband* refers to fugitive slaves who often worked as laborers for the North. (Eds.)

year, will supply their needy wives and little ones with fuel. If you, as Chief Magistrate of the Nation, will assure us of our whole pay, we are content. Our Patriotism, our enthusiasm will have a new impetus, to exert our energy more and more to aid our Country. Not that our hearts ever flagged in devotion, despite the evident apathy displayed in our behalf, but we feel as though our Country spurned us, now we are sworn to serve her. Please give this a moment's attention.

Andersonville:
". . . death stalked on every hand," 1864

. . . The prison was a parallelogram of about two to one as to its length and breadth, about eighteen acres at this time—it was enlarged July 1st to about twenty-seven acres—and one-third of this not habitable, being a swamp of liquid filth. This was enclosed by wooden walls of hewn pine logs, from eight to ten inches square, four feet buried in the ground, eighteen feet above, braced on the outside, cross-barred to make one log sustain the other, and a small platform making comfortable standing room for the guards, every one hundred feet, with above waist-high space below the top of stockade, reached by a ladder. A sloping roof to protect the guards from the sun and rain had been placed over them. Later in 1864 the second line of stockade was built and a third was partly built for protection if attacked by Federal troops, it was said, but we knew it was to discourage us from "tunneling"—the distance being too great. The Florida Artillery had cannon stationed at each corner of the stockade, thus commanding a range from any direction; four guns were so placed near the south gate and over the depressed section of stockade at which point the little stream entered the enclosure.

The "dead line" so much talked of and feared was a line of pine, four-inch boards on posts about three feet high. This line was seventeen feet from the stockade walls, thus leaving the distance all around the enclosure an open space, and incidentally reducing the acreage inside and giving the guards a clear view all about the stockade or "bull pen," the name given it by its inventor—the infamous General Winder. He was the friend of Jefferson Davis, who named him as a "Christian gentleman," and he was the architect and builder of this wooden Hell. . . .

Inside the camp death stalked on every hand. Death at the hand of the guards, though murder in cold blood, was merciful beside the systematic, studied, absolute murder inside, by slow death, inch by inch! As before

SOURCE: "Hell and the Survivor: A Civil War Memoir," *American Heritage* 33, no. 6 (October/ November 1982): 78–93. Copyright 1982 by American Heritage, a division of Forbes, Inc.

stated, one-third of the original enclosure was swampy—a mud of liquid filth, voidings from the thousands, seething with maggots in full activity. This daily increased by the necessities of the inmates, being the only place accessible for the purpose. Through this mass of pollution passed the only water that found its way through the Bull Pen. It came to us between the two sources of pollution, the Confederate camp and the cook house; first, the seepage of sinks; second, the dirt and filth emptied by the cook house; then was our turn to use it. I have known over three thousand men to wait in line to get water, and the line was added to as fast as reduced, from daylight to dark, yes, even into the night; men taking turns of duty with men of their mess, in order to hold their place in line, as no one man could stand it alone, even if in the "pink" of physical condition; the heat of the sun, blistering him, or the drenching rains soaking him, not a breath of fresh air, and we had no covering but Heaven's canopy. The air was loaded with unbearable, fever-laden stench from that poison sink of putrid mud and water, continually in motion by the activity of the germs of death. We could not get away from the stink—we ate it, drank it and slept in it (when exhaustion compelled sleep).

What wonder that men died, or were so miserable as to prefer instant death to that which they had seen hourly taking place, and so preferring, deliberately stepping within the dead line and looking their willing murderer in the eye, while a shot was sent crashing into a brain that was yet clear.

The month of June gave us twenty-seven days of rain—not consecutively, but so frequently that no one was dry in all that time. Everything was soaked—even the sandy soil. Still, this watery month was a blessing in disguise as it gave water, plenty of which was pure to drink. The boast of Winder was that the selection of this spot for his Bull Pen was the place where disease and death would come more quickly by "natural causes," when a removal of two hundred feet east would have placed us upon a living, pure, deep and clear stream of water, properly named "Sweetwater Creek," which had we been allowed to utilize would have saved thousands of lives—but no, that was not the intent of its inventor. To kill by "natural causes" was made more possible by this location. . . .

The average deaths per day for seven and a half months were 85. But during the months of July, August, September, and October the average was 100 per day. One day in August, following the great freshet,* I counted 235 corpses lying at the south gate and about. Many of those had been smothered in their "burrows" made in the side hill in which they crawled to shield themselves from sun and storm; the soil, being sandy, became rain-soaked and settled down upon the occupant and became his grave instead of a protection. Others, who had no shelter, in whom life was barely

---

*A freshet is a great overflowing of a stream caused by heavy rains. (Eds.)

existing, were rain-soaked, chilling blood and marrow, and life flitted easily away, and left but little to return to clay. These holes or burrows in both the flats and up the north slope were counted by thousands; no doubt there were some that never gave up their dead, the men buried in their self-made sepulcher. No effort was made to search unless the man was missed by a friend.

Such were Winder's "natural causes"!! . . .

Recollections of a Confederate Veteran (1865), 1899

At this time, every night, vedettes* were placed out in front to watch the Yanks. It fell to my lot one night to go. My post of duty was about one hundred yards in front, in a small grove of timber. Our instructions were to fire into any body of men and then run. I got to the post safely, sat down behind a tree and was peeping around in every direction, expecting every minute to see Grant's whole army coming at once. Of to my right, I heard a noise. Every hair on my head seemed to stand straight up and my heart was beating like a drum. Directly I heard the noise again, a little farther to my rear. I resolved to see what it was. If but one Yank, he would be captured, if more, I would fire and run. Creeping up to the spot, expecting to be shot every minute, I found a wounded turkey buzzard lying on his back. It took me several hours to get over the scare. I returned to our lines next morning feeling very thankful that I was spared to get back. In a short time, Grant pushed his lines so close to ours that the vedette post had to be abandoned. It was now hot times around Petersburg. The Yanks tried very hard to drive us out of our works.

They dug a mine under out lines, blew up one of our posts, killing a number of our boys. They got possession of a short space in our lines, but little Billy Mahone, with part of his division, soon drove them out and re-established the lines. The loss on the Federal side was greater than ours. After this, they settled down to regular siege work, planting mortar batteries and heavy siege guns.** All the heavy metal they could throw did not move us. We were there to stay for a while. Several raids were made on Weldon and Petersburg R. R. We would go down, brush them away and return to our lines, "home", as we called it. In one of these skirmishes, our Captain, D. F. Duke, was killed and T. J. Hardy, of Co. H., was placed in command and held the command till the surrender. . . .

*Vedettes were mounted sentries. (Eds.)

**This incident is vividly described in Charles Frazier's 1997 novel *Cold Mountain* and portrayed in the 2003 film version of the book. (Eds.).

SOURCE: Ada Christie Lightsey, ed., *The Veteran's Story . . . Dedicated to the Heroes who Wore the Grey* (Meridian, Mississippi News: 1899).

We crossed to the north side of the Appomattox River and headed up stream. For five days and night, we tramped, scarcely knowing where. Finally, on the 9th of April, the Yankees rounded us up at Appomattox Court House. We all knew, then, that the Southern Banner would be furled and the "Star Spangled Banner" wave in triumph. When the terms of surrender were agreed upon between Generals Lee and Grant, Lee issued his farewell address to the Army of Northern Virginia. . . .

When Gen. Lee was paroled, he mounted his old gray war-horse, Traveller, and started towards his war blighted home. As he passed through our camps, we all cheered him for the last time. The grandest chieftain the world has ever known, gave us a farewill salute. He was gracious, grand, and gallant in the sorest hour of defeat.

When we surrendered, our division commander, Billy Mahone, formed a square of his division, getting in the center of the square, and delivered his eloquent and pathetic farewell address, paying glowing tribute to his faithful men. The soldiers were paroled as fast as possible and turned loose to get home the best way they could. We had known nothing but war for four years, but the home-journey was the "tug of war". NO transportation, no rations, no money, ragged and heart-sick, with miles and miles between us and our homes "Away Down South in Dixie".

> "Through the April weather's heart-break,
> The April weather's peace,
> Past mountains steep as black despair,
> Through flowery vales of ease,
> Mocked by the liquid sunshine,
> The lilt of nesting birds.
> The men in gray went straggling home
> With grief beyond all words,
> Still in each heart there echoed
> The beat of the last tatto [sic],
> And still they thrilled to the last wild charge
> The Southland bugles blew."

Chapter 16

Reconstruction: Triumphs and Tragedies

The Howard School, founded in 1869 by African American citizens of Fayetteville, North Carolina.

In the past, depictions of the era of Reconstruction have often portrayed the African Americans of the South as, on the one hand, recipients of assistance from federal government agencies and Northern missionary societies and, on the other hand, victims of legislative and extralegal measures to deny them their rights as citizens. Recognition that blacks themselves took an active role in shaping their own destiny has occurred relatively recently. Mark Andrew Huddle's essay "To Educate a Race" tells the story of the African American residents of the textile-manufacturing center of Fayetteville, North Carolina, and their largely successful efforts to establish elementary and secondary schools as well as teacher training institutions. What characteristics of Fayetteville's black community and its leaders were of particular significance in contributing to its successes? In what ways did the actions of both Southern and Northern whites lead Fayetteville's African Americans to look "to themselves for their own elevation"?

Although even the most tenacious Southerners recognized that slavery was finished and that the South needed a new system of labor, few white Southerners could accept the freedmen as social and political equals. From 1865 to 1866, Southern politicians established Black Codes to ensure white supremacy. Huddle's essay reveals that Fayetteville's African Americans did not passively sit back and submit to efforts by the white community to restrict their freedom and efforts at self-improvement. The first document provides evidence that such assertiveness was not limited to the North Carolina town. It is a letter from a freed slave to his former master. It speaks eloquently of the conditions and humiliations that he had endured in the past and also of the better life that he had built for himself. How would you describe the general tone of the letter?

Black Codes represented efforts to maintain white dominance through legislative acts. The onset of Radical Reconstruction brought an end to this tactic. In its place, to serve the same purpose, there arose secret societies, most notably the Ku Klux Klan, which employed terror and intimidation to achieve the goal of keeping the freedmen down. The second document is an excerpt from the initiation ritual of the Knights of the White Camelia, a secret society founded in New Orleans in 1867, and very much a clone of the Ku Klux Klan. You will note that the candidate for membership is required to take an oath "to cherish" the society's "grand principles." From your reading, what do you perceive these "principles" to have been?

While the Civil War still raged, Frederick Douglass had delivered a speech that revealed his recognition that, despite the abolition of slavery and the ultimate end of the war, the attainment of equal rights for blacks would involve further struggle. The final document is an excerpt from that speech. Compare Douglass's position and arguments regarding the issues of racial superiority and inferiority, and the right to vote with those expressed by the Knights of the White Camelia.

The struggle Douglass envisioned did indeed occur and lasted for many more years than he might have expected. Beginning in the 1890s, the freedmen lost the rights and opportunities they had won during the ten years following the Civil War, as Southern whites began systematically to disfranchise African Americans and to institutionalize segregationist and discriminatory practices. Although blacks never accepted these conditions as permanent, over half a century would pass before their march toward full equality resumed with the promise of significant success.

ESSAY

To Educate a Race

Mark Andrew Huddle

In 1877 Gov. Zebulon Vance urged an education reform program upon a skeptical North Carolina legislature. Central to Vance's plan was the establishment of state-funded normal schools for the training of teachers. The first normal school for the training of white teachers was to be overseen at a special summer course to be operated at the University of North Carolina at Chapel Hill. Scholars were to be trained in a variety of disciplines and indoctrinated in the latest educational theories and practices. Interestingly, at a time when only the rudiments of public instruction existed for white North Carolinians, Governor Vance also included a call for the creation of a "state colored normal school."

In consideration of the poor condition of African American education in the immediate aftermath of the Civil War and the need for state control of any such ventures, Governor Vance called on the representatives to fund not just a summer session, but a "long-term school" in which prospective black teachers might be instructed in "appropriate" educational techniques and philosophies as well as the subjects that they would teach. The act that eventually passed the legislature in 1877 set aside $2,000 for the funding of such an institution, and a special committee of the state board of education met in June of that year to act on the governor's personal recommendation that the school be located at Fayetteville, North Carolina.

The choice of Fayetteville as the site for the school was in no way random. Soon after the passage of Governor Vance's bill, the state board of education was besieged with offers from municipalities from across the state that were interested in providing a home for the first state normal school for African Americans. A meeting of the board of education on April 10, 1877, drew more than thirty African American representatives from fifteen counties. Fayetteville sent the formidable African Methodist Episcopal Zion (AMEZ) bishop James Walker Hood to that meeting, and his efforts on behalf of the town resulted in a visit to Fayetteville by Governor Vance and state superintendent of public instruction John C. Scarborough in June 1877. Both Vance and Scarborough were favorably impressed with what they saw and recommended to the board that Fayetteville serve as the site for the school.

SOURCE: Mark Andrew Huddle, "To Educate a Race: The Making of the First State Colored Normal School, Fayetteville, North Carolina, 1865–1877," *The North Carolina Historical Review* 74 (April 1997): 135–160. Reprinted with permission of the North Carolina Office of Archives and History.

In actuality, historical precedent worked in Fayetteville's favor in the competition for the normal school. A sophisticated education effort in the town's black community had been under way since 1865. Noted African American educators Cicero and Robert Harris administered respectively the elementary Phillips School and the secondary Sumner School from 1866 until 1869, when the two schools were consolidated to form the Howard School. During the late 1860s, Fayetteville's African American schools owed much of their financial support to the northern-based American Missionary Association (AMA) and to the federal Freedmen's Bureau. It is distinctive that these schools were controlled by the African American community of Fayetteville, a community that had emerged from the war organized and with an agenda that emphasized the importance of education. In this tumultuous period, these blacks were able to maintain a remarkable independence of action in achieving their community goals. African American agency was the determining factor in the success of the Fayetteville experiment and its eventual designation as the State Colored Normal School. . . .

. . . [L]ong before the American Missionary Association (AMA) and Freedmen's Bureau began their work to establish a school among the freed people, Fayetteville had a large, organized African American community. There is significant evidence that a portion of this community was literate and that a number of free blacks actively engaged in the clandestine education of elements within the slave population. Historian John Hope Franklin has argued that among free blacks the apprenticeship system offered opportunities for the attainment of basic literacy. This desire for education certainly played a role in the urban setting of Fayetteville. From 1822 to 1824 the noted black educator and Presbyterian minister, John Chavis, whose academy in Raleigh was responsible for educating both whites and free blacks, taught at Fayetteville. There is also evidence that in 1850 a number of white elites established a short-lived day school for the training of free blacks. Finally, 1860 census data shows that approximately 11 percent of the adult (age twenty-one years and above) free black and mulatto population could read and/or write.

It is certain that a number of free blacks at Fayetteville secretly labored to teach basic reading and writing skills to slaves. When Robert Harris, the man most responsible for the success of the Howard School and the establishment of the State Colored Normal School, applied to the AMA for a teaching commission in 1864, the only experience of which he could boast was the work that he and his brother had done among the slave population at Fayetteville in the 1840s. Wrote Harris: "I have had no experience in [t]eaching except in privately teaching slaves in the South where I lived in my youth." Harris's older brother, William, also reported having taught for two years among the slaves of Fayetteville. In sum, the educational impulse was well established in Fayetteville's African American community by the end of the Civil War, when that community began a systematic effort to establish a school, train teachers, and reach out to freed people in the vicinity. All of these efforts preceded the establishment of the State Colored Normal School in 1877.

The Civil War proved particularly destructive for Fayetteville. . . . General Sherman and his troops occupied Fayetteville on March 11, [1865]. On that same day, the general issued Special Field Order No. 28, which ordered the destruction of "all railroad property, all shops, factories, tanneries, &c., and all mills save one water-mill of sufficient capacity to grind meal for the people of Fayetteville." The demolition of the railroad was not limited to the town limits but was directed to take place "as far up as the lower Little River." The cavalry was also ordered to demolish the armory and everything pertaining to it. In addition to this destruction, there was considerable pillaging: livestock was seized, and Sherman's "bummers" were said to have visited every home in the city. One wealthy Fayetteville citizen reported property losses of nearly $100,000.

Fayetteville's black community was not spared in the ensuing turmoil. In October 1865, a local African American reported to newspaper correspondent John Dennett that every black home had been ransacked during Sherman's occupation. A black man seen on the streets "with a good suit of clothes, or a new pair of shoes, was halted at once and made to exchange" with a Union soldier. As a result, Dennett reported, Fayetteville's African Americans "no longer believed that every man of Northern birth must be their friends and they more clearly [looked] to themselves for their own elevation."

Union soldiers were not the only threat to Fayetteville blacks. According to Dennett's informant, soon after Sherman's withdrawal from the city, whites moved quickly to reestablish control of the town and reinstitute elements of the antebellum slave code. Public whipping was reinstated as punishment for blacks who broke the law. Blacks were banned from meeting together for worship; they were even barred from carrying walking sticks within the city limits. Fayetteville's African American population did not simply submit to these indignities: black leaders let it be known that, if members of the white community did not desist from their attacks, they would request that a garrison of black soldiers be stationed in the town. The freed people were obviously aware of the chastening effect that such a contingent would have on the unreconstructed element in Fayetteville. In any case, the town's white leaders decided to make an accommodation with local blacks and requested that a representative of the Freedmen's Bureau be stationed in the town to serve as an arbiter for any disputes that might arise between the two groups.

In this uncertain environment, Fayetteville blacks struggled to build a community, and the center for this organizing process was Evans Chapel. One of the first of many thorny issues that had to be resolved concerned the question of denominational affiliation. The post-emancipation South witnessed the dual phenomena of northern missionaries flooding into the section to work among the freed people and the black disengagement from white southern churches. In the black mind, freedom was commensurate with independent institutions; and, along with schools, the churches had been and would continue to be the focal point of the African American community. With all of these African American souls available for salvation, northern and southern denominations engaged in an intense competition to bring the former slaves into their respective organizations.

Among the several denominations leading the first wave into the South were the African Methodist Episcopal (AME) and African Methodist Episcopal Zion (AMEZ) Churches. These northern black missionaries saw themselves as uniquely suited to work among the freed people. Both denominations were united by race and common experience with their charges; what these smaller churches lacked in resources they made up for in missionary zeal. While the AME held the organizational upper hand among blacks throughout much of the South, in North Carolina the AMEZ was supreme. . . .

The AMEZ and other black denominations resisted white charity, arguing that such largess perpetuated perceptions of white superiority among the former slaves. The church became the focus of African American life and culture as the freed people came to have their children christened, their marriages sanctified, and their funerals officiated. Black churches sponsored outings—both religious and secular—and provided necessary social services that contributed to an evolving sense of community. In a more abstract sense, these institutions provided a sense of belonging that was so important as the social organization of the slave system disappeared.

The missionary impulse had its most profound effect in the area of education. Emancipation brought opportunity to the freed people; however, without education—particularly the ability to read and write—the former slaves were unprepared to take advantage of all that could be available to them. For the missionaries, the most important part of education was teaching the freed people to read, which gave each individual personal access to the stories and lessons of the Bible. The AMEZ and other black churches took an active role in planning and implementing education programs: church buildings were used as schoolhouses, and congregations raised money to support teachers and students alike. The churches were not alone in their efforts to assist the former slaves.

Along with northern denominations that came to work among the freed people came northern benevolent societies. . . . One of the most prominent of these benevolent societies was the American Missionary Association, an abolitionist missionary organization founded in 1846 and headquartered in New York City.

The first AMA support at Fayetteville was for the educational efforts of a white Congregationalist minister, the Reverend David Dickson. In December 1865, shortly after the failure of an attempt by Fayetteville's

African American community to establish a school at Evans Chapel, the AMA dispatched Dickson and his wife, Mary, to North Carolina. Although Dickson was quite active in Fayetteville for a mere five months, his correspondence records the complex environment that fostered the founding and growth of the African American school there. The missionary's first official act was to meet with the Freedmen's Bureau agent, Major H. C. Lawrence, who, in turn, introduced him to Fayetteville's mayor and white elite. Dickson reported that he received considerable encouragement from the town's white leaders, and he later commented that the "better class of people here are in favor of having the Negro instructed." Fayetteville's white elite generally supported the combined efforts of the Freedmen's Bureau and the AMA to educate blacks. This is not to argue that the town's white populace was somehow more enlightened than the inhabitants of the rest of the Cape Fear region, where racial conflicts were severe. Early in the postwar period Fayetteville's white and black communities seem to have reached an uneasy accommodation that acknowledged a tenuous white acceptance of a literate work force in the process of economic reconstruction. Much of the AMA correspondence from the period confirms the general acceptance by local whites of black schooling. The local press periodically published articles that extolled the virtues of African American education and emphasized the need for southern white control of that process. Although occasionally Dickson lamented his treatment at the hand of those he characterized as lower-class whites, the level of white-against-black violence appears to have been lower than in other parts of North Carolina and throughout the South.

David Dickson's letters also reveal Fayetteville's African American community to be proud and well organized. In one letter the missionary vividly describes the 1866 Emancipation Day celebrations, during which blacks throughout the region met at Evans Chapel to march past the former slave market in remembrance of circumstances not long past.

More significantly, the Reverend Mr. Dickson's correspondence illustrates the explosive growth of the Fayetteville school. In the "Report of Freemen's Schools for the Southern District of North Carolina, January, 1866," the clergyman reported that in the one month in which he had served at Fayetteville, the student population had jumped from seventy-five "scholars" to 245. Although the number of students fluctuated from season to season, especially at planting and harvest times, the African American school exhibited steady growth. By the middle of February, Dickson was forced to hire two black assistants and expand the school's offerings to include two day-sessions and one night-school. His report to the AMA for February 1866 noted 272 students enrolled in these classes.

David Dickson's tenure among Fayetteville's freed people was cut short in April 1866. After suffering a "bilious attack," the clergyman was forced to undergo a period of convalescence. Mary Dickson attempted to carry on her husband's work. But when an attack of dysentery further weakened the AMA missionary, a local physician recommended that the Dicksons leave Fayetteville immediately. Rev. David Dickson died while in transit to Philadelphia.

The AMA moved quickly to replace David Dickson. Local blacks took an active role in this process and lobbied for a black replacement. The ideal choice was Robert W. Harris, who had been born in 1840 to free black parents in Fayetteville. . . .

In Virginia, Robert Harris [had] quickly established himself not only as a talented teacher but also as an advocate for the rights of the former slaves. In March 1866, he boldly offered the readers of the *American Missionary* his prescription for racial uplift in the South, calling on "northern capitalists" to purchase large tracts of land, which could be divided into small plots and sold to the freed people at cost. He also declared that the condition of black southerners was dependent upon the continued activism of a victorious North. Yet, he demonstrated a great deal of tact when dealing with local whites, a talent learned through hard experience. He was especially respected by AMA officials for his zealous temperance activities. All of these factors played a role in the decision by the AMA to consider Harris for the Fayetteville vacancy in the autumn of 1866.

Another important element in the decision to send Robert Harris to North Carolina was the active participation of Fayetteville's African American community in the process. The AMA queried local black leader John S. Leary about conditions in the town. He assured officials that a school would flourish there and went on to stress the importance of a "native teacher" in the success of any such venture. Leary then took an active role both in arranging for the leasing of two buildings for the school and in securing a commitment from the Freedmen's Bureau for financial assistance.

Robert Harris arrived in Fayetteville in late November 1866. His first act as AMA superintendent of schools was to name his younger brother, Cicero, as his assistant. Next, he divided his students into primary and intermediate grade levels based on their educational attainments. Cicero Harris was given responsibility for the primary grades, which were designated as the "Phillips School"; Robert Harris assumed control of the intermediate levels, which were called the "Sumner School." In his first report from the North Carolina field, Harris declared a total enrollment of 321 students in the school.

Despite the uncertainties of these years, the African American school at Fayetteville exhibited tremendous growth well into the 1870s. Although enrollment tended to fluctuate wildly depending on the season, the institution boasted as many as six hundred students. . . .

Initially, the school was in session from September to May. However, by 1869 the Harris brothers were seeking financial support to keep the school open throughout the summer months. Citing the "urgings of the people" and the need to prepare a group of young people to fill teaching responsibilities in the small, rural schools of the region, Robert Harris felt compelled to keep the doors open. According to the educator, his school was so inextricably "connected with the educational, religious, social and industrial affairs of the people that we cannot be spared."

The curriculum at Fayetteville emphasized practicality. The majority of instruction in the school focused on reading and writing. Students were also taught arithmetic with an emphasis on the types of problem-solving skills that would be useful when negotiating for one's labor. As the educational apparatus became more sophisticated, the curriculum boasted geography and science classes, the latter of which revolved around the school's acquisition of a telescope in 1869.

The Harrises' school provided special attention to the moral development of its students. This aspect of the curriculum reflected the close ties of the school to the AMEZ Church. Not only were classes often held in the church—the only structure large enough to house the student body—but the Harris brothers also taught the Sunday school at Evans Chapel. They used their ties to the Congregationalist-based American Missionary Association to procure religious tracts for distribution among their pupils. . . .

Another facet of this moral education was temperance. One of the first primers used by Robert Harris was entitled *The Temperance Almanac,* which contained stories concerning the evils of overindulgence and the glories of overcoming the "demon rum." In December 1868, Harris announced the organization of a "Band of Hope." Members pledged themselves to abstain from alcohol, tobacco, and profane language. Children, in particular, were singled out for membership; and a periodical titled the *Youth's Temperance Banner* was the reading material of choice in the Fayetteville Band of Hope. Members' rules also included a prohibition against marble-playing "for keeps," a practice that Robert Harris equated with gambling. Between December 1868 and January 1872, the Harrises' Band of Hope had as many as 136 members.

The success of black education efforts at Fayetteville stemmed in part from the willingness of the white community to countenance those efforts. An integral element in this tenuous accommodation was the unusually high esteem accorded to both the local Freedmen's Bureau agent and the contingent of federal troops stationed in the town. The local newspaper often expressed the appreciation of white Fayetteville to bureau officials who "labored in . . . responsible and gentlemanly fashion." According to the Fayetteville *News,* "No negro felt any injustice, and no white man felt annoyed or troubled with the officious interference which has occasioned elsewhere so much complaint." On one notable occasion, the *News* rose to the defense of the federals when they were accused by the Raleigh *Progress* of using an altercation at a local house of prostitution to foment a "war of the races." The *News* blasted the *Progress* for its "bad taste and lack of dignity" and further remarked that "the best feelings prevail between the citizens and soldiers here."

It would be inaccurate to portray postbellum Fayetteville as some sort of racial Shangri-La.* There were bitter, sometimes violent, conflicts. In May 1866, the *News* reported that a mob "got up by mullattoe scamps" had attempted to free a black male from the town jail. Local whites, especially "all returned soldiers," were admonished to arm themselves. The news story concluded with the warning that "[p]repared we have nothing to fear; unprepared we might lose some of our best citizens." In February 1867, a black man, Archie Beebe, was arrested for attacking a white woman, Mrs. Elvina Massey. While being transported to jail after an arraignment, Beebe and the sheriff's deputies protecting him were attacked by an angry white mob. In the ensuing melee, Beebe was murdered. The *News* commented on the event: "It is one of those instances where awful justice speaks from the mouth of the people and the bloody mark of vengeance is stamped by man's hand."

With the onset of radical Reconstruction in the spring of 1867, the community became increasingly politicized, and black-white relations were placed under increasing strain. The center for black political activity, not surprisingly, was the Evans Chapel AMEZ Church, which was also flourishing under the adroit leadership of the Reverend James Walker Hood. The Republican Party held its first organizational meeting in Cumberland County at the chapel on April 4, 1867. Addressing the gathering were Rev. J. W. Hood and John S. Leary; Cicero Harris also took an active role in the proceedings. Noticeably absent from that meeting (and all subsequent political gatherings) was Robert Harris. Although the educator often commented on local politics in his private correspondence, his public pronouncements on political issues were exceedingly rare.

As a native of Fayetteville, Harris no doubt recognized the political and social complexities in the town. The success of his school was contingent upon the goodwill of local whites and his own personal standing among them. The local white elite generally favored the educational work among the freed people—if the efforts were controlled by the "Southern states." While Harris's ties to the northern-based AMA and the federal Freedmen's Bureau were public knowledge, he was quick to downplay these affiliations by shifting the focus of any query toward his North Carolina upbringing. It is testimony to Robert Harris's diplomatic skills that his school never fell into disfavor with the white community. His studious avoidance of politics was matched only by his strenuous efforts to bring stability and self-sufficiency to the school. . . .

---

*An imaginary land of beauty, peace, and harmony described in James Hilton's novel *Lost Horizon*. (Eds.).

The most important accomplishment in Robert Harris's bid for independence and institutional stability was the construction of a new building to permanently house the Phillips and Sumner Schools under one roof. Soon after arriving in Fayetteville, the educator began soliciting assistance from the Freedmen's Bureau and the AMA to build a new structure for the school. In September 1867, he queried the bureau's superintendent of education, F. A. Fiske, as to whether there was "any hope for a school-house in Fayetteville?" Fiske replied in the affirmative; and, in November, Harris informed AMA officials that members of the community had purchased two lots for the school and that a deed for the property had been forwarded to the Freedmen's Bureau offices for approval. In March 1868, Cicero Harris was able to report that a contract to build a "large and commodious school-building" had been awarded and that construction would soon commence. . . . The building was dedicated in early April 1869; and the Howard School, named after Freedmen's Bureau chief Gen. O. O. Howard, opened for its first official session the following September.

Robert Harris's most enduring legacy to North Carolina education was in the training of teachers. . . . In the beginning, it was necessity that forced Harris beyond providing basic literacy to Fayetteville's freed people. The crush of students descending on the school placed great strains on the teachers, and Harris's repeated requests for northern teachers went unheeded by AMA officials. In one of his first reports, the educator acknowledged that he had employed two local blacks as temporary instructors. While both of these women, Mary Payne and Caroline Bryant, were literate, neither met with his complete approval. Still, the large number of scholars at the Phillips and Sumner Schools forced Harris to continue the practice of hiring locals. In December 1867, he announced that he had hired two of his most promising students as assistants in the primary school. Interestingly, these teachers did not receive commissions, and their salaries were to be paid by local subscription. The success of this system was soon readily apparent, and Harris's regular requests for northern teachers ceased.

The impact of training the most talented students for the classroom was felt most in the small rural schools in Cumberland and surrounding counties. In the immediate postwar period, the records of the Freedmen's Bureau include numerous requests for teachers and material support throughout the region. There were so many requests, in fact, that many outlying schools began using Robert Harris as an intermediary between themselves and the bureau. A great source of anxiety for rural teachers was the insecurity caused by the rapid turnover of the Freedmen's Bureau agents. A remedy for this uncertainty was to give Harris the responsibility for placing teachers in appropriate schools and seeing to their needs. In June 1868, he reported that there was a great demand for teachers in rural Cumberland and Moore Counties. Harris was soon placing his most promising students in teaching positions at Beaver Creek, Lower Rockfish, Black River, and Manchester in Cumberland

County and at Jonesboro in Moore County. By January, his operation had spread to Harnett and Bladen Counties, and as many as fifteen schools fell under his purview. Thus, by supplying teachers to black schools in neighboring towns and counties, Robert Harris's Fayetteville institution was functioning as a normal school a full decade before the State of North Carolina officially established it as the South's first "state colored normal school."

By the end of 1870, the Freedmen's Bureau ceased providing educational assistance to the former slaves. The last trickle of aid to the Howard School from the American Missionary Association ended in 1872. By then the school had established its independence and a well-defined sense of mission. Robert Harris continued to train young black men and women as educators until his death in 1879. . . .

The State Colored Normal School has had a lasting legacy in North Carolina history. . . . In 1939 the State Colored Normal School was renamed as Fayetteville State Teachers College, and in 1963 as Fayetteville State College. Since 1969, when it joined the University of North Carolina system, the school has operated as Fayetteville State University. The institution has come a long way from the anxious days of Reconstruction. The long-term vision of Fayetteville's African American community—in both slavery and in freedom, passed down through the generations—continues to have a profound influence on that city, North Carolina, and the nation.

DOCUMENTS

A Letter "To My Old Master," c. 1865

TO MY OLD MASTER, COLONEL P. H. ANDERSON,
BIG SPRING, TENNESSEE

Sir: I got your letter, and was glad to find that you had not forgotten Jourdon, and that you wanted me to come back and live with you again, promising to do better for me than anybody else can. I have often felt uneasy about you. I thought the Yankees would have hung you long before this, for harboring Rebs they found at your house. I suppose they never heard about your going to Colonel Martin's to kill the Union soldier that was left by his company in their stable. Although you shot at me twice before I left you, I did not want to hear of your being hurt, and am glad you are still living. It would do me good to go back to the dear old home again, and see Miss Mary and Miss Martha and Allen, Esther, Green, and Lee.

SOURCE: L. Maria Child, *The Freedmen's Book* (1865).

Give my love to them all, and tell them I hope we will meet in the better world, if not in this. I would have gone back to see you all when I was working in the Nashville Hospital, but one of the neighbors told me that Henry intended to shoot me if he ever got a chance.

I want to know particularly what the good chance is you propose to give me. I am doing tolerably well here. I get twenty-five dollars a month, with victuals and clothing; have a comfortable home for Mandy—the folks call her Mrs. Anderson—and the children—Milly, Jane, and Grundy—go to school and are learning well. The teacher says Grundy has a head for a preacher. They go to Sunday school, and Mandy and me attend church regularly. We are kindly treated. Sometimes we overhear others saying, "Them colored people were slaves" down in Tennessee. The children feel hurt when they hear such remarks; but I tell them it was no disgrace in Tennessee to belong to Colonel Anderson. Many darkeys would have been proud, as I used to be, to call you master. Now if you will write and say what wages you will give me, I will be better able to decide whether it would be to my advantage to move back again.

As to my freedom, which you say I can have, there is nothing to be gained on that score, as I got my free papers in 1864 from the Provost-Marshal-General of the Department of Nashville. Mandy says she would be afraid to go back without some proof that you were disposed to treat us justly and kindly; and we have concluded to test your sincerity by asking you to send us our wages for the time we served you. This will make us forget and forgive old scores, and rely on your justice and friendship in the future. I served you faithfully for thirty-two years, and Mandy twenty years. At twenty-five dollars a month for me, and two dollars a week for Mandy, our earnings would amount to eleven thousand six hundred and eighty dollars. Add to this the interest for the time our wages have been kept back, and deduct what you paid for our clothing, and three doctor's visits to me, and pulling a tooth for Mandy, and the balance will show what we are in justice entitled to. Please send the money by Adam's Express, in care of V. Winters, Esq., Dayton, Ohio. If you fail to pay us for faithful labors in the past, we can have little faith in your promises in the future. We trust the good Maker has opened your eyes to the wrongs which you and your fathers have done to me and my fathers, in making us toil for you for generations without recompense. Here I draw my wages every Saturday night; but in Tennessee there was never any pay-day for the Negroes any more than for the horses and cows. Surely there will be a day of reckoning for those who defraud the laborer of his hire.

In answering this letter, please state if there would be any safety for my Milly and Jane, who are now grown up, and both good-looking girls. You know how it was with poor Matilda and Catherine. I would rather stay here and starve—and die, if it come to that—than have my girls brought to shame by the violence and wickedness of their young masters. You will also please state if there has been any schools opened for the colored children in your neighborhood. The great desire of my life now is to give my children an education, and have them form virtuous habits.

Say howdy to George Carter, and thank him for taking the pistol from you when you were shooting at me.

FROM YOUR OLD SERVANT,
JOURDON ANDERSON

The Knights of the White Camelia, 1868

Questions

1. Do you belong to the white race? *Answer.*—I do.
2. Did you ever marry any woman who did not, or does not, belong to the white race? *Ans.*—No.
3. Do you promise never to marry any woman but one who belongs to the white race? *Ans.*—I do.
4. Do you believe in the superiority of your race? *Ans.*—I do.
5. Will you promise never to vote for anyone for any office of honor, profit, or trust who does not belong to your race? *Ans.*—I do.
6. Will you take a solemn oath never to abstain from casting your vote at any election in which a candidate of the Negro race shall be opposed to a white man attached to your principles, unless or prevented by severe illness or any other physical disability? *Ans.*—I will.
7. Are you opposed to allowing the control of the political affairs of this country to go in whole or in part into the hands of the African race, and will you do everything in your power to prevent it? *Ans.*—Yes.
8. Will you devote your intelligence, energy, and influence to the furtherance and propagation of the principles of our Order? *Ans.*—I will.
9. Will you, under all circumstances, defend and protect persons of the white race in their lives, rights, and property against all encroachments or invasions from any inferior race, and especially the African? *Ans.*—Yes.
10. Are you willing to take an oath forever to cherish these grand principles and to unite yourself with others who, like you, believing in their truth, have firmly bound themselves to stand by and defend them against all? *Ans.*—I am.

SOURCE: Walter L. Fleming, ed., *Documents Relating to Reconstruction* (Morgantown, W.Va.: 1904), no. 1.

The commander shall then say: If you consent to join our Association, raise your right hand and I will administer to you the oath which we have all taken:

Oath

I do solemnly swear, in the presence of these witnesses, never to reveal, without authority, the existence of his Order, its objects, its acts, and signs of recognition; never to reveal or publish, in any manner whatsoever, what I shall see or hear in this Council; never to divulge the names of the members of the Order or their acts done in connection therewith. I swear to maintain and defend the social and political superiority of the white race on this continent; always and in all places to observe a marked distinction between the white and African races; to vote for none but white men for any office of honor, profit, or trust; to devote my intelligence, energy, and influence to instill these principles in the minds and hearts of others; and to protect and defend persons of the white race in their lives, rights, and property against the encroachments and aggressions of an inferior race.

I swear, moreover, to unite myself in heart, soul, and body with those who compose this Order; to aid, protect, and defend them in all places; to obey the orders of those who, by our statutes, will have the right of giving those orders; to respond at the peril of my life to a call, sign, or cry coming from a fellow member whose rights are violated; and to do everything in my power to assist him through life. And to the faithful performance of this oath, I pledge my life and sacred honor. . . .

Frederick Douglass Demands the Franchise, c. *1865*

. . . I know that we are inferior to you in some things—virtually inferior. We walk about among you like dwarfs among giants. Our heads are scarcely seen above the great sea of humanity. The Germans are superior to us; the Irish are superior to us; the Yankees are superior to us; (laughter); they can do what we cannot, that is, what we have not hitherto been allowed to do. But while I make this admission, I utterly deny that we are originally, or naturally, or practically, or in any way, or in any important sense, inferior to anybody on this globe. (Loud applause.) This charge of inferiority is an old dodge. It has been made available for oppression on many occasions. It is only about six centuries since the blue-eyed and fair-haired Anglo-Saxons were considered inferior by the haughty Normans,

SOURCE: Frederick Douglass, "What the Black Man Wants," in *The Equality of All Men Before the Law* (Boston, 1865), 37–38.

who once trampled upon them. If you read the history of the Norman Conquest, you will find that this proud Anglo-Saxon was once looked upon as of coarser clay than his Norman master, and might be found in the highways and byways of old England laboring with a brass collar on his neck, and the name of his master marked upon it. *You* were down then! (Laughter and applause.) You are up now. I am glad you are up, and I want you to be glad to help us up also. (Applause.)

I hold that the American people are bound, not only in self-defence, to extend this right to the freedmen of the South, but they are bound by their love of country, and by all their regard for the future safety of those Southern States, to do this—to do it as a measure essential to the preservation of peace there. But I will not dwell upon this. I put it to the American sense of honor. The honor of a nation is an important thing. It is said in the Scriptures, "What doth it profit a man if he gain the whole world, and lose his own soul?" It may be said, also, What doth it profit a nation if it gain the whole world, but lose its honor? I hold that the American government has taken upon itself a solemn obligation of honor, to see that this war—let it be long or let it be short, let it cost much or let it cost little—that this war shall not cease until every freedman at the South has the right to vote. (Applause.) It has bound itself to it. What have you asked the black men of the South, the black men of the whole country, to do? Why, you have asked them to incur the deadly enmity of their masters, in order to befriend you and to befriend this Government. You have asked us to call down, not only upon ourselves, but upon our children's children, the deadly hate of the entire Southern people. You have called upon us to turn our backs upon our masters, to abandon their cause and espouse yours; to turn against the South and in favor of the North; to shoot down the Confederacy and uphold the flag—the American flag. You have called upon us to expose ourselves to all the subtle machinations of their malignity for all time. And now, what do you propose to do when you come to make peace? To reward your enemies, and trample in the dust your friends? Do you intend to sacrifice the very men who have come to the rescue of your banner in the South, and incurred the lasting displeasure of their masters thereby? Do you intend to sacrifice them and reward your enemies? Do you mean to give your enemies the right to vote, and take it away from your friends? Is that wise policy? Is that honorable? Could American honor withstand such a blow? I do not believe you will do it. I think you will see to it that we have the right to vote. . . .

Suggestions for Further Reading

For general social and economic changes before the Civil War, several books are useful. Among them are Sean Wilentz, *Chants Democratic: New York City and the Rise of the American Working Class, 1785–1850* (1984); Daniel Walkowitz, *Worker City, Company Town: Iron and Cotton-Worker Protest in Troy and Cohoes, New York, 1855–1884* (1978); and Alan Dawley, *Class and Community: The Industrial Revolution in Lynn* (1976). Those interested in delving further into the subject of Thomas Dublin's essay will want to consult *Transforming Women's Work: New England Lives in the Industrial Revolution* (1994). For economic and political issues during this period, see Charles Sellers, *The Market Revolution: Jacksonian America, 1815–1846* (1991). An interesting treatment of the cotton cloth industry in southeastern New England is Mary H. Blewett, *The Politics of Industrial Life in Nineteenth Century New England* (2000).

On the removal policy of American Indians to the West, see Ronald Satz, *American Indian Policy in the Jacksonian Era* (1975). On removal itself, see Arthur DeRosier, *The Removal of the Choctaw Indians* (1970); Wilkins Thurman, *Cherokee Tragedy: The Story of the Ridge Family and the Decimation of a People* (1970); and John Ehle, *Trail of Tears: The Rise and Fall of the Cherokee Nation* (1988). For background knowledge of Cherokee history and culture, William G. McLoughlin, *Cherokees and Missionaries, 1789–1839* (1984), is excellent. For President Thomas Jefferson, see *Jefferson and the Indians: The Tragic Fate of the First Americans* (1999), and for Andrew Jackson, see Robert Remini, *Andrew Jackson and His Indian Wars* (2001). Philip Weeks, *Farewell, My Nation: The American Indian in the Nineteenth Century* (2000), covers the entire period.

On the westward movement generally, particularly recommended is Richard White, *"It's Your Misfortune and None of My Own": A History of the American West* (1991), and two studies by Ray Billington: *The Far Western Frontier, 1830–1860* (1956) and *Westward Expansion* (1974). See also John D. Unruh, Jr., *The Plain Across: The Overland Emigrants and the Trans-Mississippi West, 1840–1860* (1979). For women and the West, consult John M. Faragher, *Women and Men on the Overland Trail* (1979), and Julie Roy Jeffrey, *Frontier Women: The Trans-Mississippi West, 1840–1880* (1979). A vivid description of family life in the Oregon Territory is included in Lillian Schlissel, Byrd Gibbens, and Elizabeth Hampsten, *Far from Home: Families of the Westward Journey* (1989). For the frontier as experienced by children, see Eliot West, *Growing Up with the Country, Children on the Far Western Frontier* (1989). Susan Lee Johnson, *The Roaring Camp: The Social World of the California Gold Rush* (2000), also covers the California gold rush. Walter Nugent, *Into the West: The Story of Its People* (1999), deals with the West generally.

There is a growing literature on women's history. Two general works of value are Alice Kessler-Harris, *Out to Work: A History of Wage Earning*

Women in America (1982), and Carl Degler, *At Odds: Women and the Family from the Revolution to the Present* (1981). On plantation women, see Catherine Clinton, *The Plantation Mistress* (1982), and Ann Firor Scott, *The Southern Lady: From Pedestal to Politics, 1830–1930* (1970). On women in American culture, consult Ann Douglas, *The Feminization of American Culture* (1977); Nancy Cott, *The Bonds of Womanhood: "Woman's Sphere" in New England, 1780–1835* (1977); Mary Ryan, *Cradle of the Middle Class: The Family in Oneida County, New York, 1790–1865* (1981); and Katherine Kish Sklar, *Catharine Beecher: A Study in American Domesticity* (1973). For black women, see Jacqueline Jones, *Labor of Love, Labor of Sorrow: Black Women, Work and the Family from Slavery to the Present* (1985). Especially interesting on the relationships of black men and white women is Martha Hodes, *White Women, Black Men: Illicit Sex in the Nineteenth Century South* (1997).

For religion in early-nineteenth-century America, an older but useful work is Whitney Cross, *The Burned-Over District: A Social and Intellectual History of Enthusiastic Religion in Western New York, 1800–1855* (1950). A more recent examination of the same region is Michael Barkun, *Crucible of the Millennium: The Burned-Over District of New York in the 1840s* (1986). See also Paul Conkin, *Cane Ridge: America's Pentecost* (1990), John B. Boles, *The Great Revival* (1972). For a comprehensive study of revivalism, consult William McLoughlin, *Modern Revivalism: Charles Grandison Finney to Billy Graham* (1959). A more recent view is found in Paul E. Johnson, *A Shopkeeper's Millennium: Society and Revivals in Rochester, New York, 1815–1837* (1978). Marianne Perciaccante, *Calling Down the Fire: Charles Grandison Finney and Revivalism in Jefferson County, New York* (2003) is also useful.

For immigration before the Civil War, see David Gerber, *The Making of an American Pluralism: Buffalo, New York, 1825–1860* (1989), and Brian C. Mitchell, *The Paddy Camps: The Irish of Lowell, 1821–1861* (1988). Other accounts are Jay Dolan, *Immigrant Church. New York's Irish and German Catholics. 1815–1865* (1975); Robert Ernst, *Immigrant Life in New York City, 1812–1863* (1949); Oscar Handlin, *Boston's Immigrants, 1790–1880: A Study in Acculturation* (1970); and Lawrence McCaffrey, *The Irish Diaspora* (1976). A highly regarded study of women immigrants is Hasia R. Diner, *Erin's Daughters in America: Irish Immigrant Women in the Nineteenth Century* (1983). An important survey of Irish emigration is Kirby Miller, *Emigrants and Exiles: Ireland and the Irish Exodus to North America* (1985). A classic study of anti-immigrant sentiment is Ray Allen Billington, *The Protestant Crusade, 1800–1860: Study of the Origins of American Nativism* (1938). More recent are Dale T. Knobel, *"America for Americans": The Nativist Movement in the United States* (1997) and Tyler Anbinder, *Nativism and Slavery: The Northern Know-Nothings and the Politics of the 1850s* (1992). Ethnic culture in the Midwest is examined in Jon Gerdje, *The Minds of the West: Ethnoculture in the Rural Midwest, 1830–1917* (1997).

For reform movements, useful general works are Alice Felt Tyler, *Freedom's Ferment* (1944), and Ronald G. Walters, *American Reformers, 1815–1860* (1978). On the antislavery movement, see Louis Filler, *The Crusade Against Slavery* (1960); Blanche Glassman Hersh, *The Slavery of Sex: Feminist-Abolitionists in America* (1978); and Eric Foner, *Free Soil, Free Labor, Free Men: The Ideology of the Republican Party Before the Civil War* (1970). For studies of the movement to improve care for the mentally ill, see David J. Rothman, *The Discovery of the Asylum: Social Order and Disorder in the New Republic* (1971), and Gerald Grob, *Mental Institutions in America: Social Policy to 1875* (1973). On the women's rights movement, the reader will profit from Ellen C. DuBois, *Feminism and Suffrage: The Emergence of an Independent Women's Movement in America, 1848–1869* (1978). Studies of the crusade for public schooling include Carl F. Kaestle, *Pillars of the Republic: Common Schools and American Society, 1780–1860* (1983); Lawrence A. Cremin, *American Education: The National Experience, 1783–1876* (1981); and Frederick M. Binder, *The Age of the Common School: 1830–1865* (1974). An important revisionist view is found in Michael Katz, *The Irony of Early School Reform* (1968). An excellent study of reforms in the education of deaf and blind children is Ernest Freeberg. T*he Education of Laura Bridgman: First Deaf and Blind Person to Learn Language* (2000).

Surveys of the several utopian movements may be found in Michael Fellman, *The Unbounded Frame: Freedom and Community in Nineteenth Century Utopianism* (1973); Mark Holloway, *Heavens on Earth* (1951); and Raymond Muncy, *Sex and Marriage in Utopian Communities: 19th Century America* (1973). Two recent accounts of American utopias are Stephen Stein, *The Shaker Experience in America* (1992), and Spencer Klaw, *Without Sin: The Life and Death of the Oneida Community* (1993).

The literature on antebellum slavery is extensive. Two important works are Brenda E. Stevenson, *Life in Black and White: Family and Community in the Slave South* (1996), and Wilma King, *Stolen Childhood: Slave Youth in Nineteenth Century America* (1996). Standard works are John Blassingame, *The Slave Community: Plantation Life in the Antebellum South* (1972); Eugene D. Genovese, *Roll, Jordan, Roll* (1974); and Herbert Gutman, *The Black Family in Slavery and Freedom, l750–1925* (1976); an account of slavery in one community is Charles Joyner, *Down by the Riverside: A South Carolina Slave Community* (1984). Those interested in the role and place of women in plantation society should turn to Elizabeth Fox-Genovese, *Within the Plantation Household: Black and White Women of the Old South* (1988). For free blacks in the South, consult Ira Berlin, *Slaves Without Masters: The Free Negro in the Antebellum South* (1975), and Michael Johnson and James Roark, *Black Masters: A Free Family of Color in the Old South* (1984). For the North, see Leon Litwack, *North of Slavery: The Negro in the Free States* (1961). A compelling survey of the history of slavery in America is Peter Kolchin, *American Slavery, 1619–1887* (1993). Newer books on slavery are Walter Johnson, *Soul by Soul: Life Inside the Antebellum Slave Market* (1999), and

John Hope Franklin and Loren Schweninger, *Runaway Slaves: Rebels on the Plantation* (1999).

Among the newer works are Ira Berlin, *Generations of Captivity: A History of African American Slaves* (2003); John Hope Franklin and Loren Schweninger, *In Search of the Promised Land: A Slave Family in the Old South* (2005); David Brion Davis, *Inhuman Bondage: The Rise and Fall of Slavery in the New World* (2006); and Fergus M. Bordewich, *Bound for Canaan: The Underground Railroad and the War for the American Soul* (2005).

The best introduction to the Civil War is James McPherson, *Battle Cry of Freedom: The Civil War Era* (1988). McPherson has also written an account of the soldiers' view of the war, *For Cause and Comrades: Why Men Fought in the Civil War* (1997). Other works on this topic are two by Bell I. Wiley: *The Life of Johnny Reb* (1943) and *The Life of Bill Yank* (1952). Also for northern soldiers see Richard Moe, *The Last Full Measure: The Life and Death of the First Minnesota Volunteers* (1993). Consult also Gerald F. Linderman, *Embattled Courage: The Experiences of Combat in the American Civil War* (1988). The experiences of black soldiers are described in Dudley R. Cornish, *The Sable Arm* (1966). For treatments of the home front, consult Robert Meyers, *The Children of Pride* (1972), for a Southern view. See George Winston Smith and Charles Burnet Judah, *Life in the North During the Civil War* (1966), and J. Matthew Gallman, *The North Fights the Civil War: The Home Front* (1994), for the Northern view. For contributions of women to the war effort, see Mary E. Massey, *Bonnet Brigades* (1966). Benjamin Quarles, *The Negro in the Civil War* (1953), reveals the impact of the war on blacks. A new book on the Civil War is Barnet Schecter, *The Devil's Own Work: The Civil War Draft Riots and the Fight to Reconstruct America* (2005).

On Southern black Americans after the Civil War, consult two works by Eric Foner: *Nothing But Freedom: Emancipation and Its Legacy* (1983) and his impressive *Reconstruction: America's Unfinished Revolution, 1863–1967* (1988). See also John Hope Franklin, *Reconstruction After the Civil War* (1961); Leon Litwack, *Been in the Storm So Long: The Aftermath of Slavery* (1979); and Howard Rabinowitz, *Race Relations in the Urban South, 1865–1890* (1980). On black poverty, see Jay R. Mandle, *The Roots of Black Poverty* (1978). C. Vann Woodward, *The Strange Career of Jim Crow* (1966), remains an important work. Very comprehensive is Leon F. Litwack, *Trouble in Mind: Black Southerners in the Age of Jim Crow* (1998).